elixir

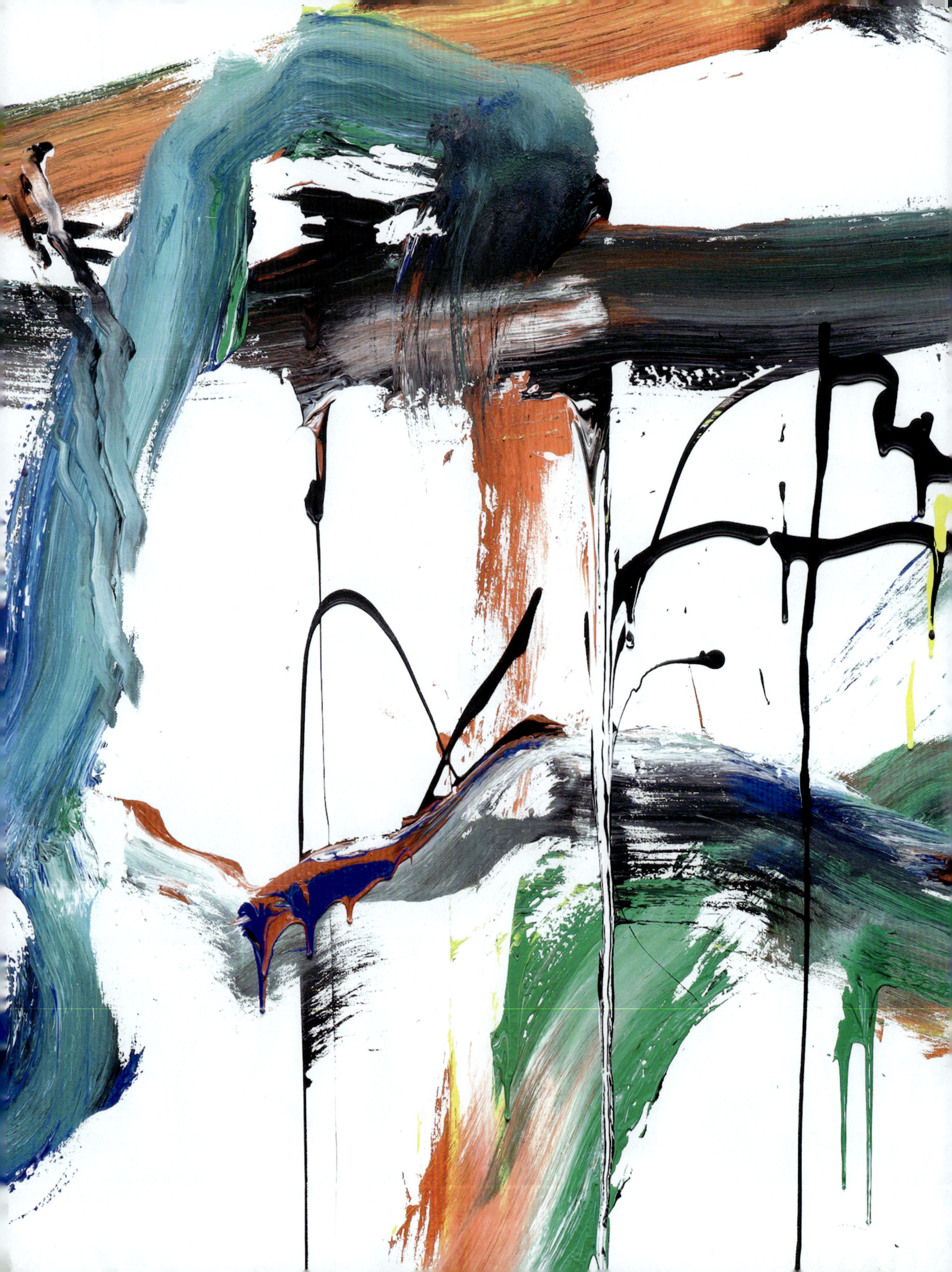

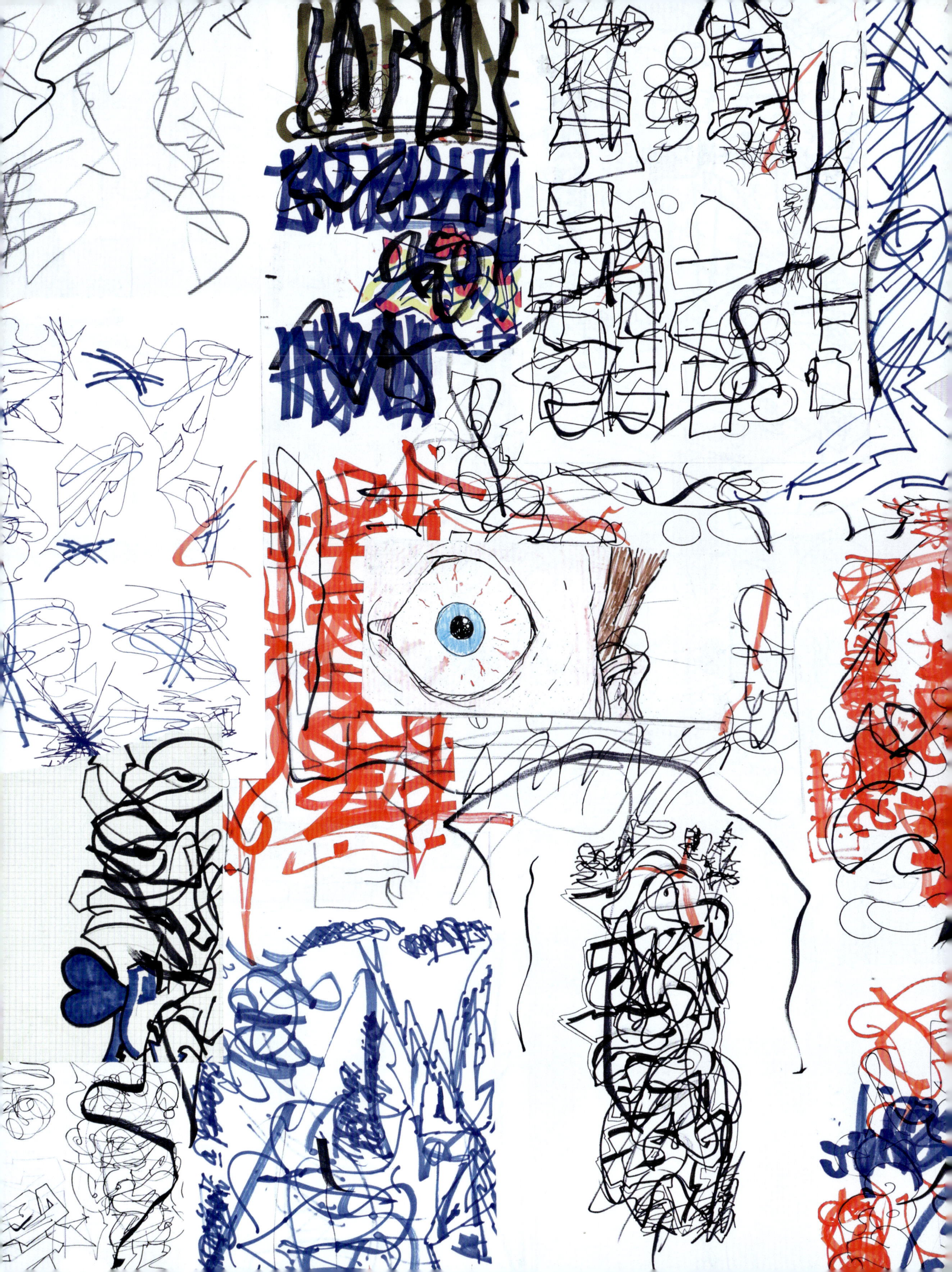

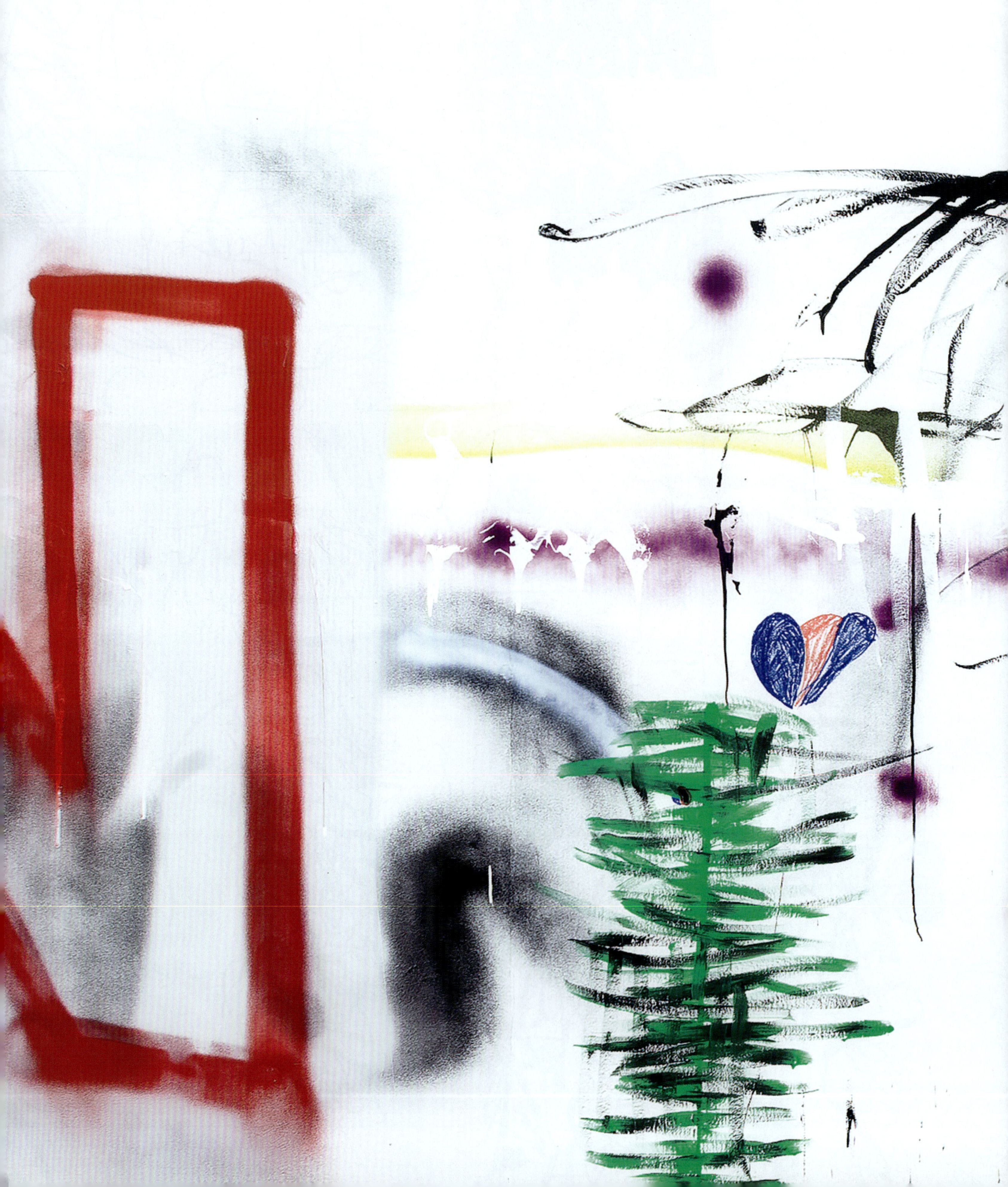

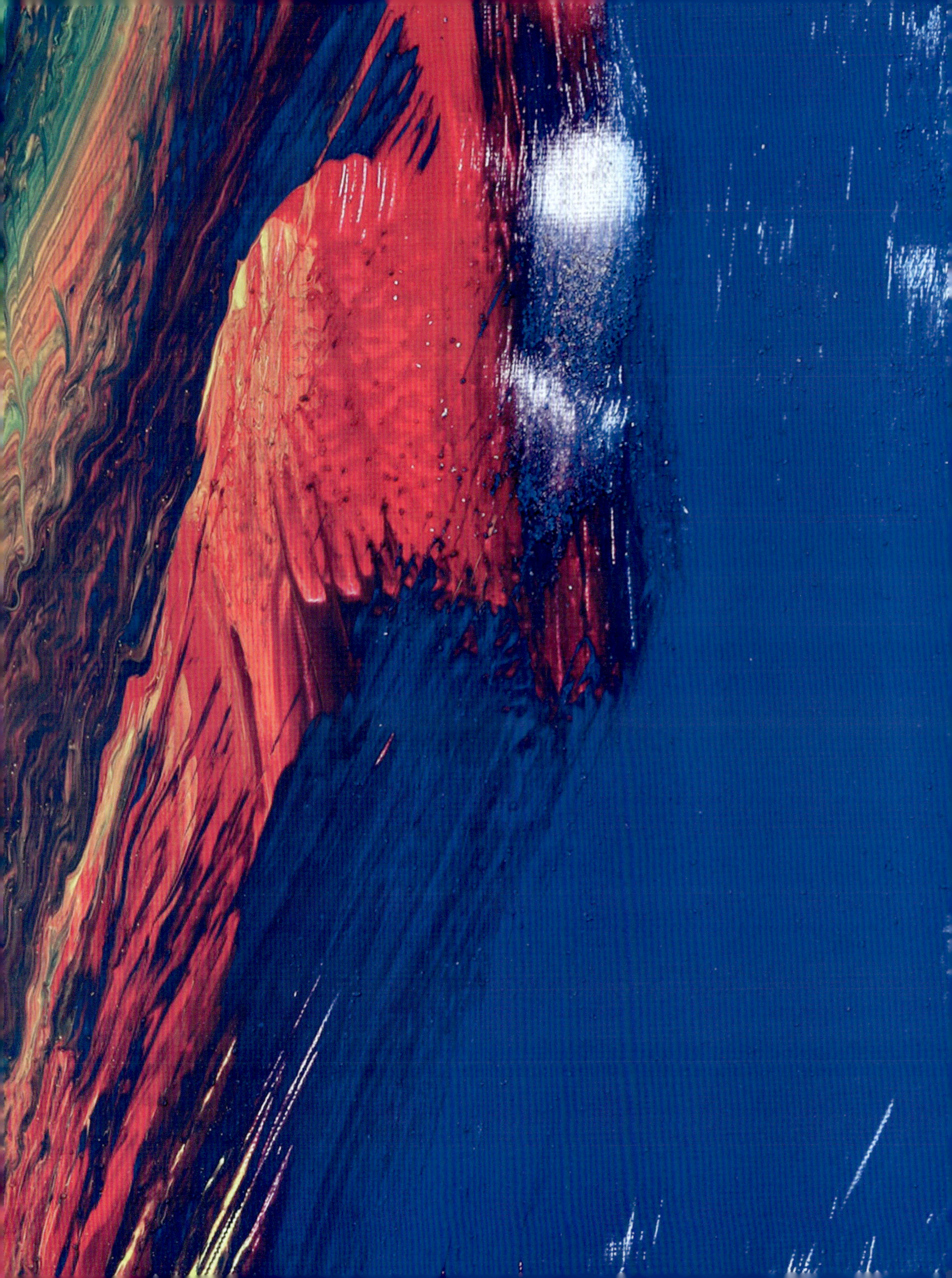

WORK

TEXT

PROMPTING MOVEMENT: QUESTIONS FOR CHRISTIAN FALSNAES

Aaron Bogart: In a recent interview, when asked about the relation between the immateriality of performance and the materiality of the objects that are often an outcome of your work, you say: "Immaterial artworks don't exist. Human beings are material as well. It's not about the medium but the kind of experience facilitated."
Are you saying that the bodily *actions* performed by an artist, which are ephemeral and fleeting and have traditionally been taken to be the sine qua non of performance art, are not artworks?

Christian Falsnaes: Not at all. I do see performances as artworks, but I don't accept the notion that performance is "immaterial." The people attending and performing the work are material and must be dealt with as such. The physical confrontation with bodies, movements, space, and composition is far from the supposed "immateriality" of purely conceptual works.
For me, performance, painting, installation, and video are different media, but when a video recording from a performance is published on YouTube or a performance is used as a production facility for a painting they overlap and become intertwined. The viewing habits, rules, and rituals of interaction change with the media, and that's one of the reasons why I find it interesting to work with various production and presentation formats. While I work across multiple media and contexts, most of my works relate to performance, either as a process or as a way to activate the viewer.

AB: Why is performance important for you? What is the potential of performance?

CF: I think performance can be used to establish an intimate relation to the viewer. One of the problems with the exhibition format is that it facilitates a mode of addressing the viewer that is distanced and often disengaged. I see great potential in the reflective and analytical visitor, conscious about her/his interaction with the work, but I feel that the focus of the exhibition needs to be on the experience that the works facilitate rather than on the significance of the displayed works themselves. Otherwise the result can be a fundamental disengagement and separation between viewer and art. For me, the potential of performance is in its ability to address the viewer directly and place her/his experience at the center of the exhibition. Because performance generates situations and moments rather than images and objects, it always creates a direct relation to the viewer as they become part of the generated situation.

AB: How do you work with the audience as material? (Reference to the statement: "The audience is my main material.")

CF: I try to push the relation between viewer and artwork even further by making the individual exhibition visitor an integrated and inseparable part of the work itself. Instead of exhibiting the result of an interesting process, I let the viewer be part of an interesting process. I engage the viewers by telling them: *Without you there would be no work.* When I say that the audience is the main material of my work, I mean that what I try to form is the reactions, emotions, and behavior of the people who experience them. Instead of looking at a work that exists independently of oneself, you are looking at yourself as the work.

AB: You studied under Daniel Richter, in his painting class at the Akademie der bildende Künste in Vienna; what did painting teach you about performance art and vice versa?

CF: I started out with graffiti, which is related to both performance and painting, and so my interest in performance initially developed from painting—and it is still an important part of my practice. There is a rich history of intersections between painting and performance that I feel related to. When I started to work with performance, I became interested in the circumstances under which a work is created rather than the end result, so I started to focus more on the process. That also influenced my approach to painting. In my *One* paintings, for example, I work with visitors to produce paintings. I stage the production circumstances as a performance, but the performance is basically a production facility for the paintings. Even though I have specific ideas about the overall direction of each painting and try to control the process in that direction, I delegate the expression, the brushstrokes, and the sensibility of painting to the viewer. Since the paintings are always painted by more than one visitor a collective mode of expression replaces an individual one.

AB: Sticking with Vienna, how does your work relate to Viennese Actionism, if at all? *Opening* (2013), for example, is transgressive and action-oriented, and there are numerous pieces where confrontational or agitated behavior is encouraged. Do you aim at politicizing the space surrounding a performance?

CF: When I studied in Vienna, I used to study the history of performance art, including Viennese Actionism. There are definitely elements that interest me, the relation between action and image for instance, but I feel that my work is embedded in a different tradition. Regarding the performance history in Vienna, I have been much more influenced by an artist like VALIE EXPORT.

Some of my works do have elements of transgression and confrontation, but the purpose is never merely to provoke. I am interested in all kinds of behavior, not only agitated or confrontational, and I often try to evoke a series of emotions and reactions within one single work in order to make the situations leading to specific behavior as visible as possible. I definitely see political potential in the awareness that participation in such constructed situations can enable through self-reflection.

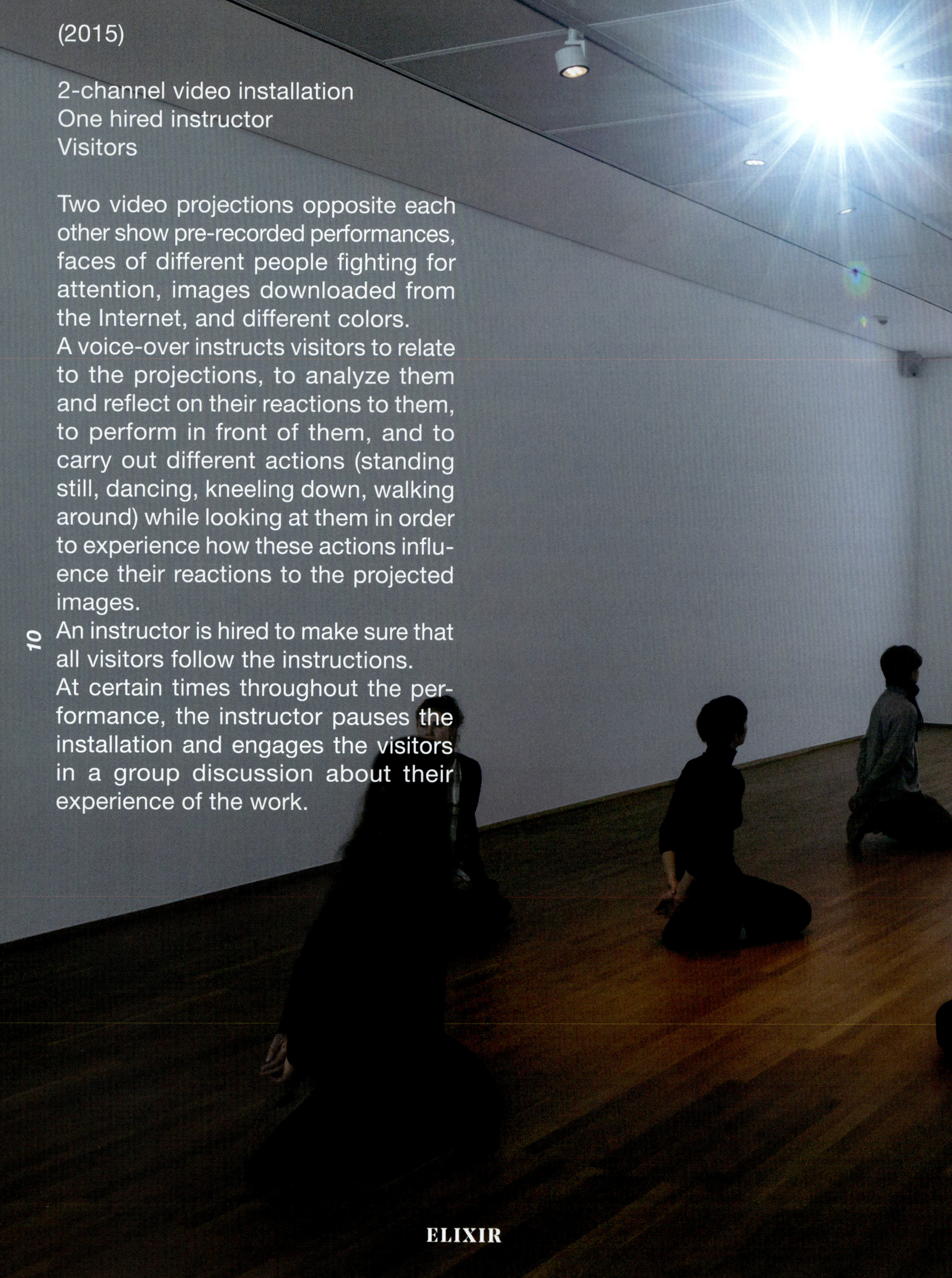

(2015)

2-channel video installation
One hired instructor
Visitors

Two video projections opposite each other show pre-recorded performances, faces of different people fighting for attention, images downloaded from the Internet, and different colors.
A voice-over instructs visitors to relate to the projections, to analyze them and reflect on their reactions to them, to perform in front of them, and to carry out different actions (standing still, dancing, kneeling down, walking around) while looking at them in order to experience how these actions influence their reactions to the projected images.
An instructor is hired to make sure that all visitors follow the instructions.
At certain times throughout the performance, the instructor pauses the installation and engages the visitors in a group discussion about their experience of the work.

MOV–
ING
IMAGES

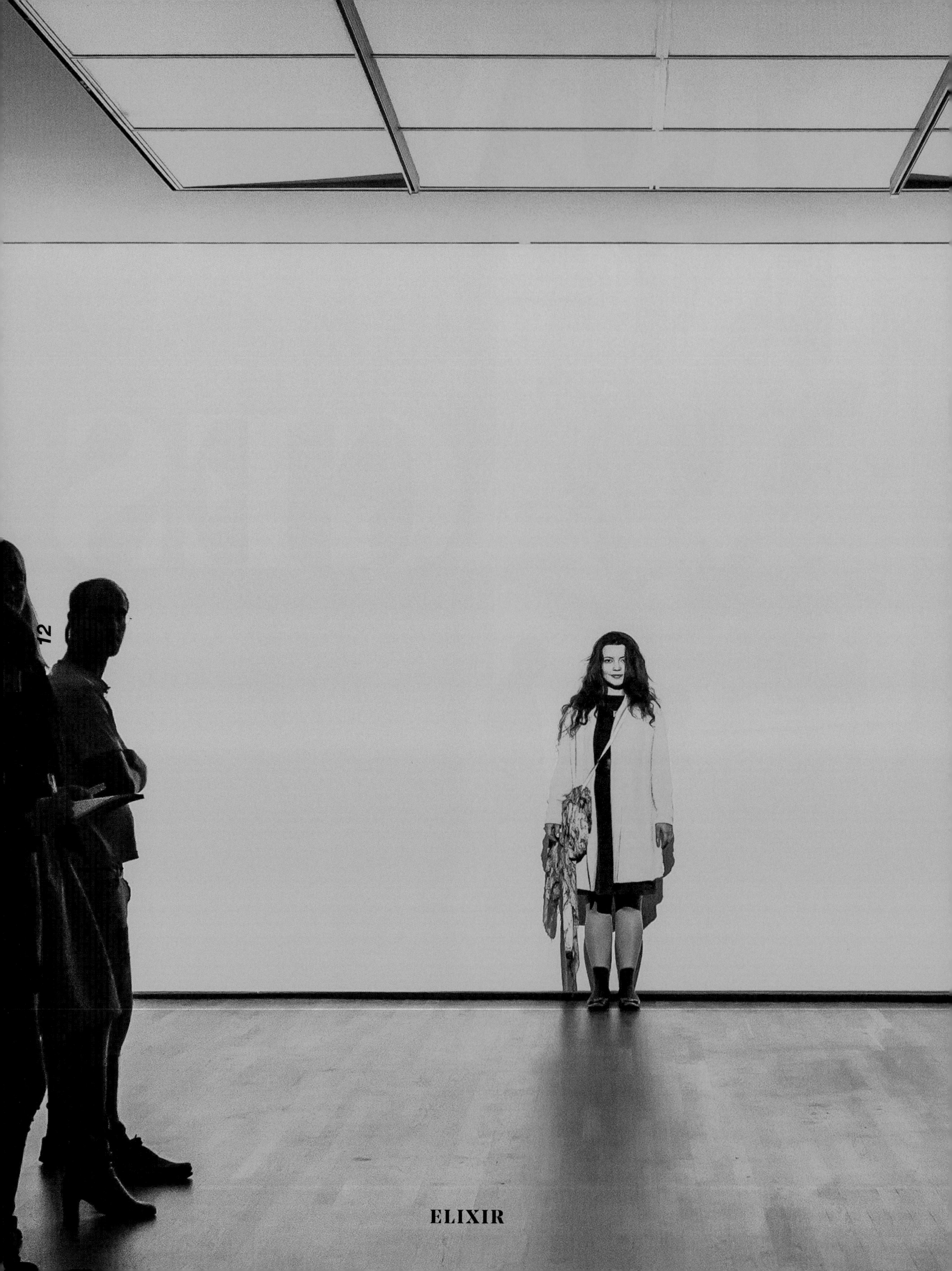

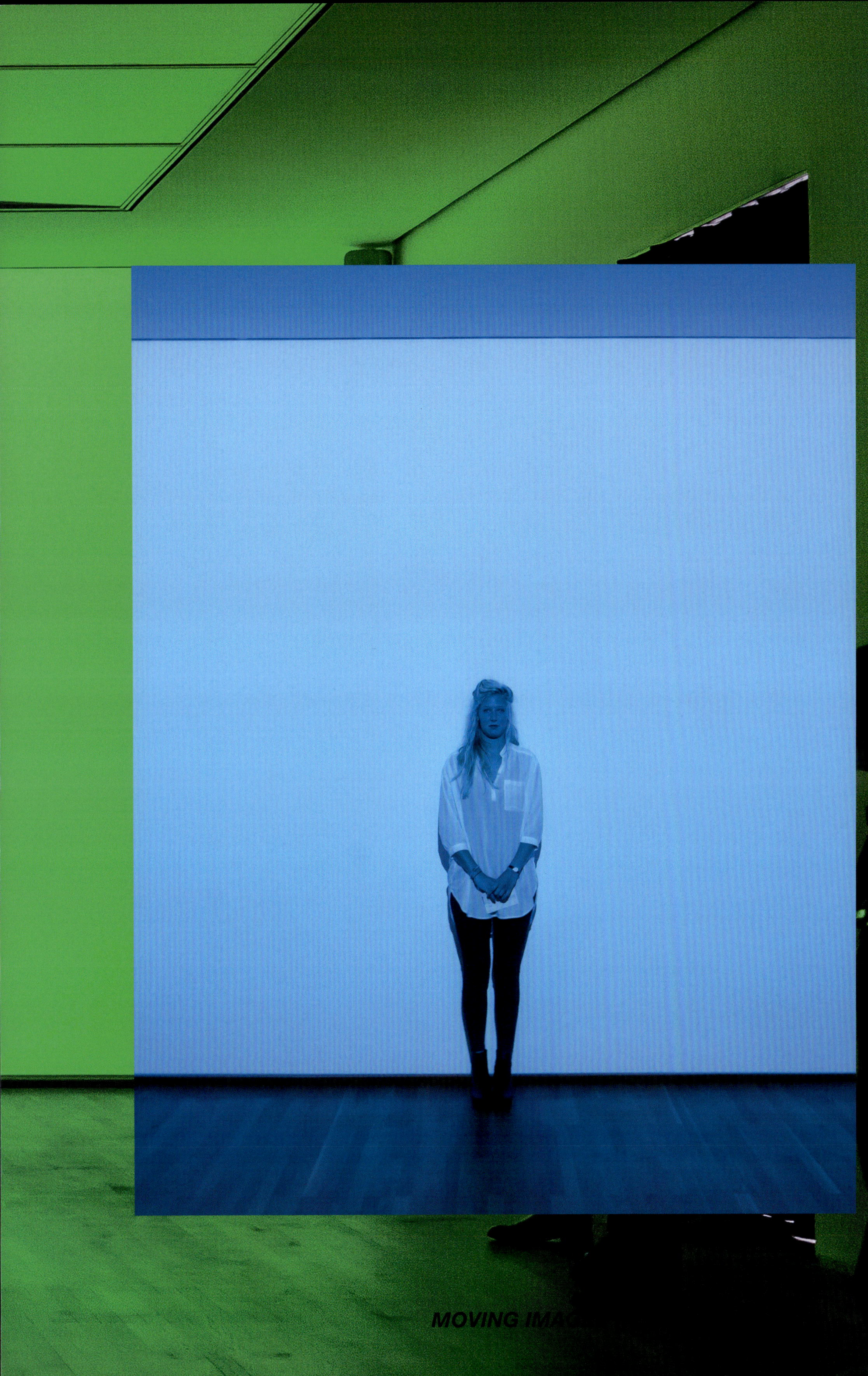
MOVING IMA

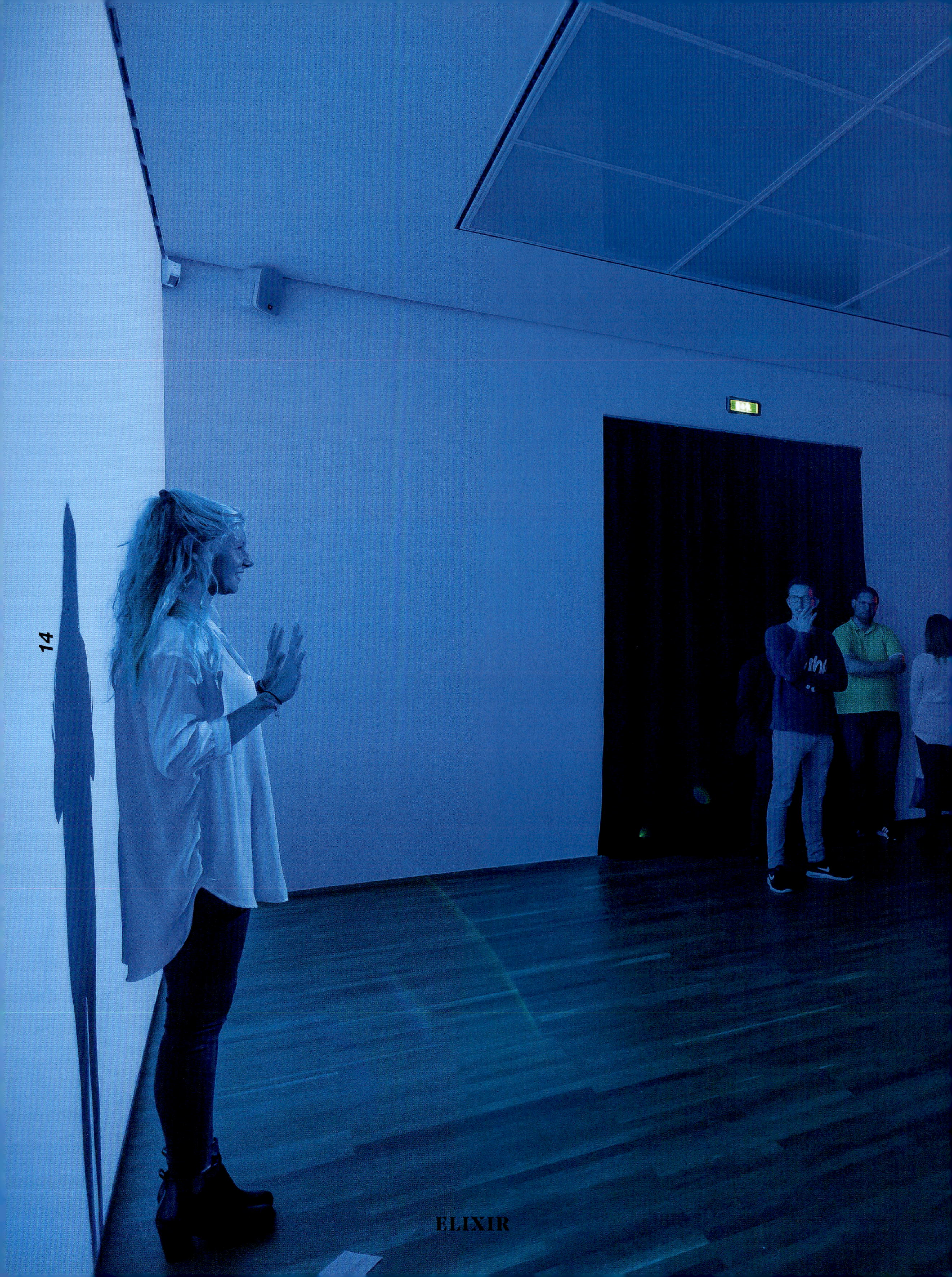

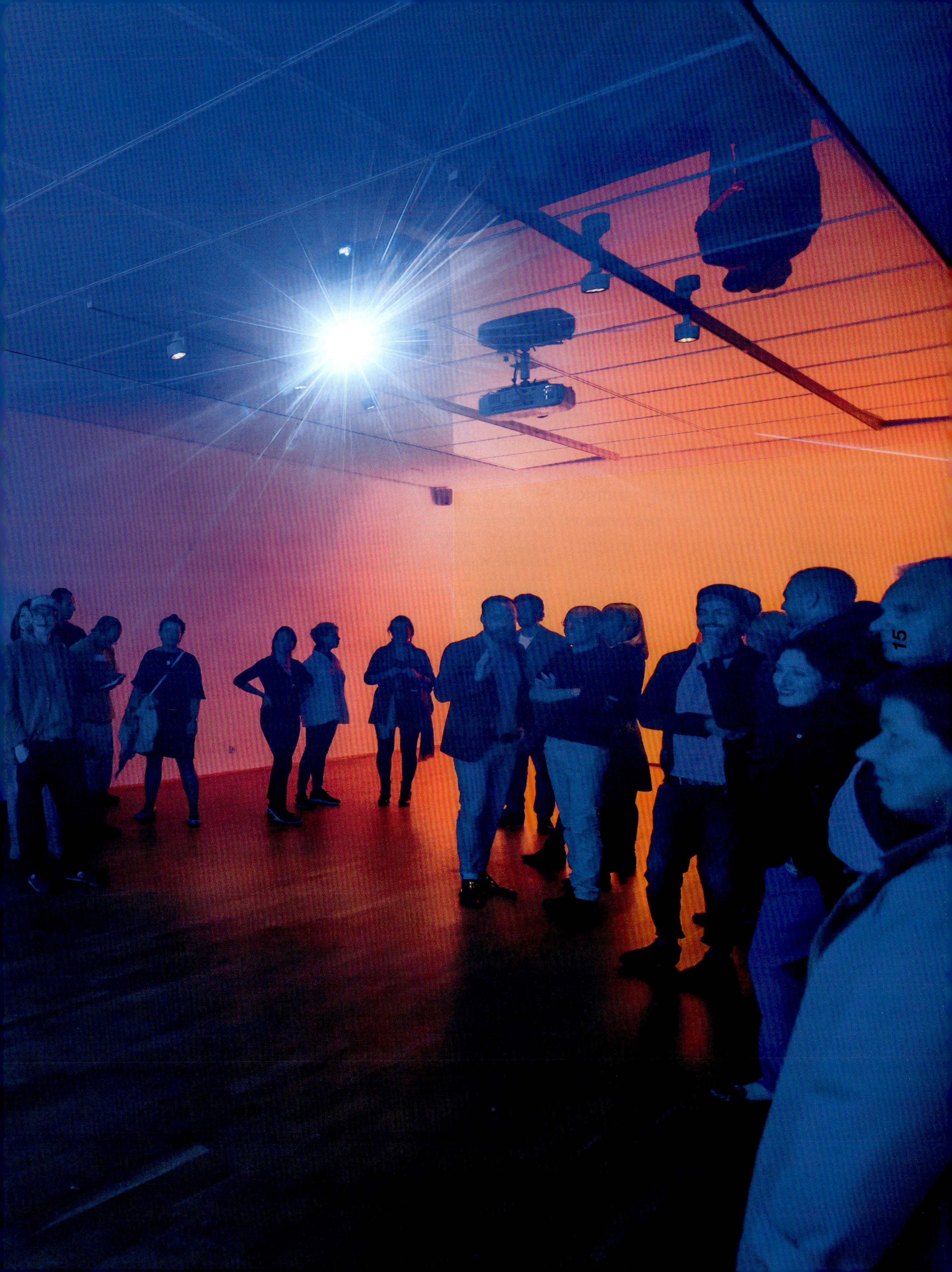

MOVING IMAGES

Text by Anna-Catharina Gebbers

In his 2015 contribution to an exhibition at the Hamburger Bahnhof for the shortlist of the artists nominated for the Preis der Nationalgalerie, Christian Falsnaes expanded the possibilities of performance art in a surprising way. Caught off guard immediately upon entering the exhibition space—as with prior works of Falsnaes—the visitors were confronted with the question of whether they wanted to be a part of participatory performances. But as in *Justified Beliefs* (2014), Falsnaes had created situations where he was not physically present. Instead, he showed two *delegated performances*,[1] whose execution he had entirely handed over to the viewers, to performers instructed by him—and to instructions recorded by him, as well as technical elements. With this joint presentation of the installation environments *Moving Images* (2015) and *The Title Is Your Name* (2015), Falsnaes put a reflection on the role of media at the heart of an exhibition more centrally than ever.

< 1
Cf. Claire Bishop, *Delegated Performance: Outsourcing Authenticity*, CUNY Academic Works, New York 2012, www.academicworks.cuny.edu/gc_pubs/45 (last visited July 15, 2016).

Until then, it had been above all the unpredictable and the uncontrollable that were hallmarks of Christian Falsnaes's performances: He has neither worked with professional actors nor with an exact script, but rather left it up to the audience how to implement his instructions. His communicative action alone and the power of his rhetorical influence in the actual confrontation with the audience starkly produced the focused presentation of a social situation; and only in the subsequent video work did Falsnaes intervene through montage, turning the presentation in the performance situation into a representation through moving images.

Moving Images confronts the viewer entering the room and the performative situation with two juxtaposed video screenings, produced beforehand. The images each show actors of a prior performance: different images and protagonists of this performance face each other on the images in the room and more or less directly vie for the viewer's attention. Between these scenes, staccato-like sequences from image material found on the Internet have been inserted. This *found footage* is sorted by the most popular topics, which the algorithms of search engines such as Google, Bing, or Yahoo have long known: sex, violence, baby animals. However, in the exhibition space, it is not left up to the audience to submit to these images or to perceive them in passing, quickly crossing the room. Rather, upon entering the room, *Moving Images* lets the viewers step into the images. The images flow across their bodies, the sound envelops them, and in the middle of the room a performer receives them. Moreover, a male voice comes from the speakers at regular intervals giving the viewers of the images instructions: to kneel and fold their arms behind their backs or dance.

In the film produced for *Moving Images*, the documented situation is not designed as a happening with random visitors. Instead, Falsnaes developed a targeted performative staging for the film. The protagonists shown in the film are not professional actors, but their activities follow a more or less concrete shooting schedule and script. These participants, too, received instructions. For example, Falsnaes asked them to yell "Look at me!" into the camera: as a message to later viewers. He also told them to perform different group activities: to sing as a choir, to cheer wildly, to perform dance choreographies, and to direct each other. Everything directed at the camera.

In the final video itself, Falsnaes is not present: as a participant of the performance, the producing artist makes himself his own material and is visible to the other participants; as the film's producer, he simultaneously becomes the intermediate, omniscient author. This authorial, hegemonial role is emphasized by the omission of his person in the images. Through the recorded instructions, he subsequently seeks to also influence the viewers of the film. This succession of roles (on the one hand making himself, on the other hand making the audience the material) is then again repeated in the screening of the film in the same exhibition space where the film was made: A commenting performer interacts with the film and its viewers by interrupting the film and entrapping the viewers in performative actions. As a group, they discuss the images seen and their experience. The degrading role to follow orders, to be asked to kneel or to dance in front of others, but also the pornographic flood of images are opened for discussion once more from outside—by the performer.

The exhibition at the Hamburger Bahnhof was put in yet another reflective context by a second immersive situation, which Falsnaes created in an adjacent room. In contrast to the first room, the actions in *The Title Is Your Name* (2015) are embedded into a one-on-one situation: only a single visitor can enter the room. Unlike in the preceding room, there is no integration into a group here. And the distance to the people depicted in the film images is exchanged for the perceived lack of distance to a person as they appear in Skype or Periscope. The lack of distance we feel in these forms of communication, which have become natural to us, lets video images become an extension of our bodies. We interact with the images as if they were real people. They trigger similar emotions, thoughts, and bodily experiences.

With the works *The Title Is Your Name* (2015) and the work *Moving Images* (2015), Christian Falsnaes creates immersive situations in which filmic work, exhibition space, and performance are interwoven. Presentation and representation, materiality of the performance and its transformation into other media, as well as physical presence and filmic documentation merge.

In both works, performance and video film intertwine. The audience both assumes the role of a viewer and becomes part of a performance. The mutual influence of performer and audience (feedback loop) is only partially present; there is no direct influence of the acting viewer on images transmitted in real time, as in closed-circuit installations. What matters, rather, is the image that those acting in the performance create. Falsnaes amplifies a resulting analytic viewing of the images by letting different actors repeat the actions in the film, but also in the exhibition space, and by letting the experiences from *The Title Is Your Name* (2015) and *Moving Images* (2015) build upon each other. The perspective on the images of performing people changes once one has been a performing person oneself.

Christian Falsnaes thus expands traditional parameters of performance art, such as physicality, space, sound, and temporality. He demonstrates the ostensive distance between active physical presentation and the distanced passive perception of representation. The aesthetics of production, of reception, and of the work can no longer be separated, neither with respect to the artistic work nor to a society influenced by media. Falsnaes demonstrates to the viewers what active role they play in the all but unavoidable representation of one's own person in seemingly private images, as well as in social media or in the staging of images in the media.

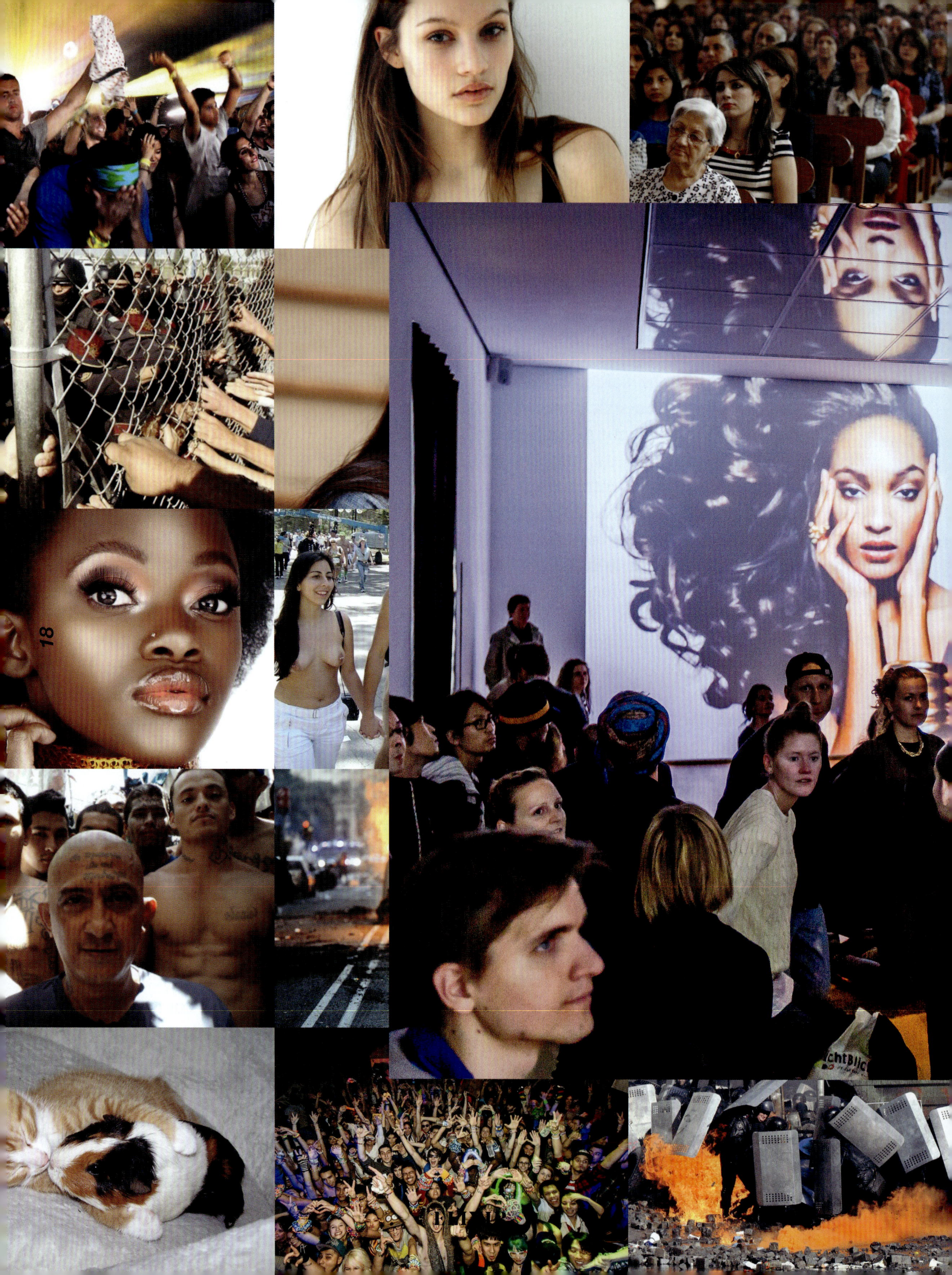

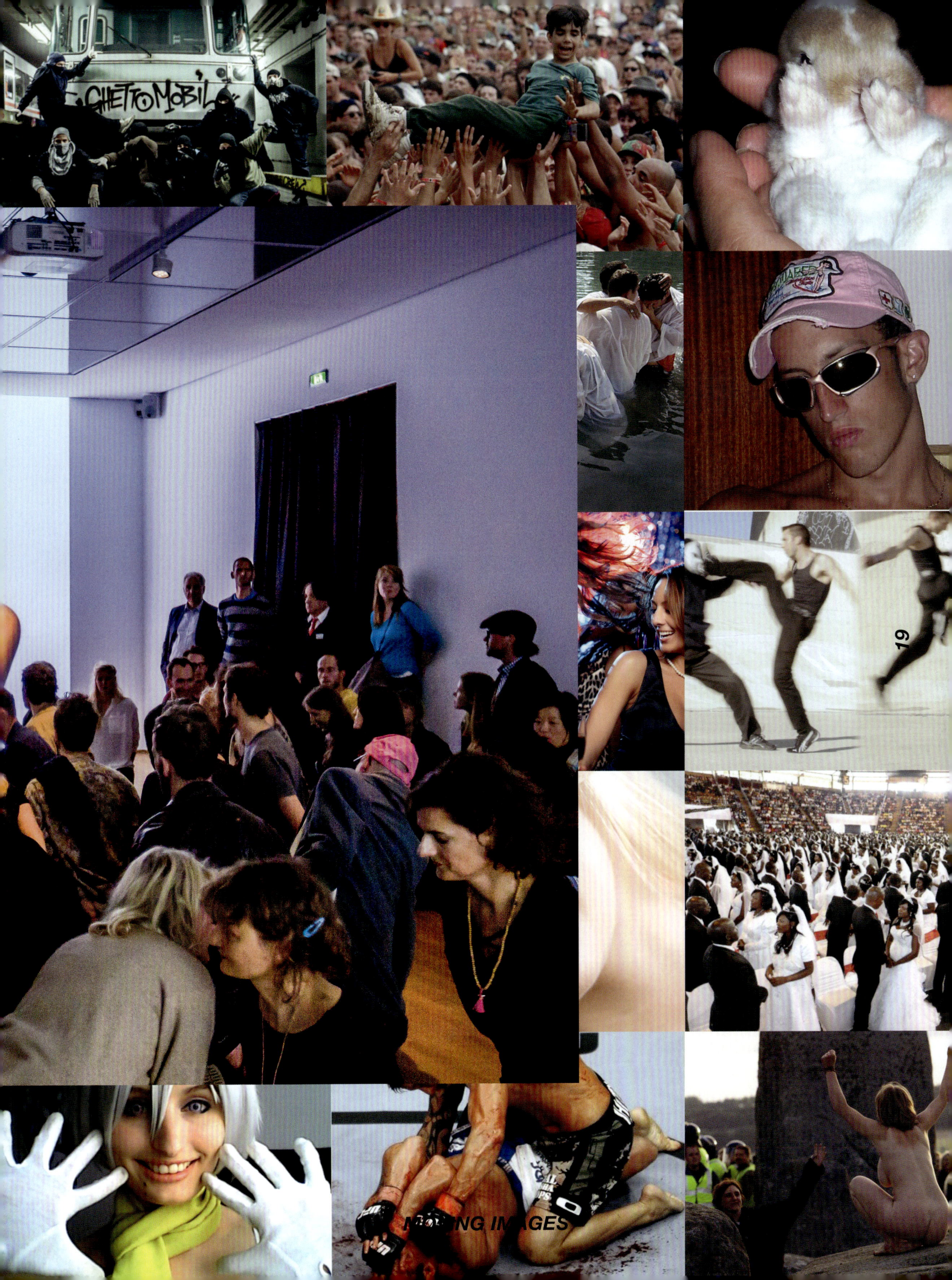
GHETTOMOBIL

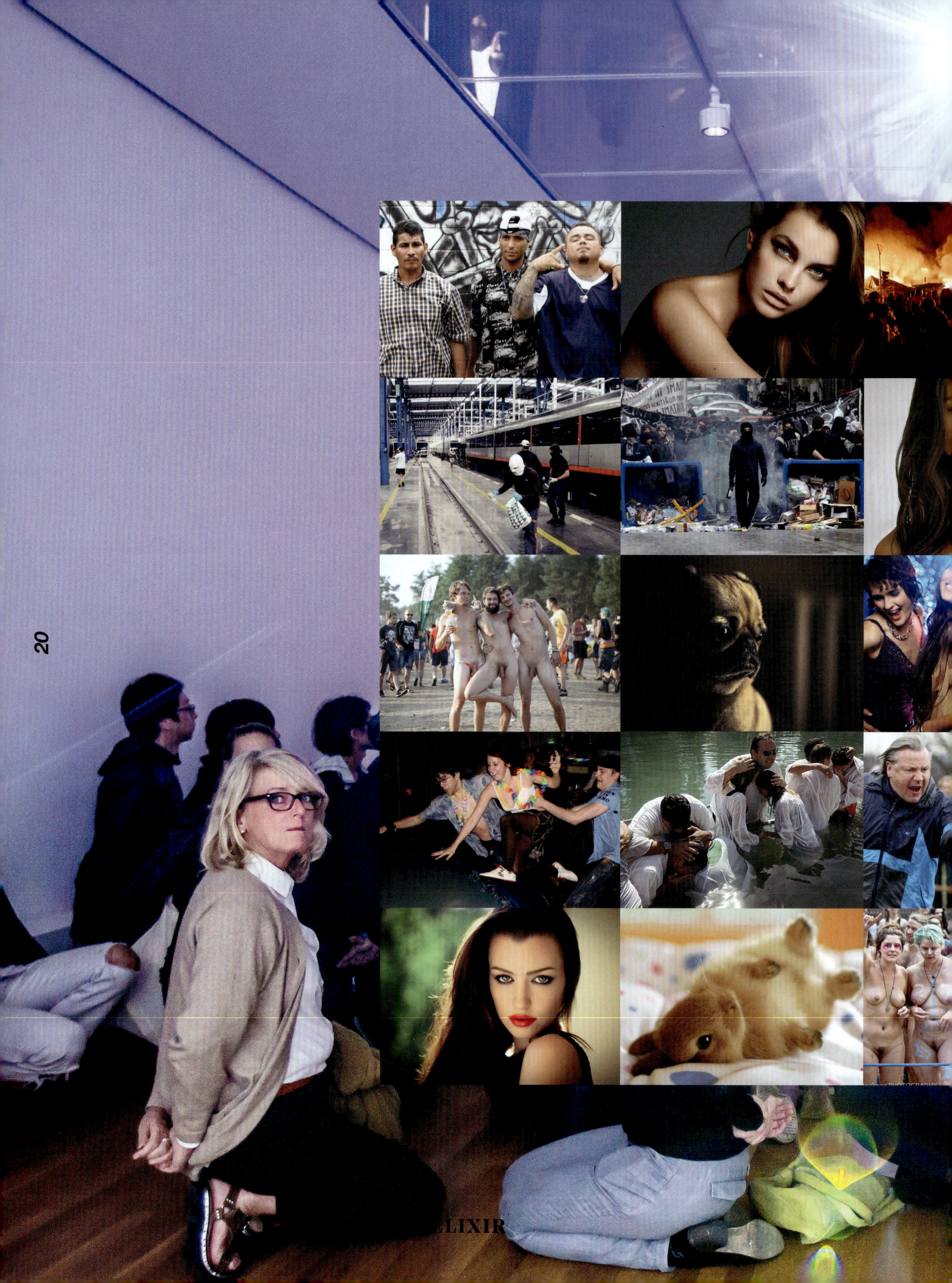
ELIXIR

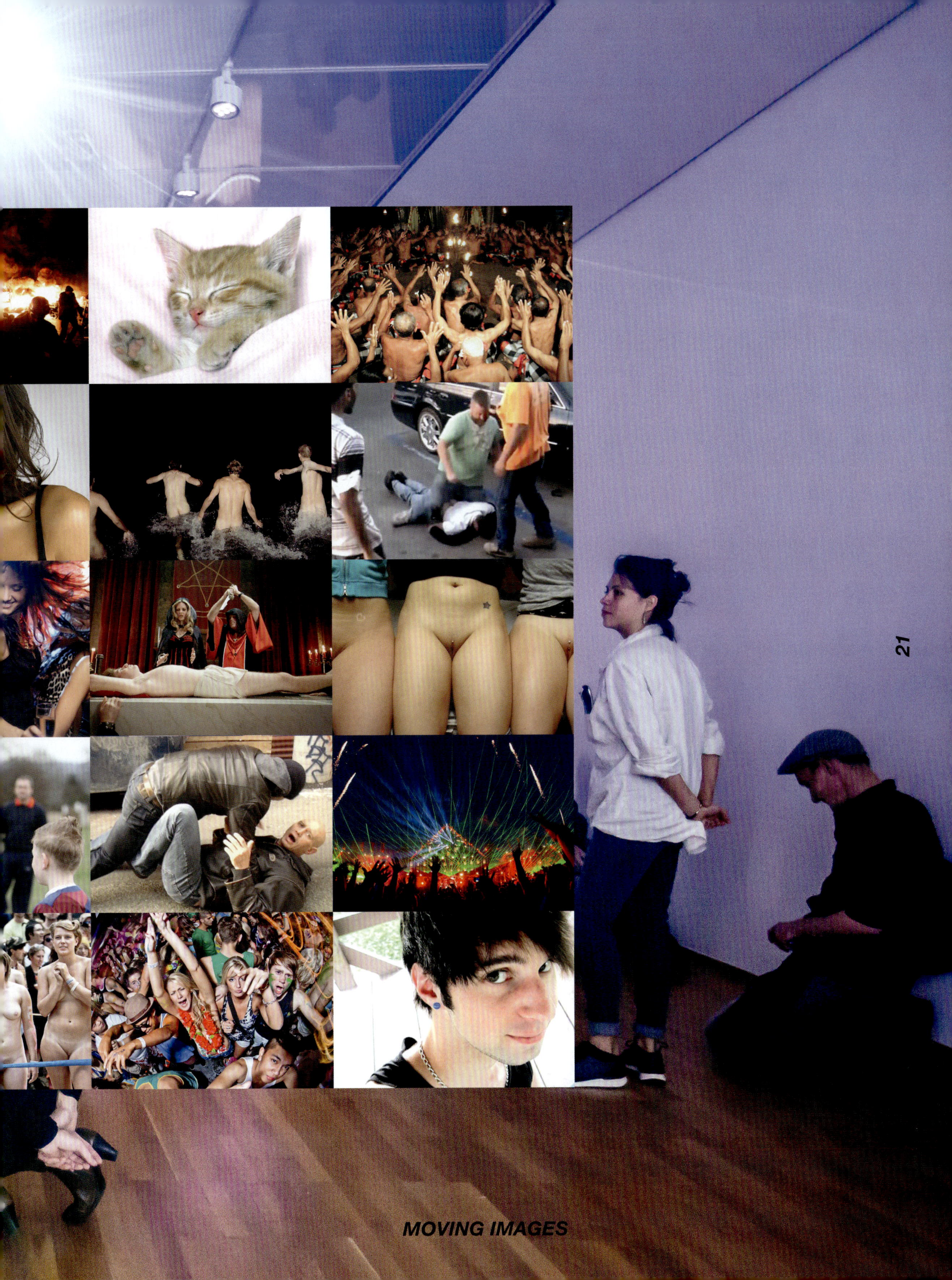

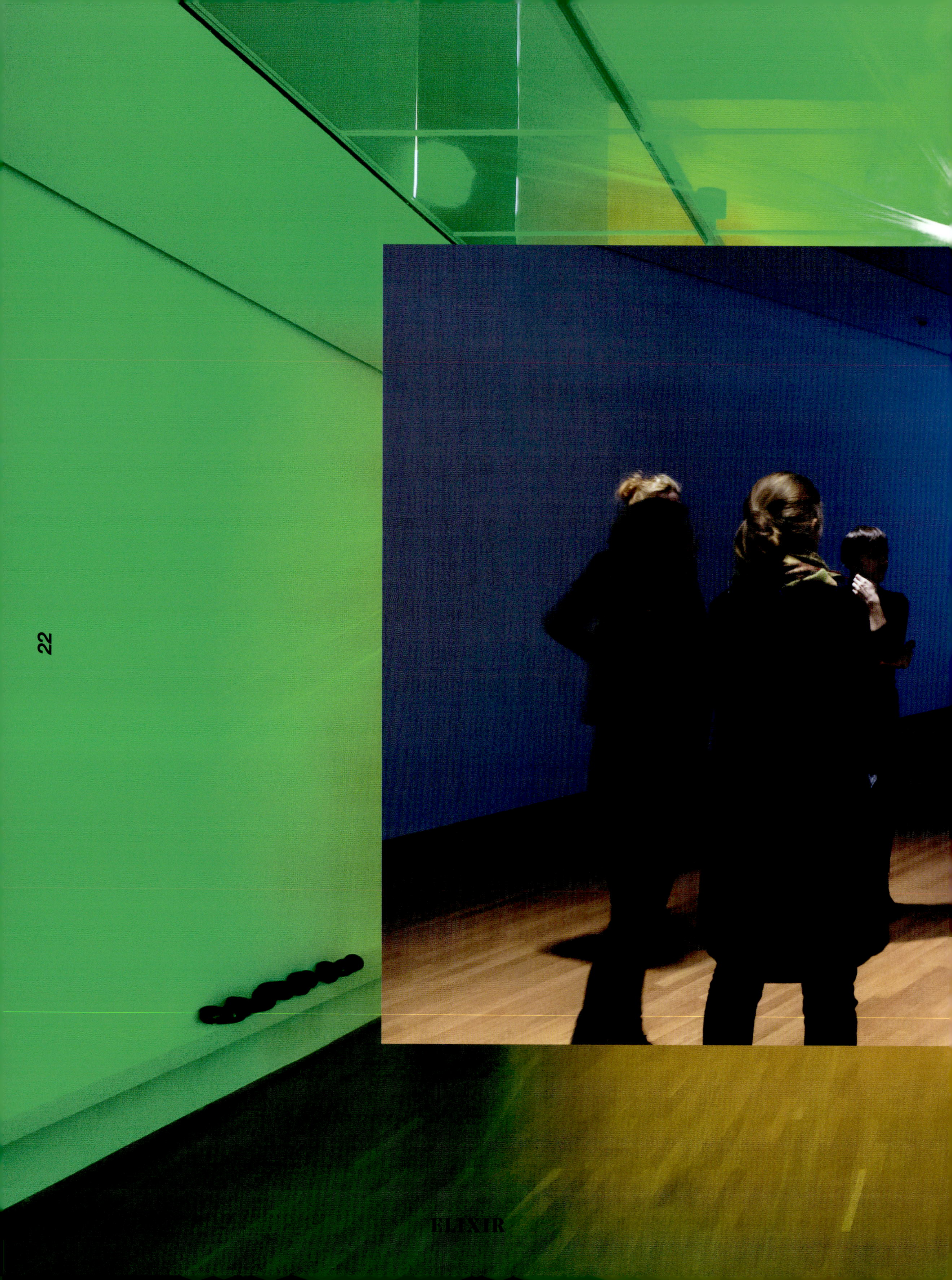

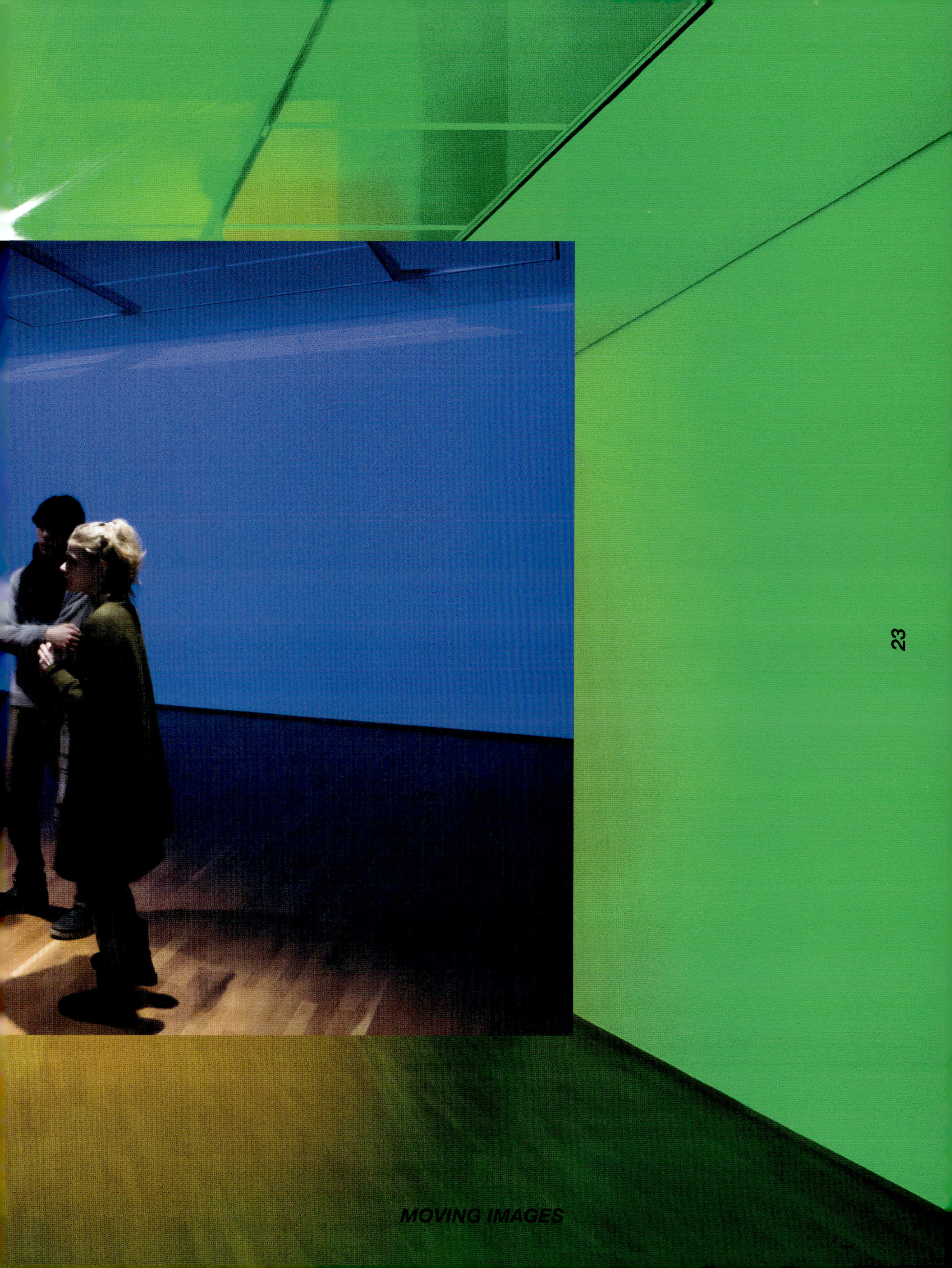

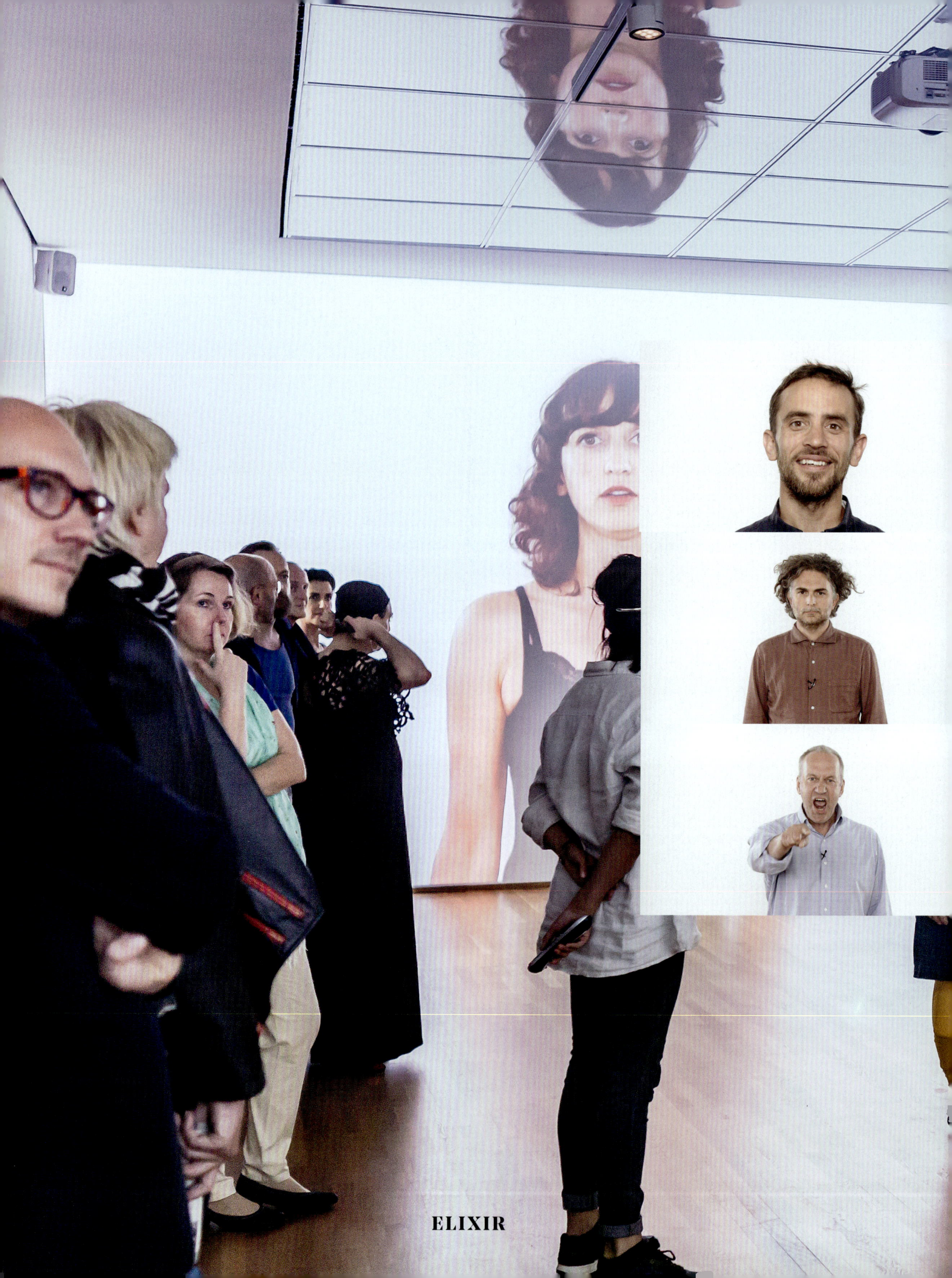

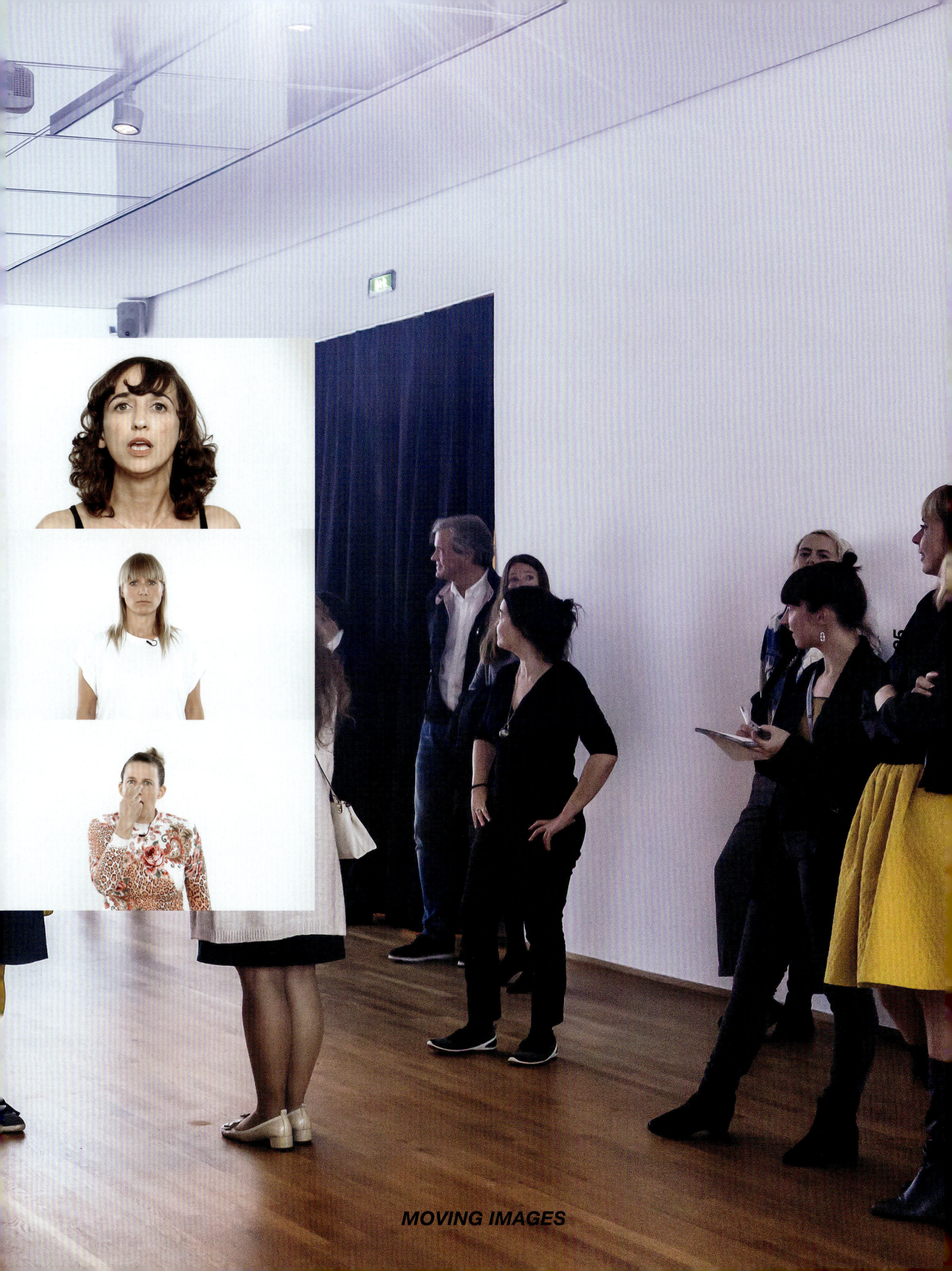

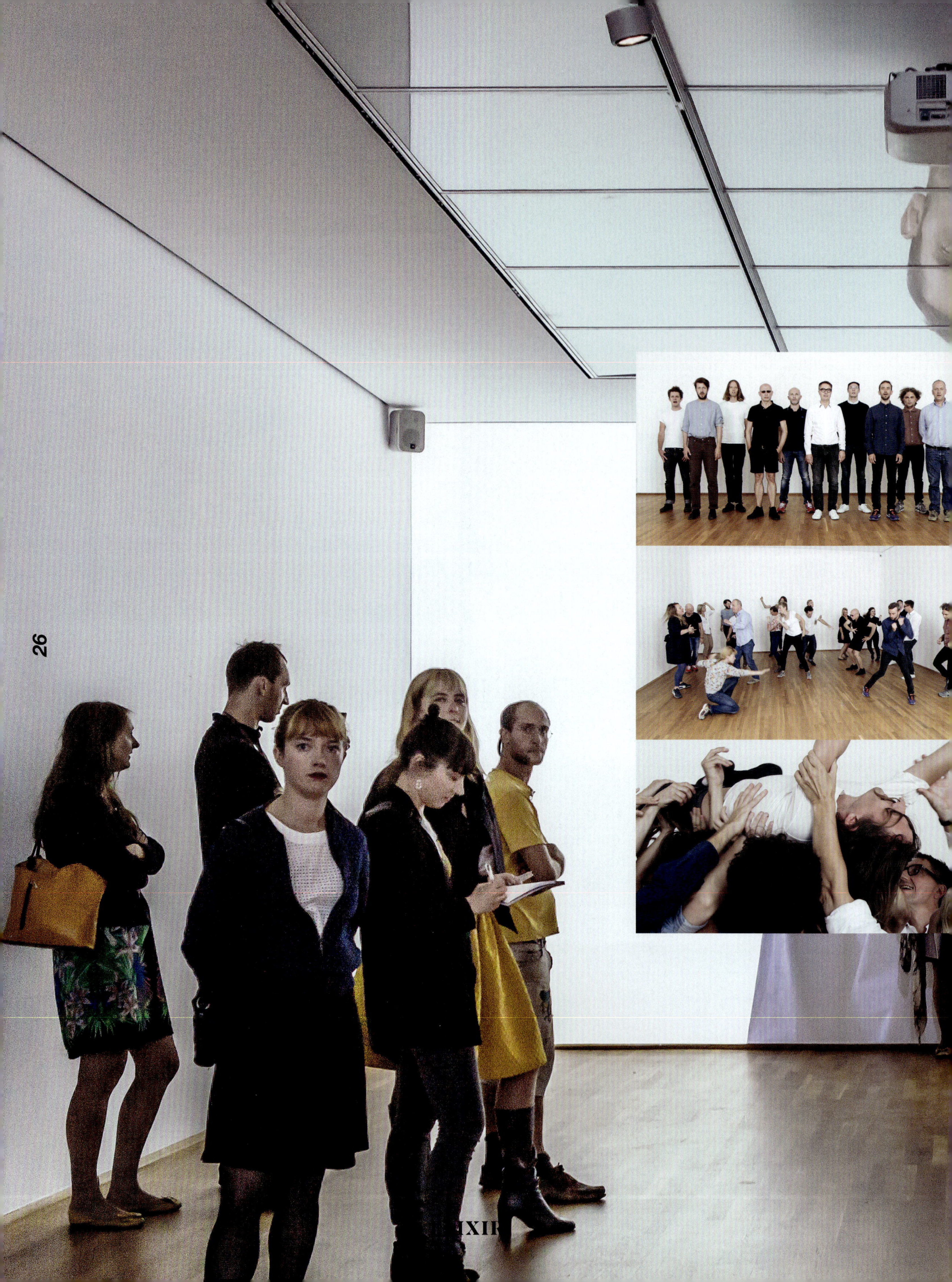

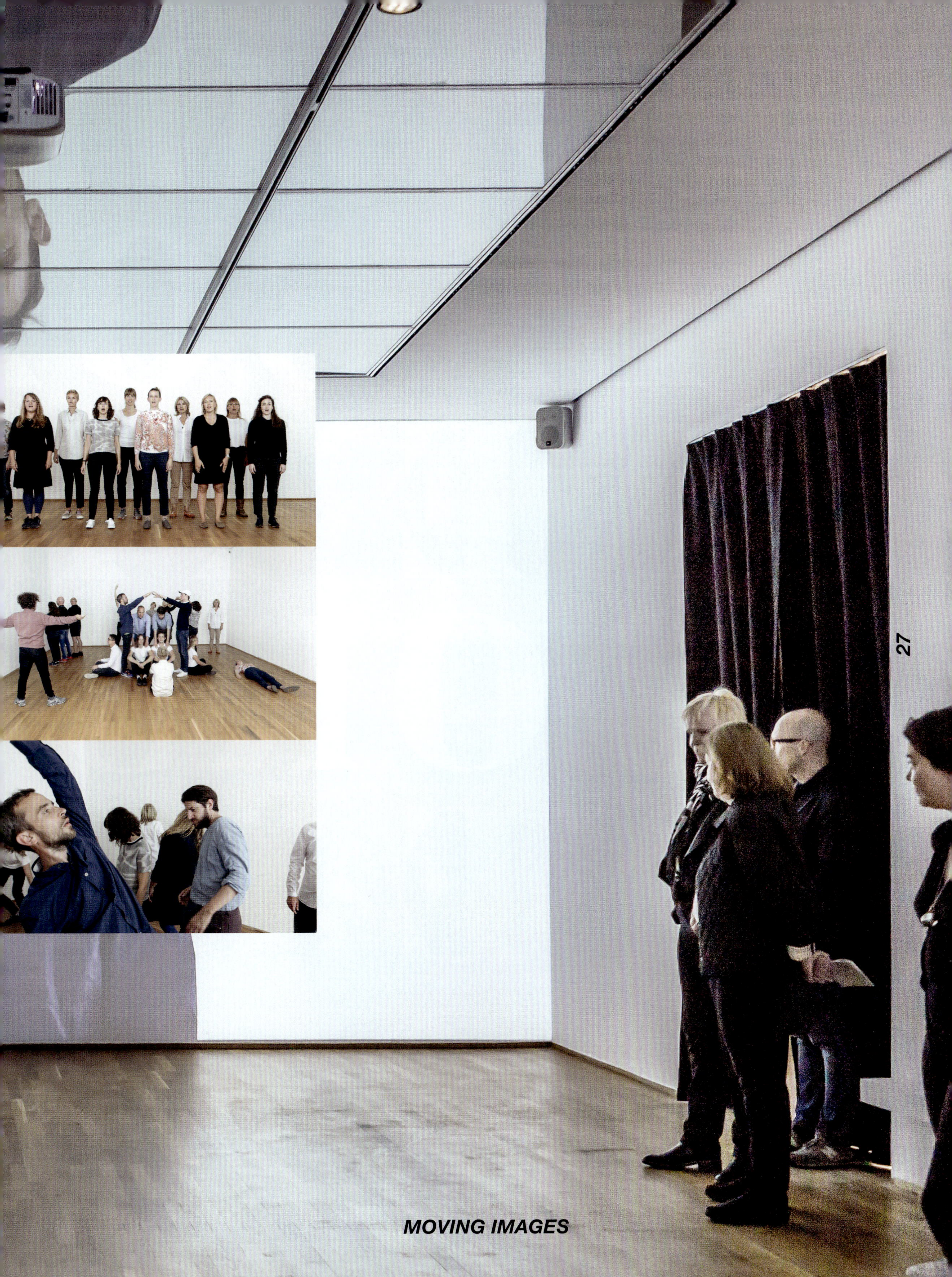

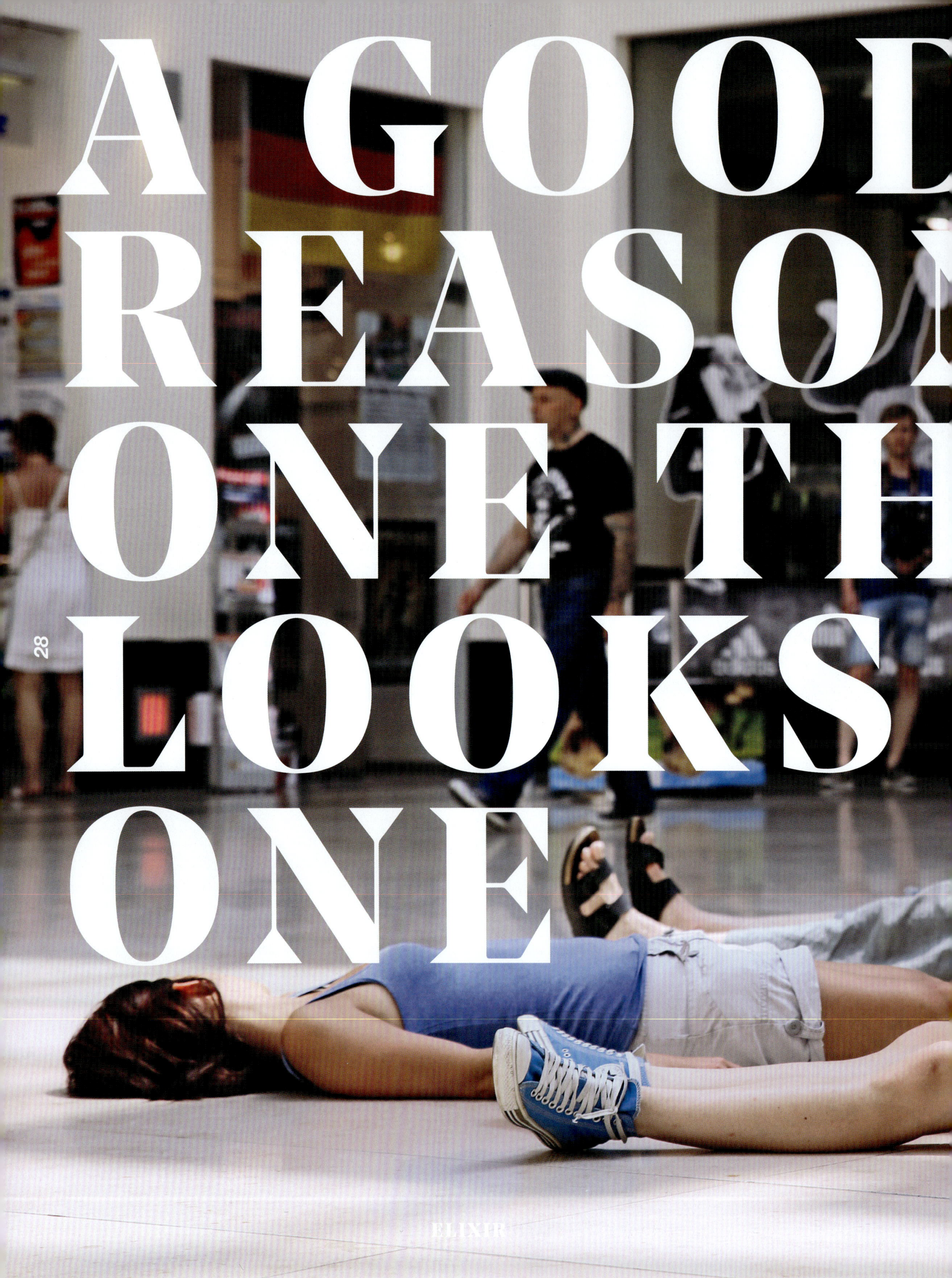
A GOO
REASO
ONE TH
LOOKS
ONE

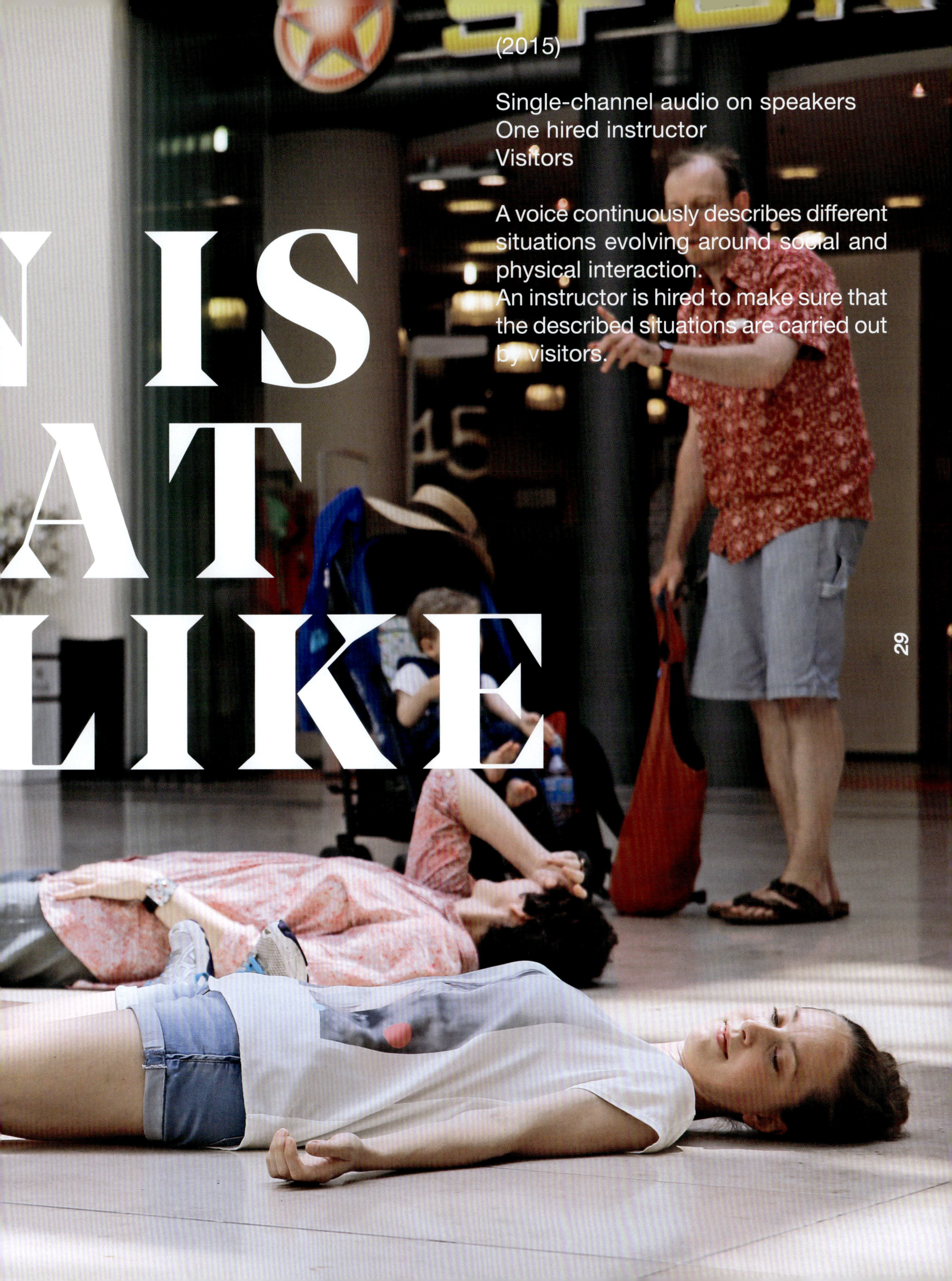

IS
AT
LIKE

(2015)

Single-channel audio on speakers
One hired instructor
Visitors

A voice continuously describes different situations evolving around social and physical interaction.
An instructor is hired to make sure that the described situations are carried out by visitors.

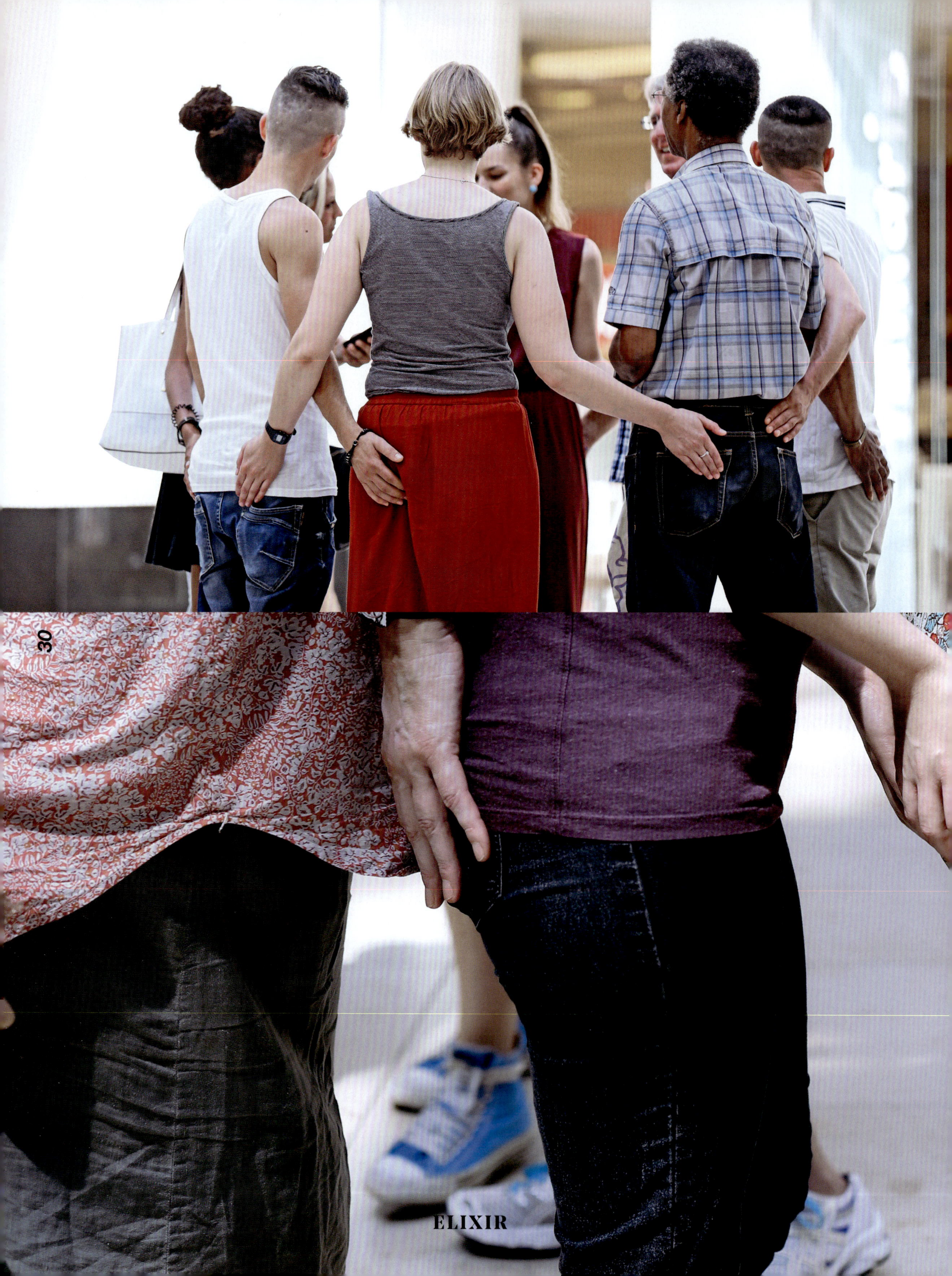

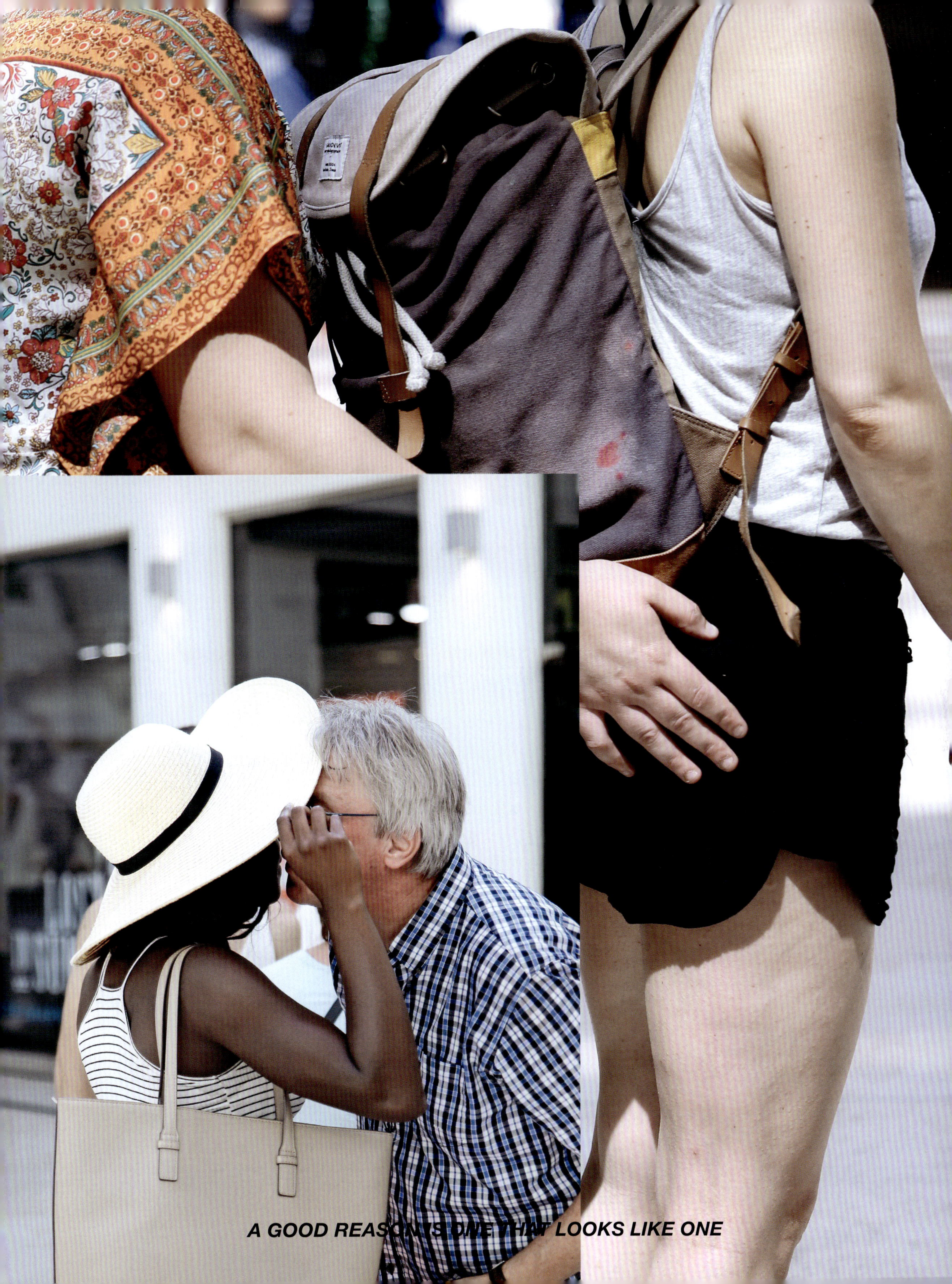
A GOOD REASON IS ONE THAT LOOKS LIKE ONE

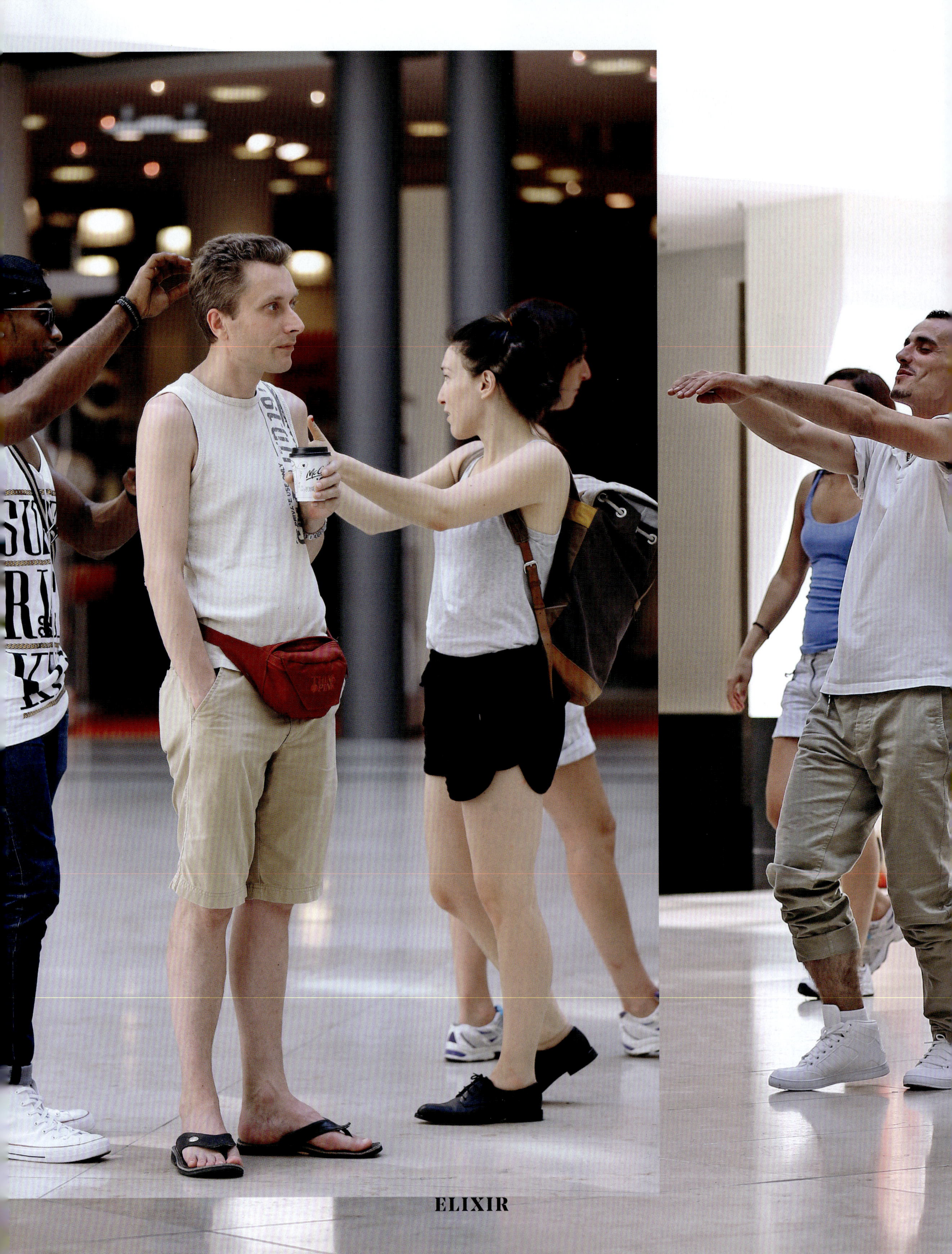

ELIXIR

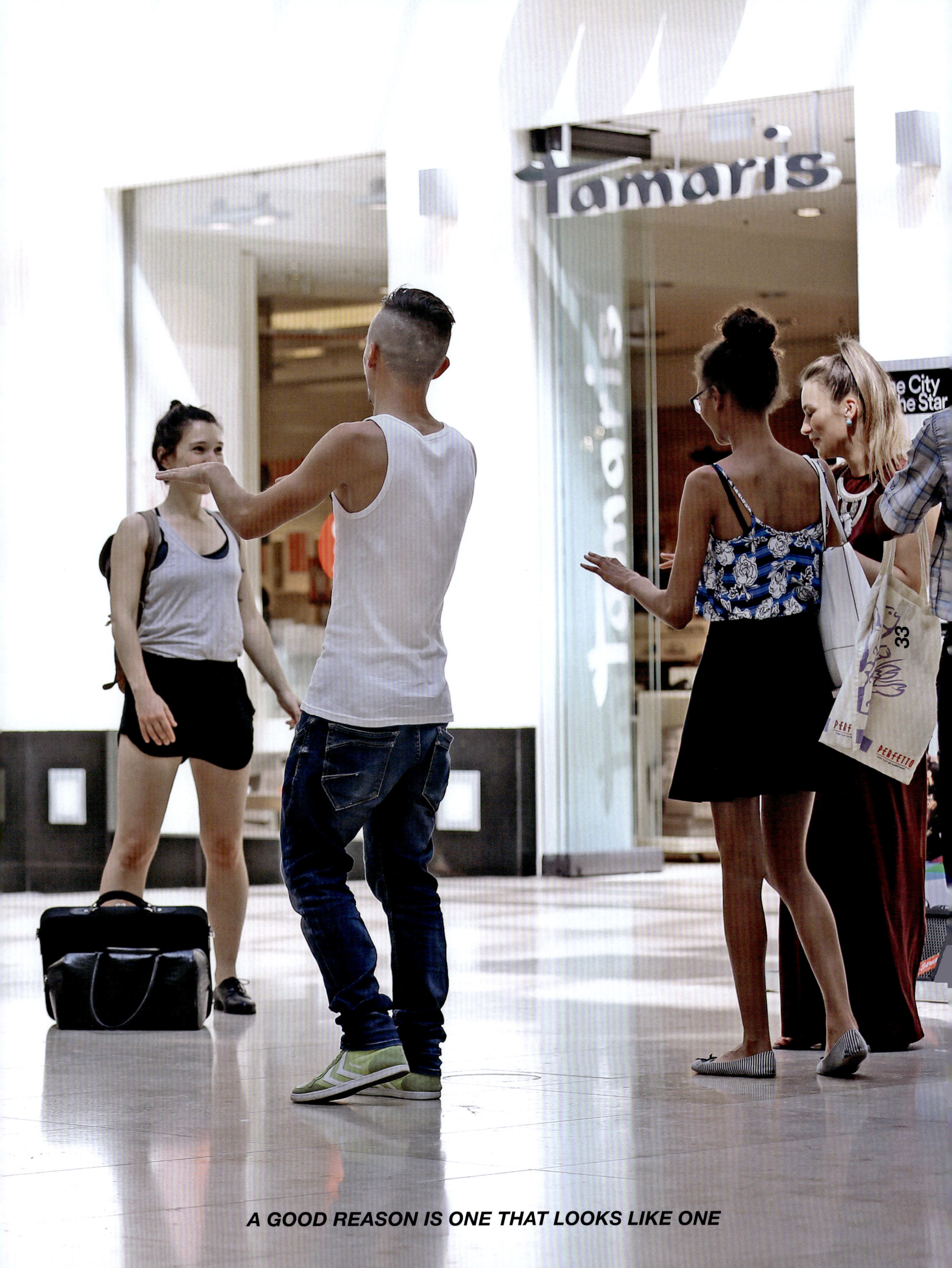

A GOOD REASON IS ONE THAT LOOKS LIKE ONE

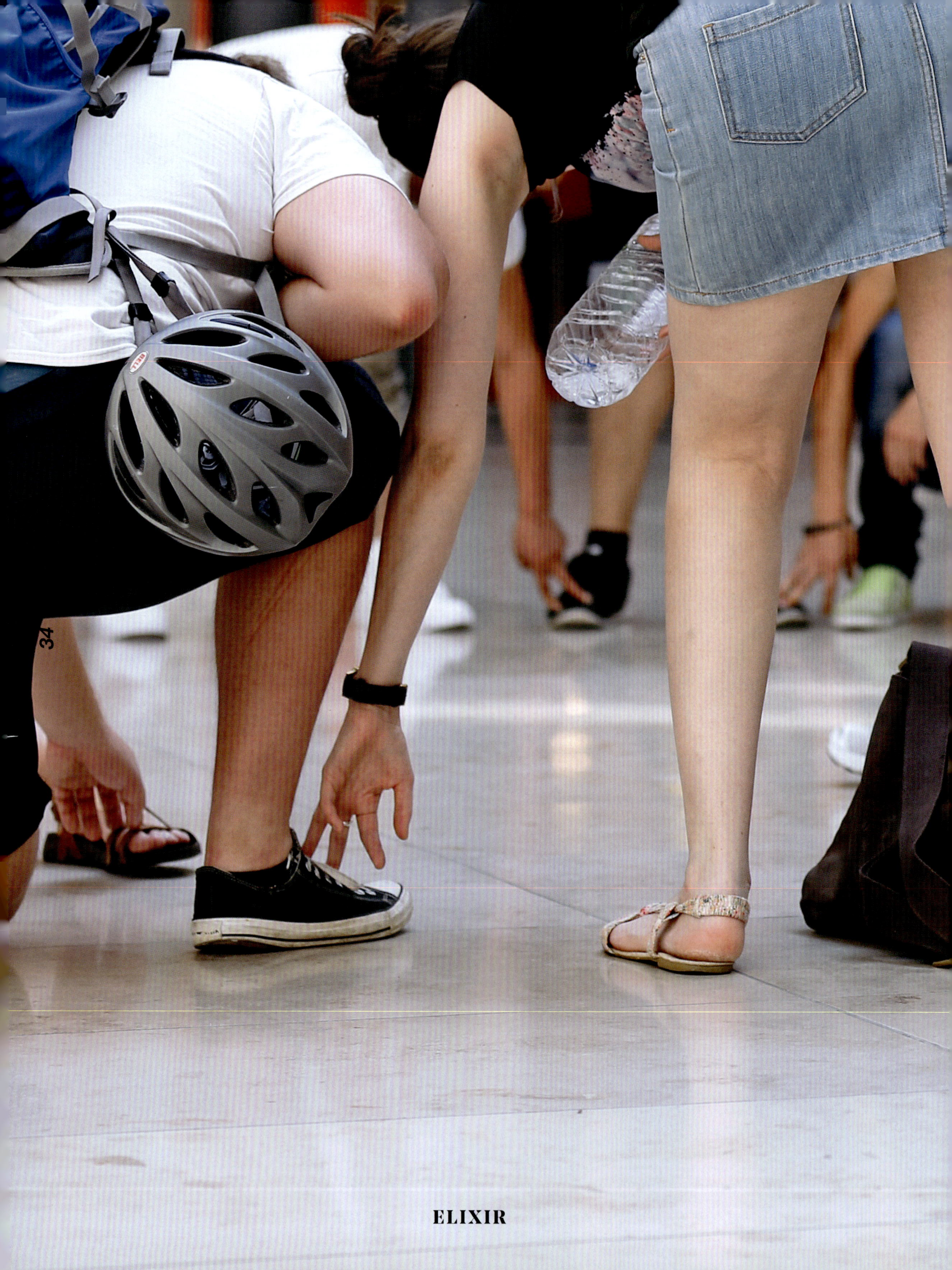

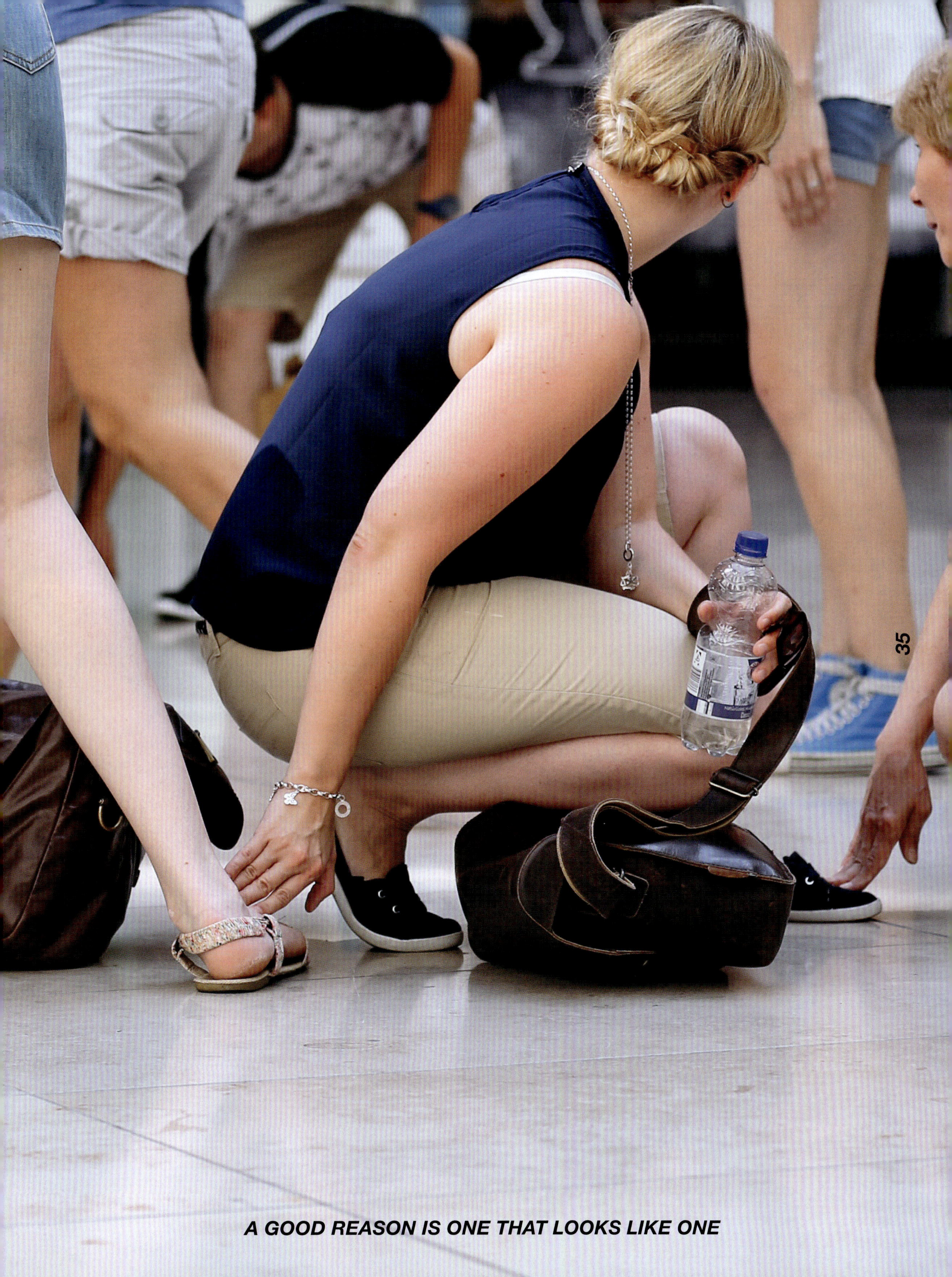

A GOOD REASON IS ONE THAT LOOKS LIKE ONE

Performance
Spray-painted OSB plates on wood structure, ca. 300 x 1500 cm
Video

A large white wood wall is placed in one location.
An audience is brought to the wall and instructed to spray-paint it and saw it into pieces.
The pieces from the wall are carried to another location by the audience and rebuilt as a collective monument.
The audience kneels down in front of the work they have created and look at it.
The instructor makes the audience cheer and display euphoric behavior throughout the performance.
The performance is recorded on video.

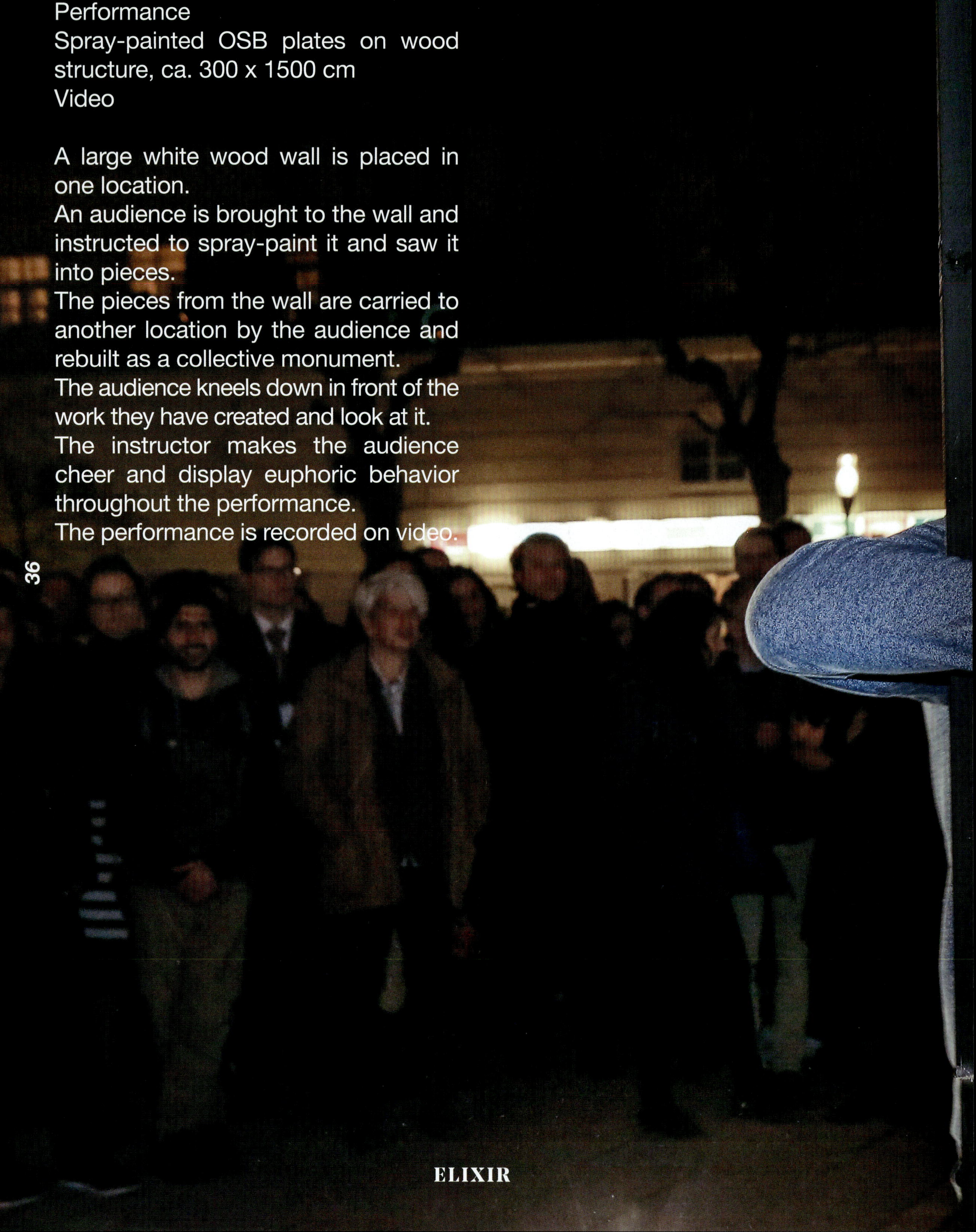

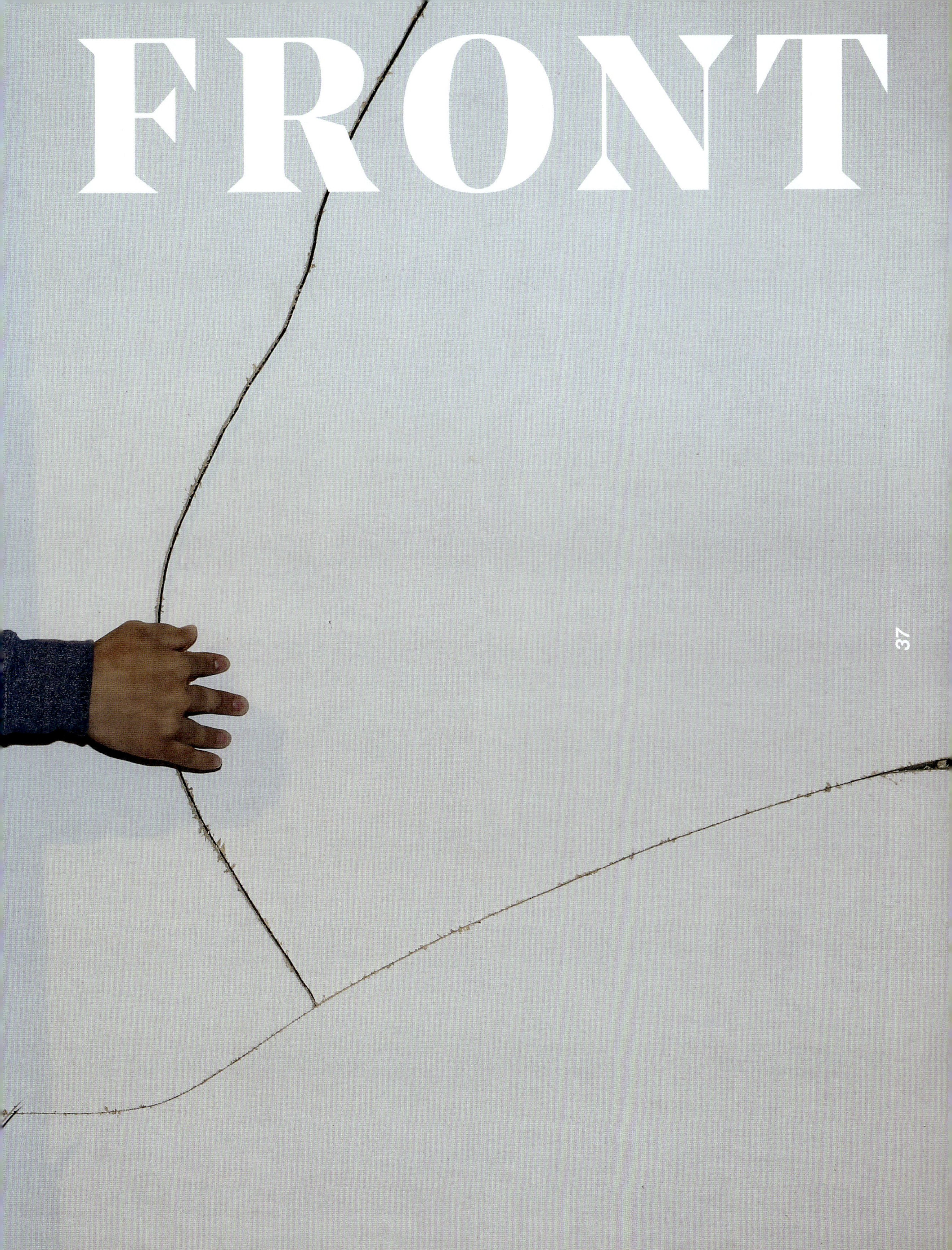
FRONT
37

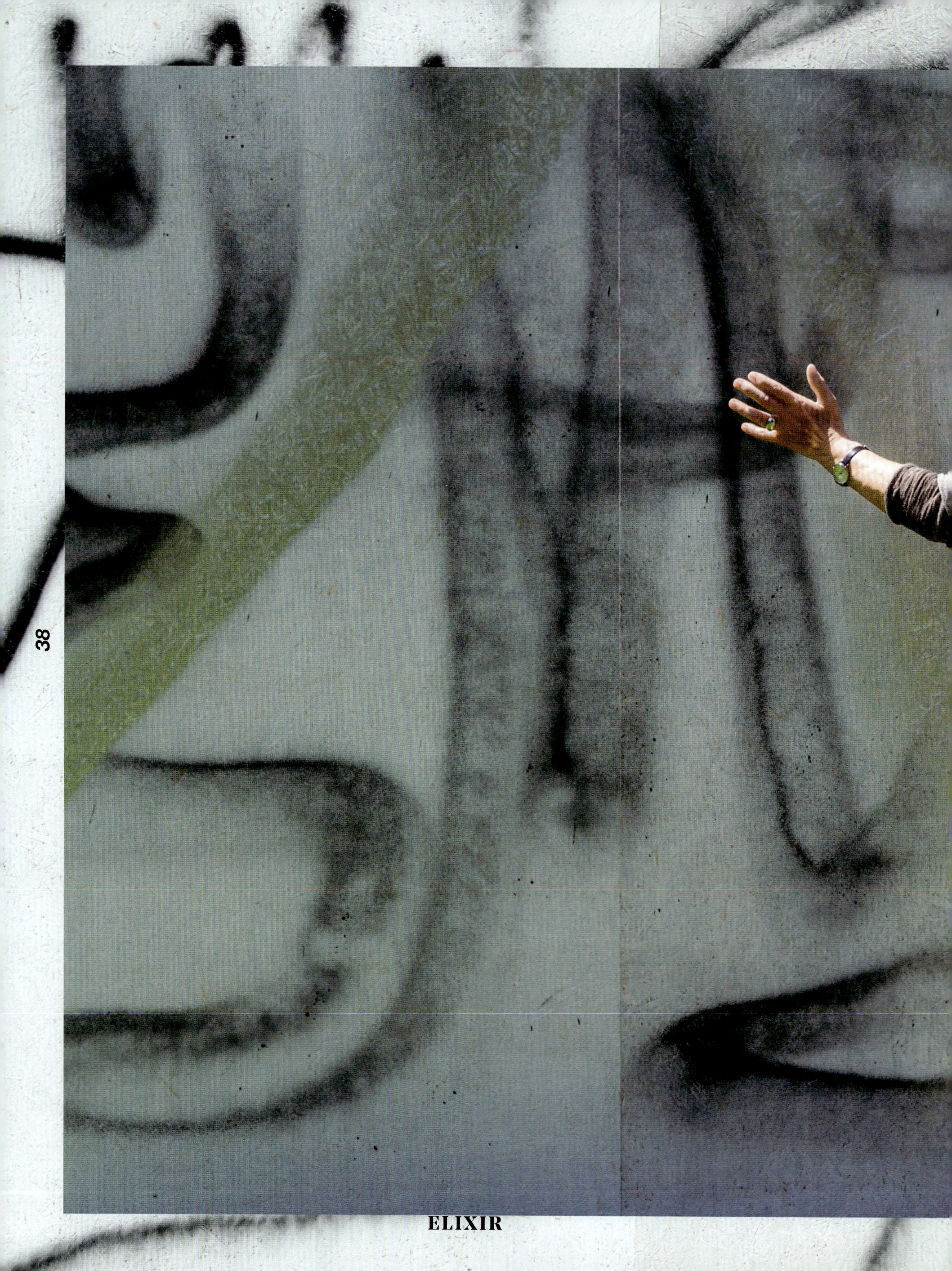

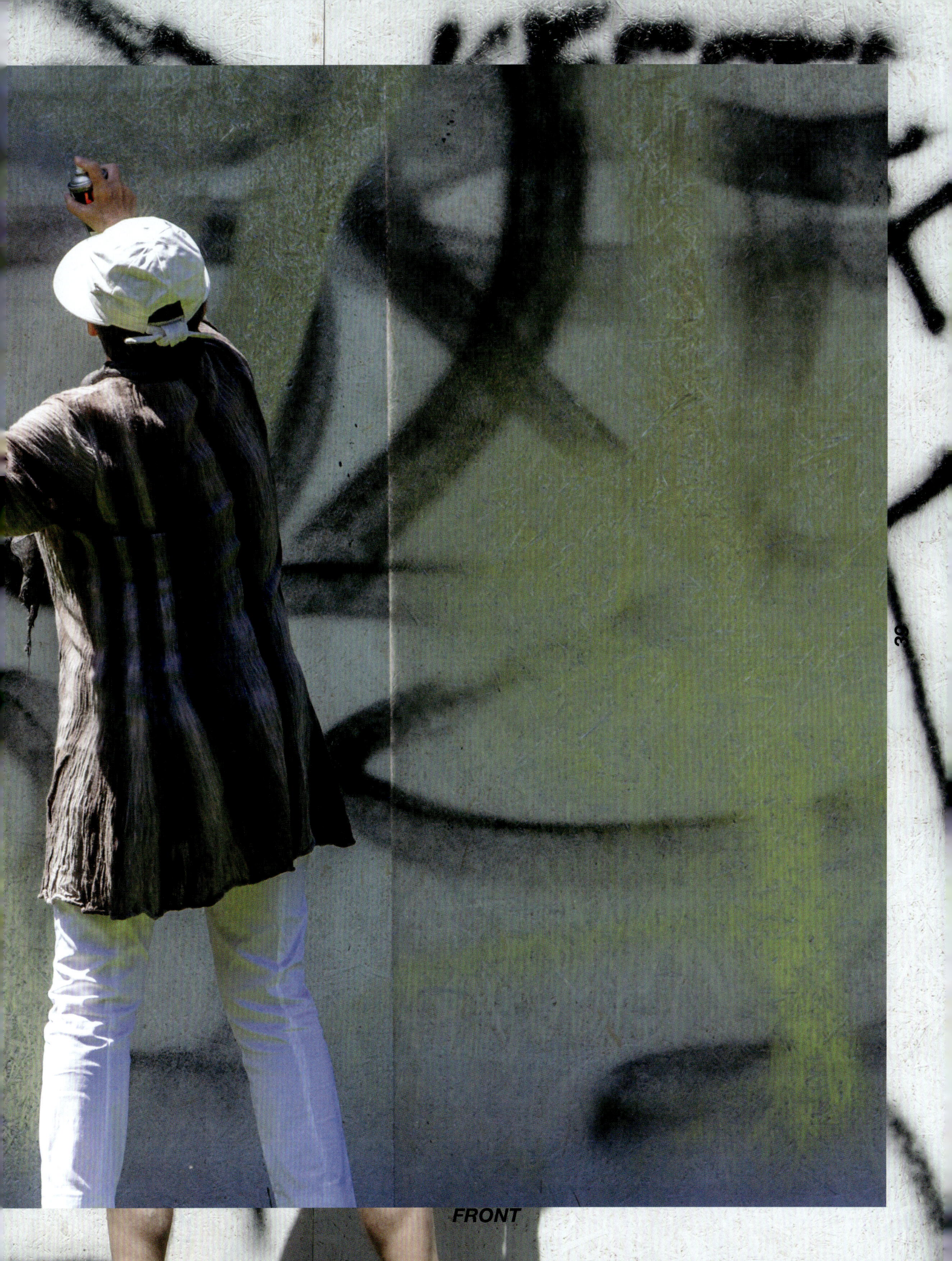

FRONT

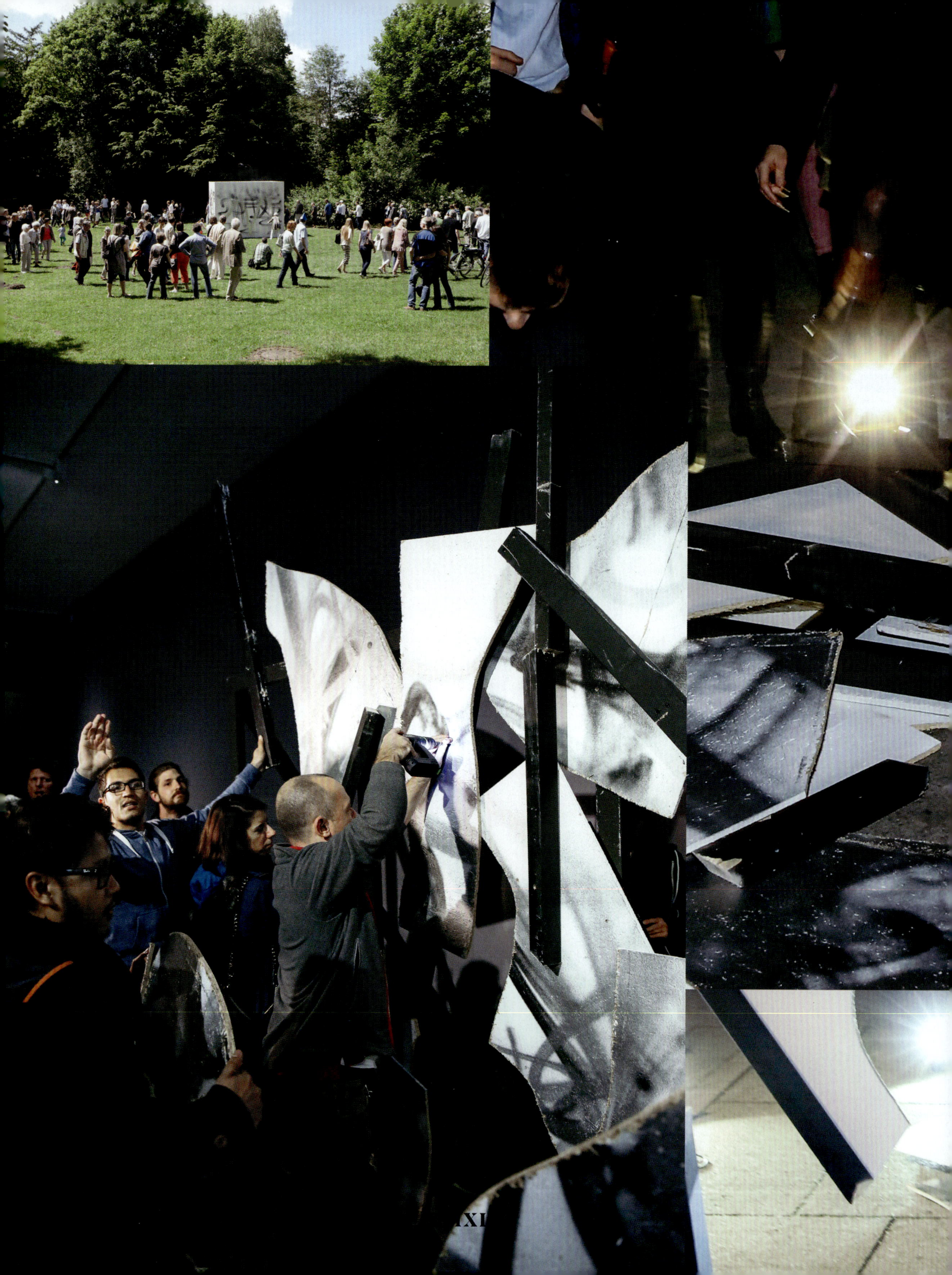

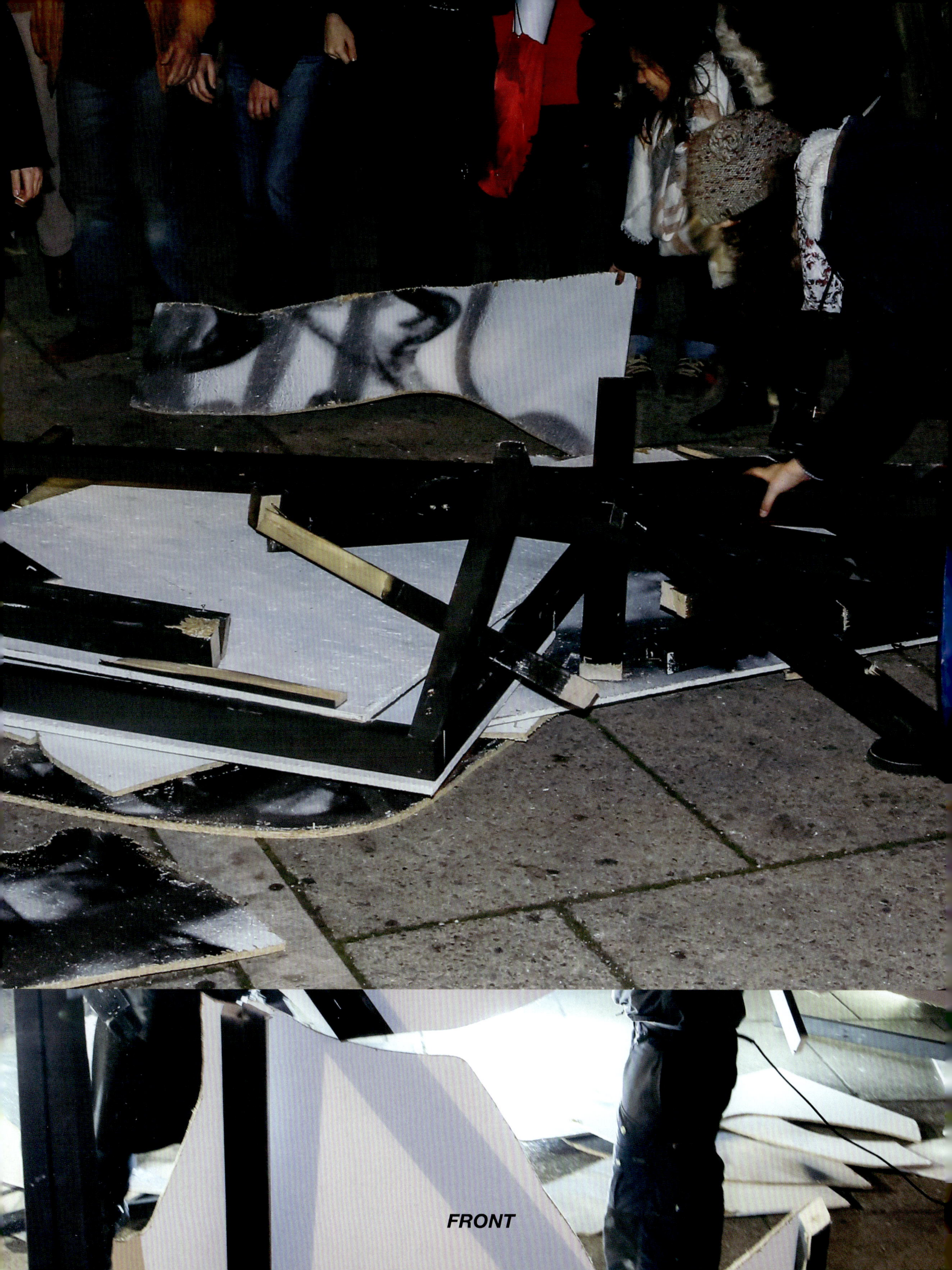
FRONT

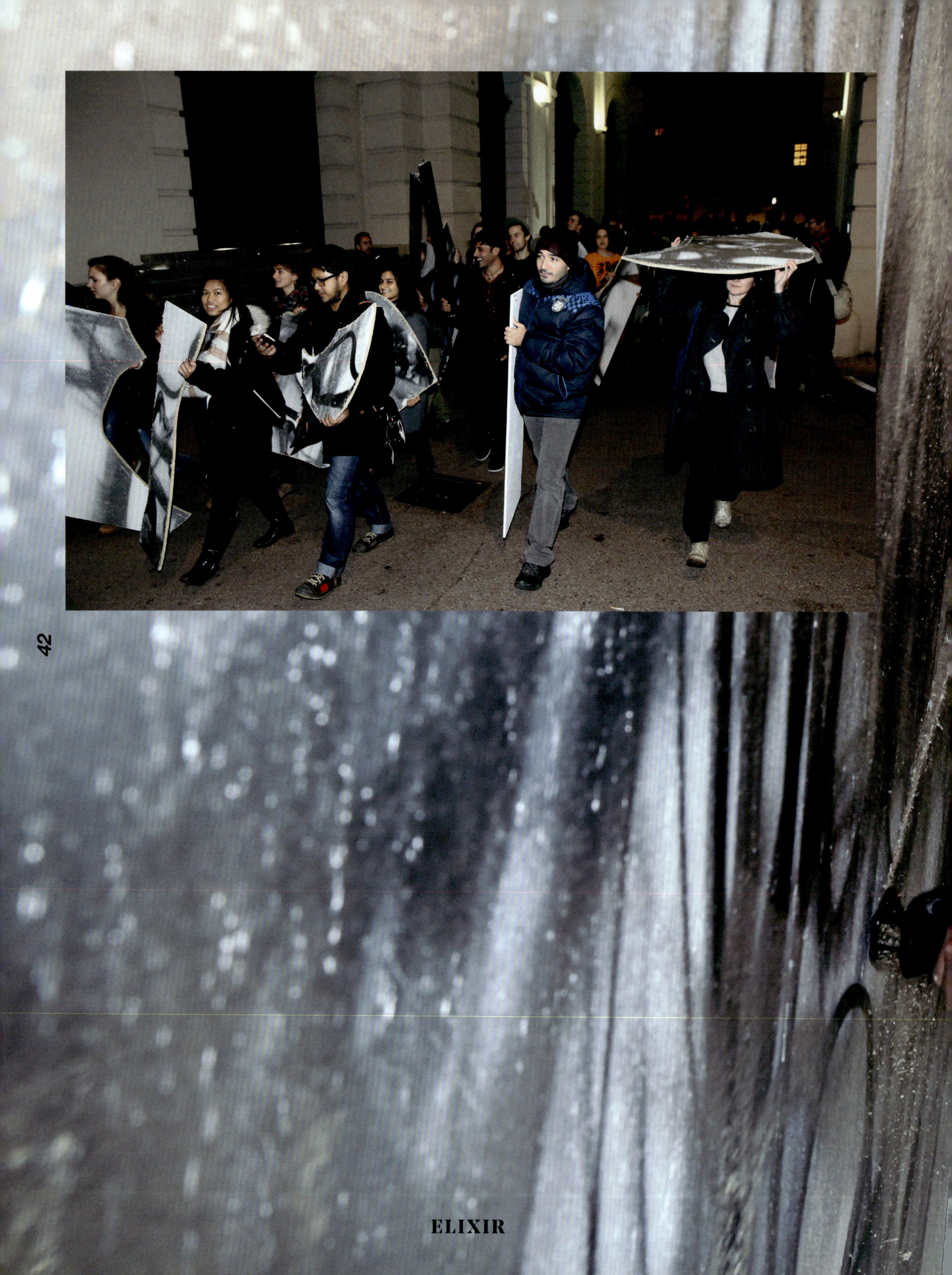

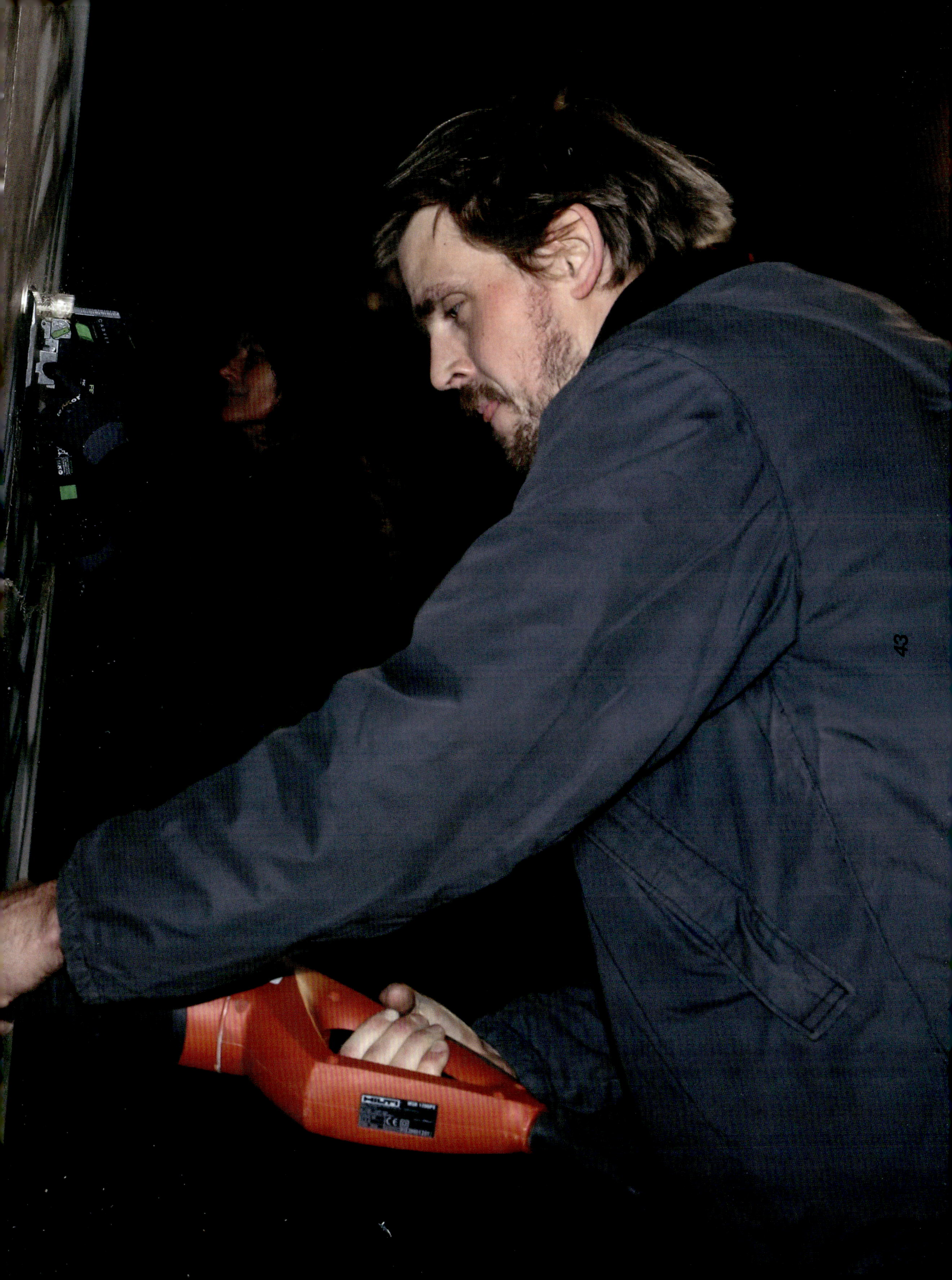

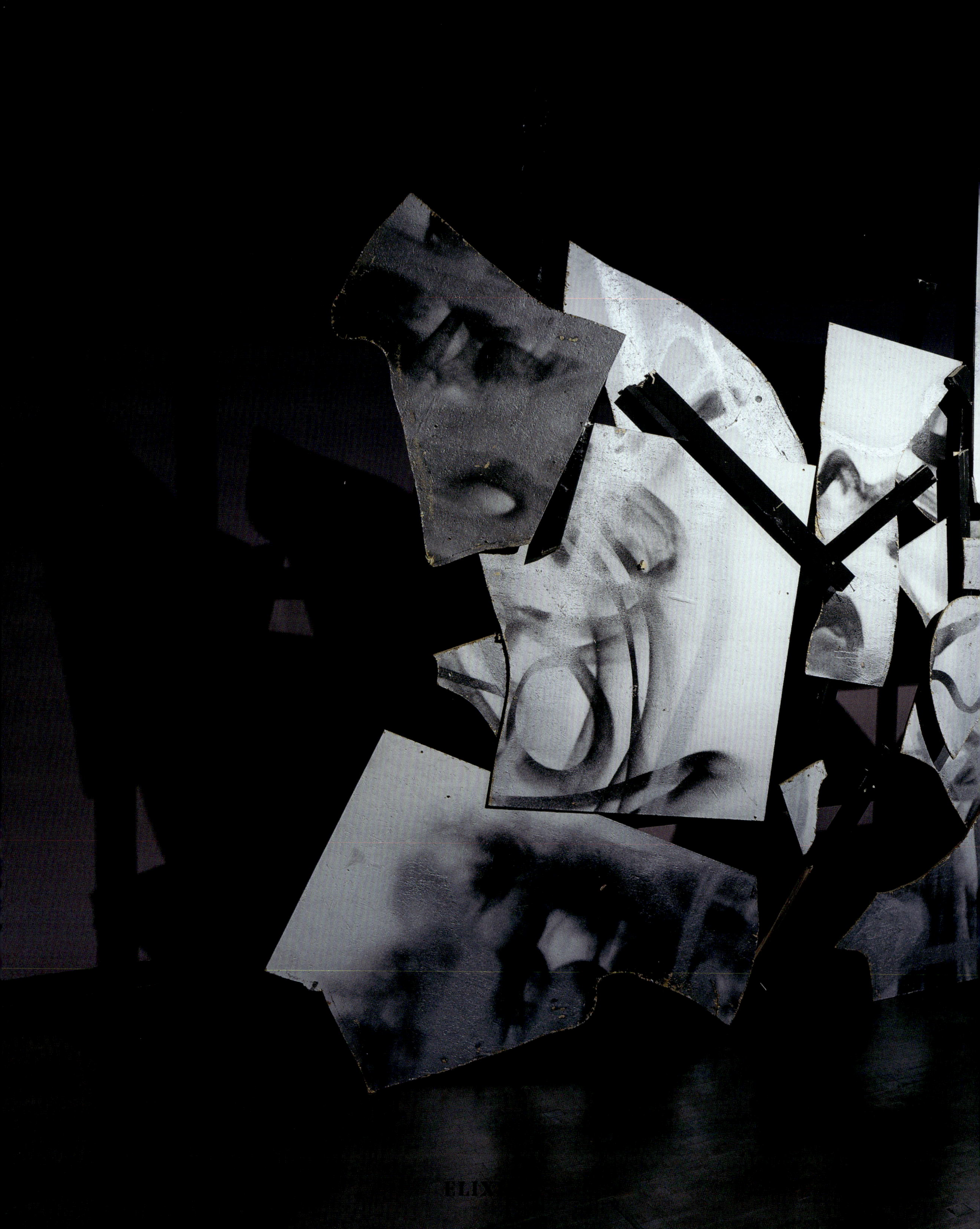
ELIX

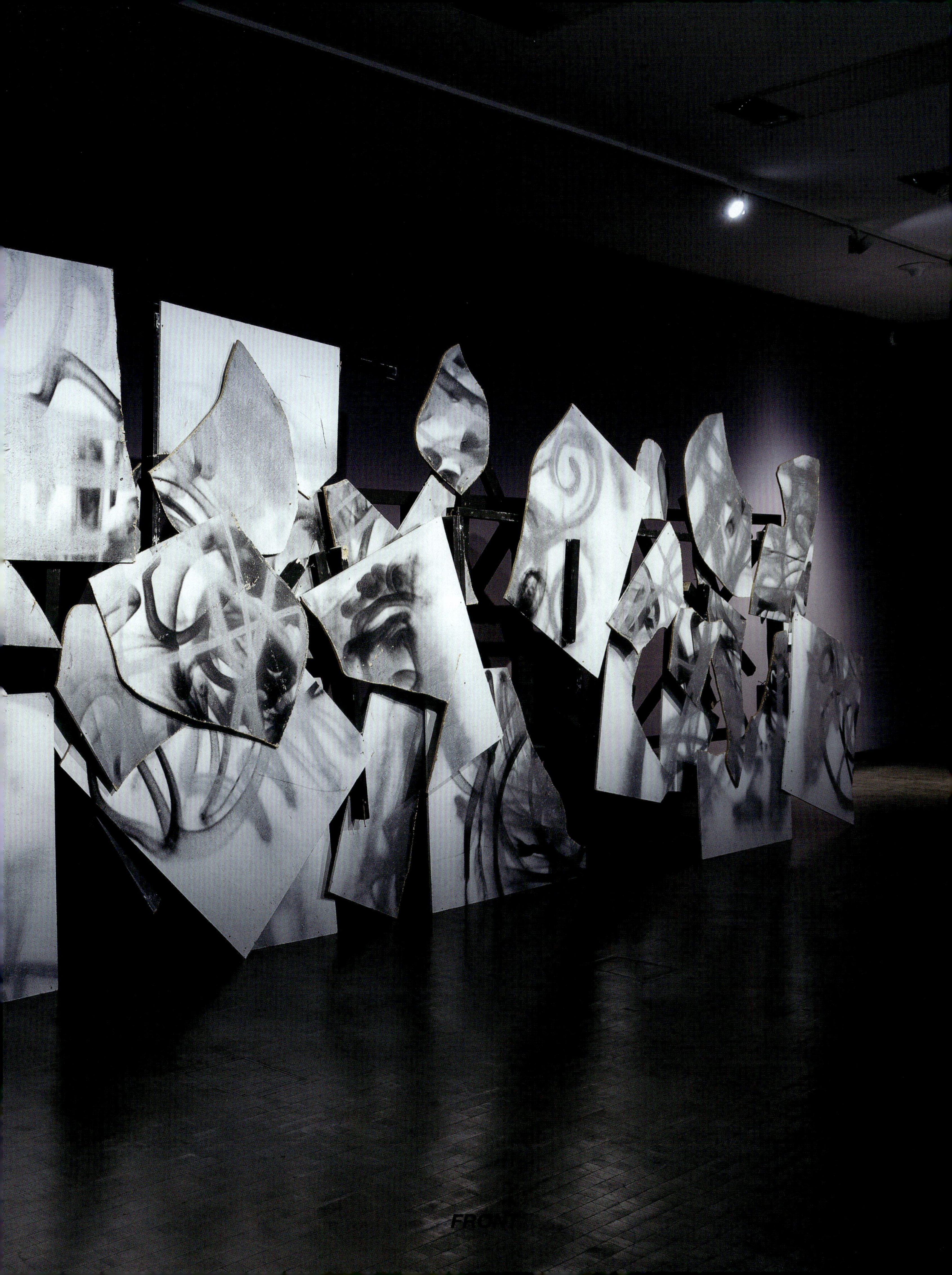
FRONT

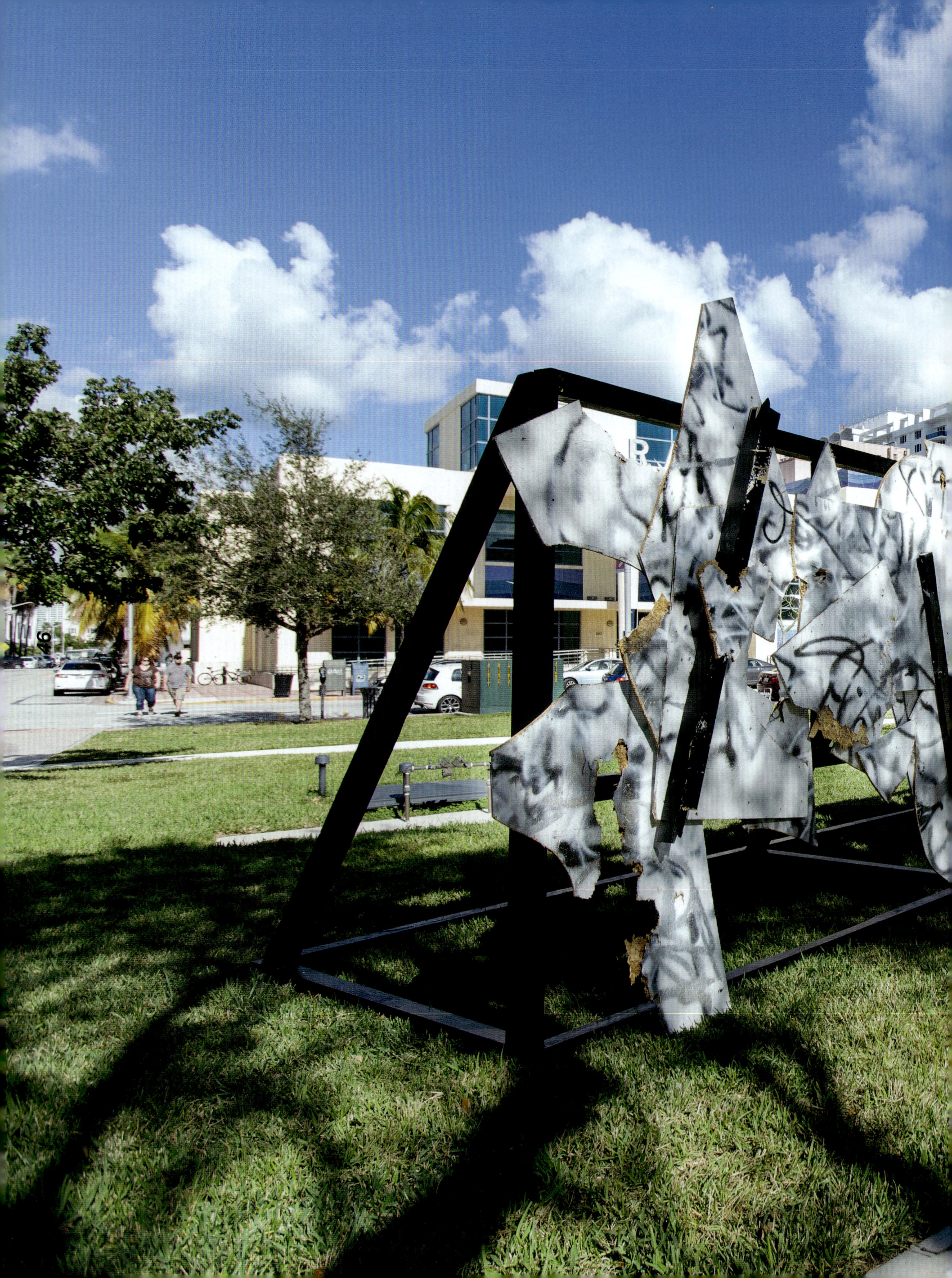

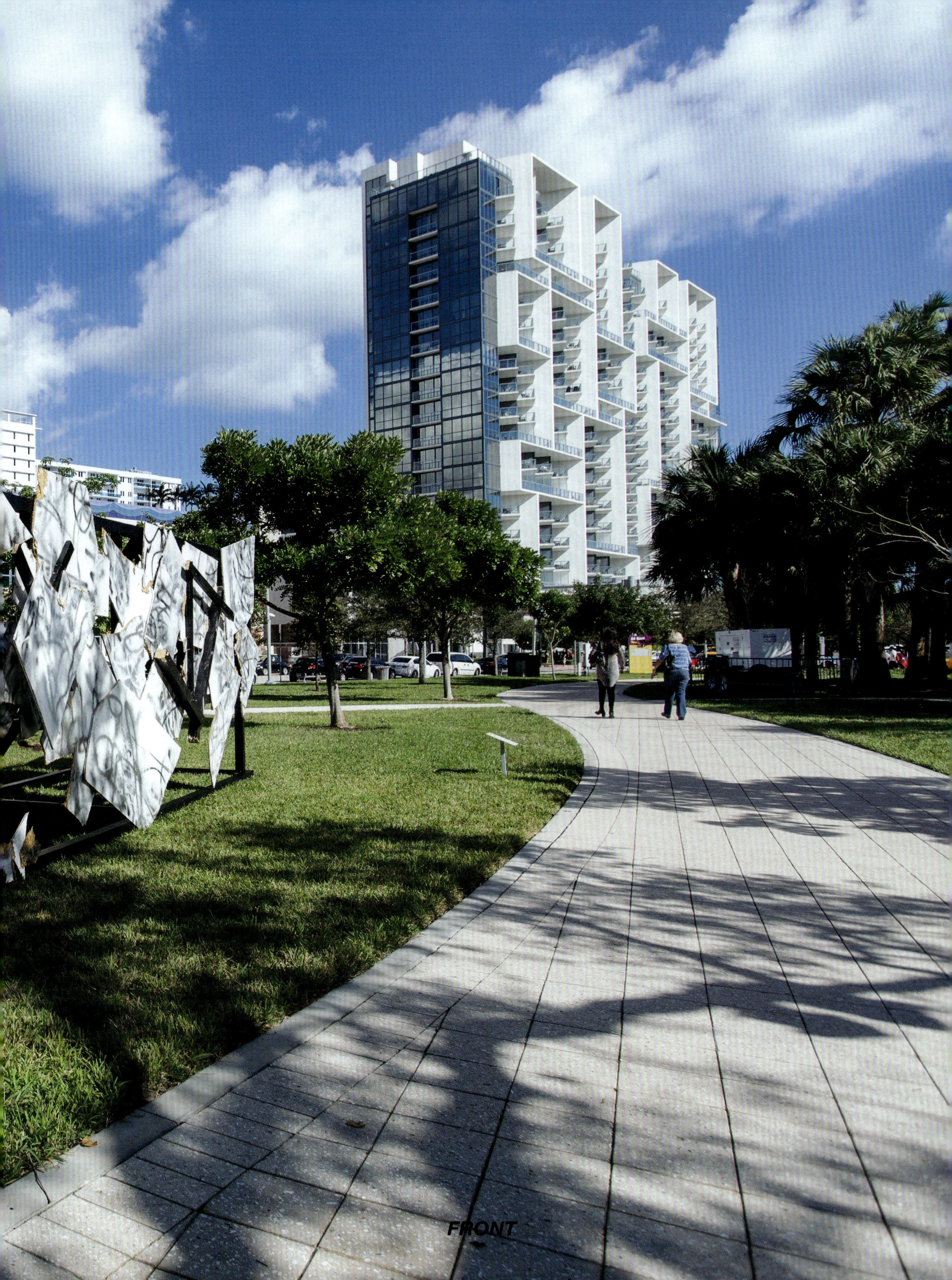
FRONT

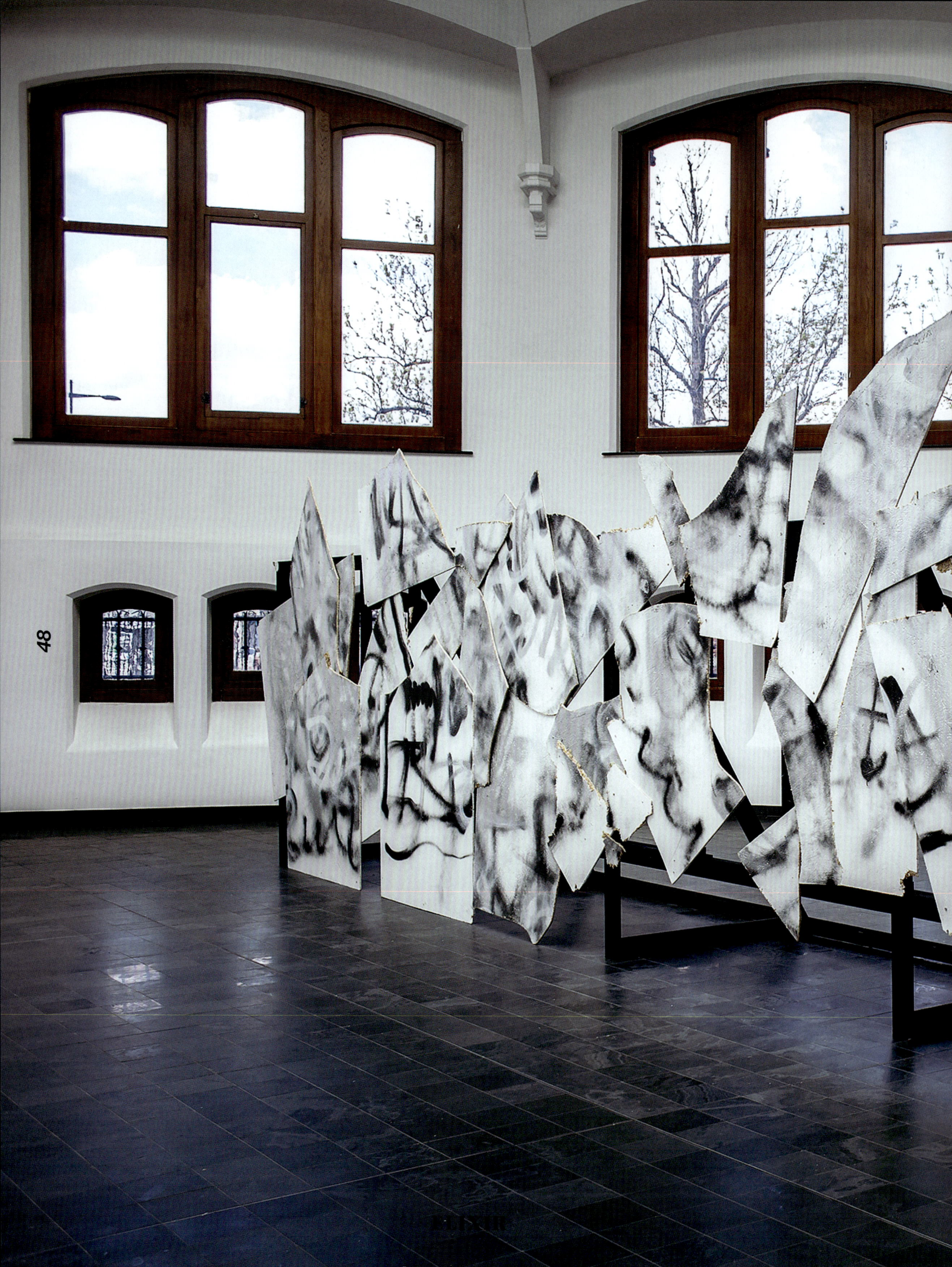

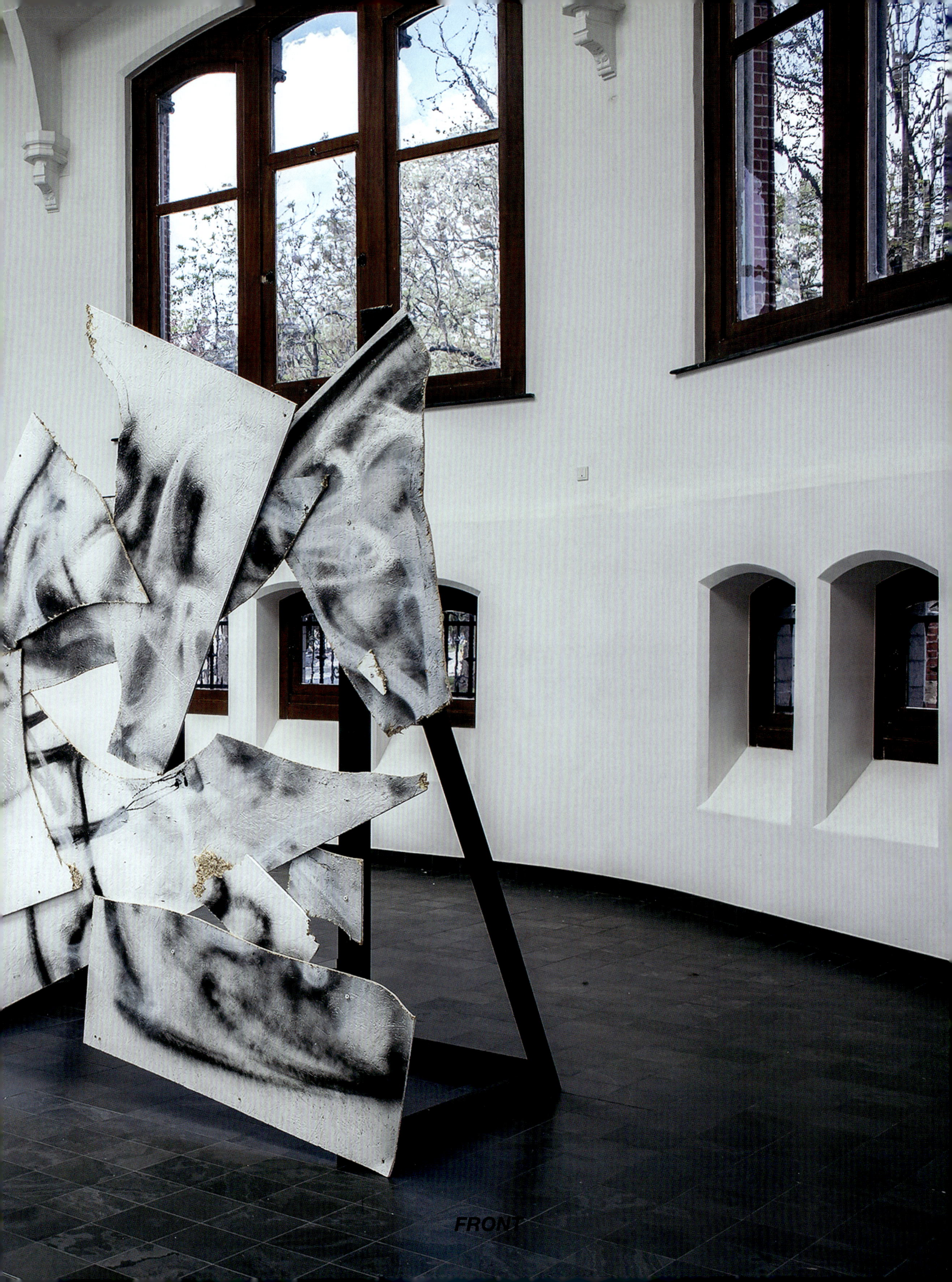
FRONT

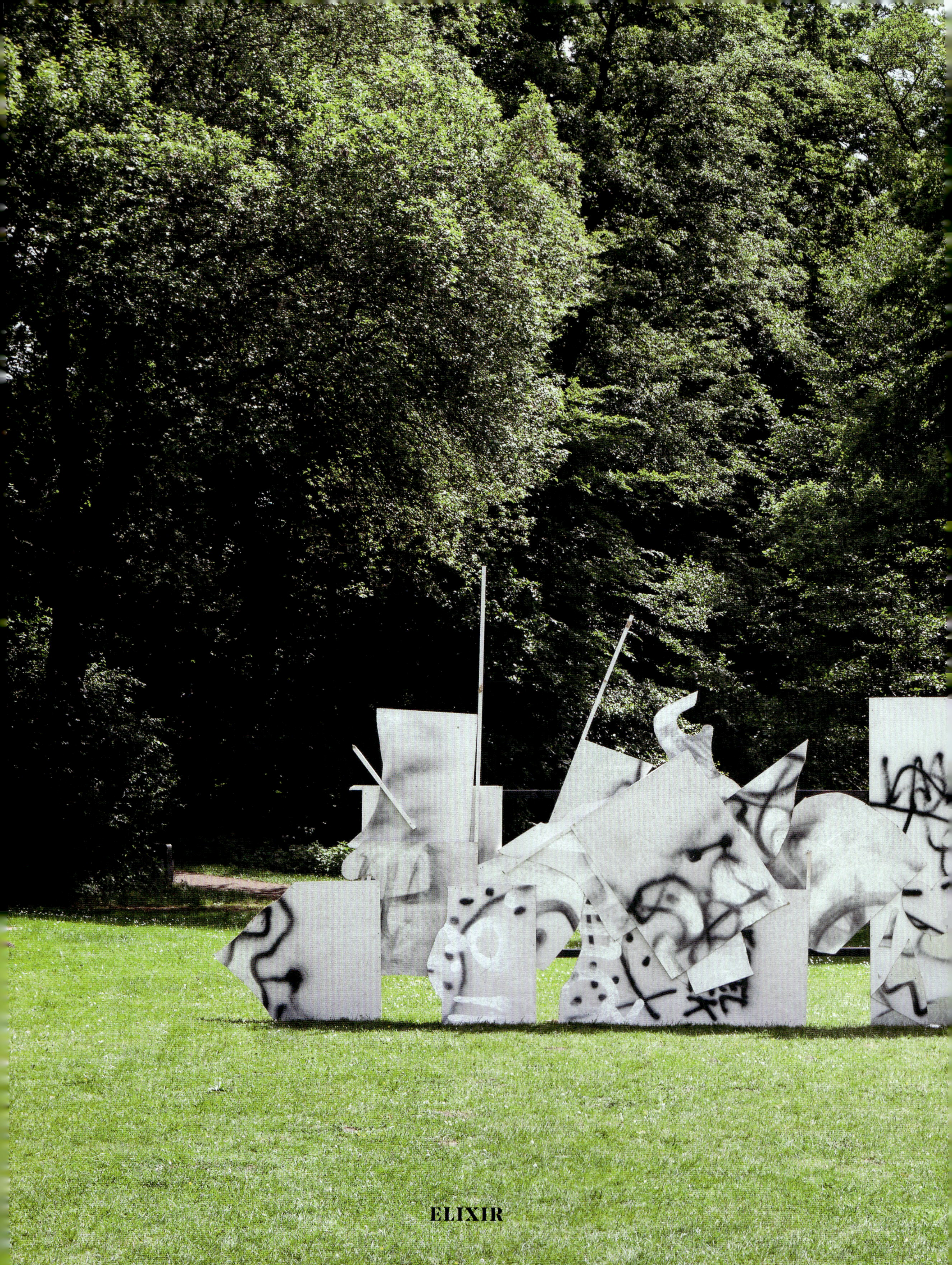

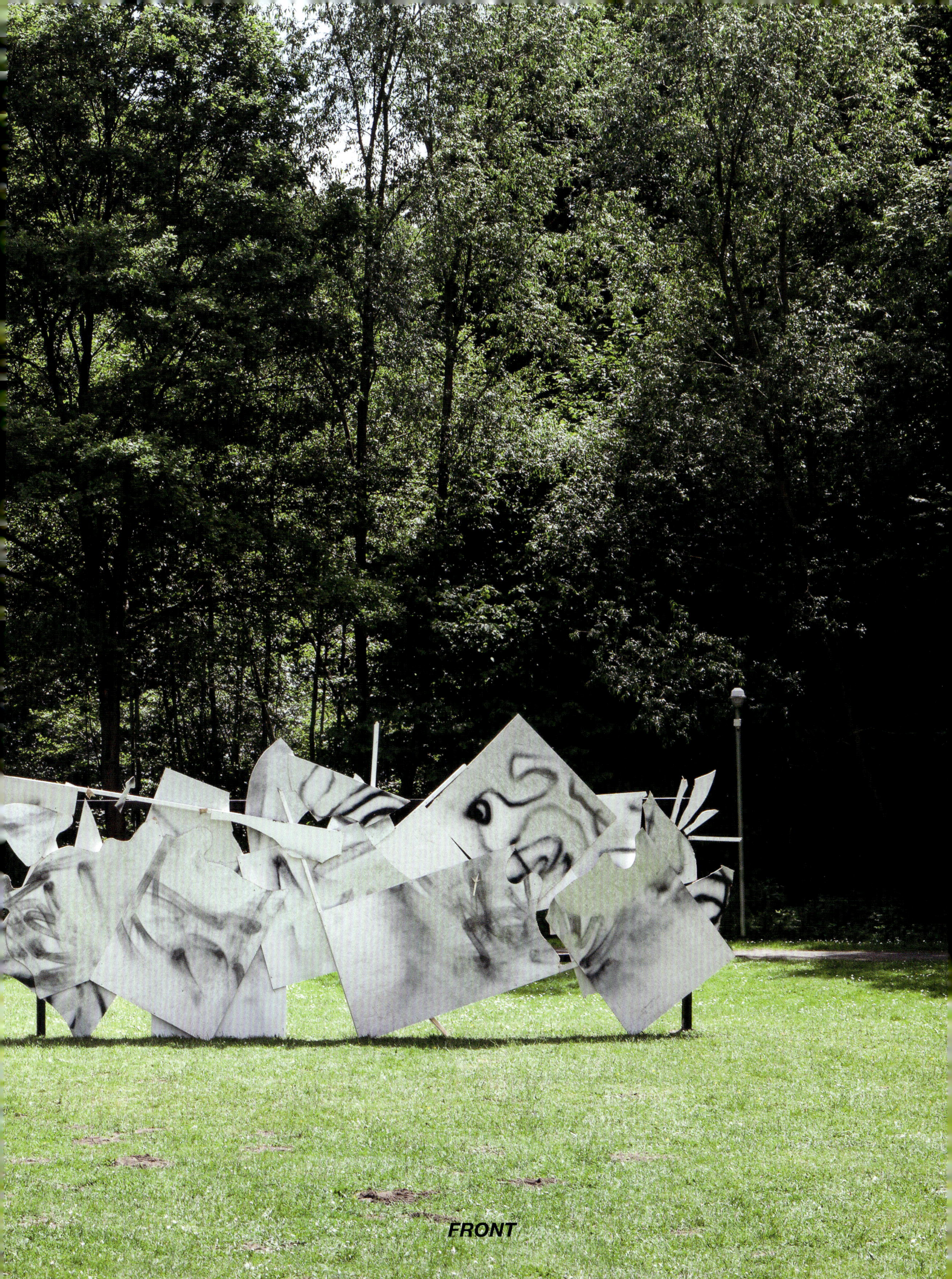

FRONT

(2015)

Mobile phone
Visitors

Whenever *Available* is shown, Christian Falsnaes agrees to the following conditions:
Throughout the opening hours of the exhibition, visitors can call him and receive instructions for performances that they carry out.
Every caller receives instructions for a personalized performance.
Christian Falsnaes agrees to be available during the opening hours of the entire duration of the exhibition.

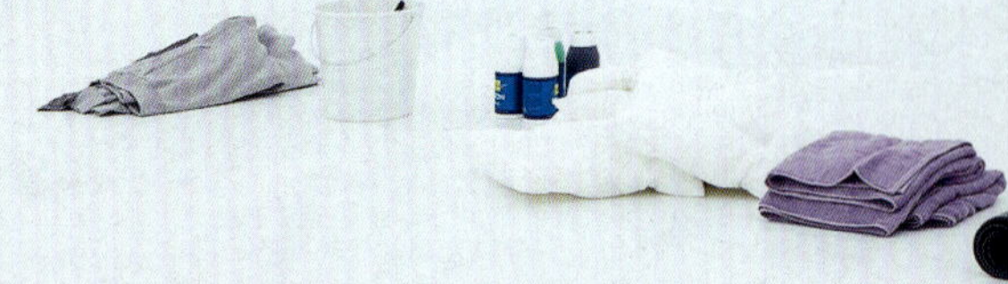

AVAIL-
ABLE

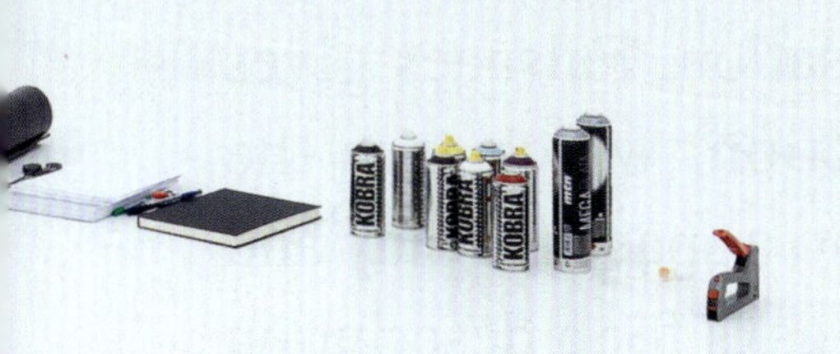

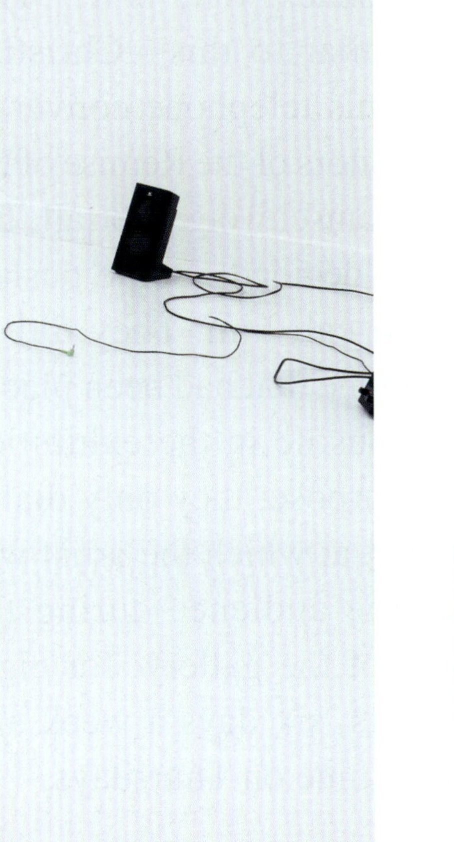

"[I] was inexorably delivered over to the voice that now sounded. There was nothing to allay the violence with which it now pierced me. Powerless, I suffered, seeing that it obliterated my consciousness of time, my firm resolve, my sense of duty. And just as the medium obeys the voice that takes possession of him from beyond the grave, I submitted to the first proposal that came my way through the telephone."
Walter Benjamin, *Berlin Childhood around 1900*[1]

< 1
Walter Benjamin, Berlin Childhood around 1900, in *Selected Writings, VOL. 3: 1935–1938* eds. Howard Eiland and Michael W. Jennings, trans. Edmund Jephcott, Howard Eiland et al. (Cambridge, MA and London: Belknap Press, 2002 [1938]), 344, 350.

ON PRESENCE AND AVAILABILITY: THOUGHTS ON CHRISTIAN FALSNAES'S AVAILABLE

Text by Jule Hillgärtner

Let's start with the beginning: "Hello, this is Christian Falsnaes. Who is it?" This is how—or similar to this—Christian Falsnaes starts his telephone conversations with the visitors of the Remise of the Kunstverein Braunschweig. Not all, but several of them decided—some pushed themselves—to call him. They did so from the cell phone that had been placed on the small console in the exhibition room for this purpose; they only dialed a single number, at which the artist was available for the audience during the opening hours of the gallery: for eight exhibition weeks, six days a week and six hours a day, nine on Thursdays.

With *Available*, Christian Falsnaes takes a risk, performs an experiment, and makes a binding promise at the same time, the effect of which on his private and artistic life he can hardly assess beforehand. Availability, a contemporary phenomenon hailed and lamented, is probably experienced by almost everyone who constantly carries a cell phone as crux and opportunity, appeal and doom, desire and frustration, benefit and constant potential for interference. It is this very incongruity that Falsnaes faces head on when he declares himself the sovereign, who certainly decided on the rules and the basic conditions of *Available*, but within which he himself will be most tightly caught. Whether the artist will remain the definitive authority at one end of the line or become a service provider delivering ideas for the one on the other end, is decided in the individual dialogue.

During the conversation, Falsnaes gives instructions for action, which turn the exhibition space into a space for play and creation. Often, he asks for a description of the current appearance of the room both to start the dialogue and to find starting points for his instructions for action. He guides the audience—individuals as well as groups of visitors—to actions that have consequences for the room, originally completely white, but equipped with all sorts of props, by letting them spray the top right corner yellow, paint parts of the floor in black and—some weeks later—white again; he lets a Rihanna song blare from loudspeakers and gets all present to dance along in a state of hilarity that is both inspiring and perplexing—and sometimes also creepy.

This clear division of roles between the one dictating the actions and those executing them by no means indicates a simple relationship of active and passive, announcement and reaction, but also brings a reverse side with it; apart from the decision to pick up the phone and thereby to claim Falsnaes's undivided attention—without even being able to guess where he is at that moment and what he is doing—there is often something demanding in the voice of the caller who wants to be put to action right now, not at some later time. The prompt, somehow also merciless demand for as clear an answer as possible to the question of "What should I do?" at first appears to contradict what Falsnaes usually likes to, and knows how to, aim at in his work: a jointly negotiated interaction between him and his counterpart, a jointly developed dynamic, which exists in the moment and delights beyond it.

Unquestionably for the concept devised for the work *Available*, filled with life in mutual conversations, the cell phone is crucial as a communication medium and the only means for artist and audience to relate with one another in real time. In this, the counterpart is in turn listened to and addressed, but in any case never seen. Unlike in some other works by Falsnaes, there is no video link, but only the voices, the language, the individual cadences of speech and sound associated with them. Everything else—on both sides—remains up to the imagination. The voice, dissociated from the body of the speaker, works like that of a "higher being" that commands, on other occasions describes its environment in a dedicated manner, or falls silent to listen to the conversation partner. As with an office or hotline, caller and called are and essentially remain strangers. Falsnaes's physical presence and charisma, which is characteristic of his performance works, is also focused in *Available*, into his address, audible through the phone. The dialogue between artist and visitor is all the more perceived as an individual, very personal experience, between the artist there and myself here. We share this time, in which we both press the phones to our ears, are closely connected via the telephone despite being strangers, and together shape—more or less consciously—all of the nuances from availability to disposability, which mark *Available*.

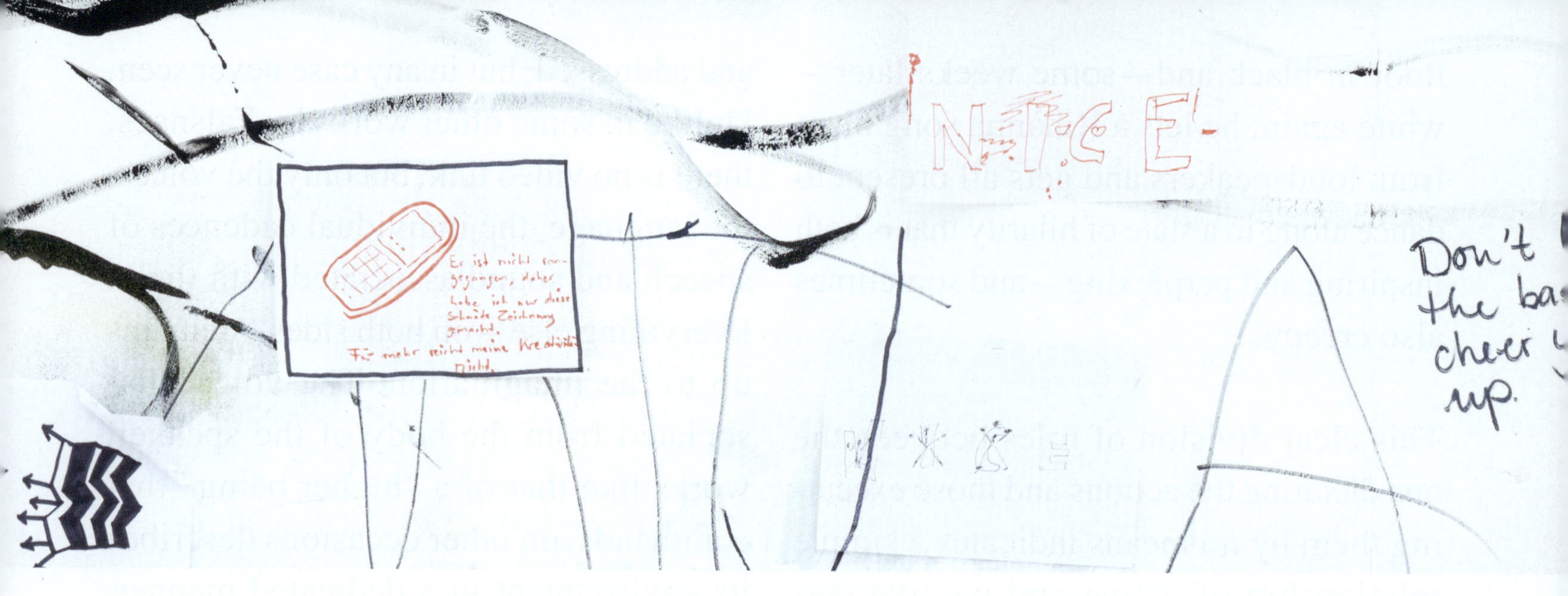

Bitte benutzen Sie das Mobiltelefon, um Christian Falsnaes anzurufen und von ihm weitere Anweisungen zu erhalten.

Sollten Sie kein Telefon vorfinden, ist es gerade in Gebrauch. Warten Sie und schauen Sie sich um: Der Anrufer befindet sich in Ihrer Nähe.

Please use the mobile phone to call Christian Falsnaes and get further instructions from him.

If there is no phone, it is currently in use. Wait and look around: the caller should be somewhere nearby.

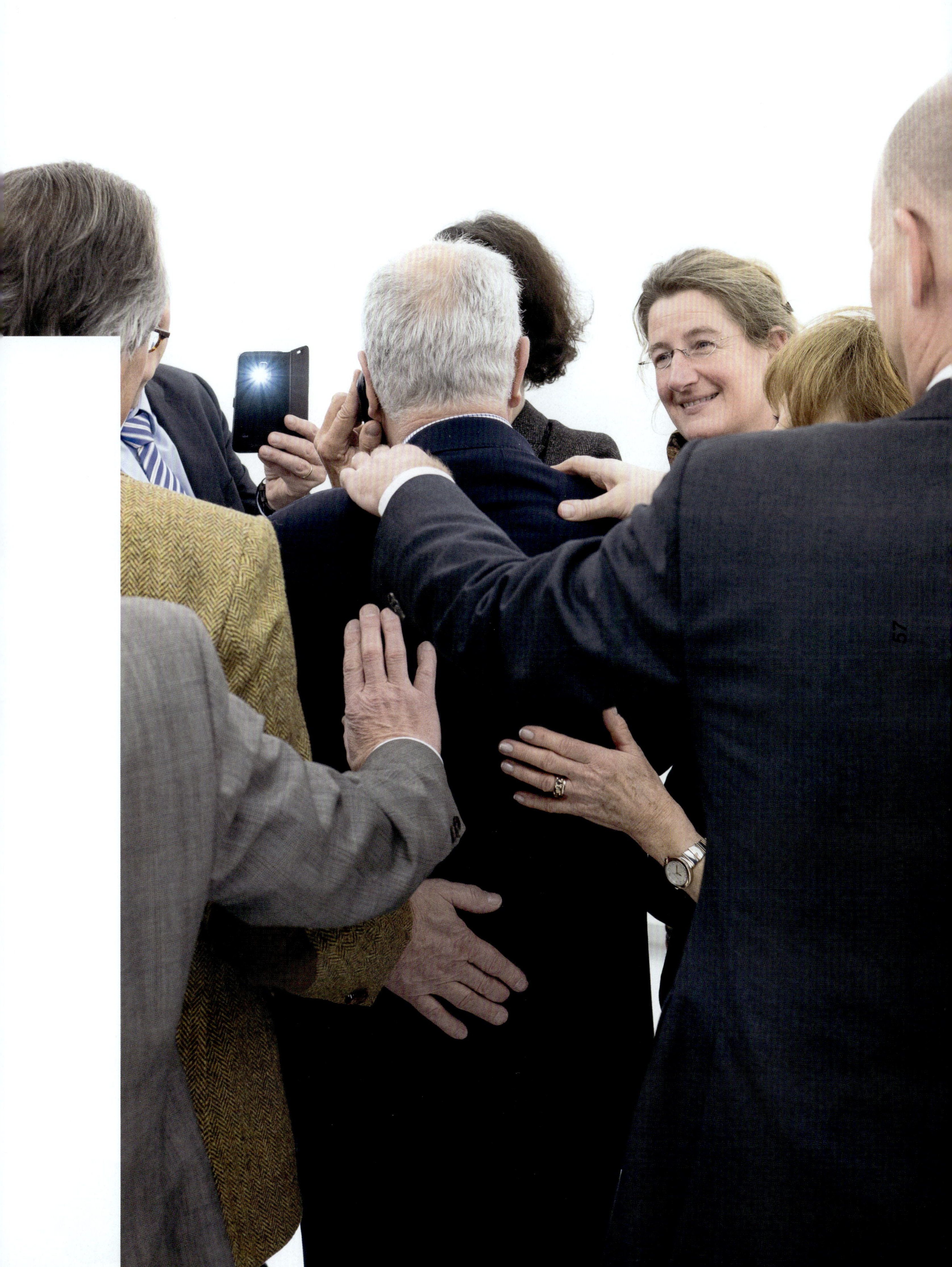

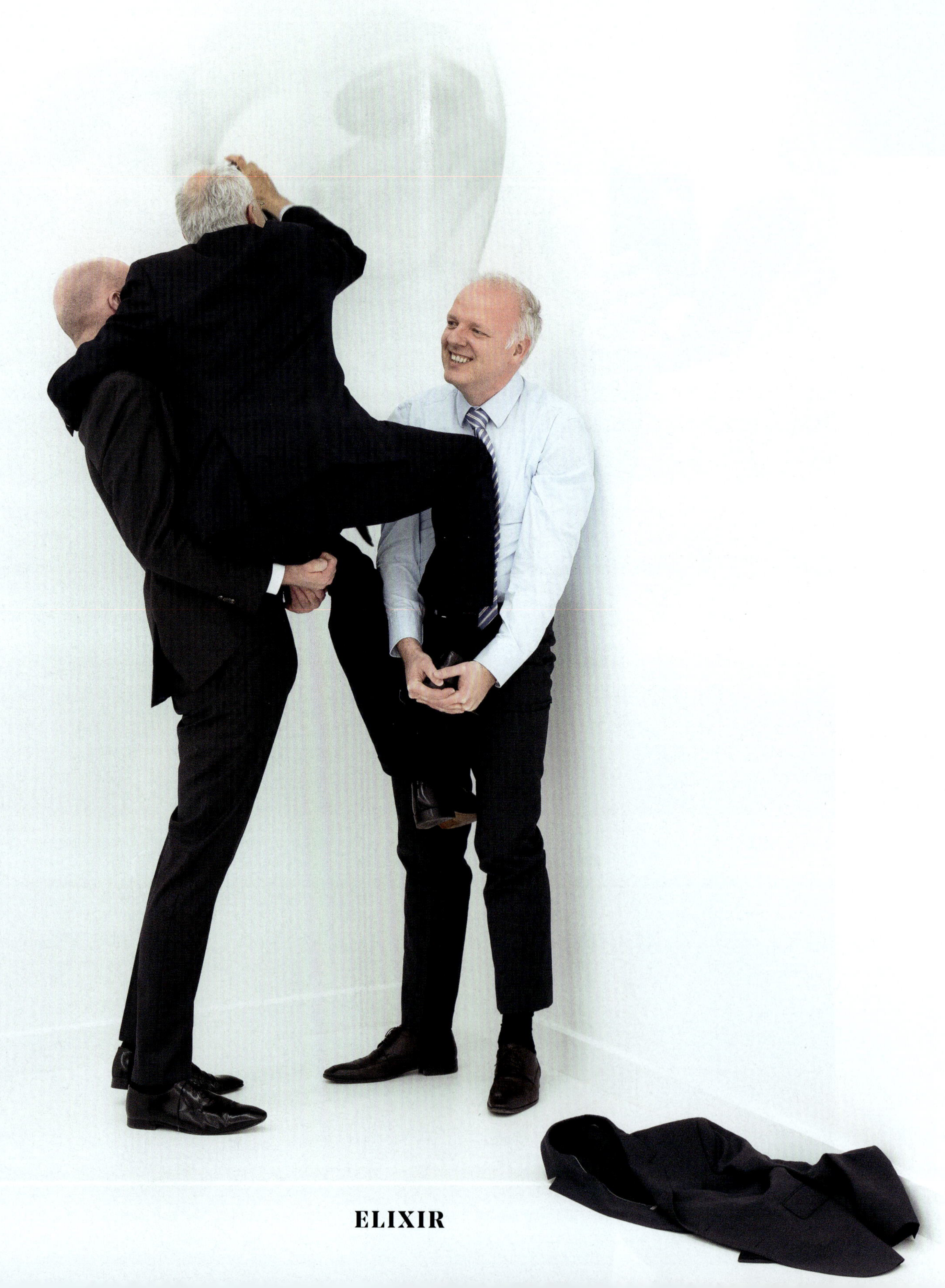

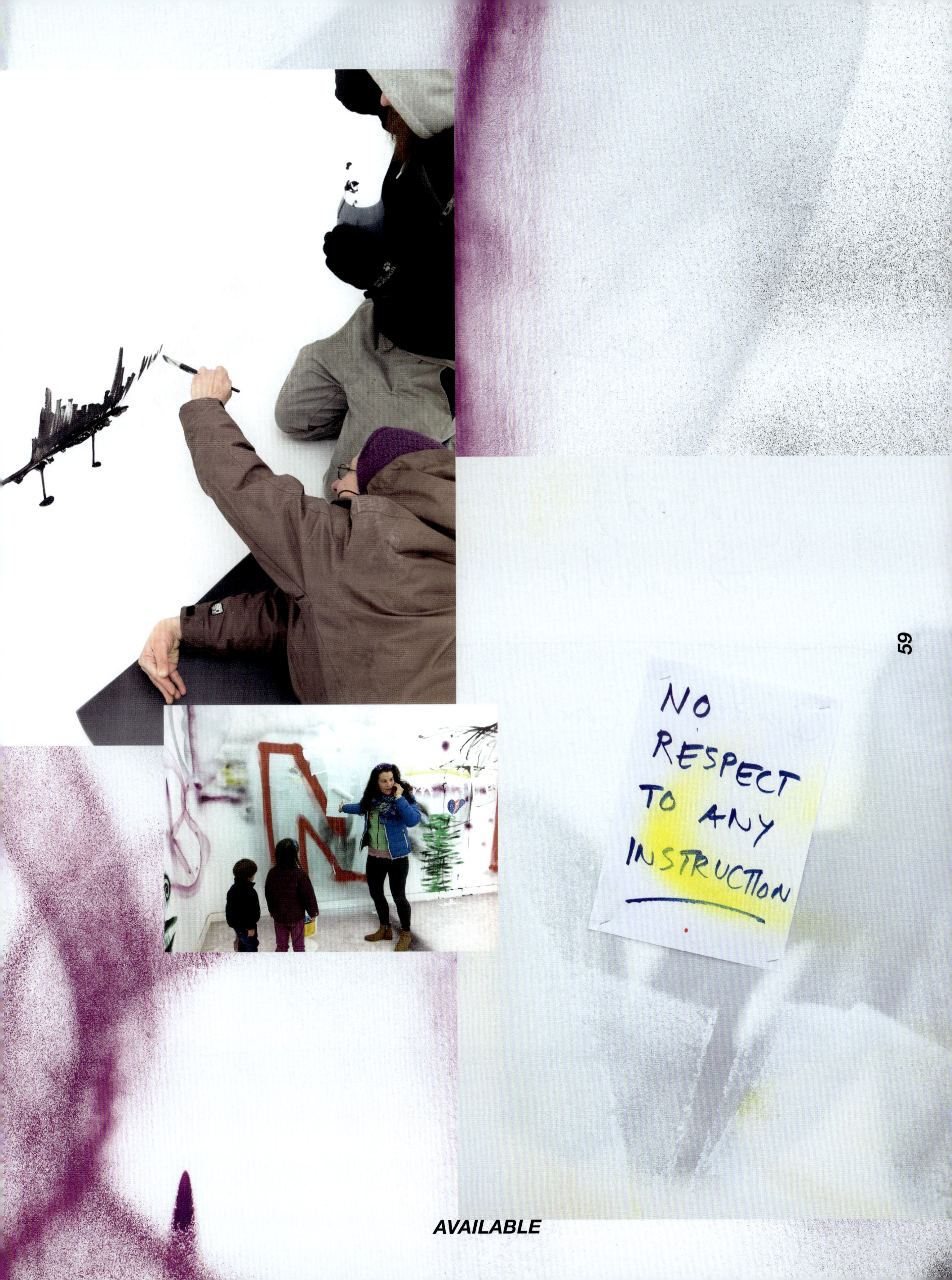
NO
RESPECT
TO ANY
INSTRUCTION

Tuesday

- late caller painted chrome all over the space (naked)
  → wrote in book

- Caller carried out instruction that was written on the paper (with red marker)
  → Absolute freedom

Thursday

I was at an Opening in Kunsthalle Wien
→ Caller imagined to be me / be in my body and walk through the exhibition (closed her eyes while i walked through the exhibition with the phone)

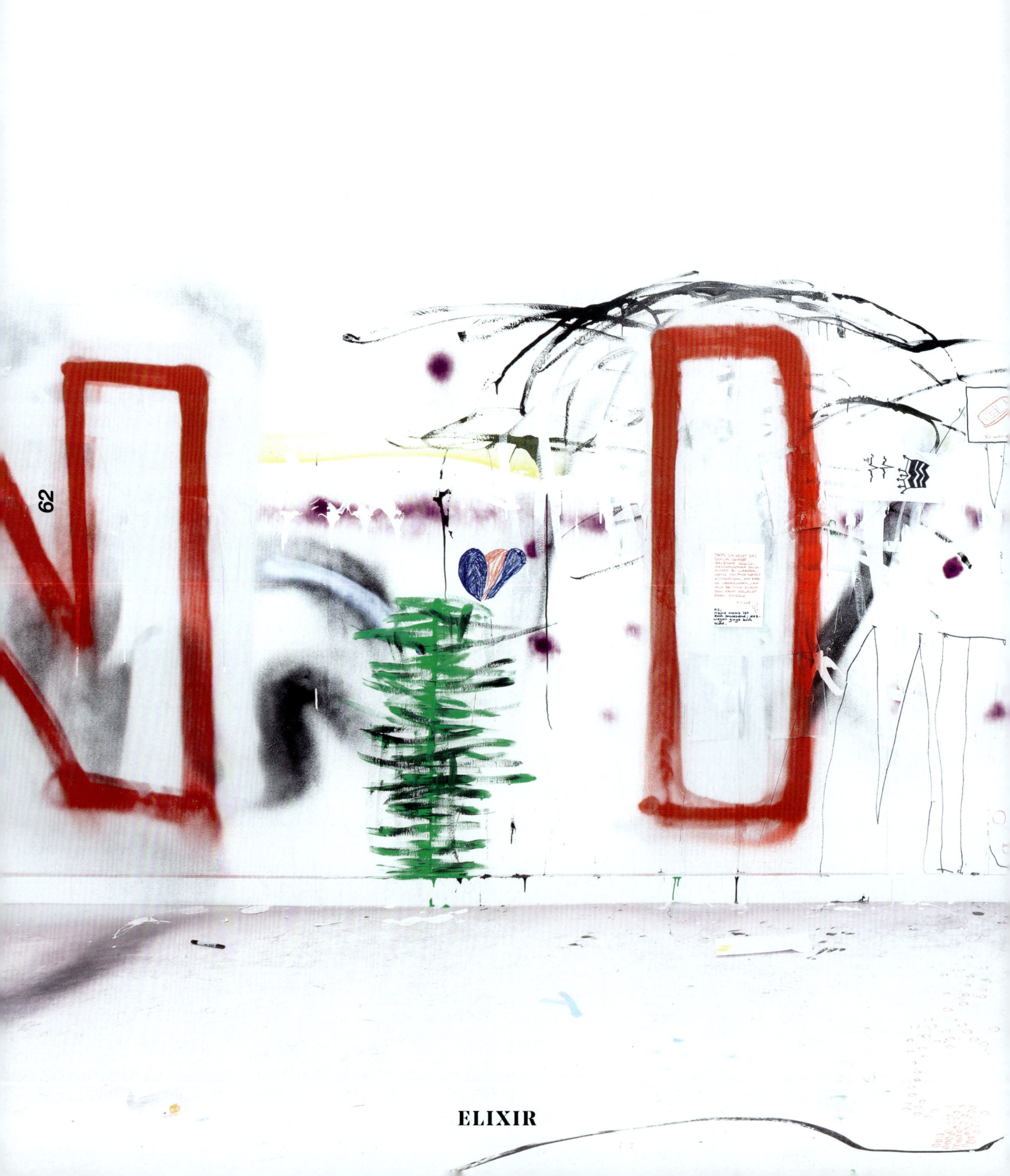

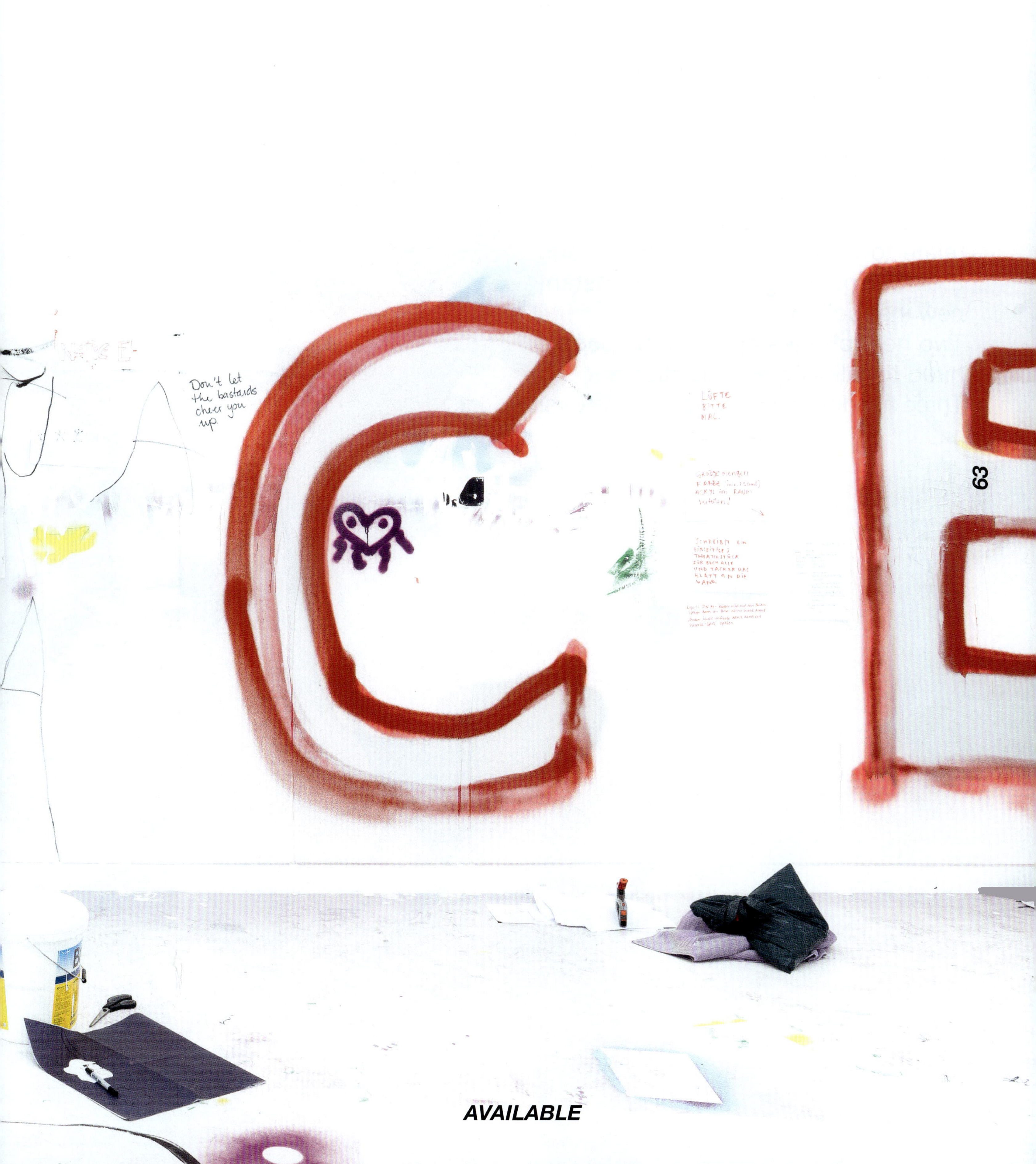

AVAILABLE

(2014)

5-channel audio on wireless headphones
Two people hired to follow instructions
Visitors

Five wireless headphones in different colors continuously play instructions directly to the people wearing them. The instructions are different, but synchronized and relate to each other. When visitors wearing headphones follow the instructions, choreographed situations develop, as they are told to relate to each other, themselves, and their surroundings through constant new instructions.
Two headphones are worn by people hired to follow the instructions.
Three headphones are worn by visitors.

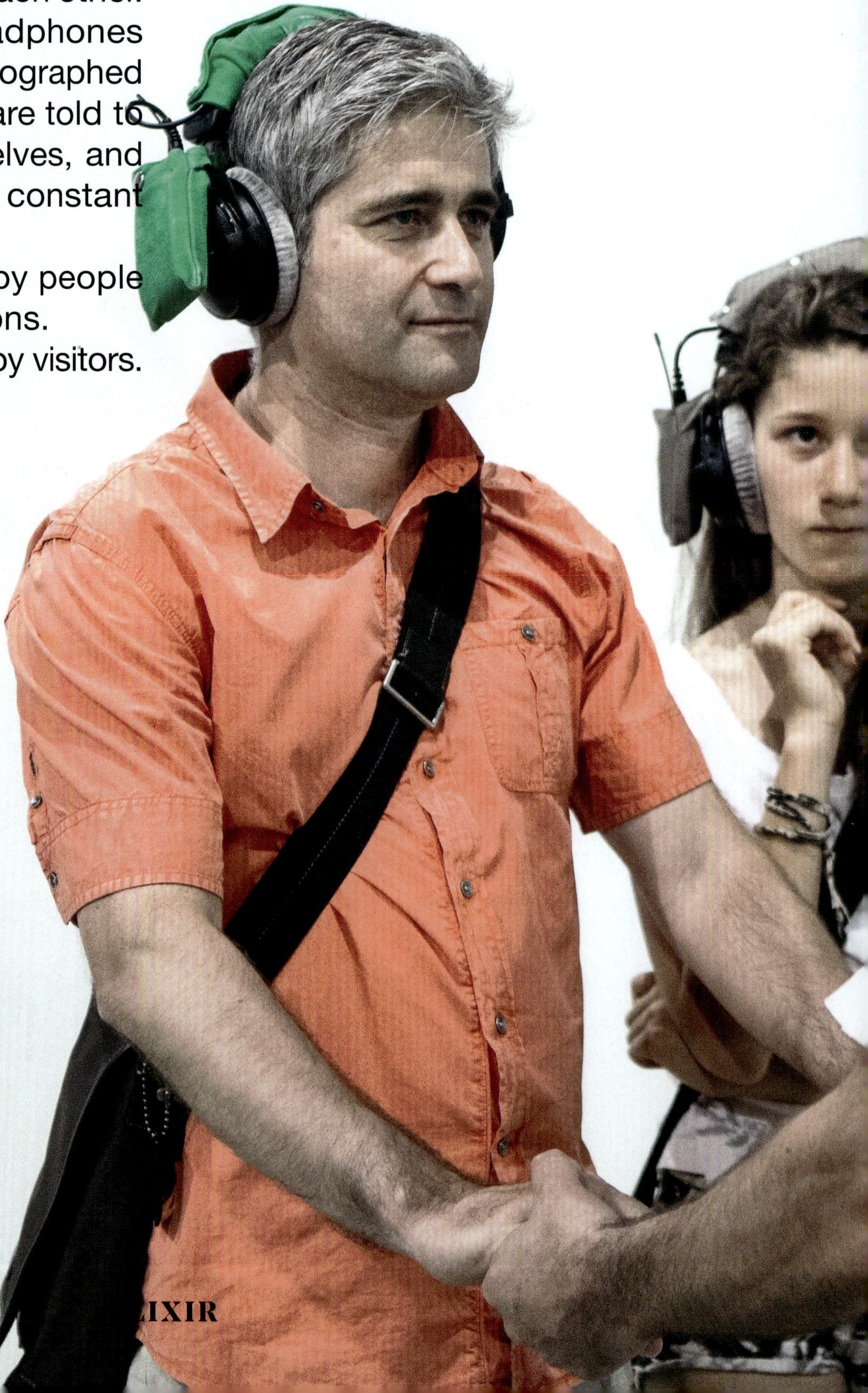

LIXIR

JUSTI-FIED BELIEFS

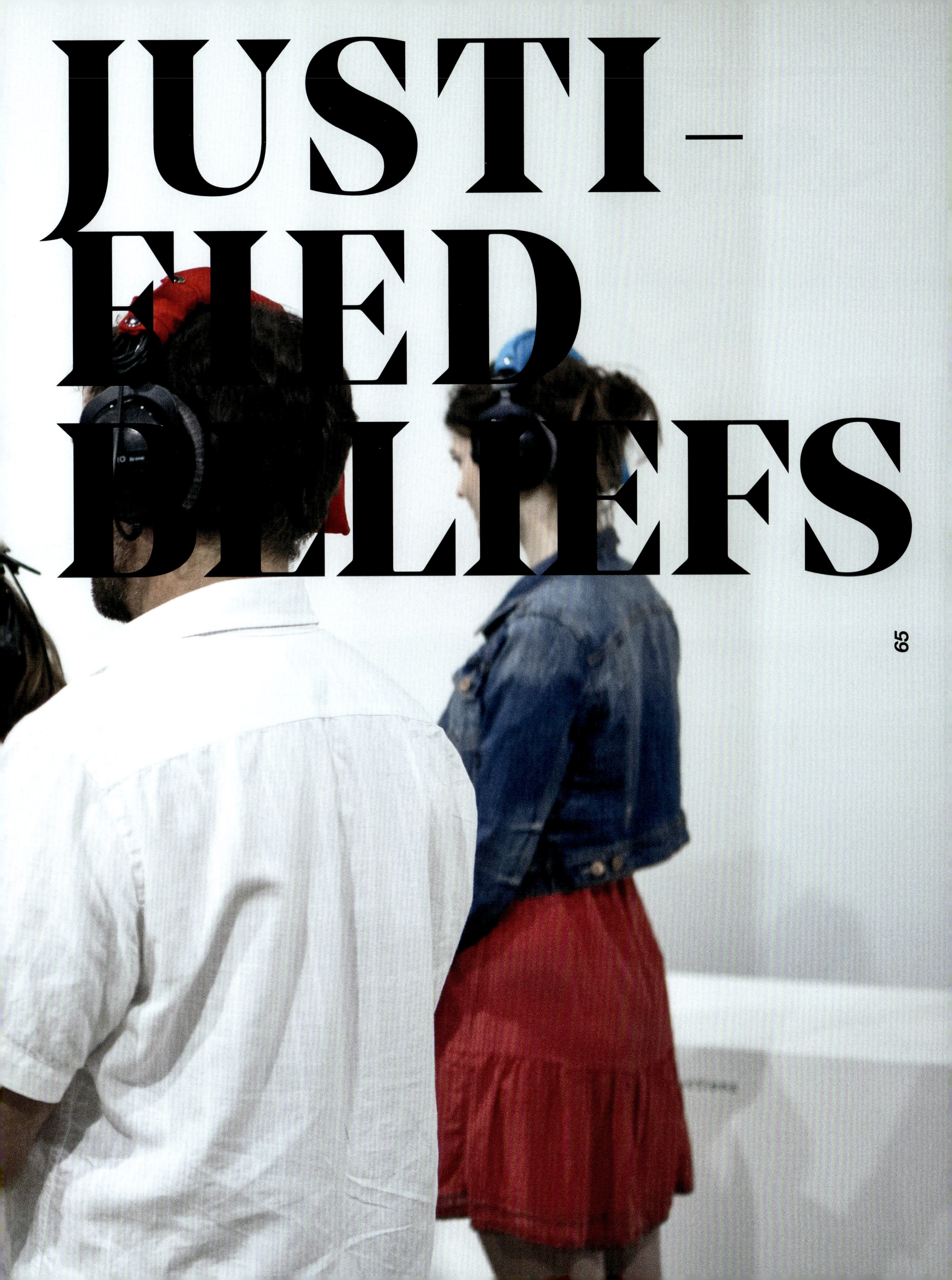

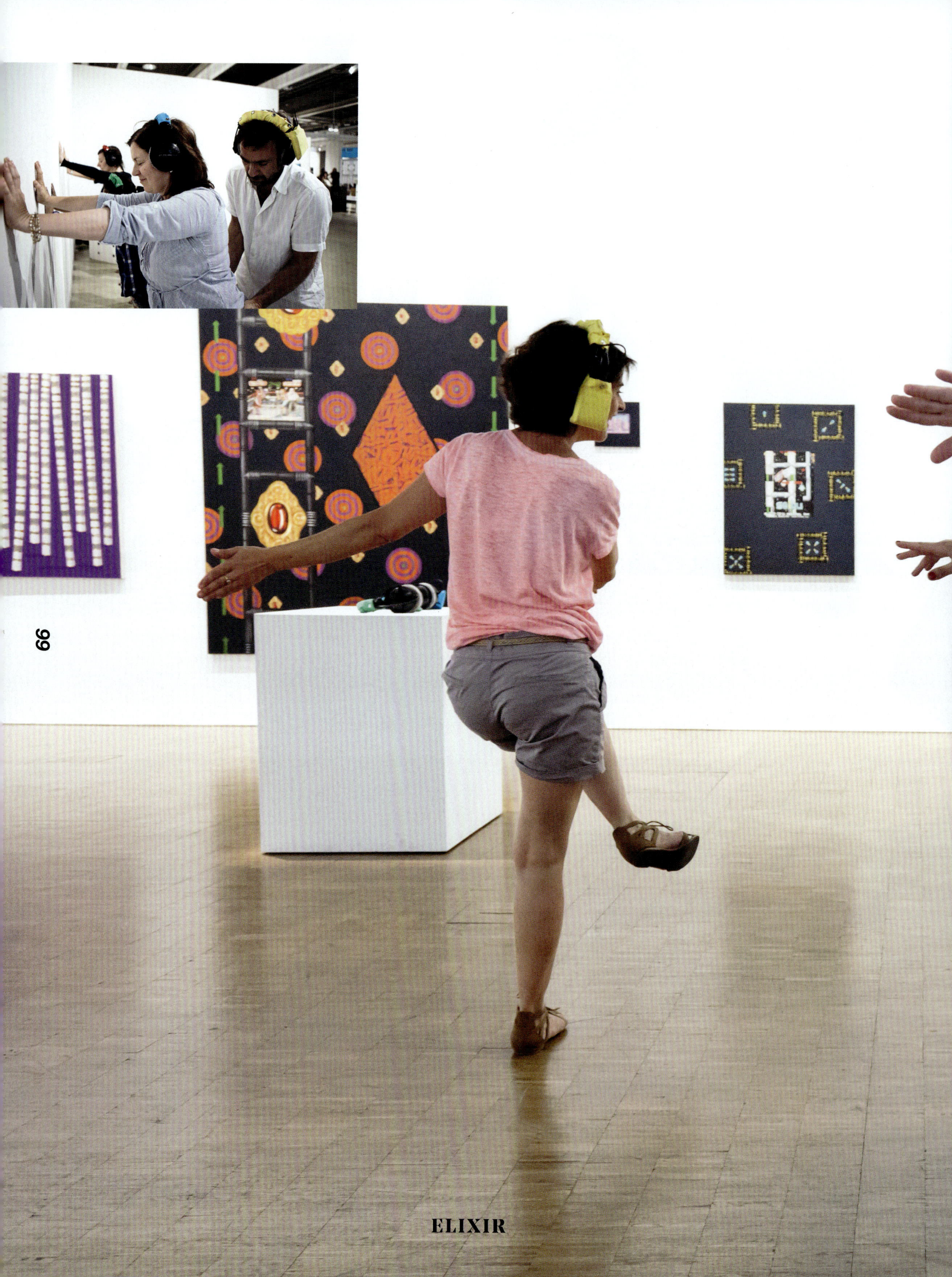

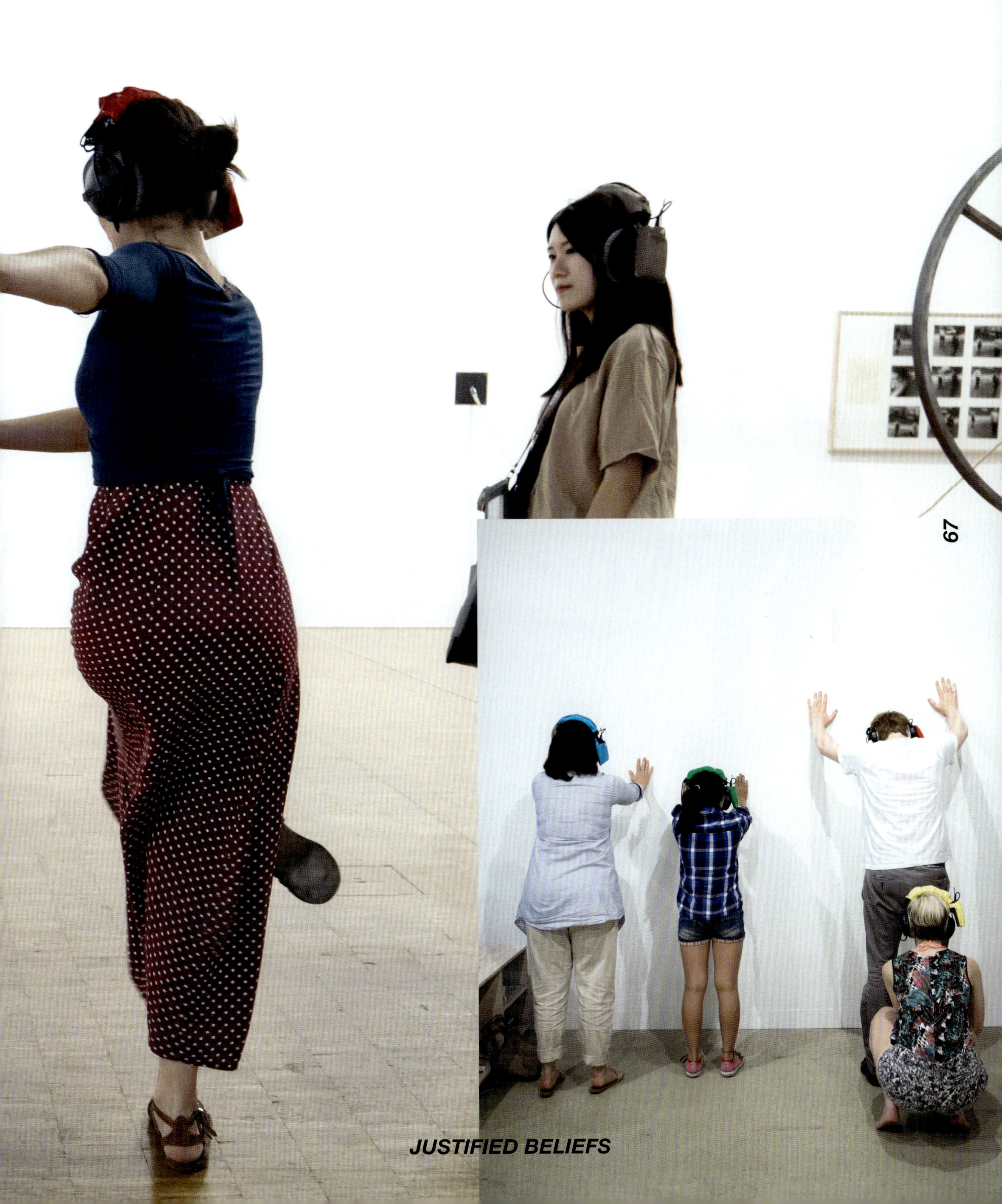

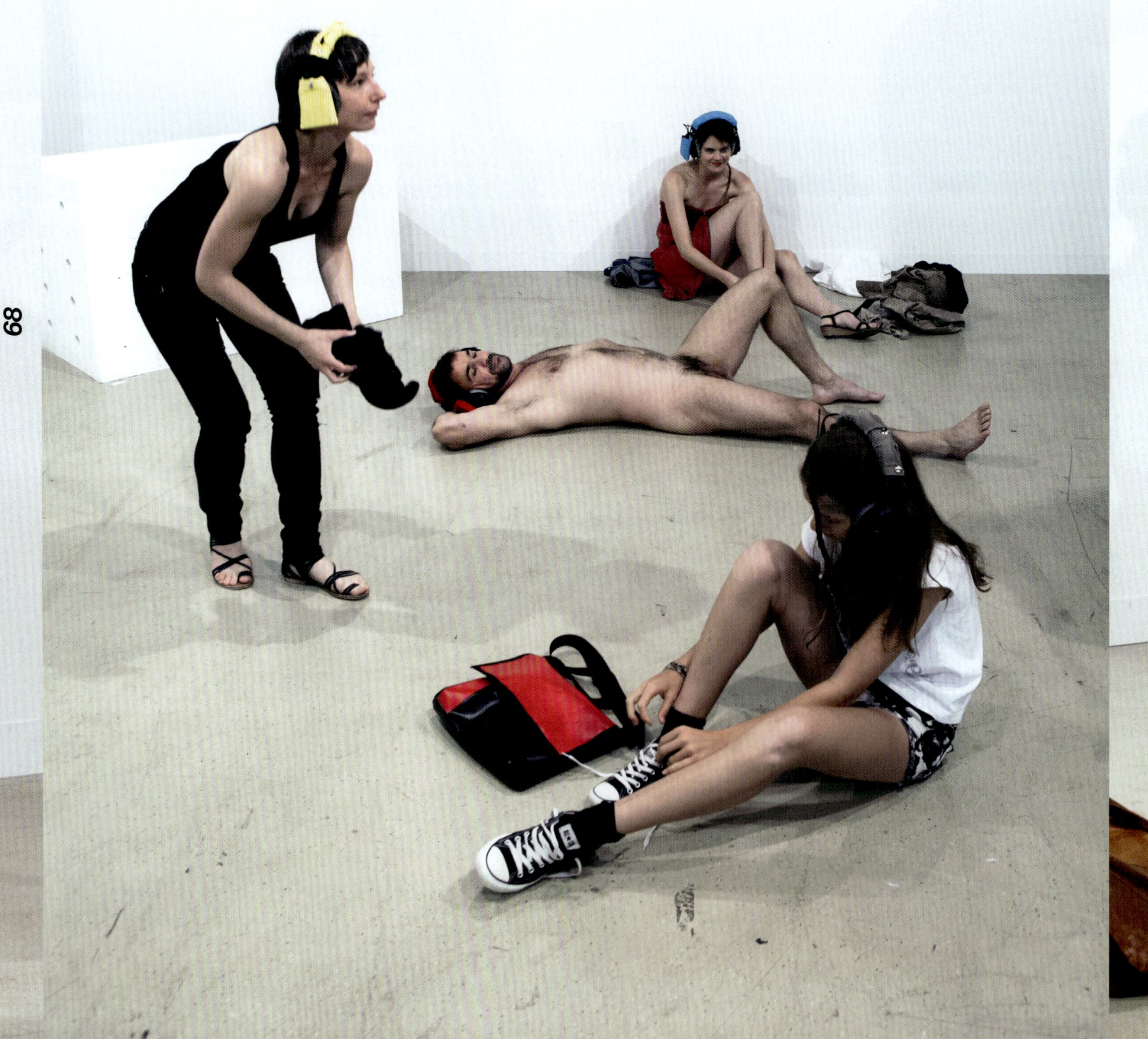

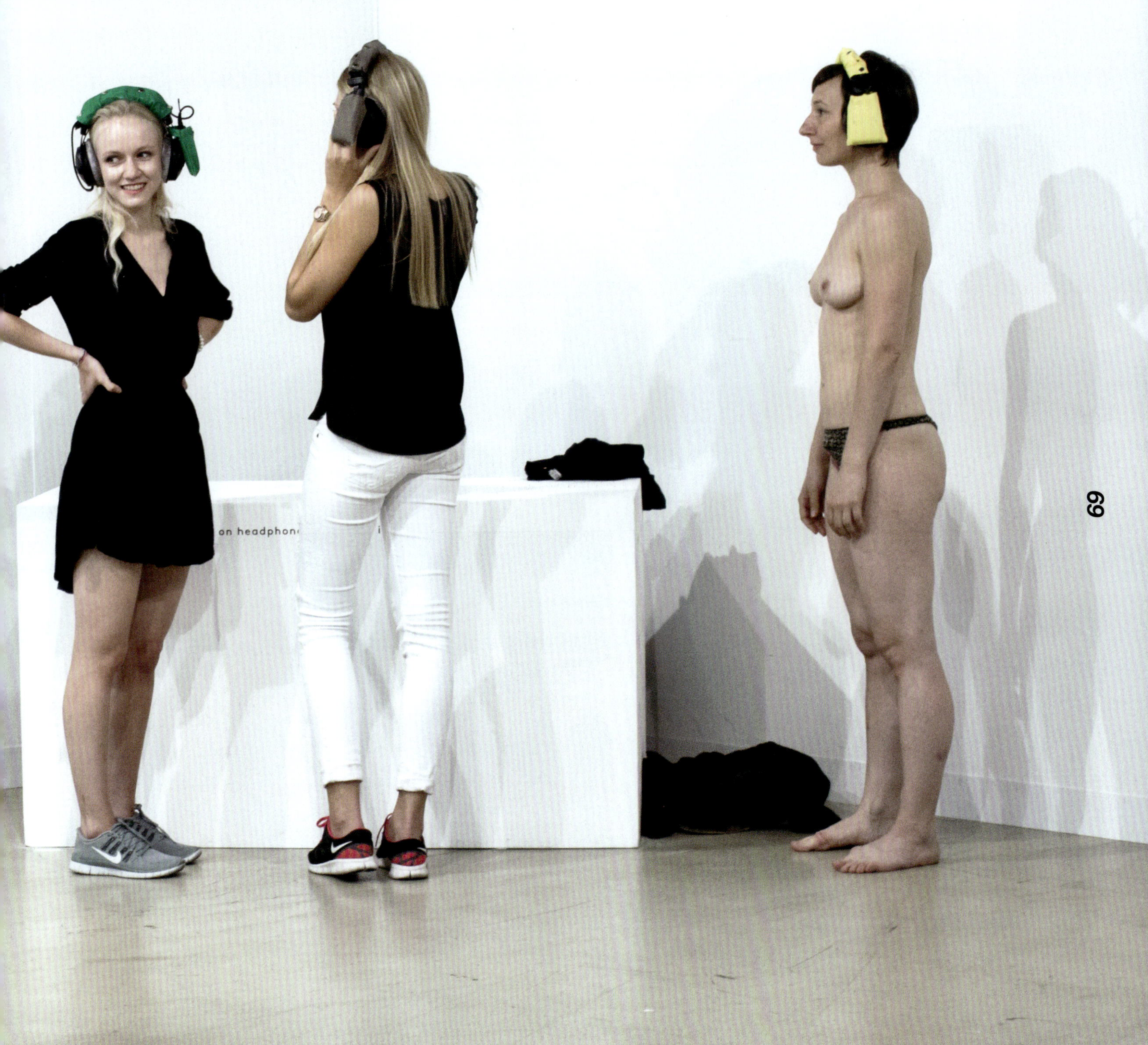

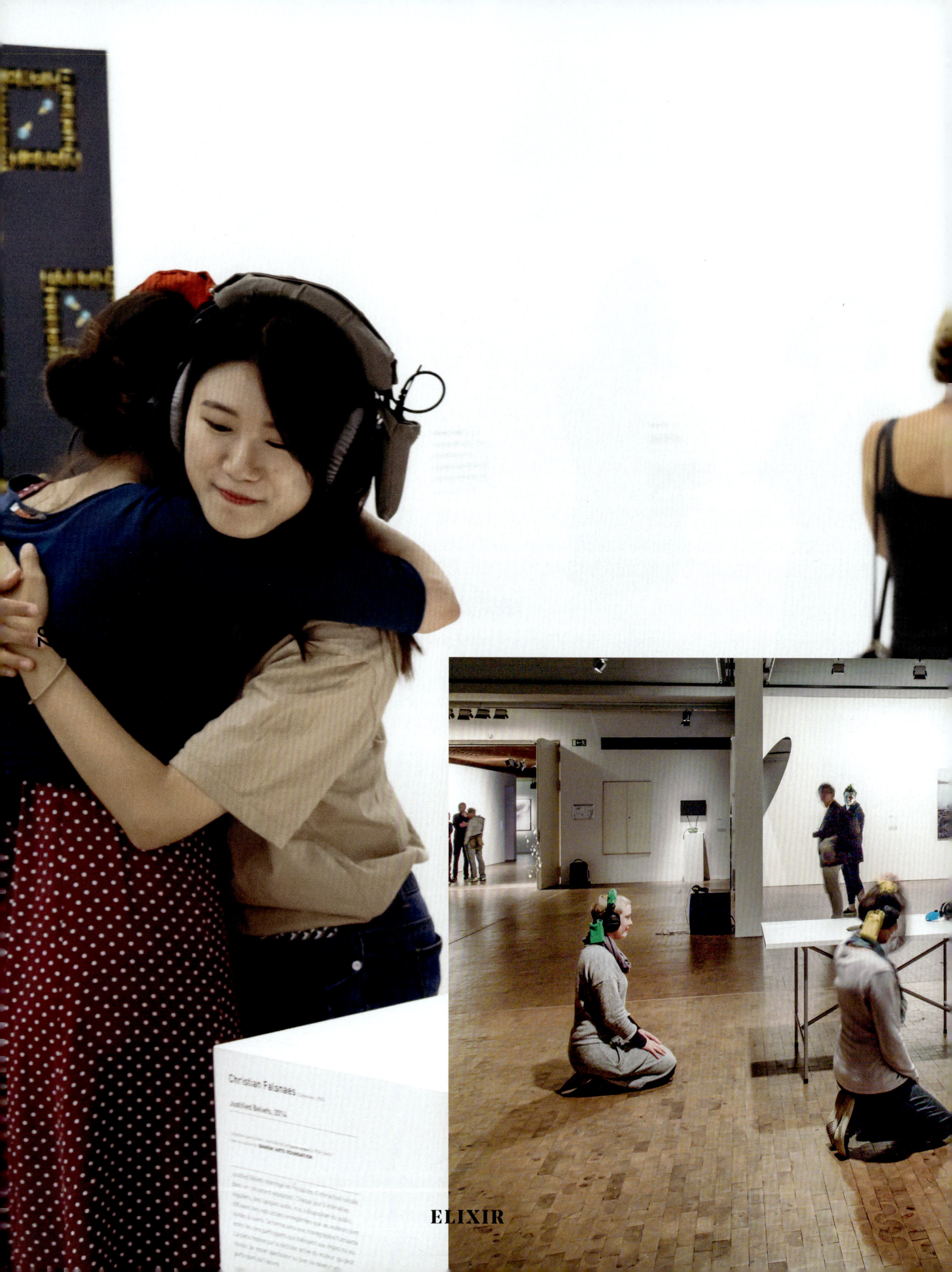

ELIXIR

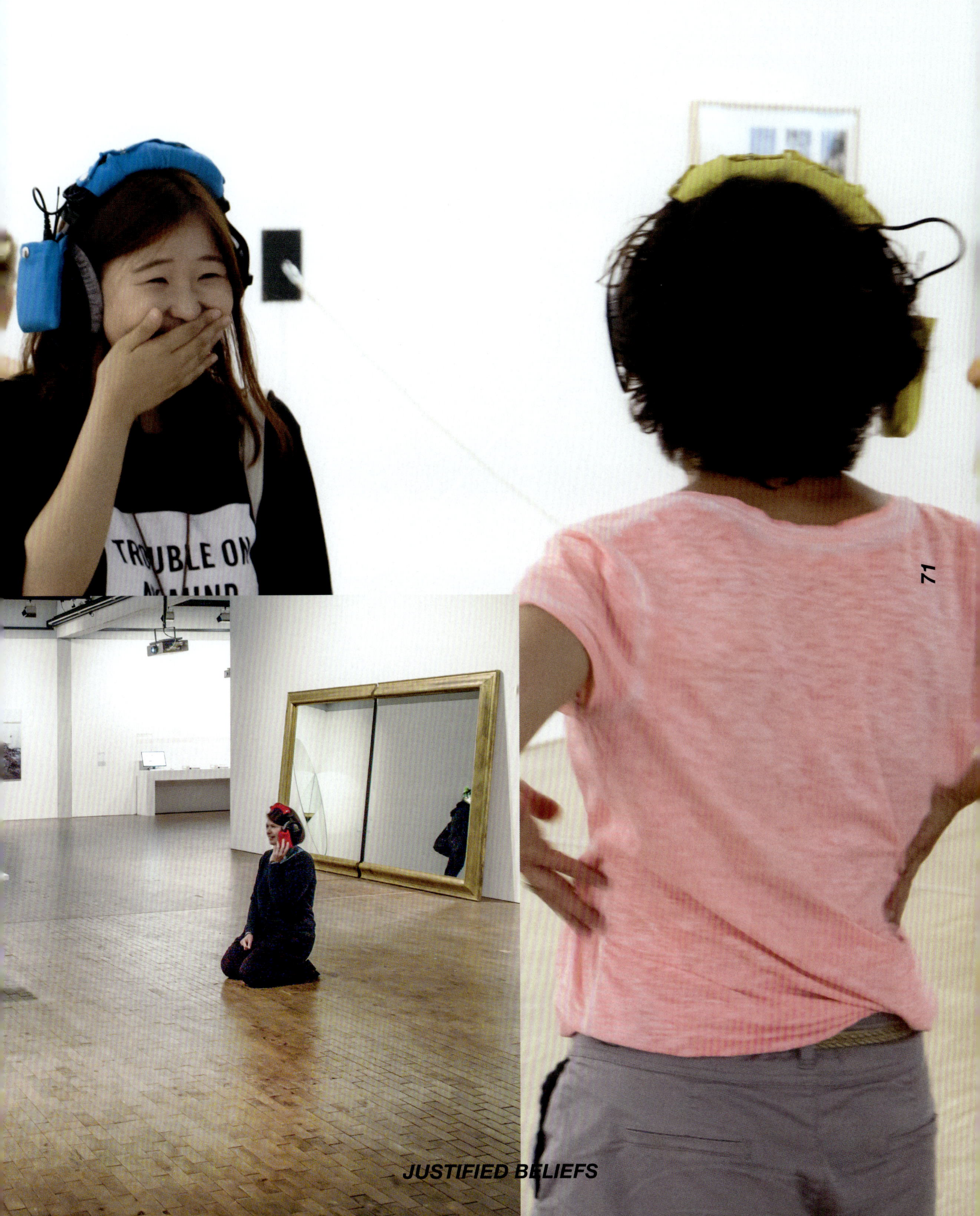

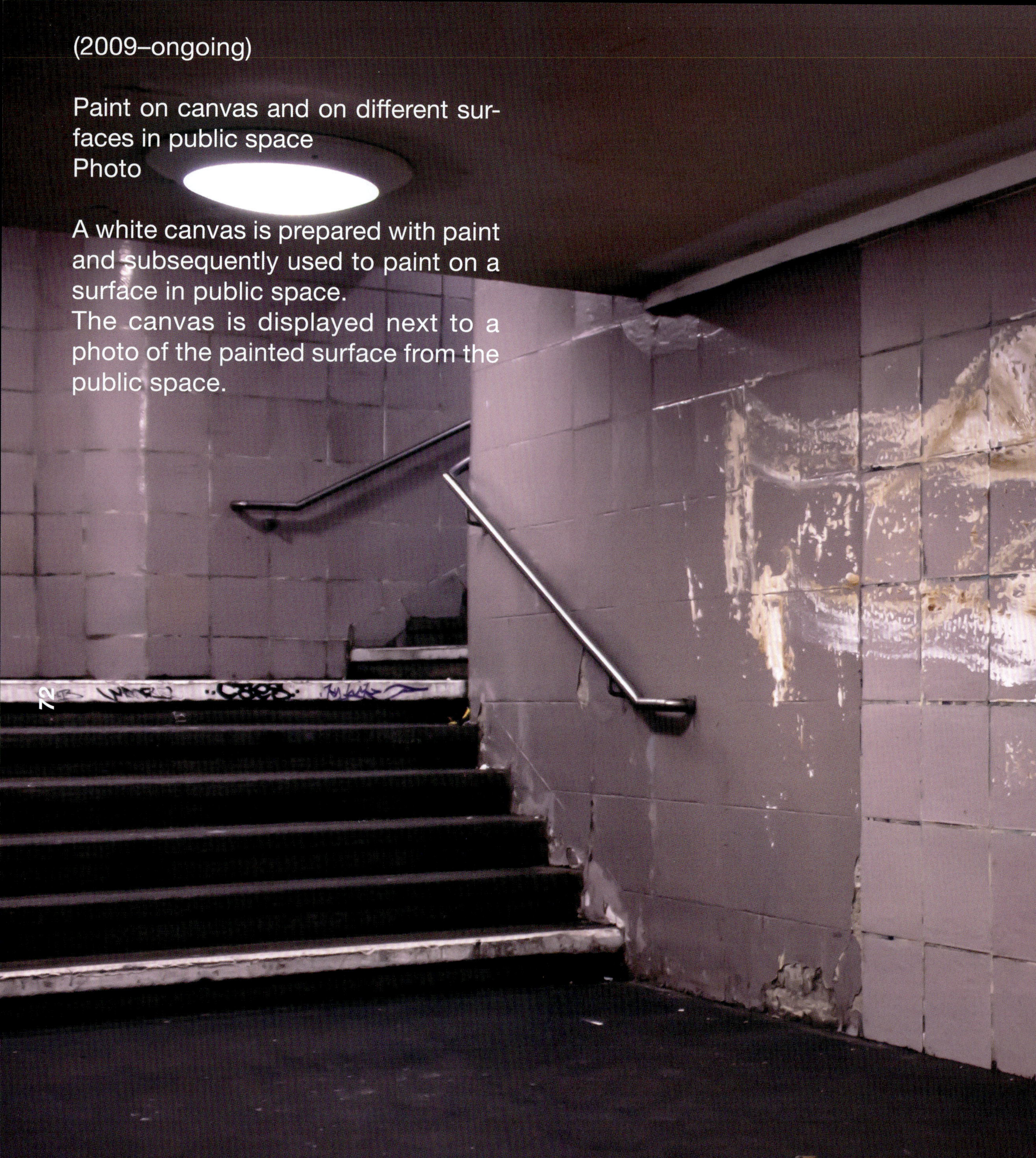

(2009–ongoing)

Paint on canvas and on different surfaces in public space
Photo

A white canvas is prepared with paint and subsequently used to paint on a surface in public space.
The canvas is displayed next to a photo of the painted surface from the public space.

SUR– FACE MEMO– RY

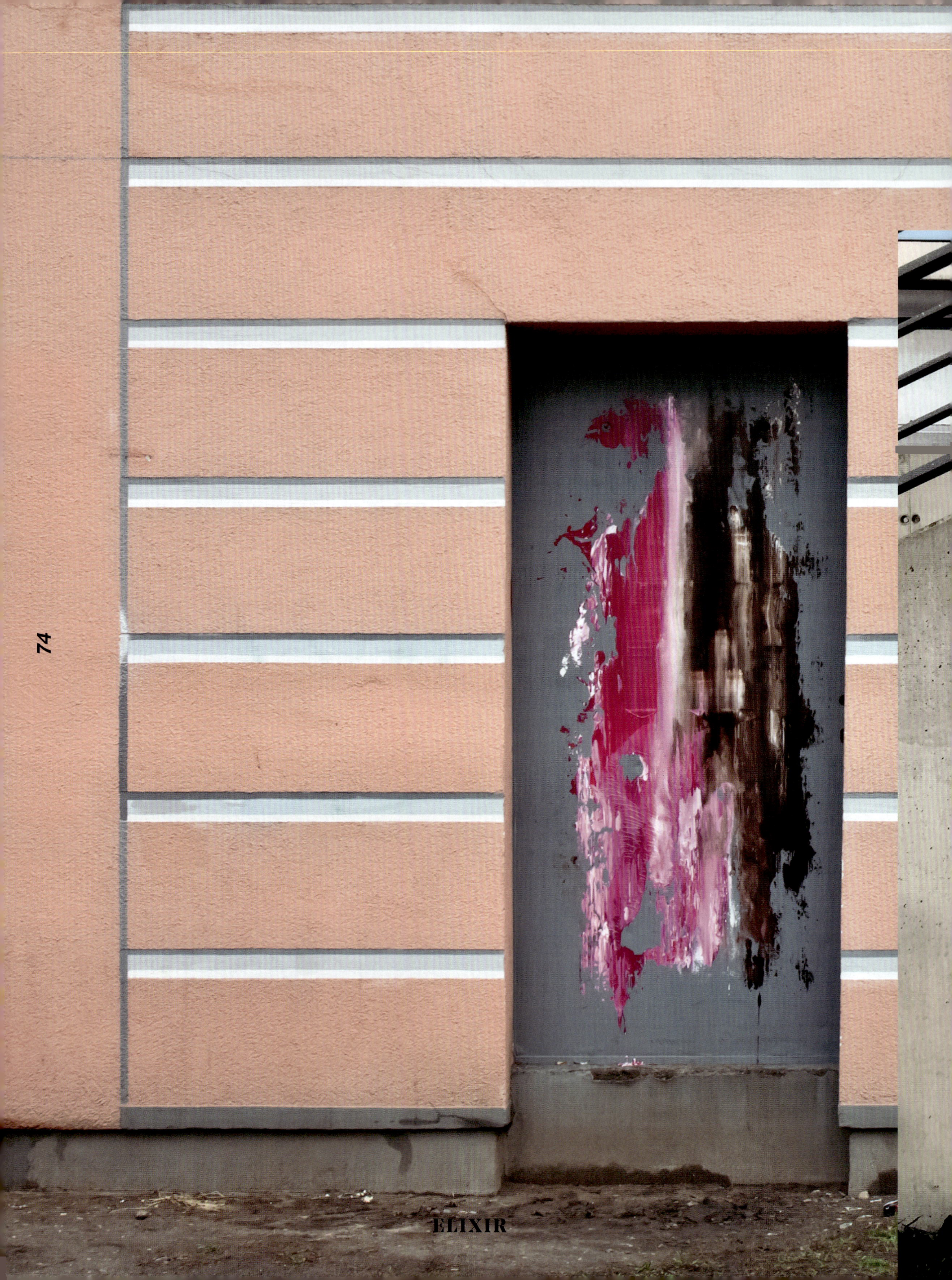

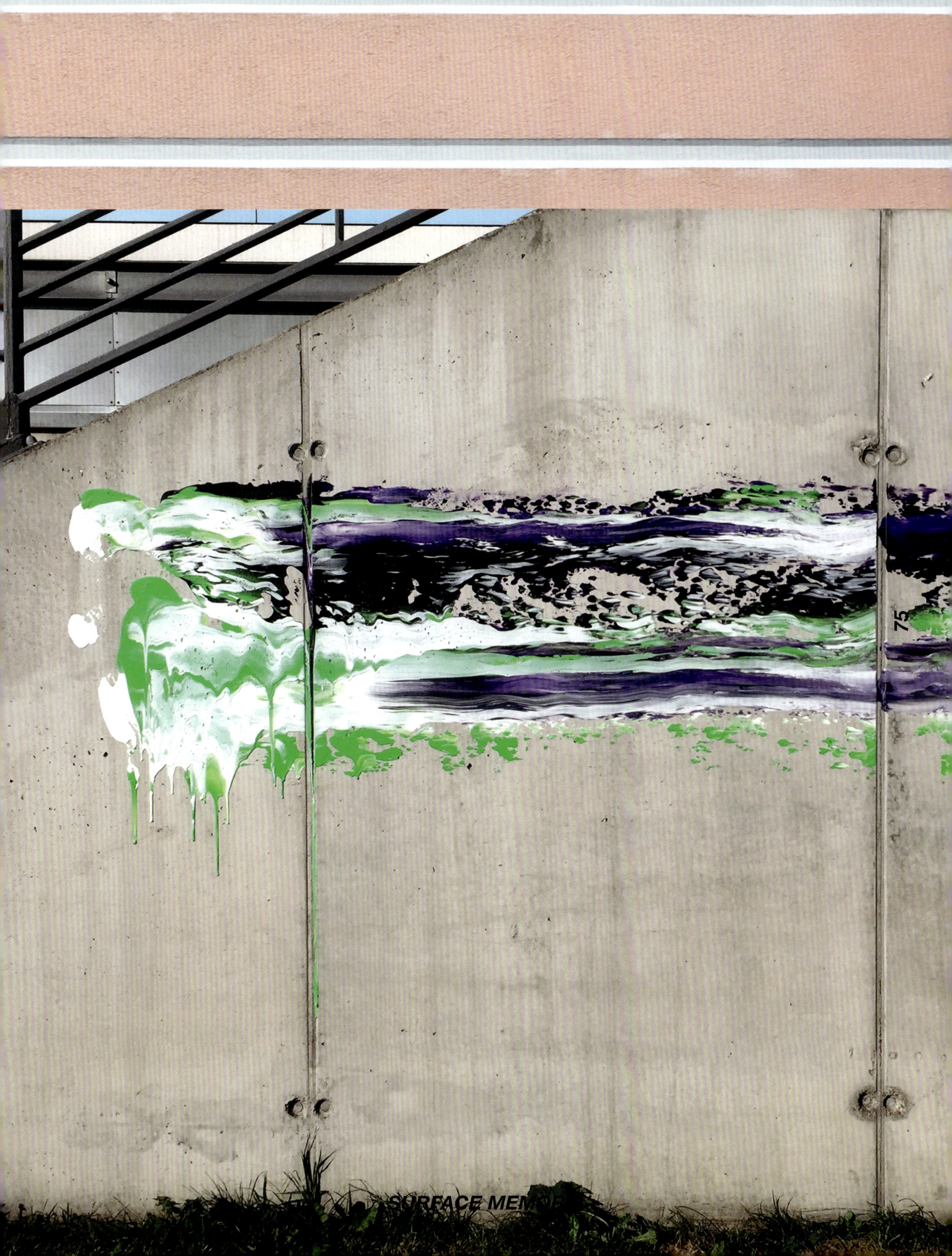

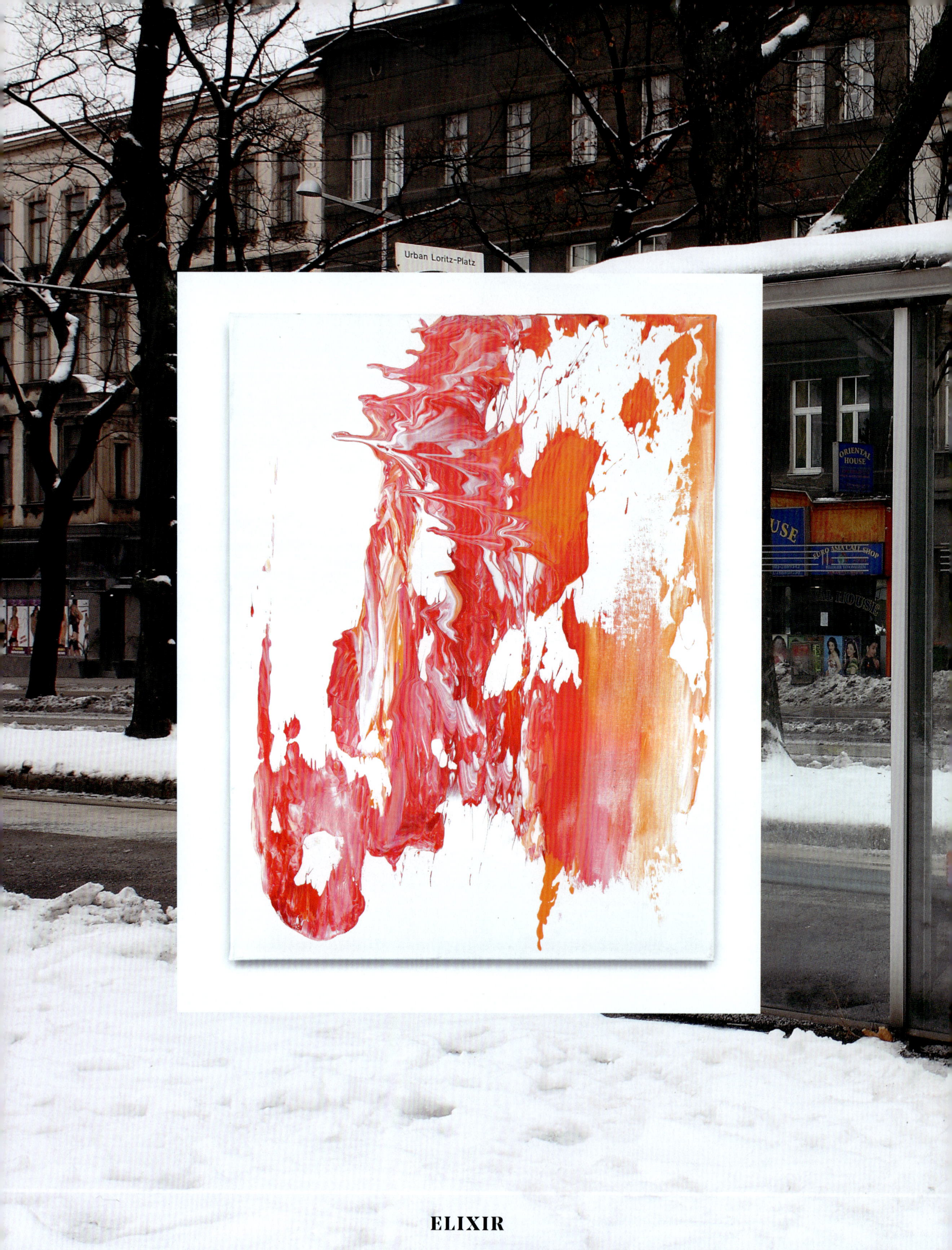

ELIXIR

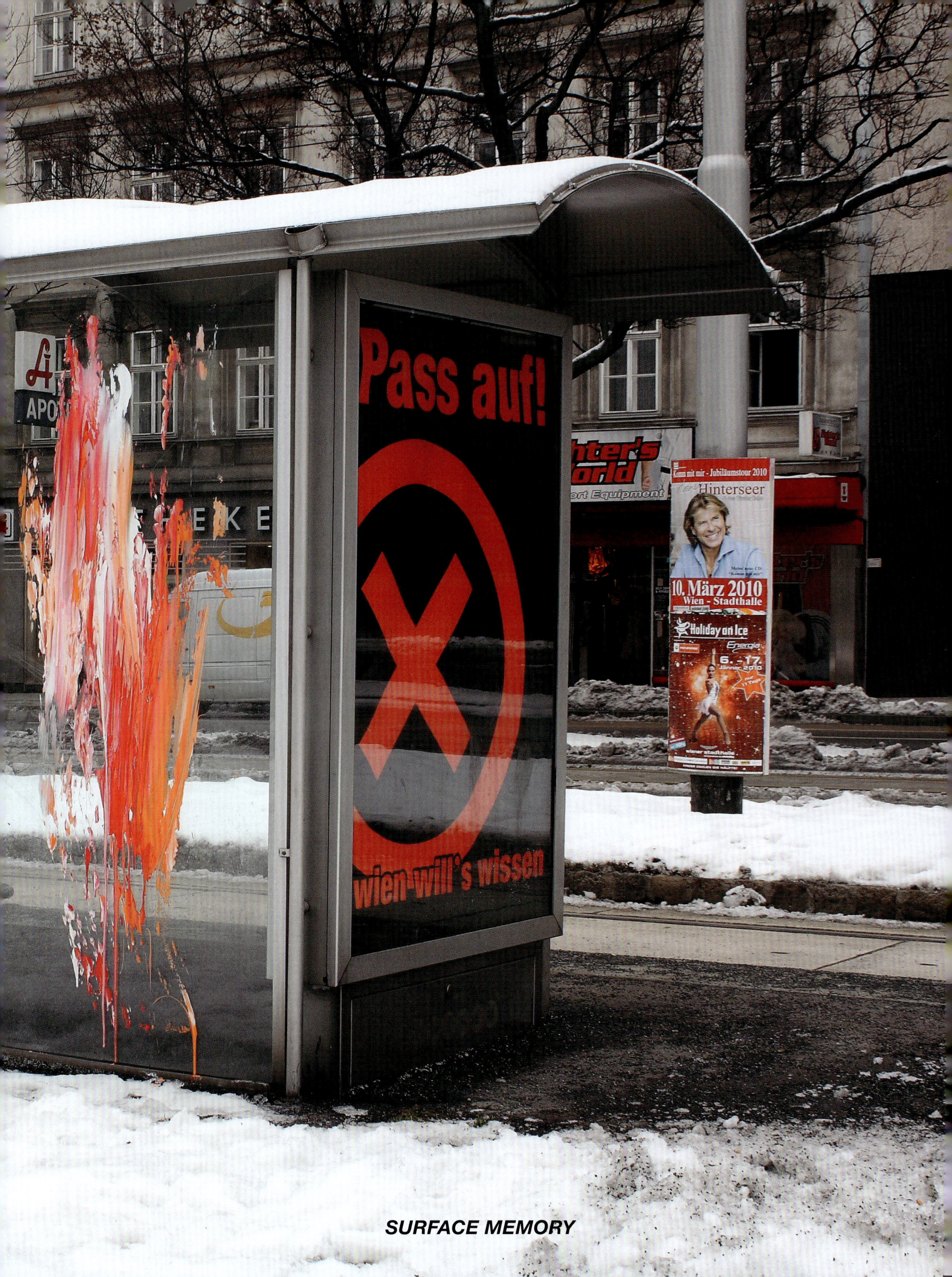

SURFACE MEMORY

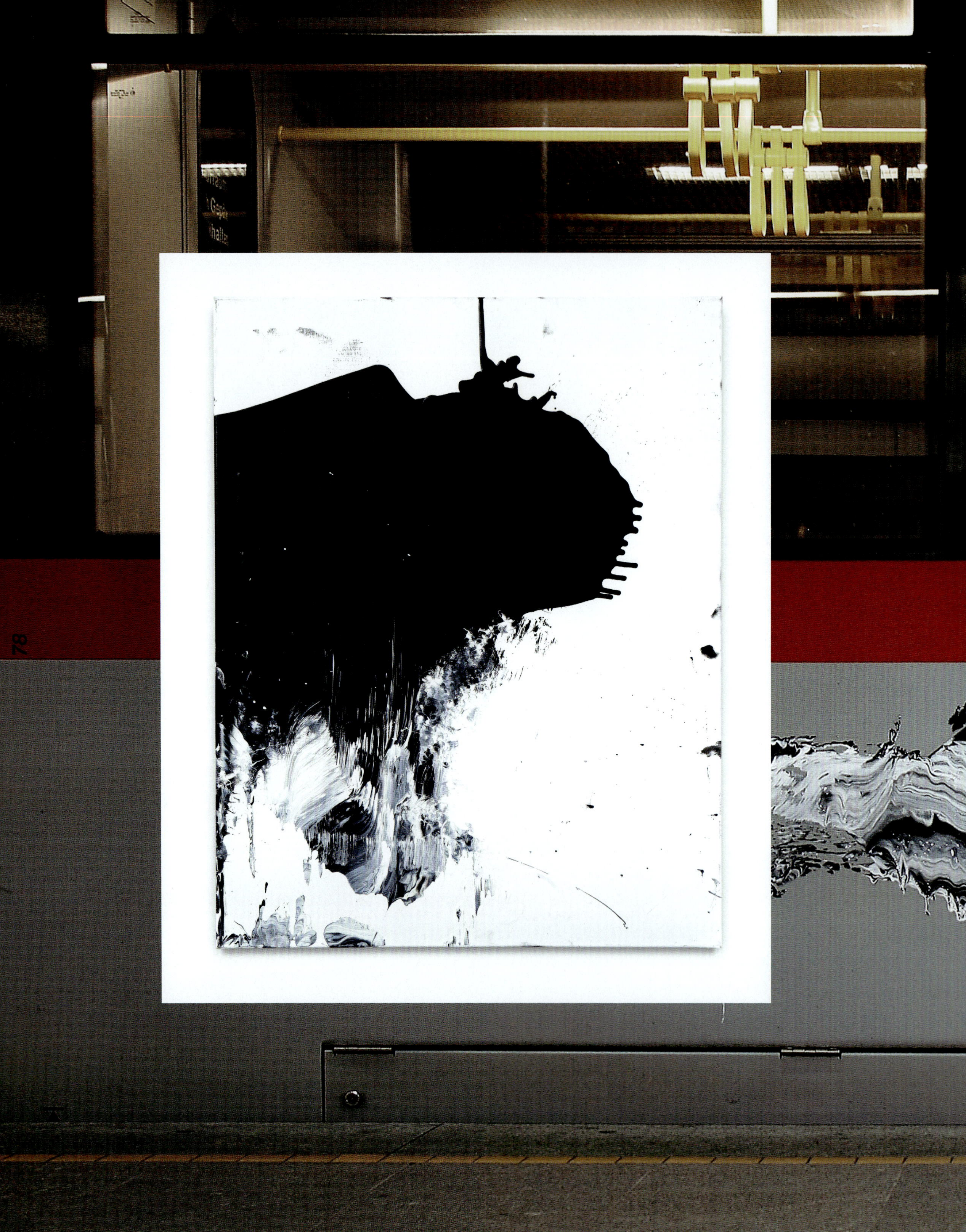

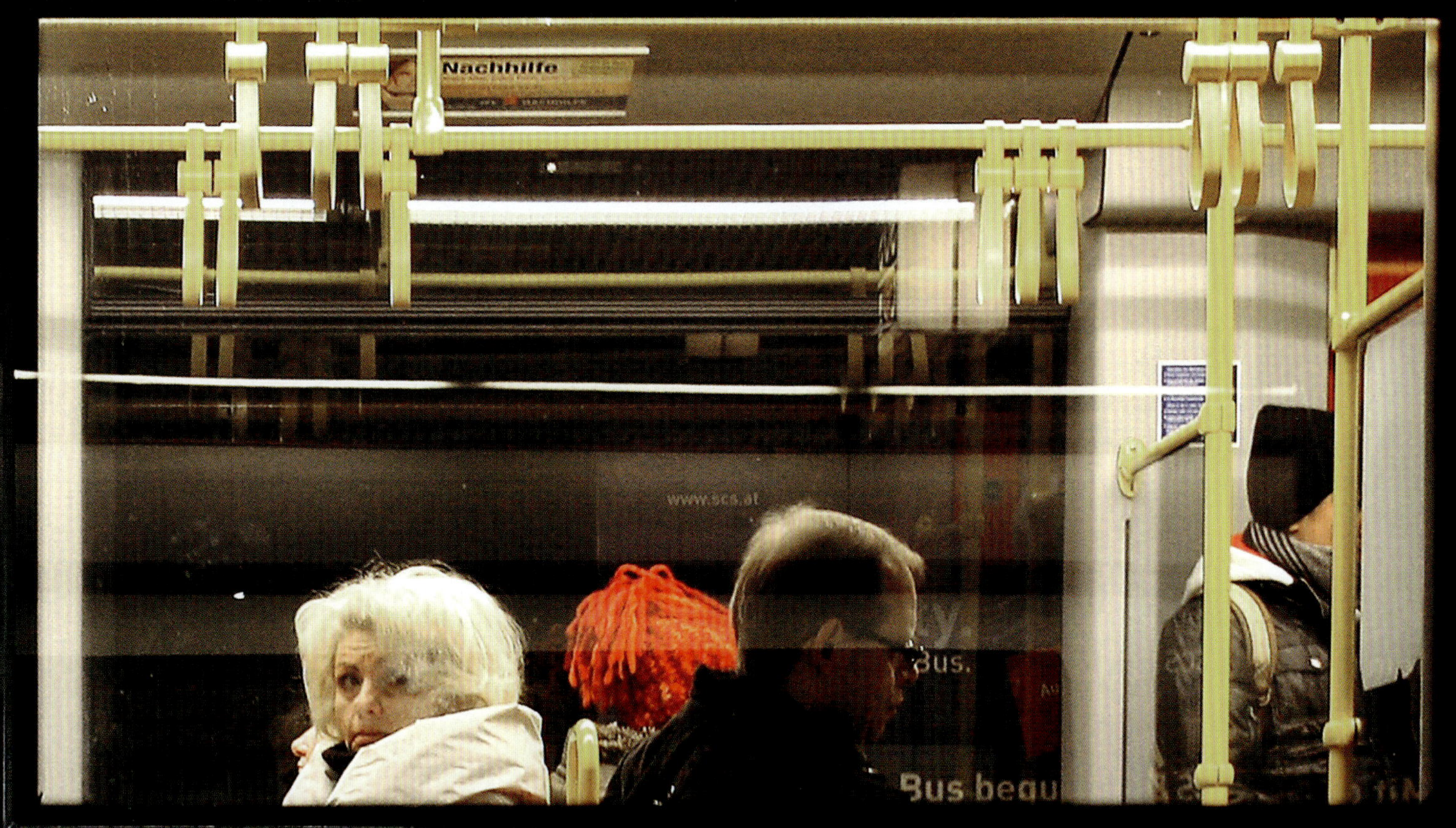
Nachhilfe
www.scs.at
Bus.

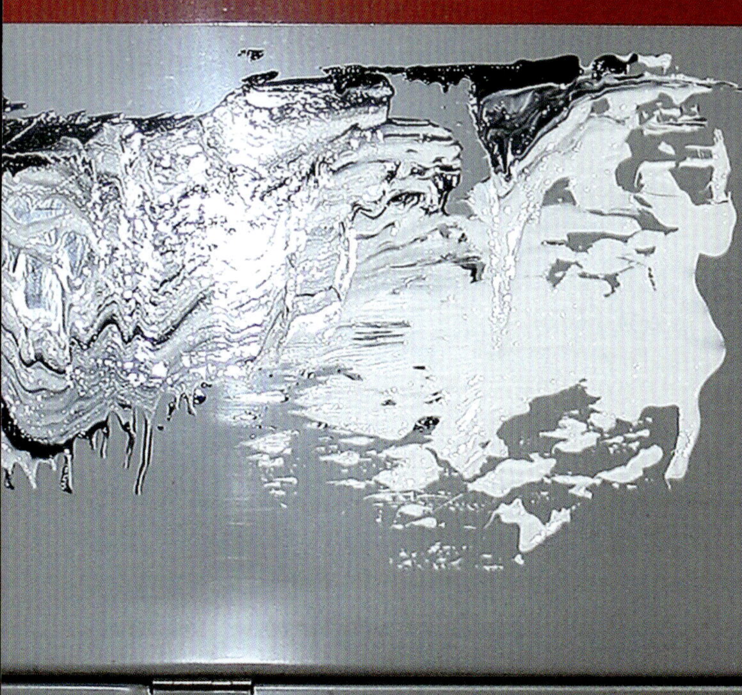

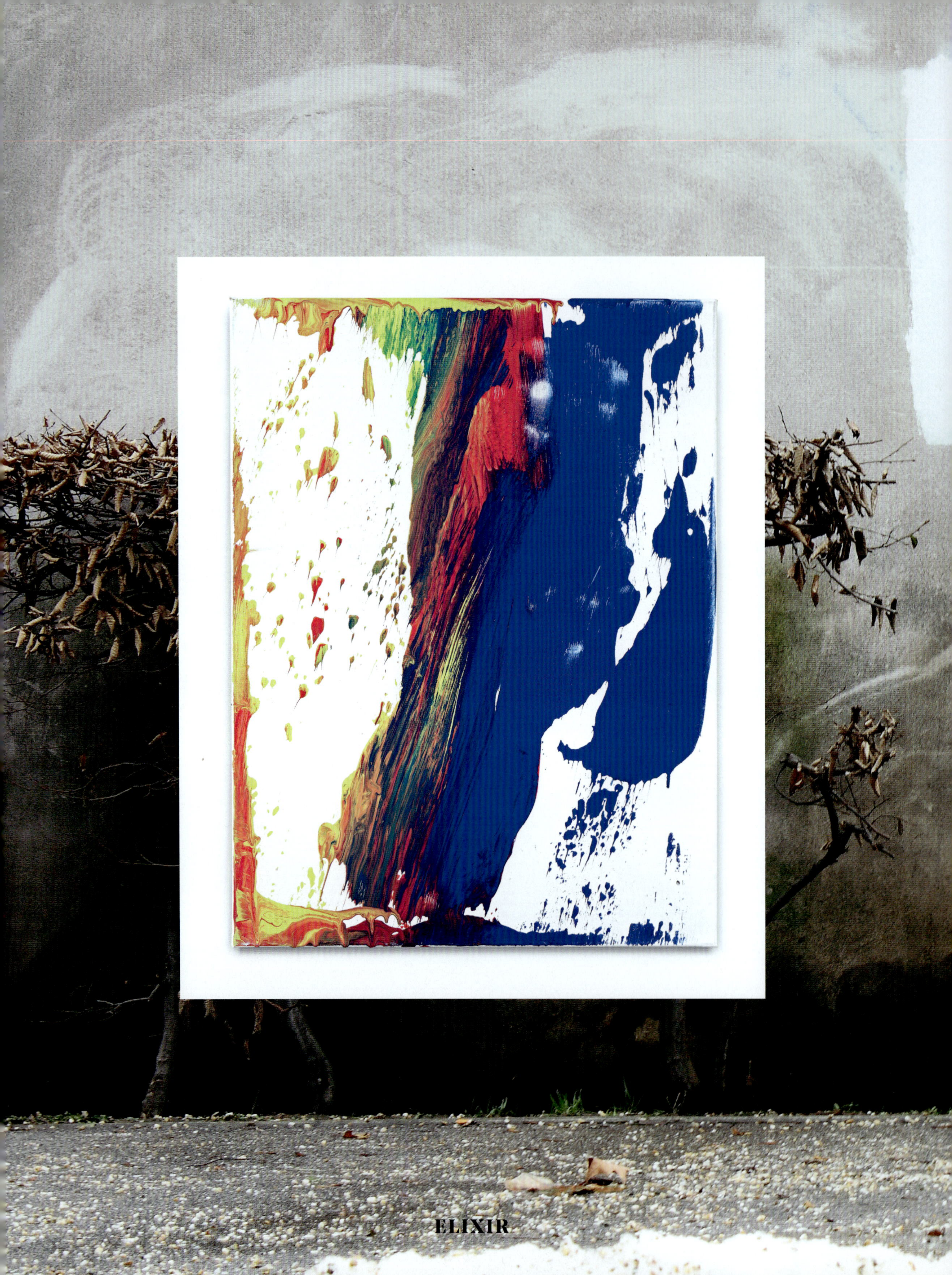

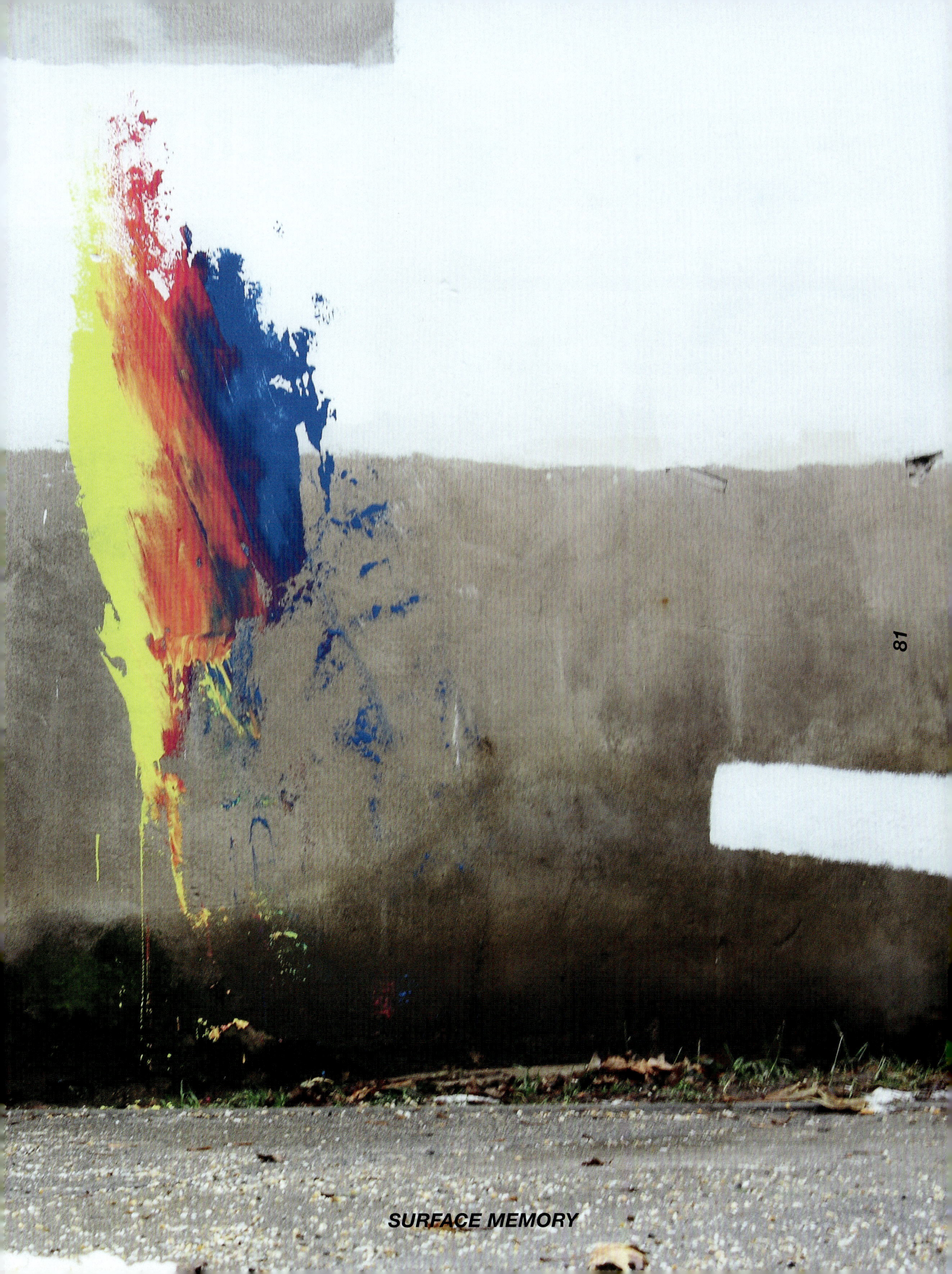

(2015)

App for Android tablet
YouTube channel
Visitors

The Title Is Your Name is not a title, but rather refers to the titles of the videos that are created whenever someone performs the work: the names of the exhibition visitors.
A room is lit by spotlights. In the middle of the room is a table and a tablet. Visitors must enter alone. Interacting with an app on the tablet, each visitor carries out a private performance. The app records the performance through the webcam. If the visitor does not want to see the recorded video, it is deleted immediately. If the visitor does want to see the video, it is uploaded to the YouTube channel *The Title Is Your Name*.

THE TITLE IS YOUR NAME

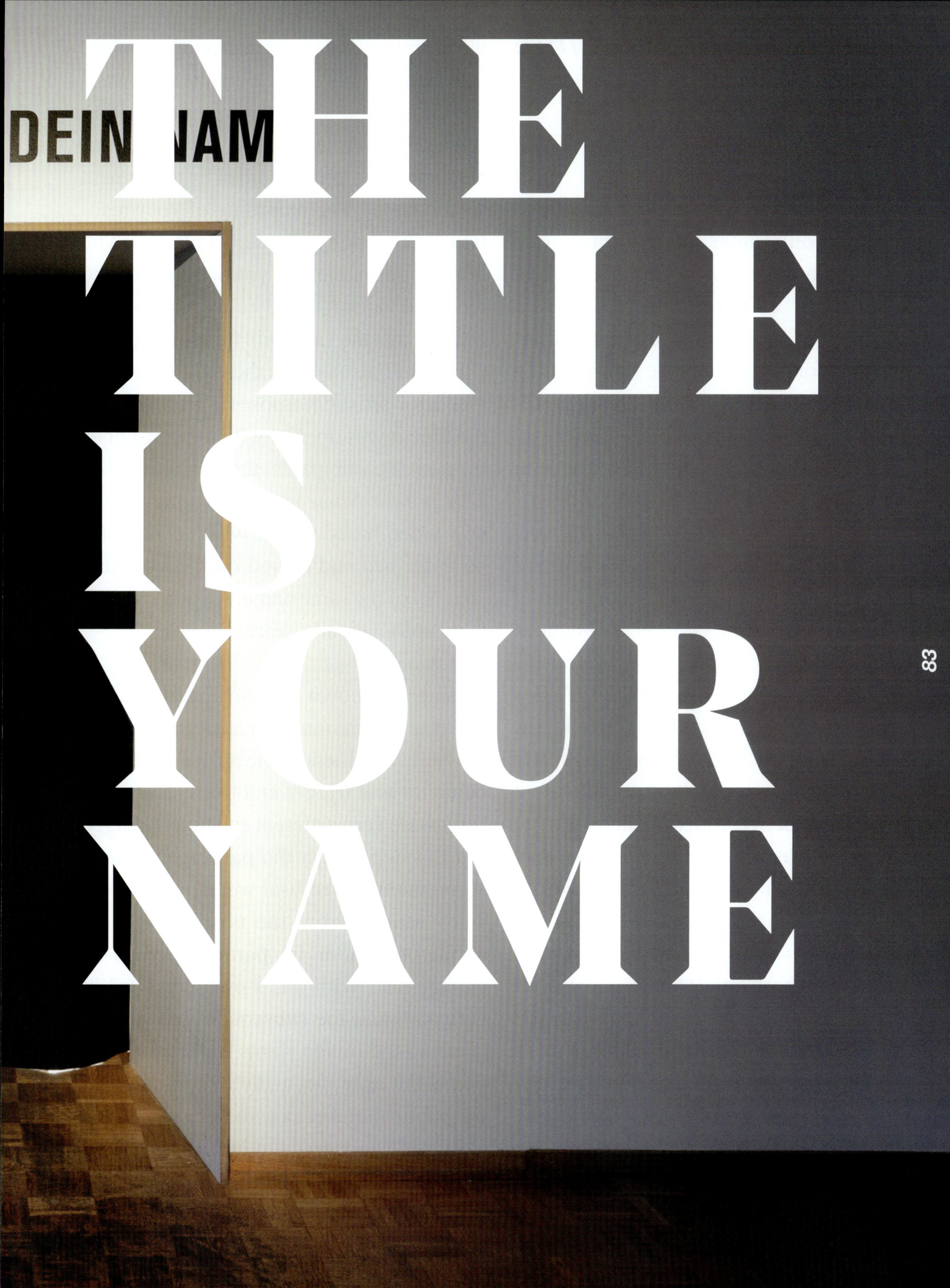

DEIN NAM

CHRISTIAN FALSNAES: THE TITLE IS YOUR NAME

Text by Thomas Thiel

Entrance, foyer, and reception. Short information with the friendly directions to please only enter the exhibition one person at a time, paired with the request to put away cell phone and jacket. Even entering the exhibition starts with an instruction for action, then the stairs leading up to the floor above. The staircase is still lit, the first room entirely dark—backstage. Only a spotlight points to the entrance to the second room: *The Title is Your Name*. Through a black curtain, suddenly surrounded by glaring light, in the middle of the room a white table and a chair. A tablet shows a play button. Off you go—action!

Christian Falsnaes's solo show *The Title is Your Name* at the Kunstverein Bielefeld was based on a single work, an app specifically developed—an application to activate a relationship between artwork and viewers. The artist was present-absent—above all not physically present as in earlier works. A dialogue with the visitors was established exclusively via a video, which Falsnaes filmed with the internal camera of the tablet before the opening in the exhibition space. Formally it resembles the aesthetic of selfie videos, tutorials, or video conferences, and shows the artist primarily at close range. However, the app not only presents the video but also, at the same time, unnoticeably documents the individual reactions in the reception and performance of the work. The visitors only learned about this toward the end of the about seven minute-long screening: "While watching the video, your reactions have been recorded by the camera on the tablet. The recording of your reactions is a work by Christian Falsnaes. The title is your name. Do you want to see the recorded video? [...] By clicking Yes, you confirm that the video will be saved and that Christian Falsnaes has the right to use the video for artistic purposes." Thus, during the time it was up, and with the consent of the active participants, the exhibition *The Title is Your Name* generated a number of new video-based works, which could later be published and shared on the YouTube channel of the same name. All other videos were automatically deleted.

Falsnaes is known for using language and physical expression to create situations that inevitably influence one's own, personal behavior and trigger emotions. The reactions were very different and, interestingly, did not depend on the participant's age. Agreement and refusal were evenly split. They ranged from the possible refusal of the conditions for participation to an engagement with one's own behavior in the room and the subsequent request for clearing the image rights for artistic purposes. For example, many visitors declined the publication because the moment in the exhibition appeared too intimate to them, the execution of the performative instructions for action too personal, or because they minded being found on the Internet later on. At the same time, it was striking that the majority of the active participants trusted the artist, using their actual name without playing with the possibilities of anonymization (pseudonyms, initials, etc.) in the title. Openness, spontaneity, improvisation, and physical activity were demanded; the artist recorded active participation just the same as a refusal to follow the rapidly sequenced instructions. Even misunderstandings in the technical use or dialogic moments in the communication with the artist were filmed. During, and certainly after, the performance there were a lot of questions: How much of myself do I reveal? Do I sing or dance with a tablet in my hands for an absent artist? Do I follow his instructions or do I avoid the artistic script? Am I being watched?

With the experimental setting *The Title is Your Name* (2015), Falsnaes first designed an interactive room installation, which moved the focus to the performative potential of viewing art, the object of which ultimately only the participants know. Until today, only the performative reactions to Falsnaes's video are known. In that sense, the work also invites an analysis of the audience. How an individual dealt with the situation could be found out not only from conversations with other visitors, but also from other recordings. Possible hints are hidden in the summary and in the non-verbal expression of the individual viewers.

In Falsnaes's work, the audience is both object and artistic material; it oscillates between voluntariness and seduction, between exclusion and participation, between individual decision and surrender. As he first did in *Justified Beliefs* (2014) and later in *Available* (2015), Falsnaes continues to explore the relationship between artist and audience, but the works no longer require the physical presence of the artist for their performance. At the same time, from the perspective of the artist, the work is only completed through the performance of the individual viewers. *The Title is Your Name* is also therefore a joint venture, which as a result remains where it was produced and as documentation after the performance. The quality and form of participation determines the artistic result and thereby escapes the control of the artist, is part of the work process and the essential conditions. What is essential is not just the result, but also the personal experience of the participants. *The Title is Your Name* documents this experience in over 1,300 videos, which since January 2015 have also been produced in other places, and in its visible result resembles an Internet meme that has lost its original. With few means—a tablet, a Bluetooth headset, an app, a video with live characters, the possibility for movement in the room—Christian Falsnaes creates not just a mirror of one's self, but also a moment of immersion, which lets the "fourth wall" between artist and audience disappear.

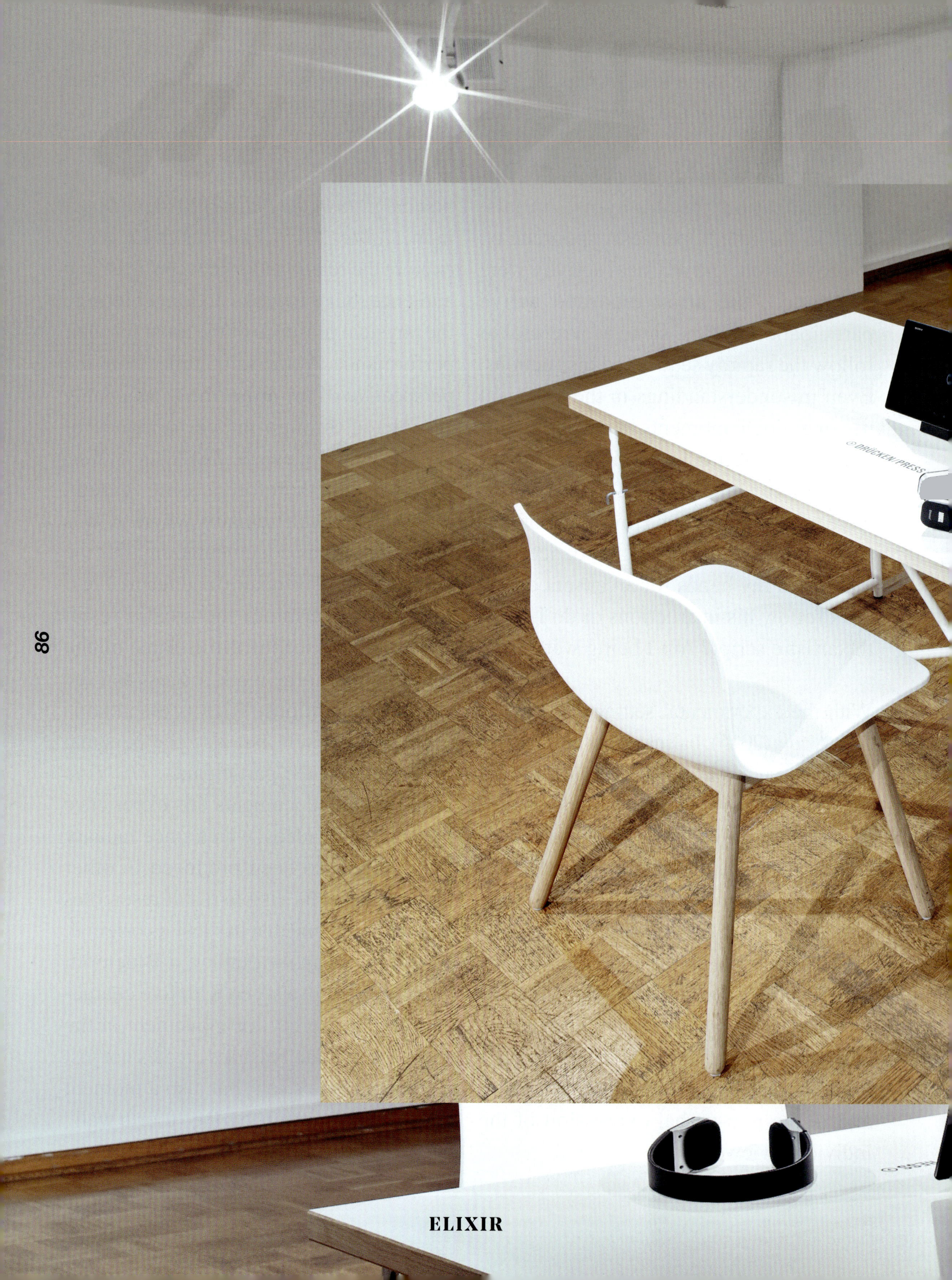
DRÜCKEN/PRESS
ELIXIR

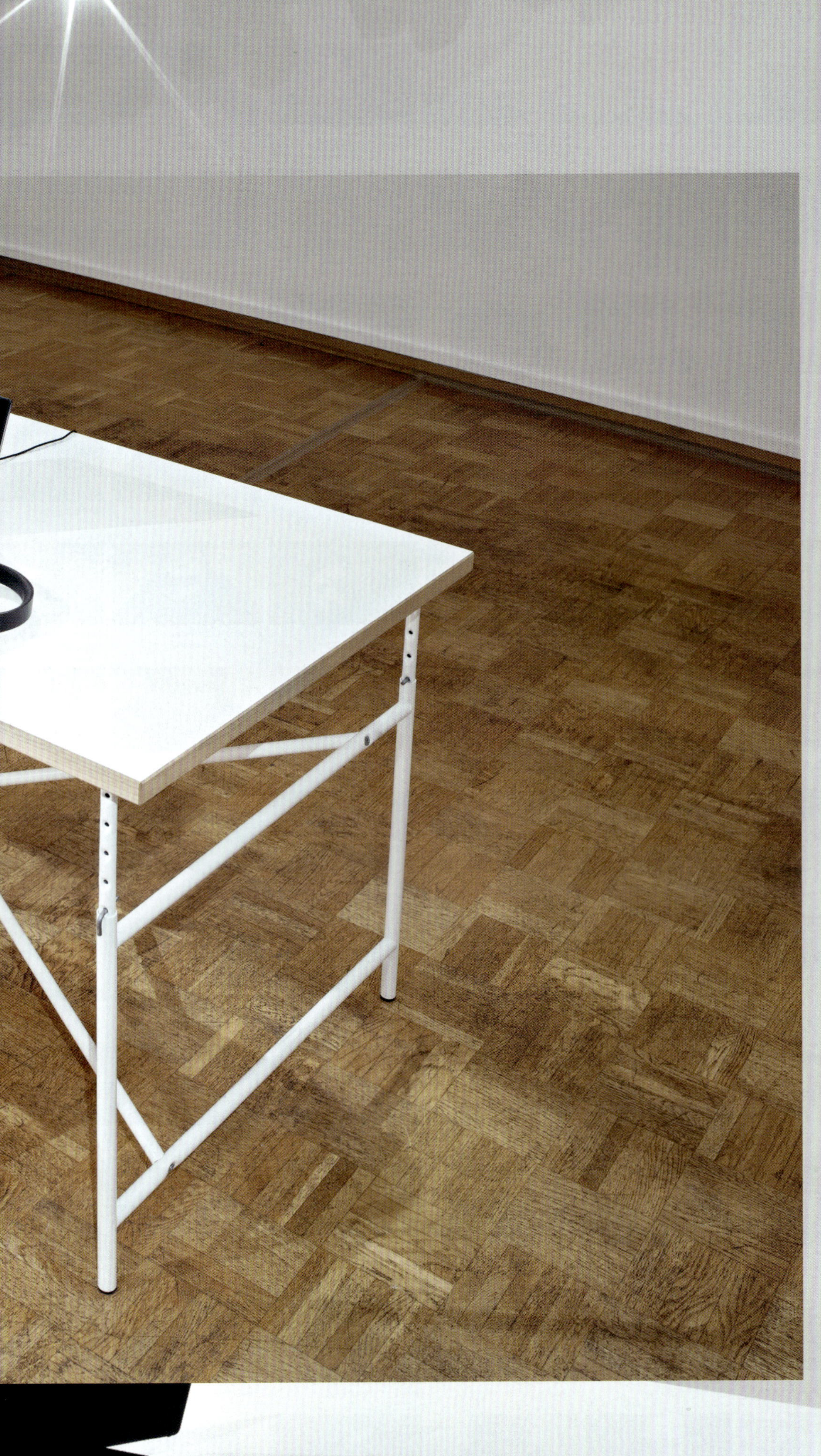

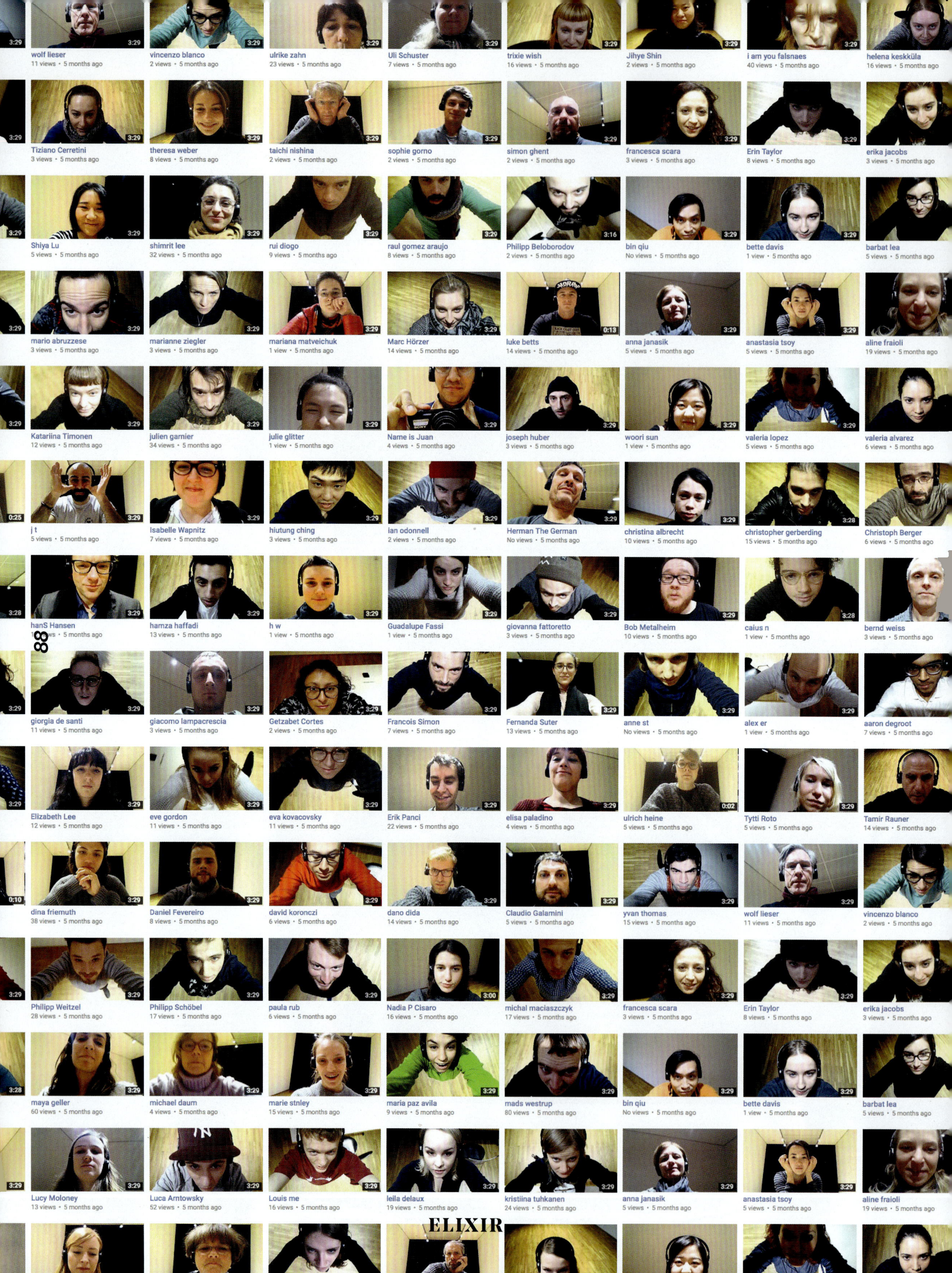
wolf lieser
11 views • 5 months ago
vincenzo blanco
2 views • 5 months ago
ulrike zahn
23 views • 5 months ago
Uli Schuster
7 views • 5 months ago
trixie wish
16 views • 5 months ago
Jihye Shin
2 views • 5 months ago
i am you falsnaes
40 views • 5 months ago
helena keskküla
16 views • 5 months ago
Tiziano Cerretini
3 views • 5 months ago
theresa weber
8 views • 5 months ago
taichi nishina
2 views • 5 months ago
sophie gorno
2 views • 5 months ago
simon ghent
2 views • 5 months ago
francesca scara
3 views • 5 months ago
Erin Taylor
8 views • 5 months ago
erika jacobs
3 views • 5 months ago
Shiya Lu
5 views • 5 months ago
shimrit lee
32 views • 5 months ago
rui diogo
9 views • 5 months ago
raul gomez araujo
8 views • 5 months ago
Philipp Beloborodov
2 views • 5 months ago
bin qiu
No views • 5 months ago
bette davis
1 view • 5 months ago
barbat lea
5 views • 5 months ago
mario abruzzese
3 views • 5 months ago
marianne ziegler
3 views • 5 months ago
mariana matveichuk
1 view • 5 months ago
Marc Hörzer
14 views • 5 months ago
luke betts
14 views • 5 months ago
anna janasik
5 views • 5 months ago
anastasia tsoy
5 views • 5 months ago
aline fraioli
19 views • 5 months ago
Katariina Timonen
12 views • 5 months ago
julien garnier
34 views • 5 months ago
julie glitter
1 view • 5 months ago
Name is Juan
4 views • 5 months ago
joseph huber
3 views • 5 months ago
woori sun
1 view • 5 months ago
valeria lopez
5 views • 5 months ago
valeria alvarez
6 views • 5 months ago
j t
5 views • 5 months ago
Isabelle Wapnitz
7 views • 5 months ago
hiutung ching
3 views • 5 months ago
ian odonnell
2 views • 5 months ago
Herman The German
No views • 5 months ago
christina albrecht
10 views • 5 months ago
christopher gerberding
15 views • 5 months ago
Christoph Berger
6 views • 5 months ago
hanS Hansen
5 months ago
hamza haffadi
13 views • 5 months ago
h w
1 view • 5 months ago
Guadalupe Fassi
1 view • 5 months ago
giovanna fattoretto
3 views • 5 months ago
Bob Metalheim
10 views • 5 months ago
caius n
1 view • 5 months ago
bernd weiss
3 views • 5 months ago
giorgia de santi
11 views • 5 months ago
giacomo lampacrescia
3 views • 5 months ago
Getzabet Cortes
2 views • 5 months ago
Francois Simon
7 views • 5 months ago
Fernanda Suter
13 views • 5 months ago
anne st
No views • 5 months ago
alex er
1 view • 5 months ago
aaron degroot
7 views • 5 months ago
Elizabeth Lee
12 views • 5 months ago
eve gordon
11 views • 5 months ago
eva kovacovsky
11 views • 5 months ago
Erik Panci
22 views • 5 months ago
elisa paladino
4 views • 5 months ago
ulrich heine
5 views • 5 months ago
Tytti Roto
5 views • 5 months ago
Tamir Rauner
14 views • 5 months ago
dina friemuth
38 views • 5 months ago
Daniel Fevereiro
8 views • 5 months ago
david koronczi
6 views • 5 months ago
dano dida
14 views • 5 months ago
Claudio Galamini
5 views • 5 months ago
yvan thomas
15 views • 5 months ago
wolf lieser
11 views • 5 months ago
vincenzo blanco
2 views • 5 months ago
Philipp Weitzel
28 views • 5 months ago
Philipp Schöbel
17 views • 5 months ago
paula rub
6 views • 5 months ago
Nadia P Cisaro
16 views • 5 months ago
michal maciaszczyk
17 views • 5 months ago
francesca scara
3 views • 5 months ago
Erin Taylor
8 views • 5 months ago
erika jacobs
3 views • 5 months ago
maya geller
60 views • 5 months ago
michael daum
4 views • 5 months ago
marie stnley
15 views • 5 months ago
maria paz avila
9 views • 5 months ago
mads westrup
80 views • 5 months ago
bin qiu
No views • 5 months ago
bette davis
1 view • 5 months ago
barbat lea
5 views • 5 months ago
Lucy Moloney
13 views • 5 months ago
Luca Arntowsky
52 views • 5 months ago
Louis me
16 views • 5 months ago
leila delaux
19 views • 5 months ago
kristiina tuhkanen
24 views • 5 months ago
anna janasik
5 views • 5 months ago
anastasia tsoy
5 views • 5 months ago
aline fraioli
19 views • 5 months ago
ELIXIR

cera — 5 months ago | Guenther zehner — No views • 5 months ago | g g — 3 views • 5 months ago | Kasia Bogumil — 19 views • 5 months ago | Karen van den Berg — 38 views • 5 months ago | jinwoojung jung — 11 views • 5 months ago | Jan Amaru Toefflinger — 3 views • 5 months ago | johanna ehl — 7 views • 5 months ago | jen m — 7 views

et — 5 months ago | cristiano bellei — 12 views • 5 months ago | christina schelhas — 1 view • 5 months ago | Jeanne Marie CC Varain — 5 views • 5 months ago | j t — 5 views • 5 months ago | Isabelle Wapnitz — 7 views • 5 months ago | hiutung ching — 3 views • 5 months ago | ian odonnell — 2 views • 5 months ago | Herma — No views

hame — 5 months ago | artem filatov — 3 views • 5 months ago | antoine lelievre — 3 views • 5 months ago | hartmut weymann — 10 views • 5 months ago | hanS Hansen — 12 views • 5 months ago | hamza haffadi — 13 views • 5 months ago | h w — 1 view • 5 months ago | Guadalupe Fassi — 1 view • 5 months ago | giovann — 3 views

a — 5 months ago | akiko ukai — 3 views • 5 months ago | Adam Dubbe — 5 views • 5 months ago | giovanna fattoretto — 10 views • 5 months ago | giorgia de santi — 11 views • 5 months ago | giacomo lampacrescia — 3 views • 5 months ago | Getzabet Cortes — 2 views • 5 months ago | Francois Simon — 7 views • 5 months ago | Fernan — 13 views

neururer — 5 months ago | stefan schmitt — 12 views • 5 months ago | Sangpil Yoo — 4 views • 5 months ago | f zett — 5 views • 5 months ago | Elizabeth Lee — 12 views • 5 months ago | eve gordon — 11 views • 5 months ago | eva kovacovsky — 11 views • 5 months ago | Erik Panci — 22 views • 5 months ago | elisa pa — 4 views

incent — 5 months ago | Carolin Schramm — 34 views • 5 months ago | brynn alred — 5 views • 5 months ago | Toby O'Leary — 14 views • 5 months ago | Tiziano Cerretini — 3 views • 5 months ago | theresa weber — 8 views • 5 months ago | taichi nishina — 2 views • 5 months ago | sophie gorno — 2 views • 5 months ago | simon — 2 views

seerieder — 5 months ago | ze ming sim — 1 view • 5 months ago | Andrew Crawford — 8 views • 5 months ago | Simeone Del Prete — 5 views • 5 months ago | Shiya Lu — 5 views • 5 months ago | shimrit lee — 32 views • 5 months ago | rui diogo — 9 views • 5 months ago | raul gomez araujo — 8 views • 5 months ago | Philipp — 2 views

89

Albuquerque Terra — 5 months ago | vanildo da silva — 3 views • 5 months ago | Valentina Smirnova — 11 views • 5 months ago | martina pasqualini — 10 views • 5 months ago | mario abruzzese — 3 views • 5 months ago | marianne ziegler — 3 views • 5 months ago | mariana matveichuk — 1 view • 5 months ago | Marc Hörzer — 14 views • 5 months ago | luke be — 14 views

vasse — 5 months ago | Raphaela Haring — 45 views • 5 months ago | r e — 1 view • 5 months ago | Lionel ESCHENBRENNER — 2 views • 5 months ago | Katariina Timonen — 12 views • 5 months ago | julien garnier — 34 views • 5 months ago | julie glitter — 1 view • 5 months ago | Name is Juan — 4 views • 5 months ago | joseph — 3 views

hn — 5 months ago | Uli Schuster — 7 views • 5 months ago | trixie wish — 16 views • 5 months ago | Jihye Shin — 2 views • 5 months ago | i am you falsnaes — 40 views • 5 months ago | helena keskküla — 16 views • 5 months ago | hanna kucera — 27 views • 5 months ago | Guenther zehner — No views • 5 months ago | g g — 3 views

et — 5 months ago | cristiano bellei — 12 views • 5 months ago | christina schelhas — 1 view • 5 months ago | perretti antonio — 12 views • 5 months ago | Per Jonsson — 1 view • 5 months ago | Per Jonsson — 5 views • 5 months ago | maya xu — 5 views • 5 months ago | maria d coll — 7 views • 5 months ago | maria a — 11 views

hame — 5 months ago | artem filatov — 3 views • 5 months ago | antoine lelievre — 3 views • 5 months ago | katharina weinstock — 21 views • 5 months ago | juan pablo coronel — 14 views • 5 months ago | jean noel — 6 views • 5 months ago | jane calm — 2 views • 5 months ago | hao li — 2 views • 5 months ago | hanna k — 6 views

ka — 5 months ago | akiko ukai — 3 views • 5 months ago | Adam Dubbe — 5 views • 5 months ago | gabriele caffagni — 7 views • 5 months ago | Frank Wertke — 4 views • 5 months ago | fen de winter — 18 views • 5 months ago | feli romero — 4 views • 5 months ago | federico bazzoli — 22 views • 5 months ago | Emily C — 15 views

THE TITLE IS YOUR NAME

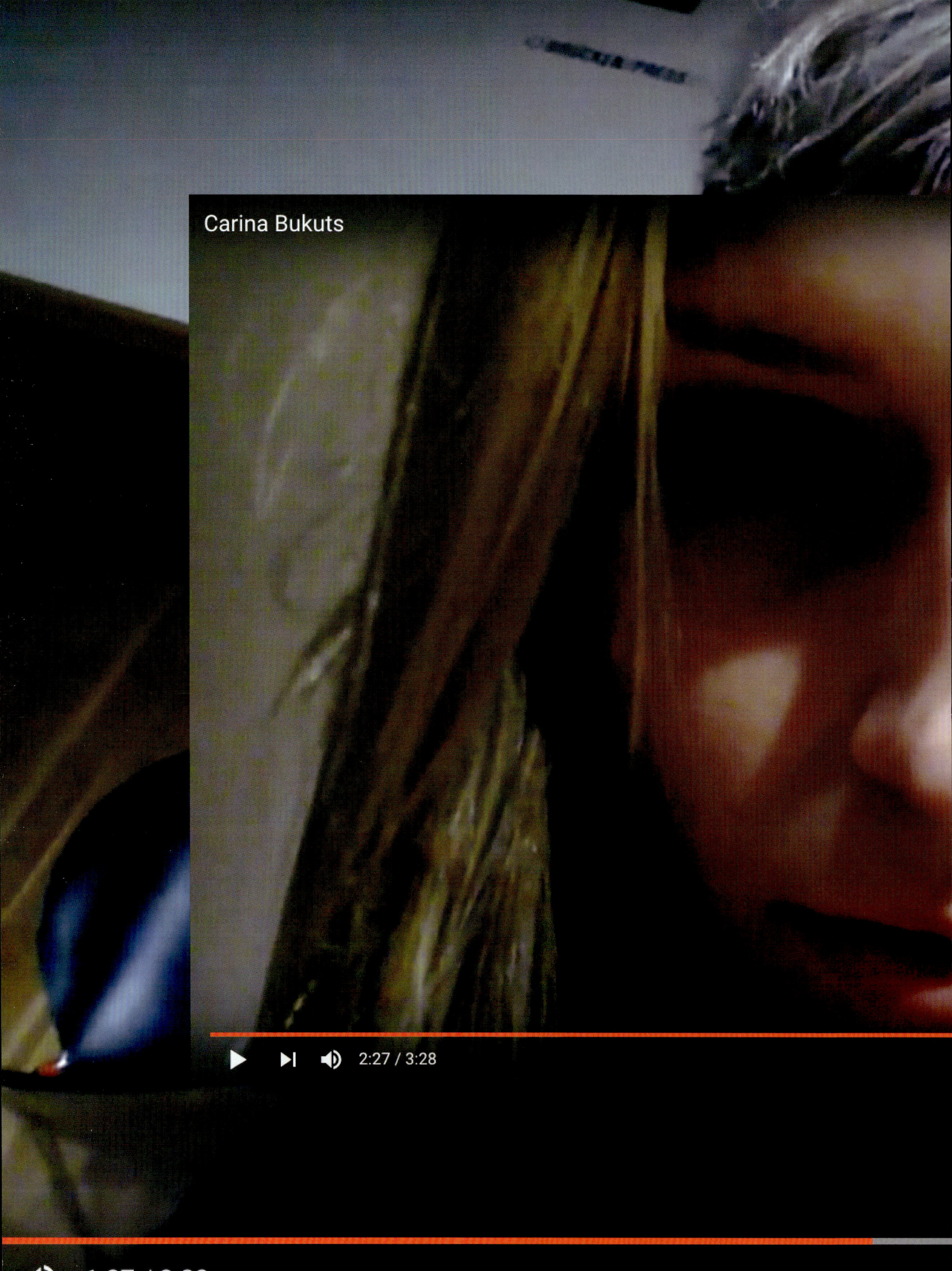
Carina Bukuts
2:27 / 3:28

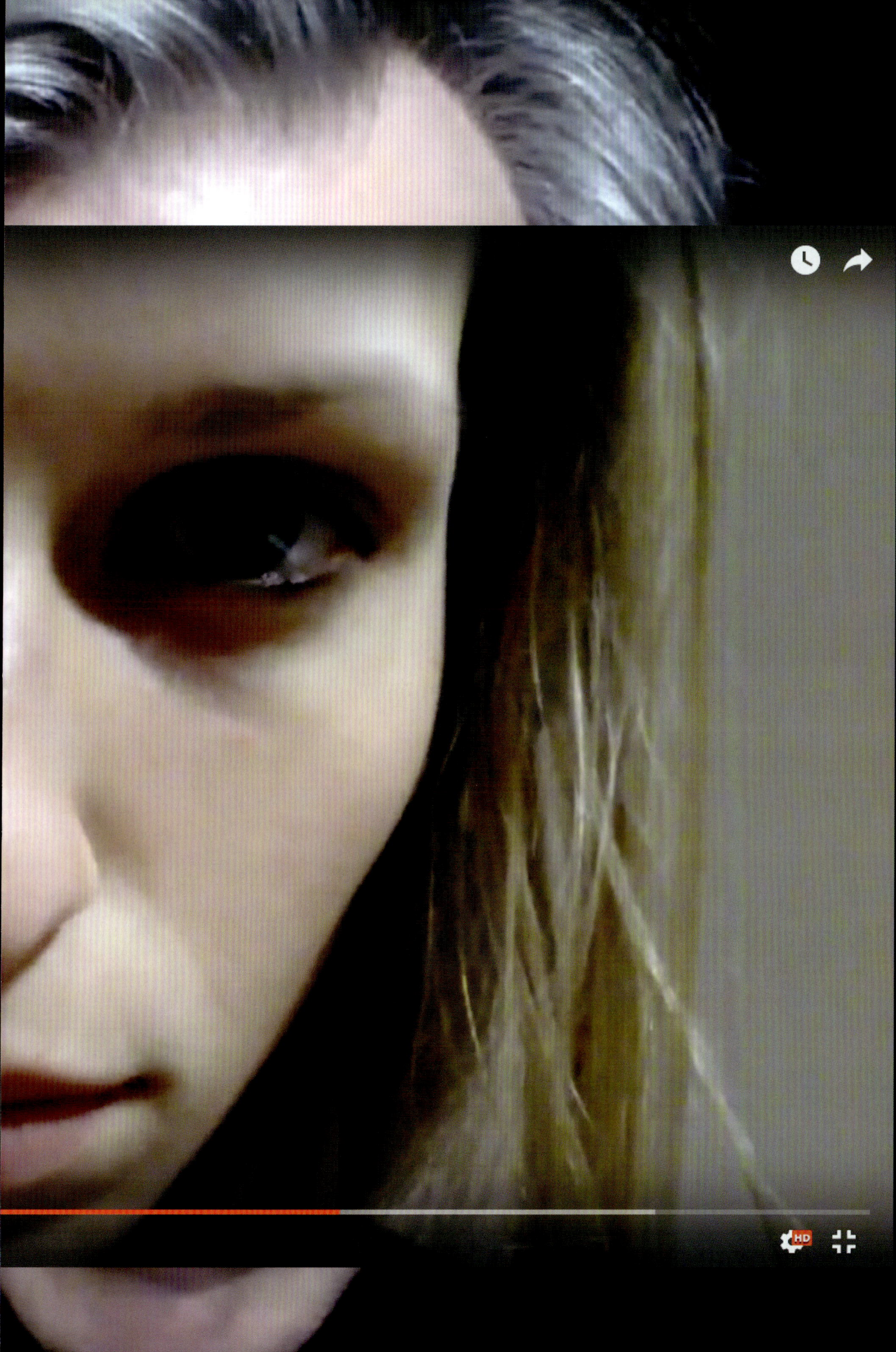
HD

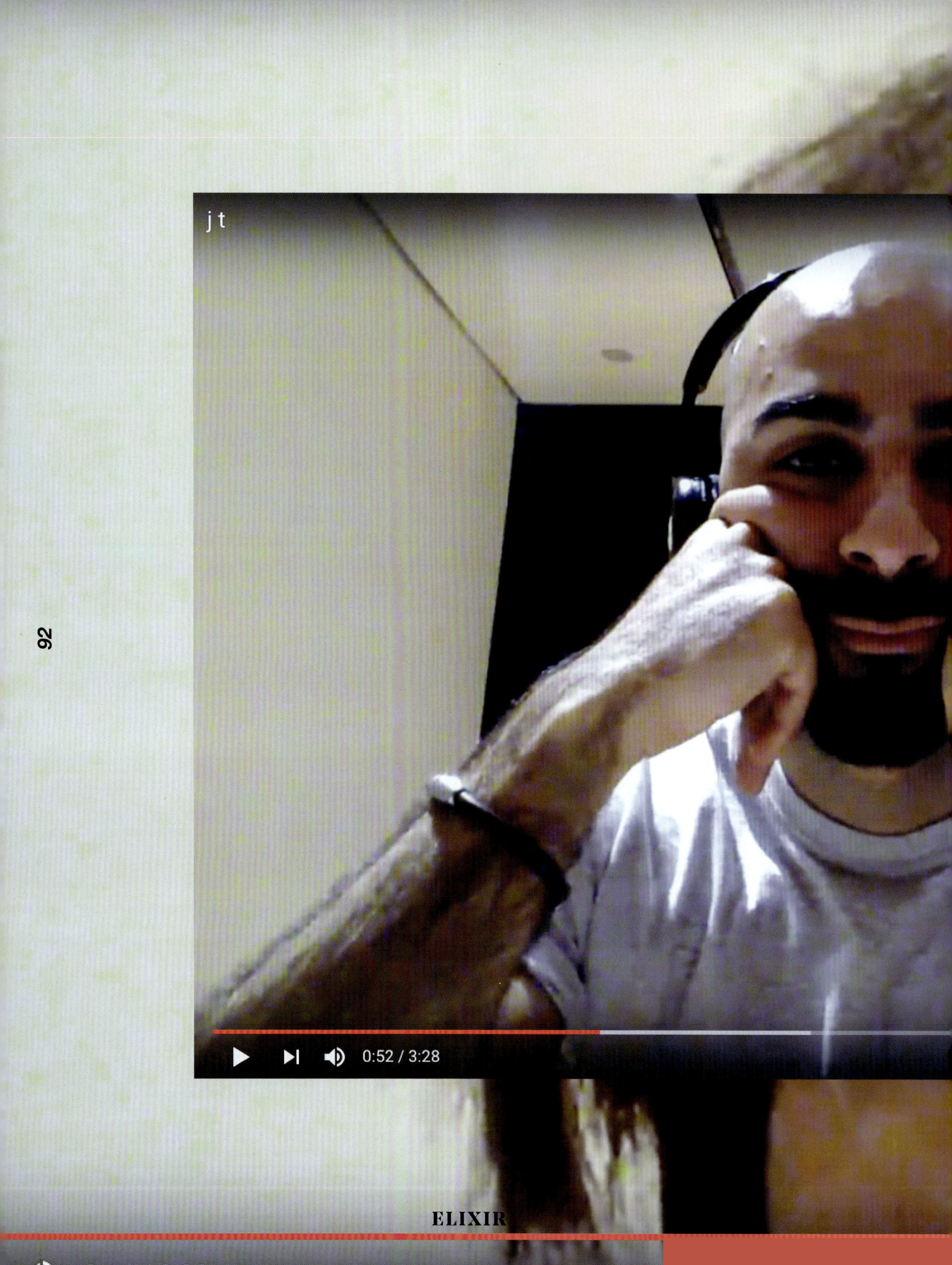
j t
0:52 / 3:28

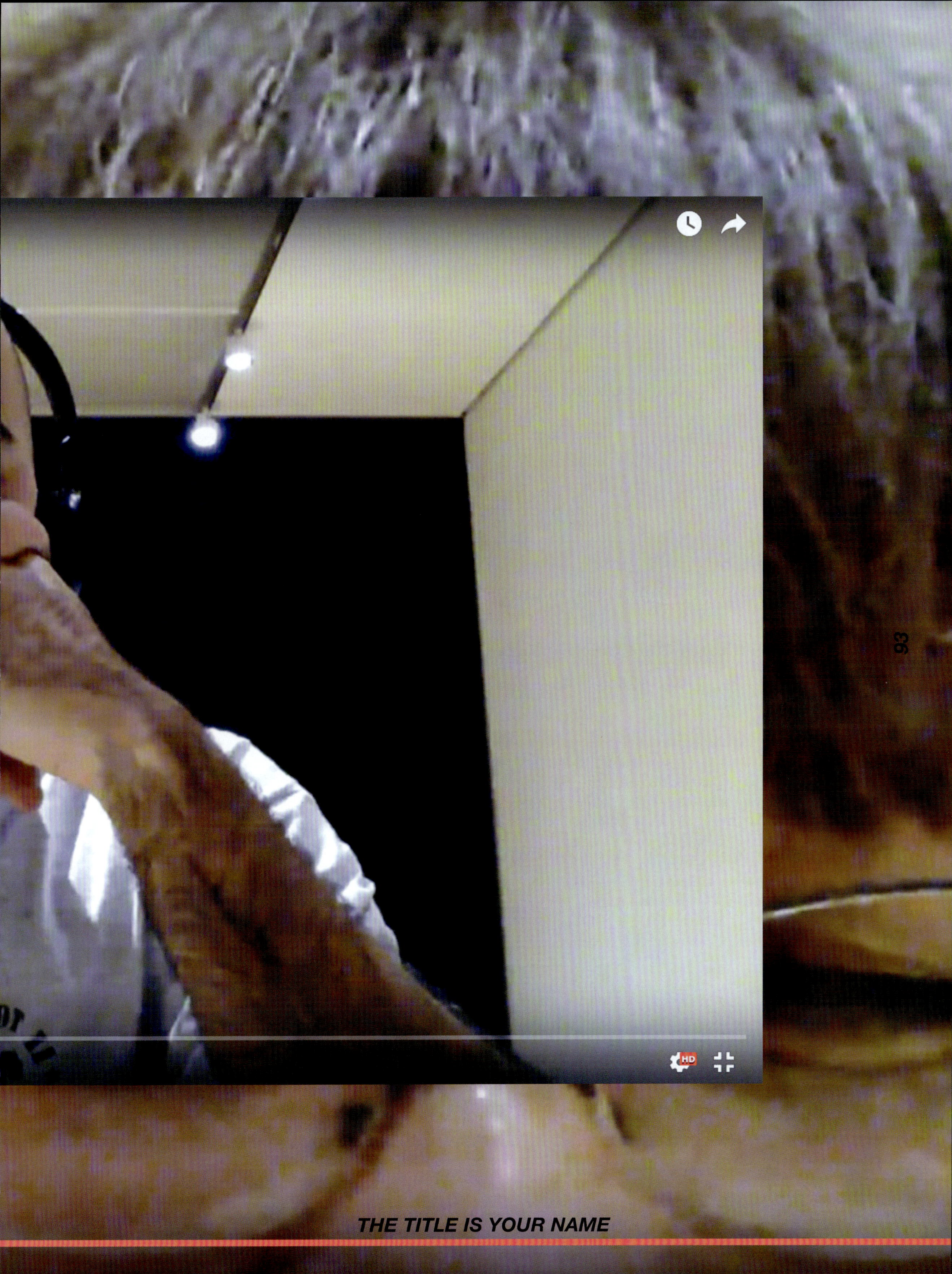

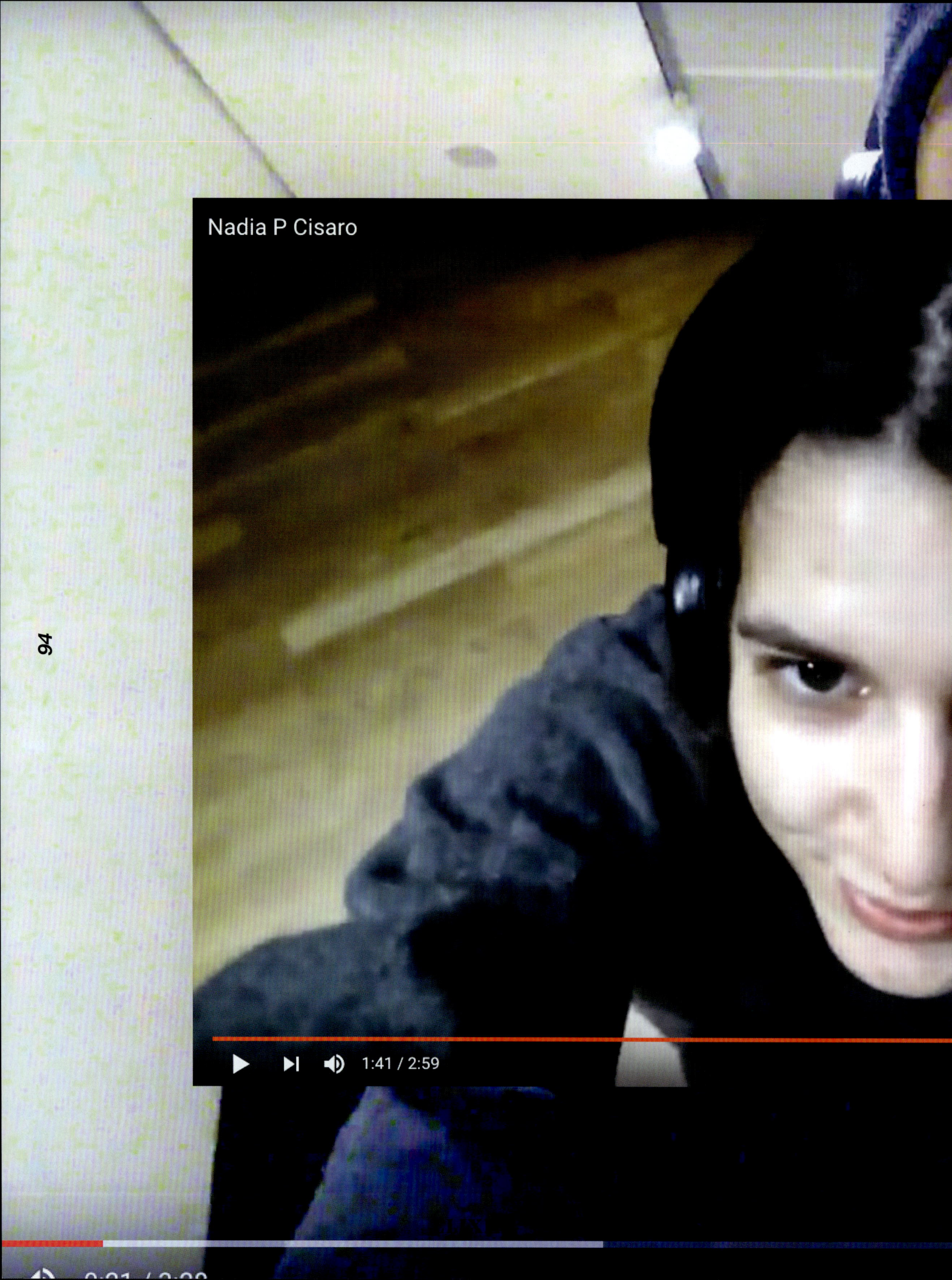
Nadia P Cisaro
1:41 / 2:59

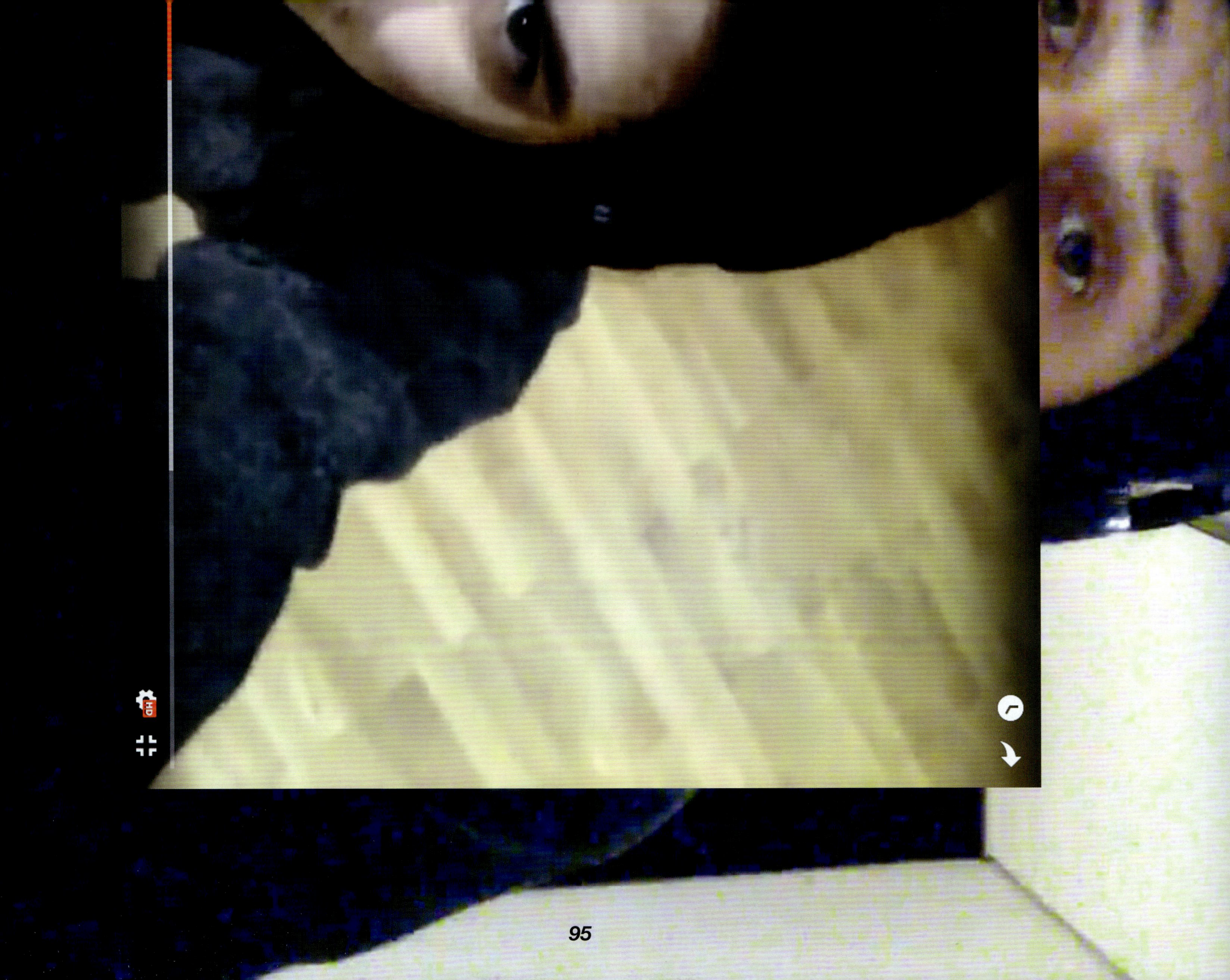
HD

(2014)

Performance
Video

The audience is instructed to sit down, to watch silently, to smile, to clap, to cheer, to stand up and cheer as loud as possible, to scream, to chant “Rise!”, to storm the stage, to dance wildly, to dance slow and sexily, to touch each other and keep dancing, to stop and look around, to leave the space.
No further content is presented.

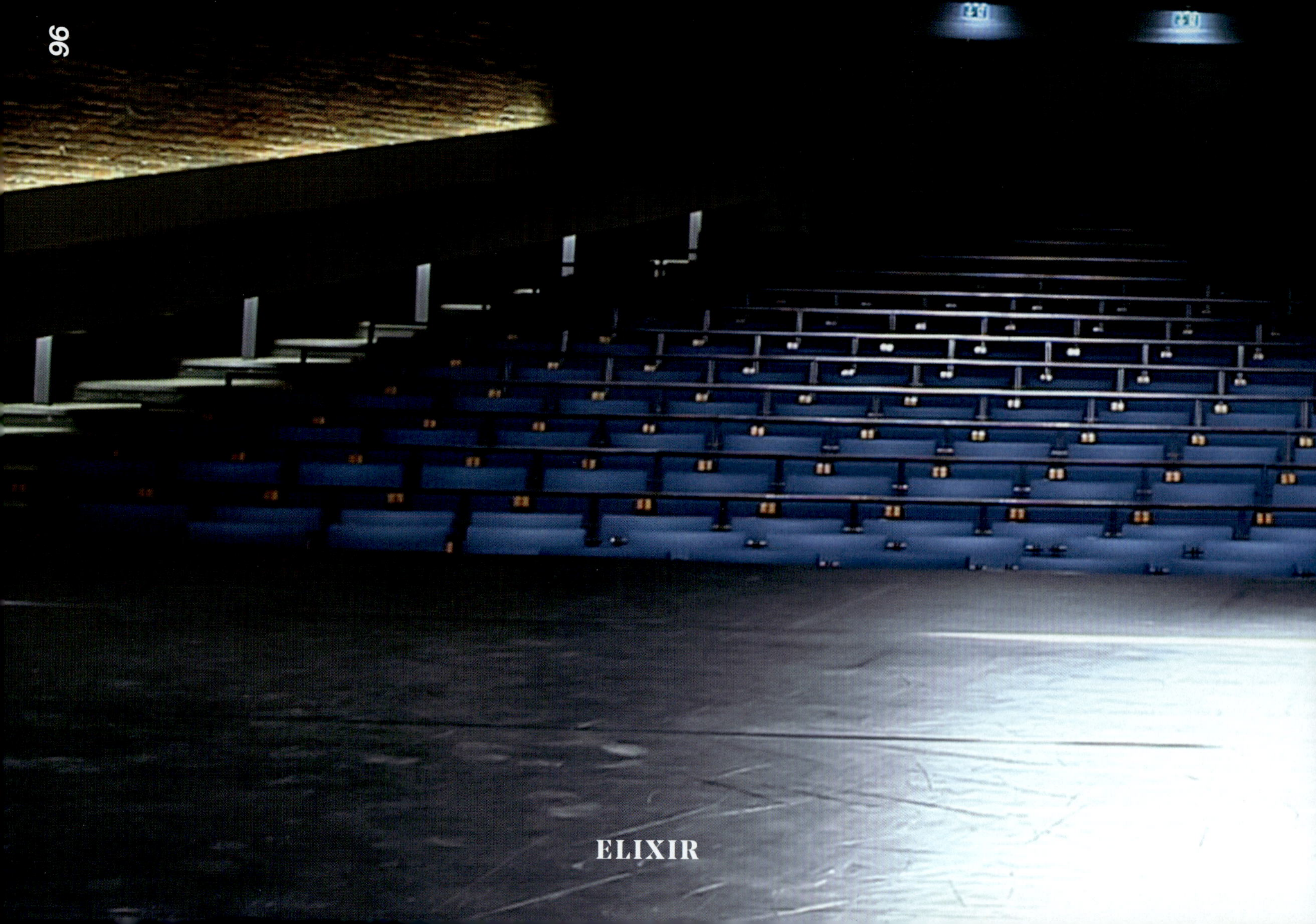

ELIXIR

RISE

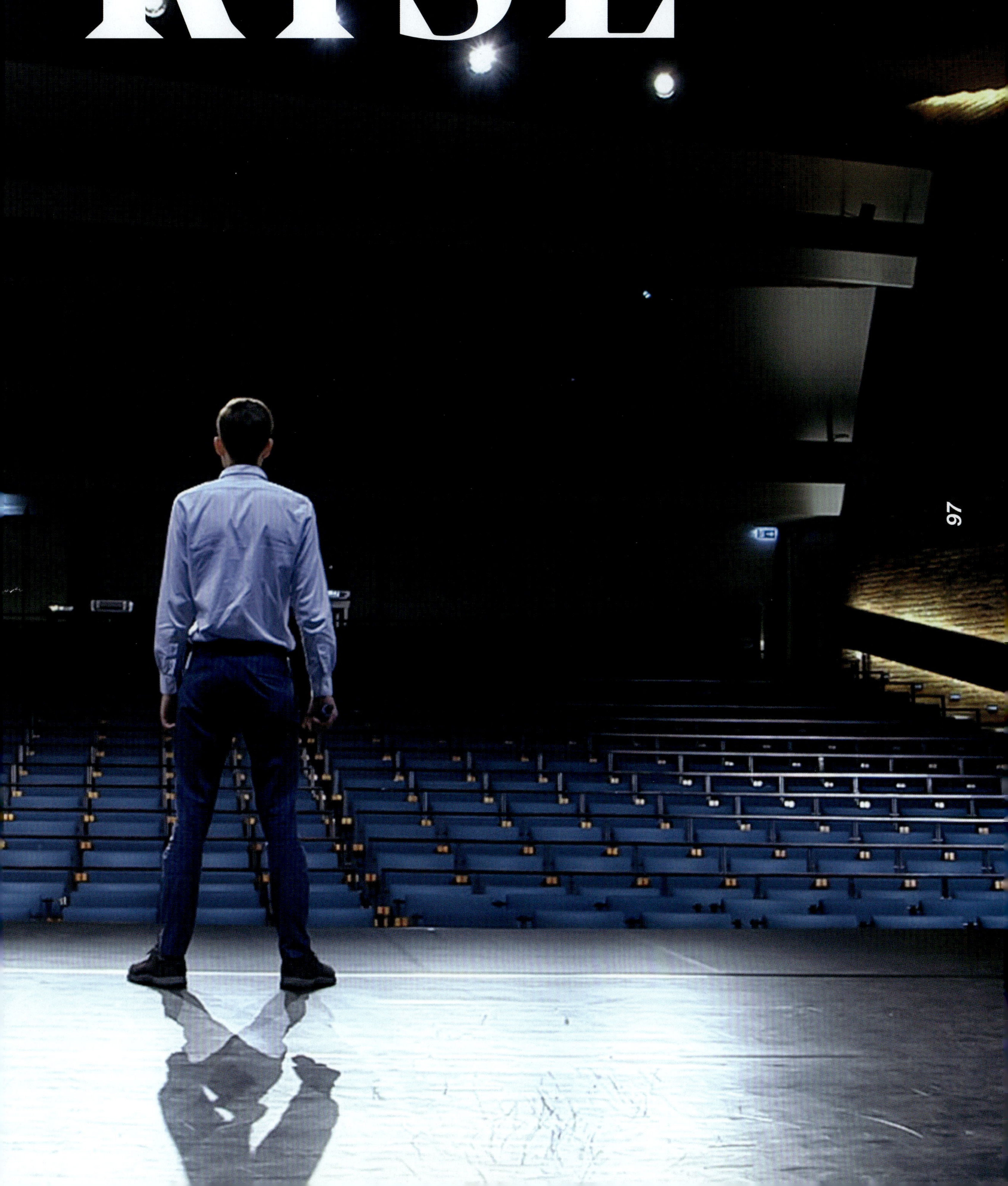

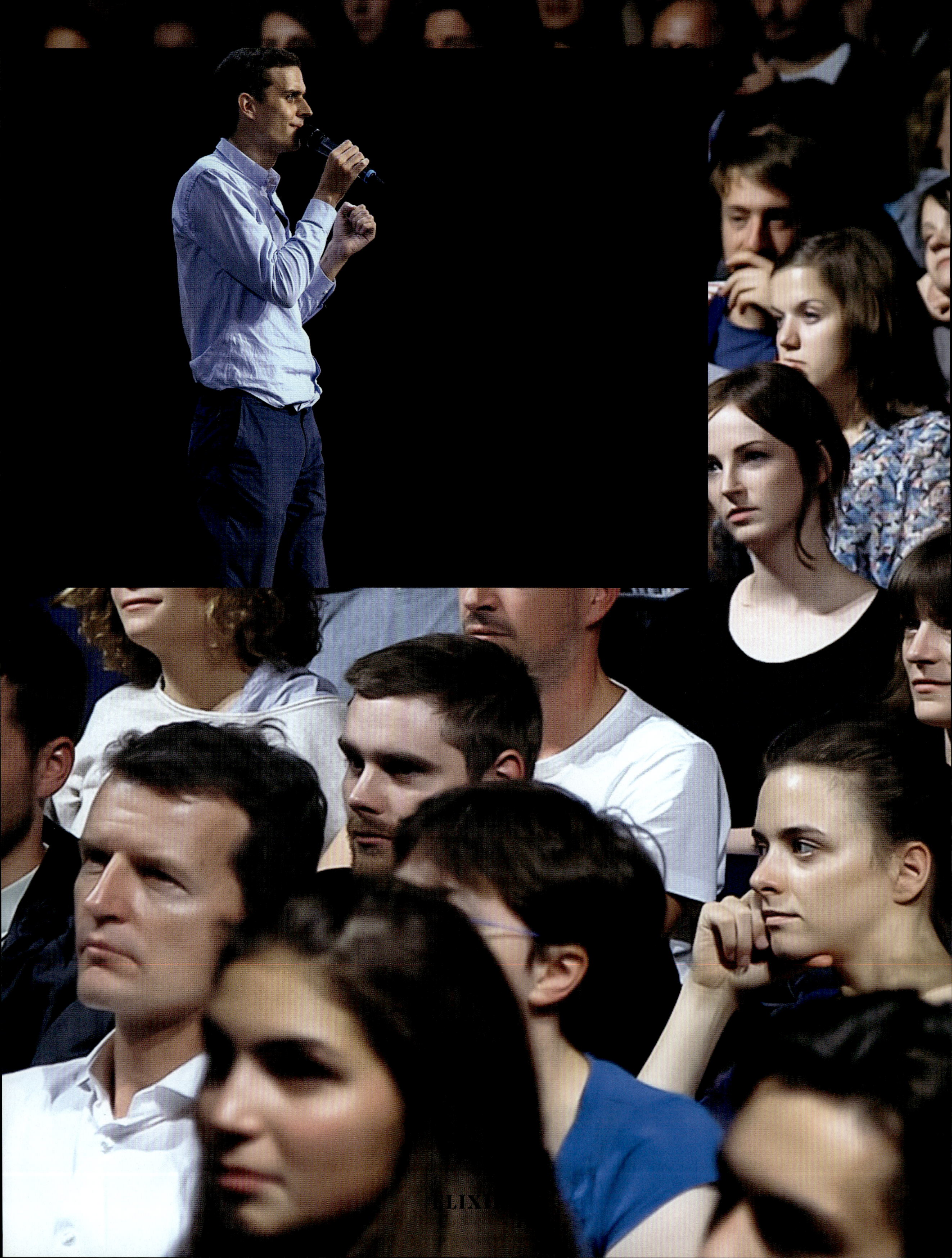

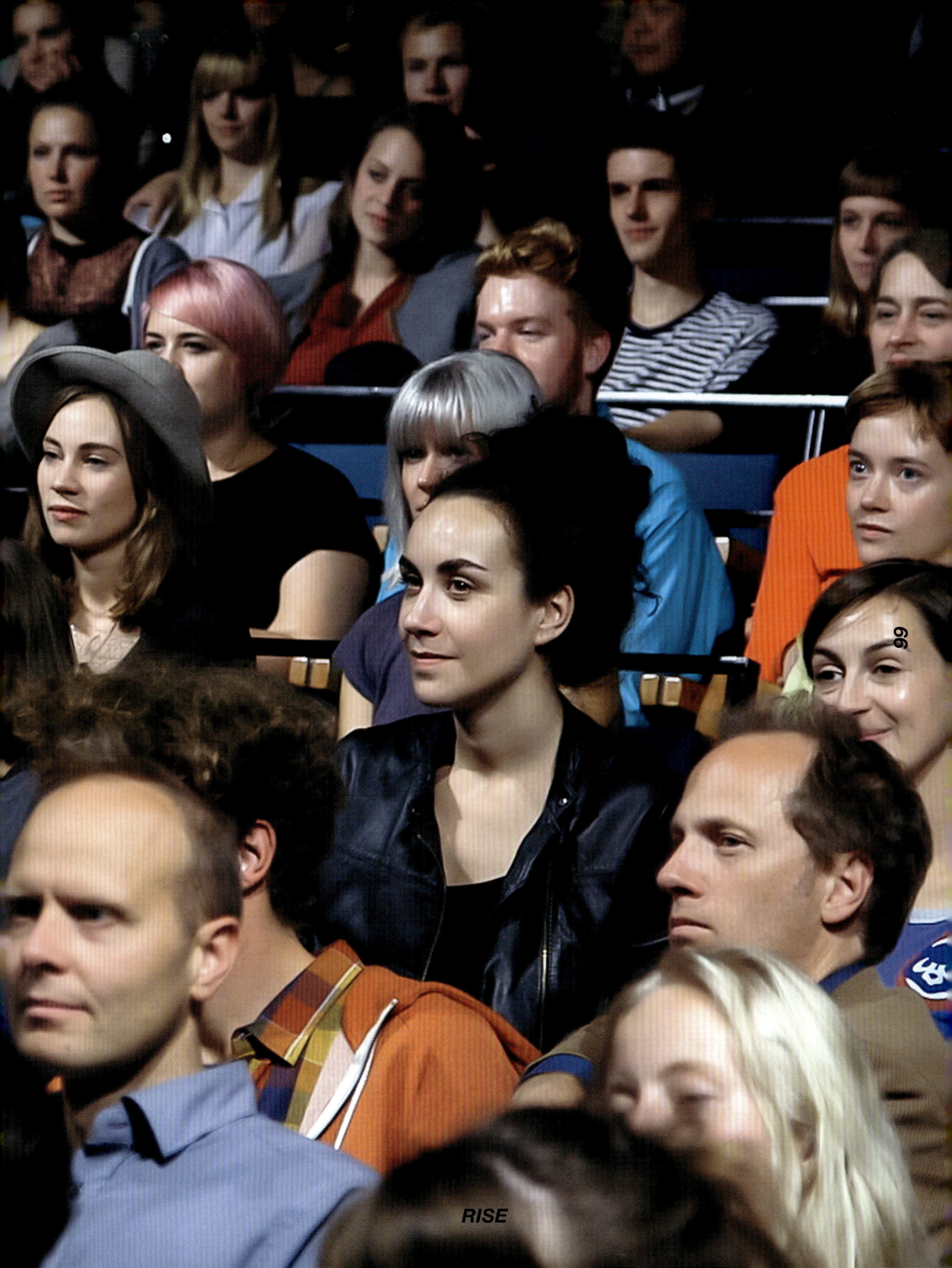

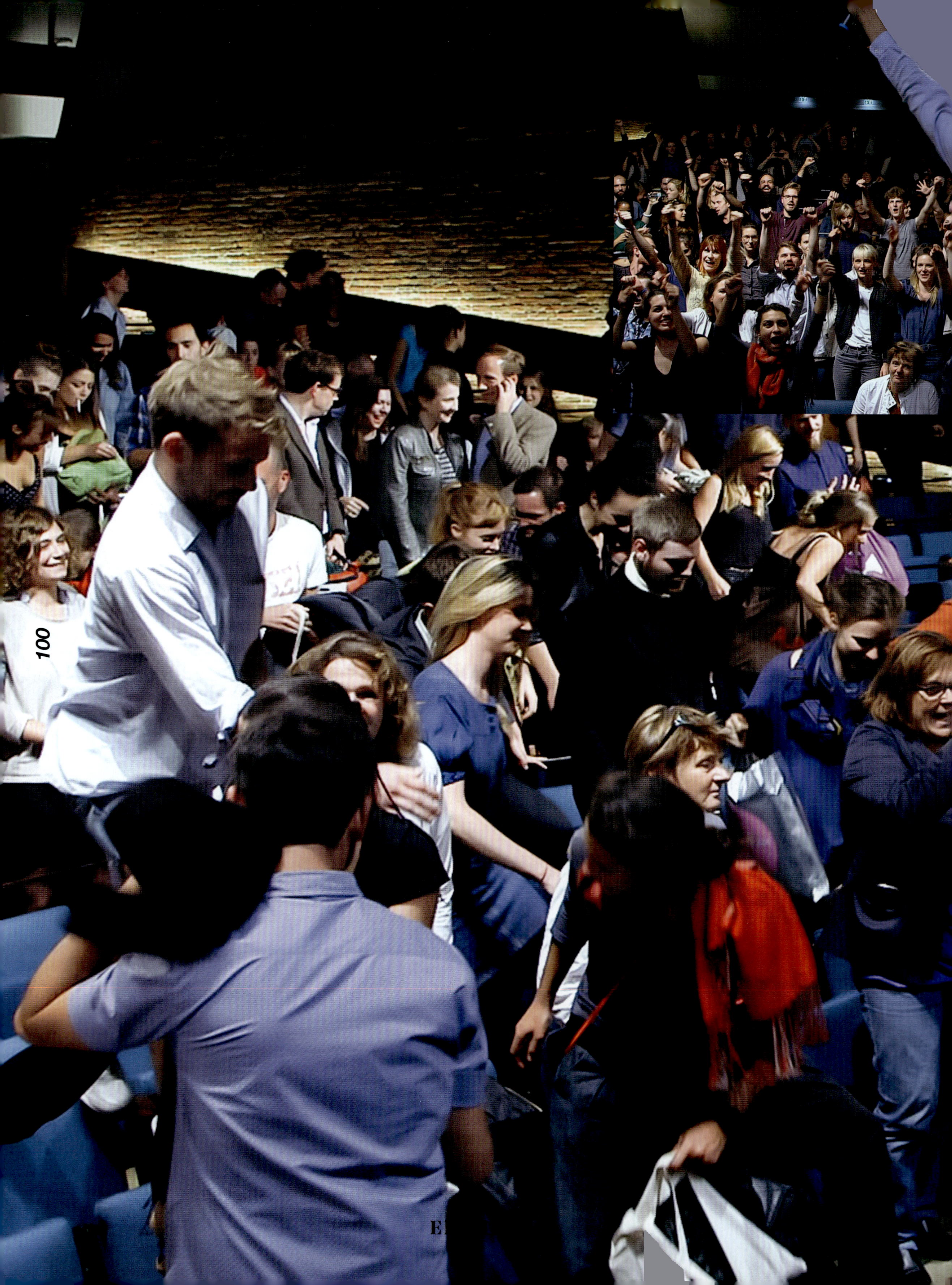

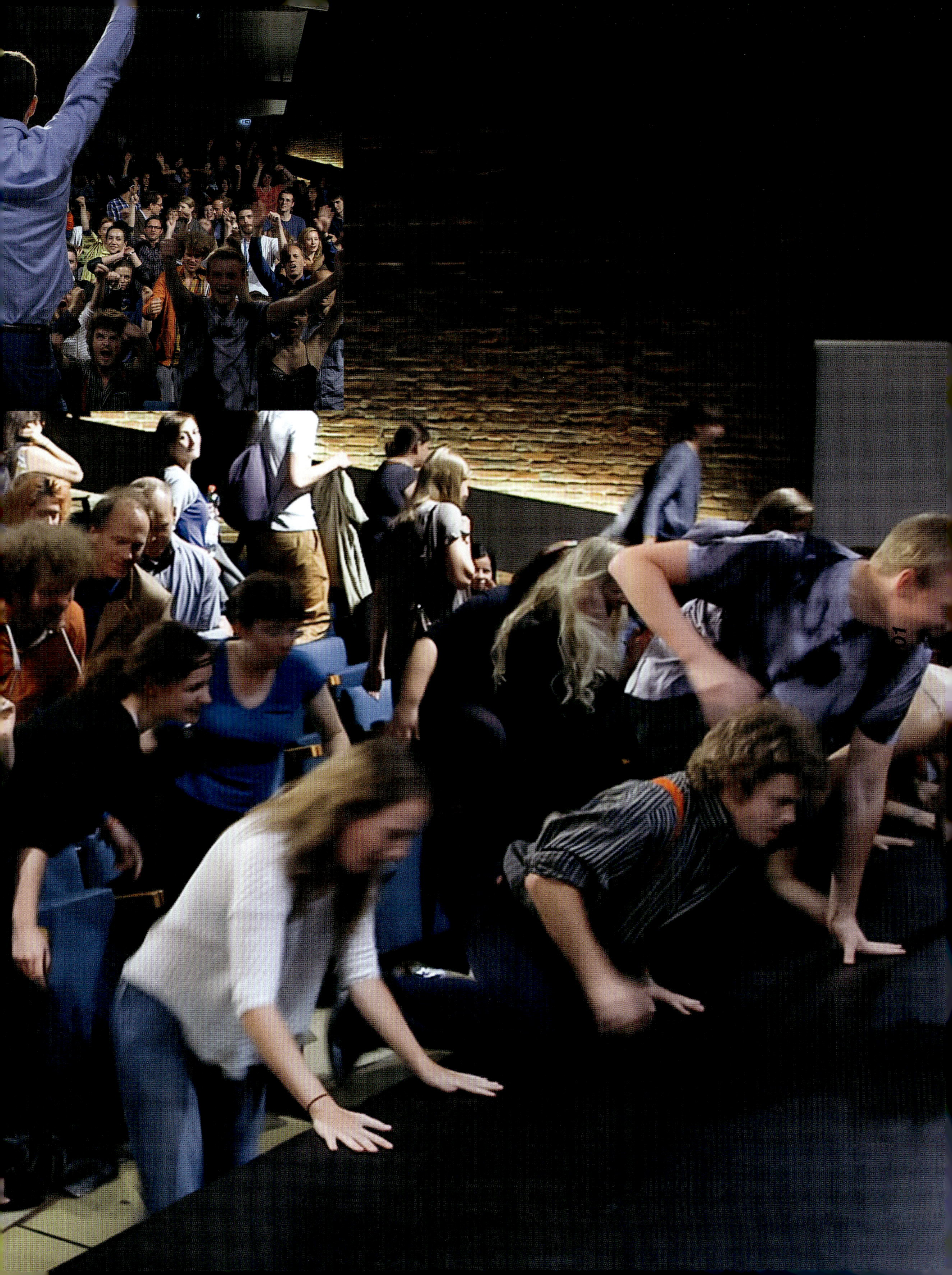

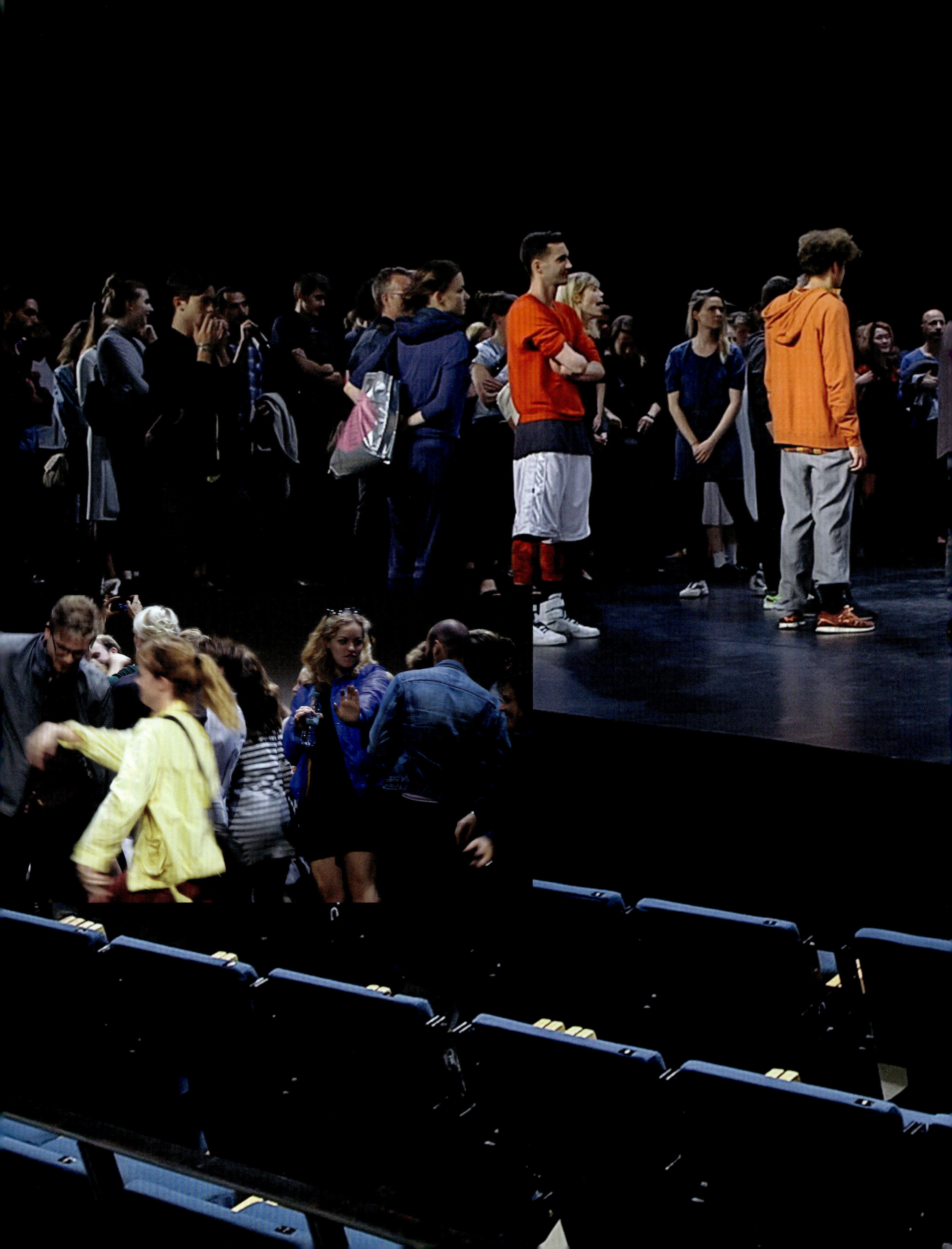

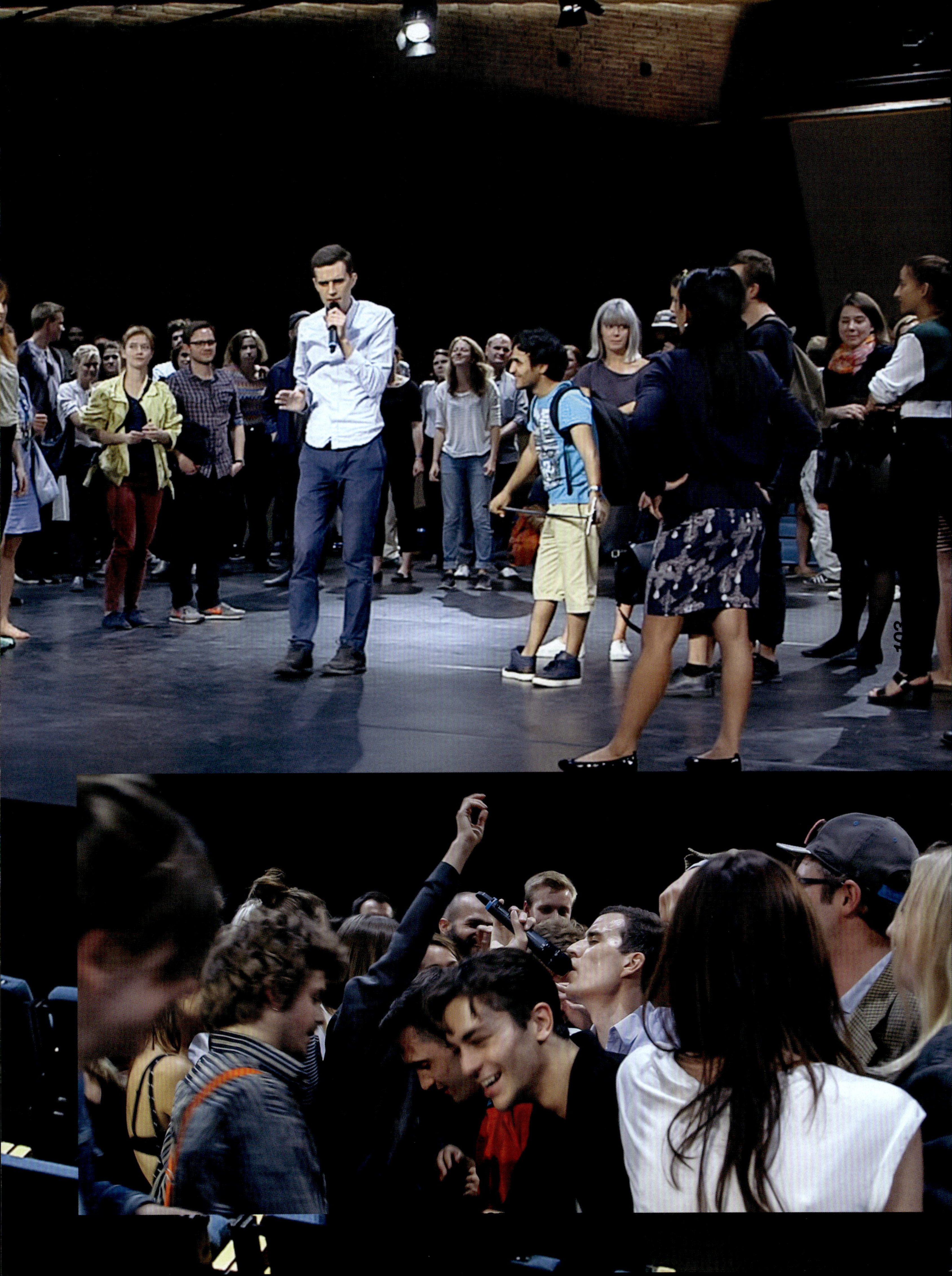

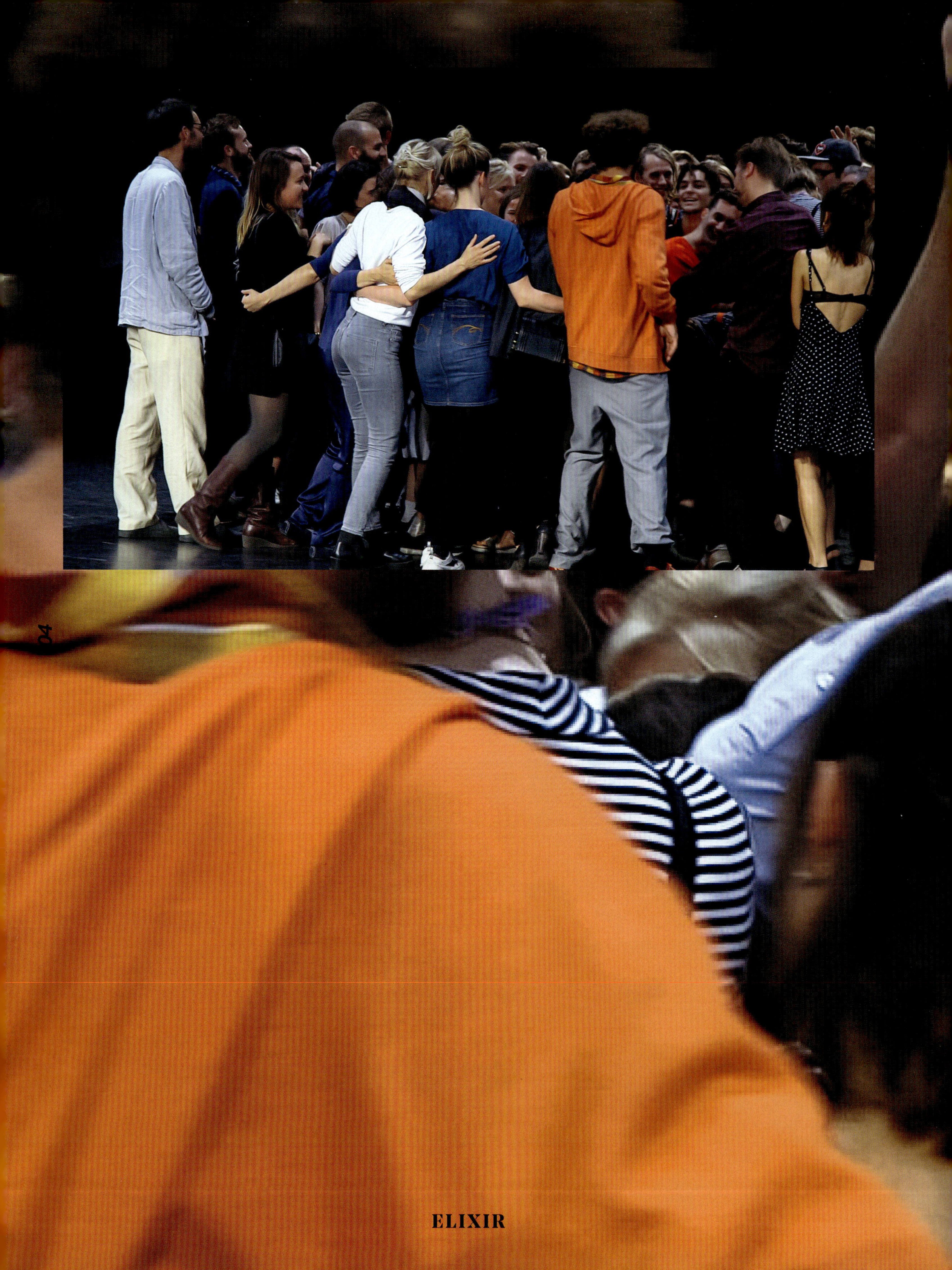

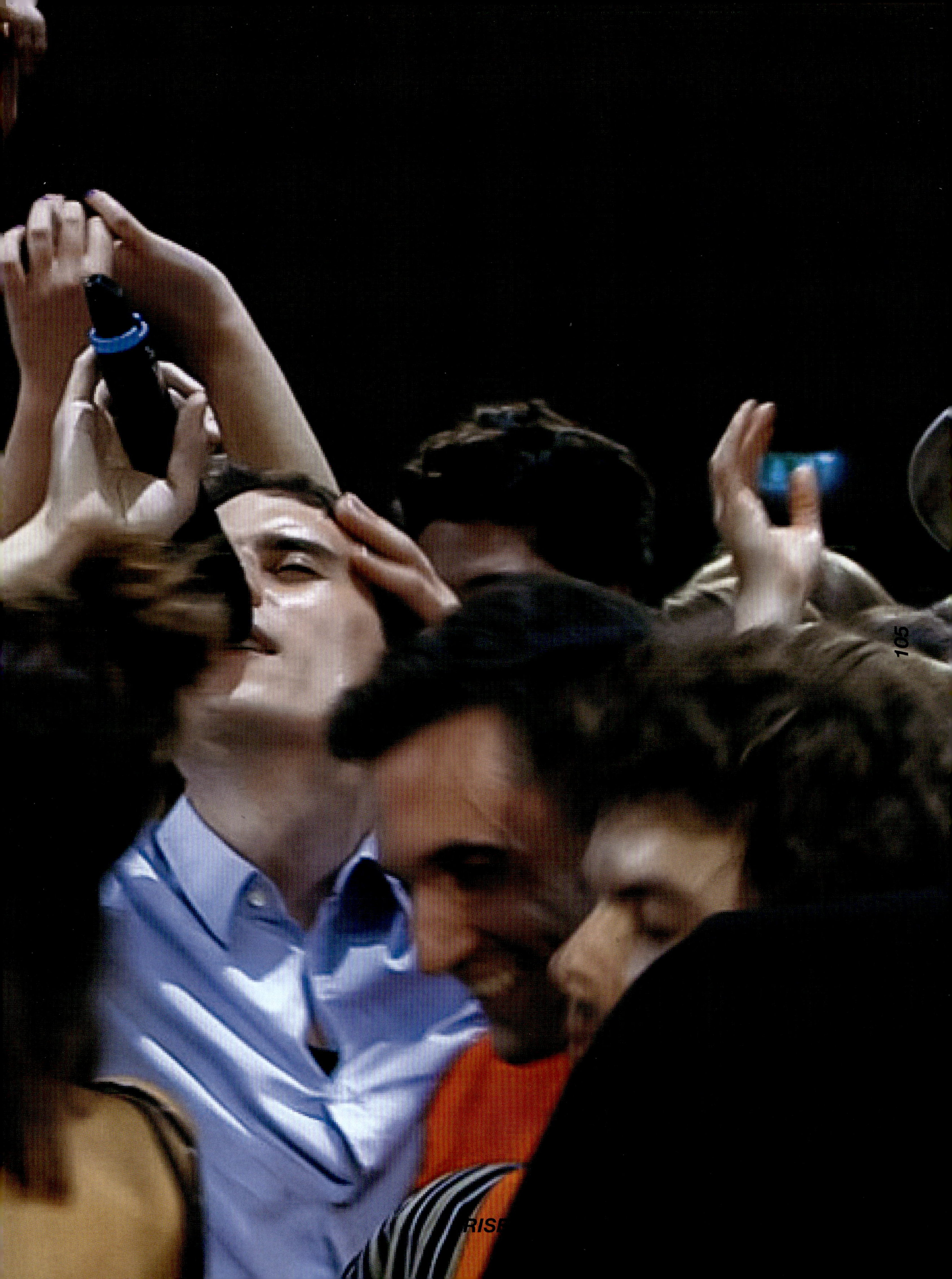

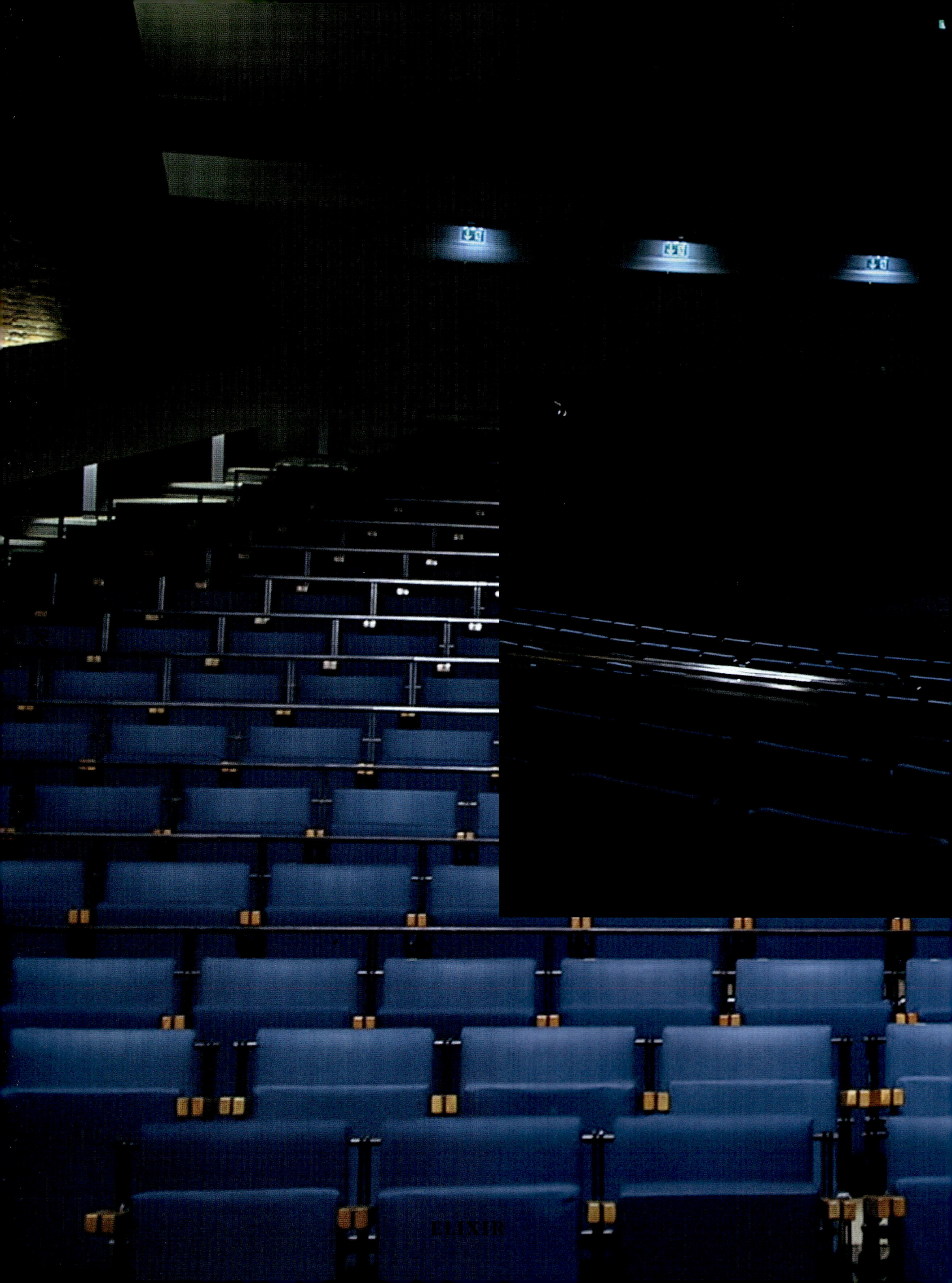

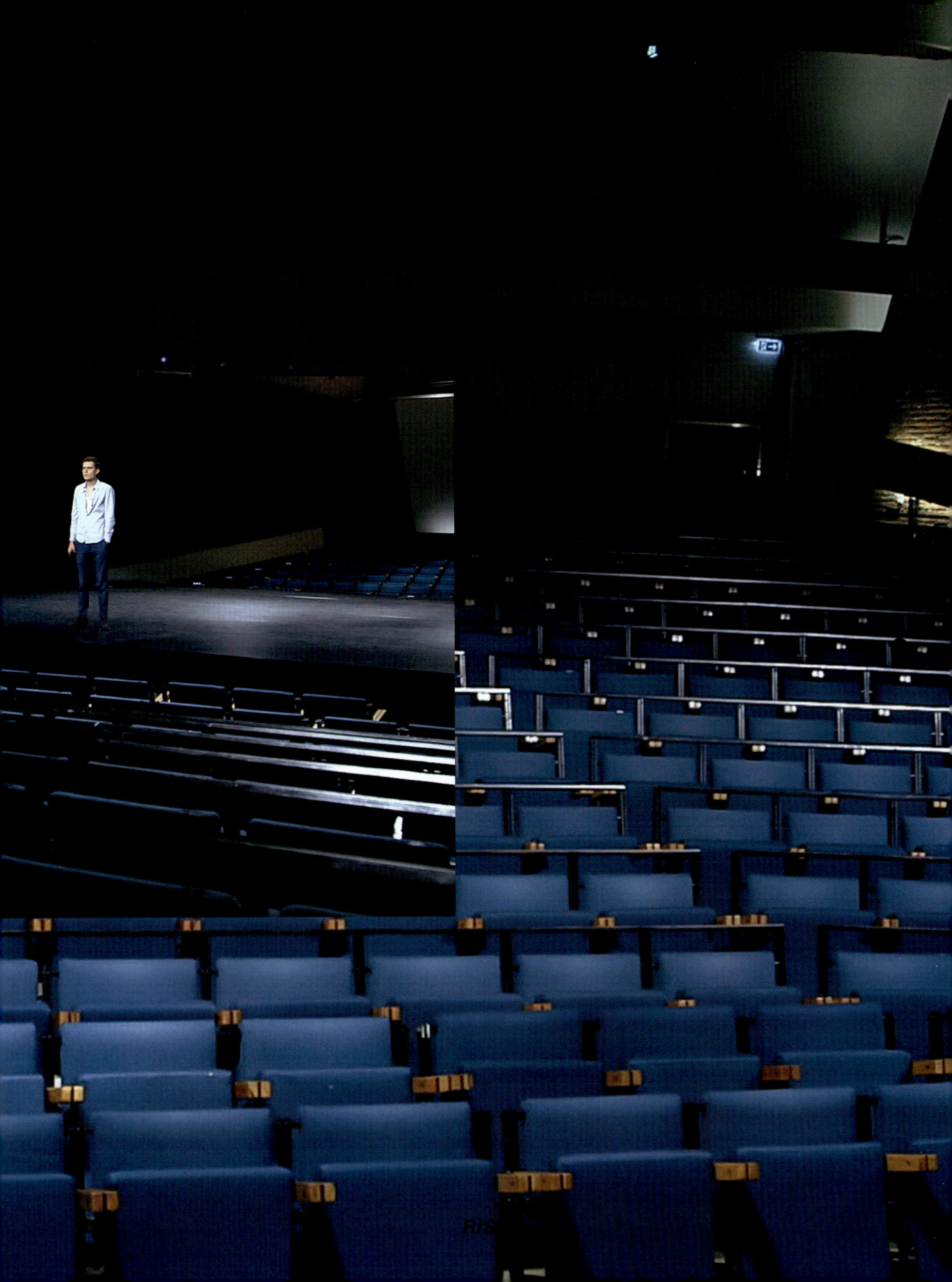

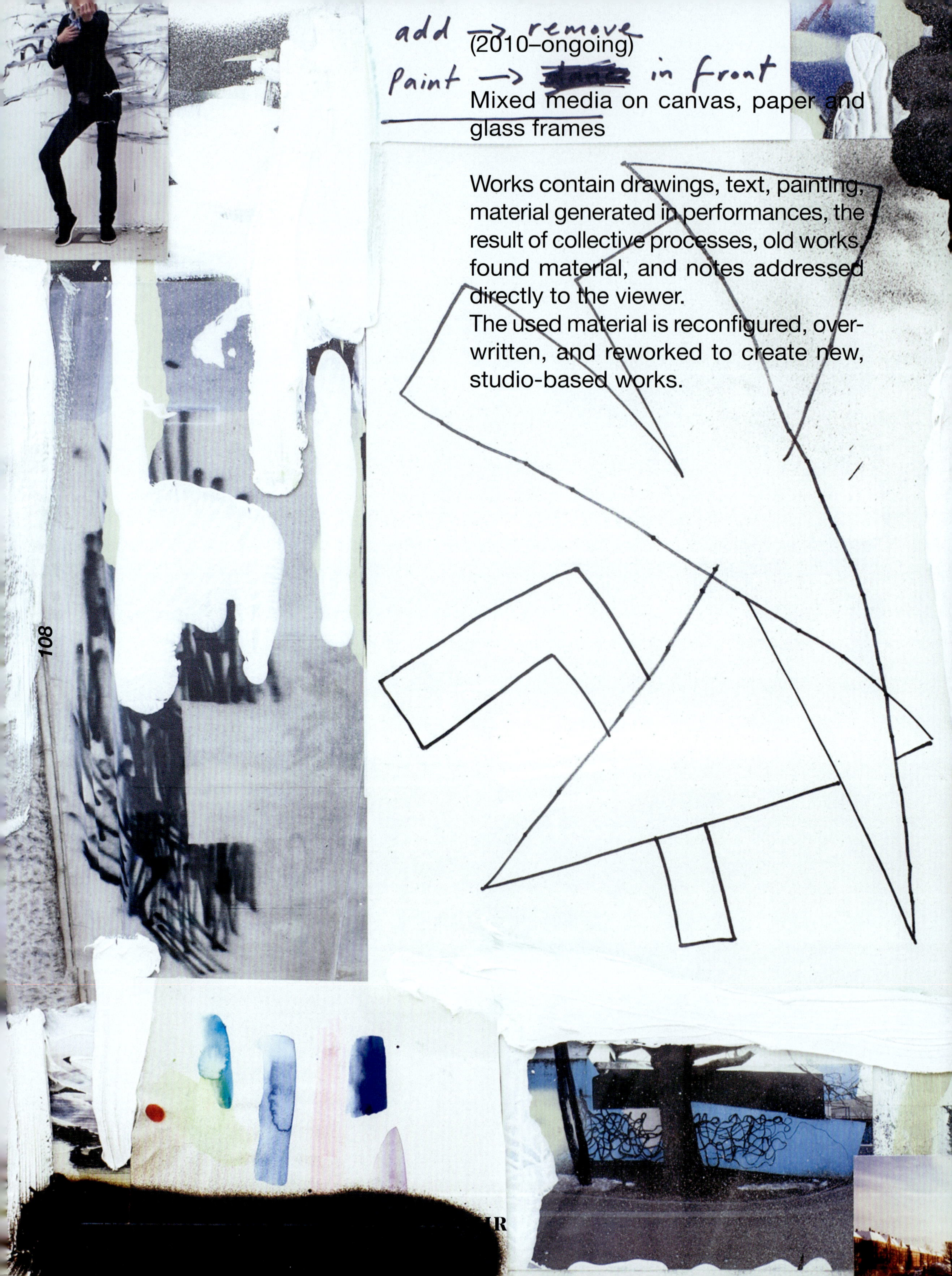

(2010–ongoing)

Mixed media on canvas, paper and glass frames

Works contain drawings, text, painting, material generated in performances, the result of collective processes, old works, found material, and notes addressed directly to the viewer.
The used material is reconfigured, over-written, and reworked to create new, studio-based works.

LOOK
FOLL–
OW
LIKE
CONN–
ECT

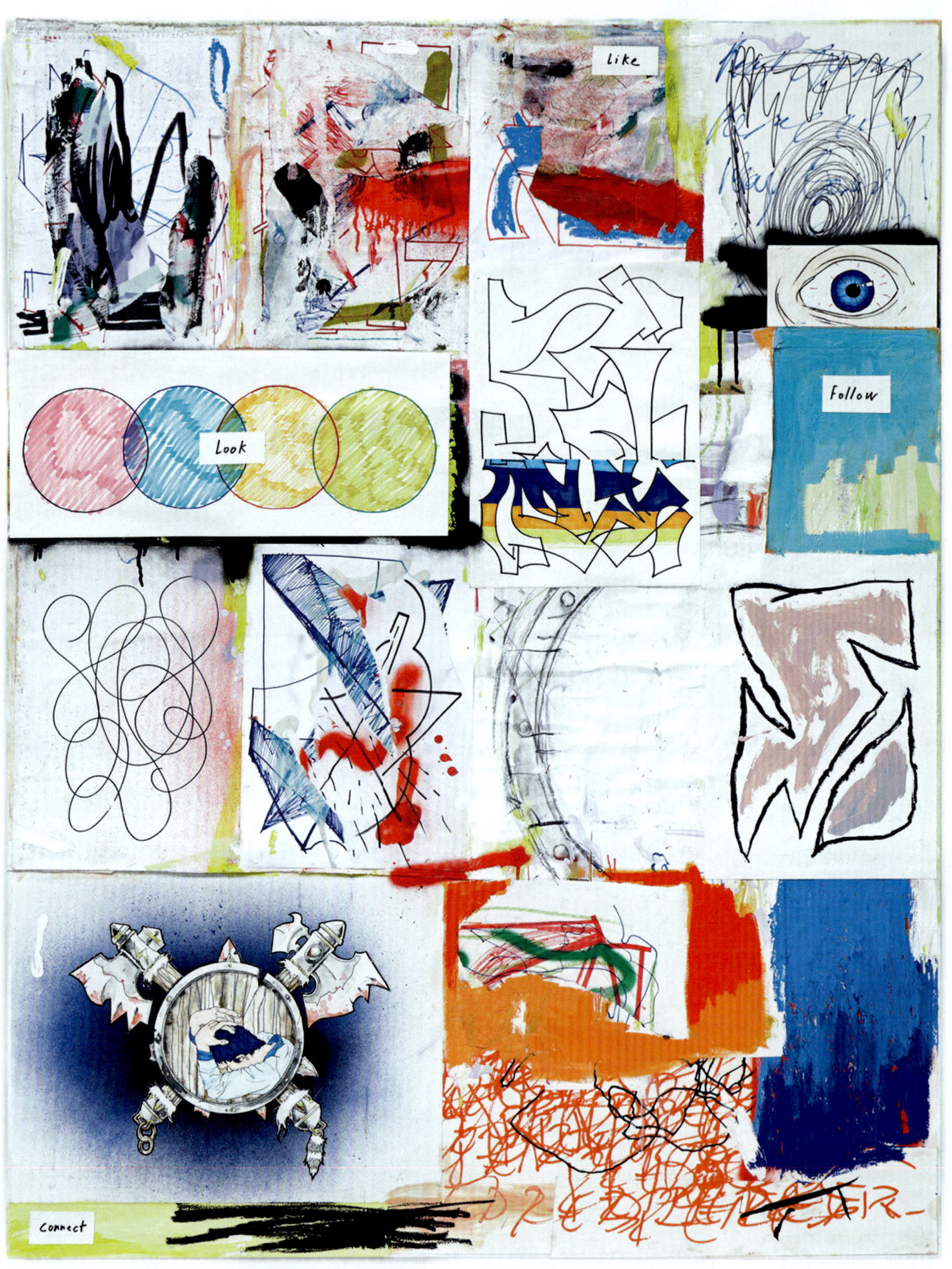
Like
Look
Follow
Connect

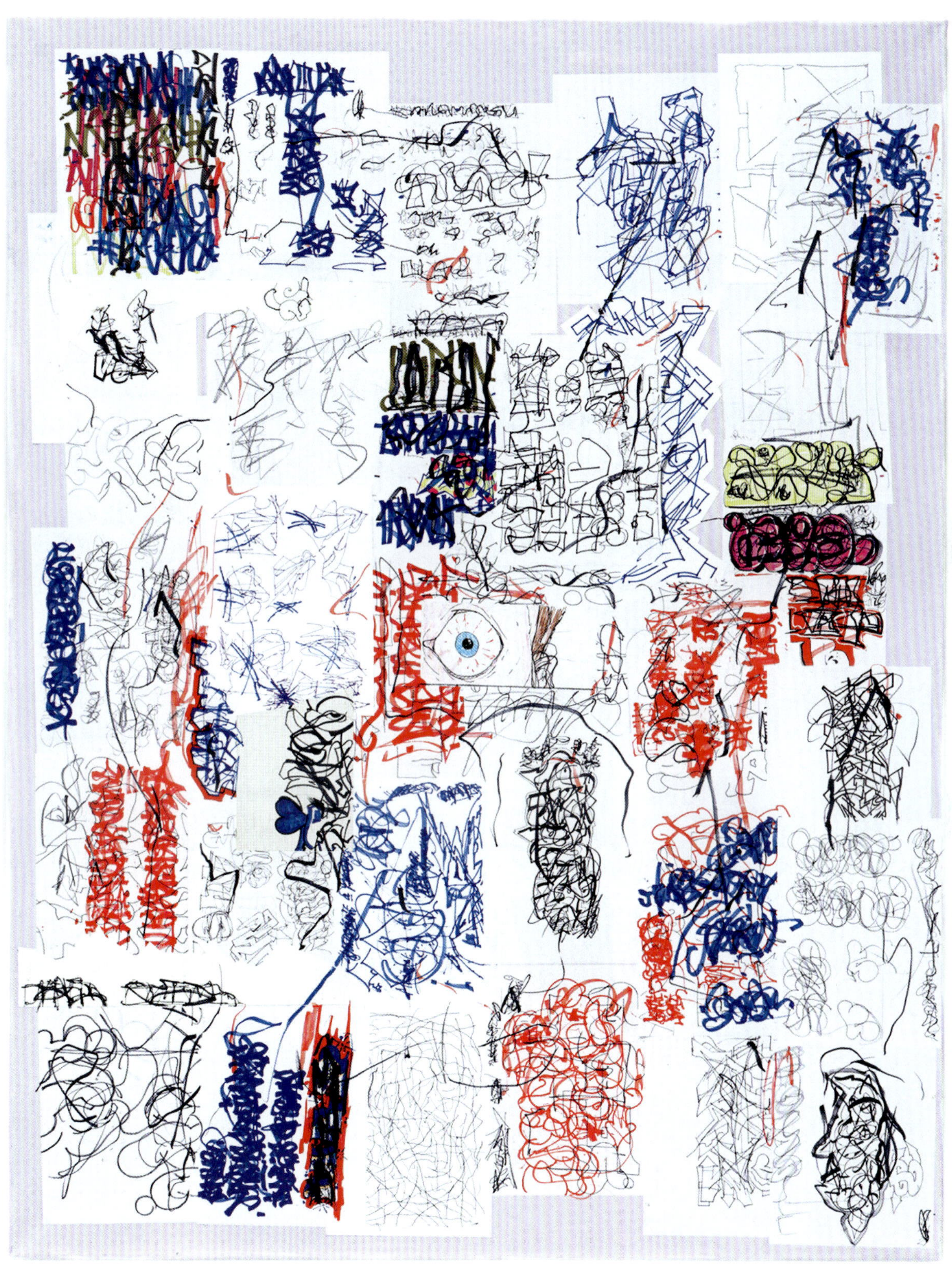

Love and Security
intense and conscious
being-in-the-moment
targetting perfect
surface / media / body
per for METRO
subway body steel
vulnerable cum-shot!

LOOK FOLLOW LIKE CONNECT

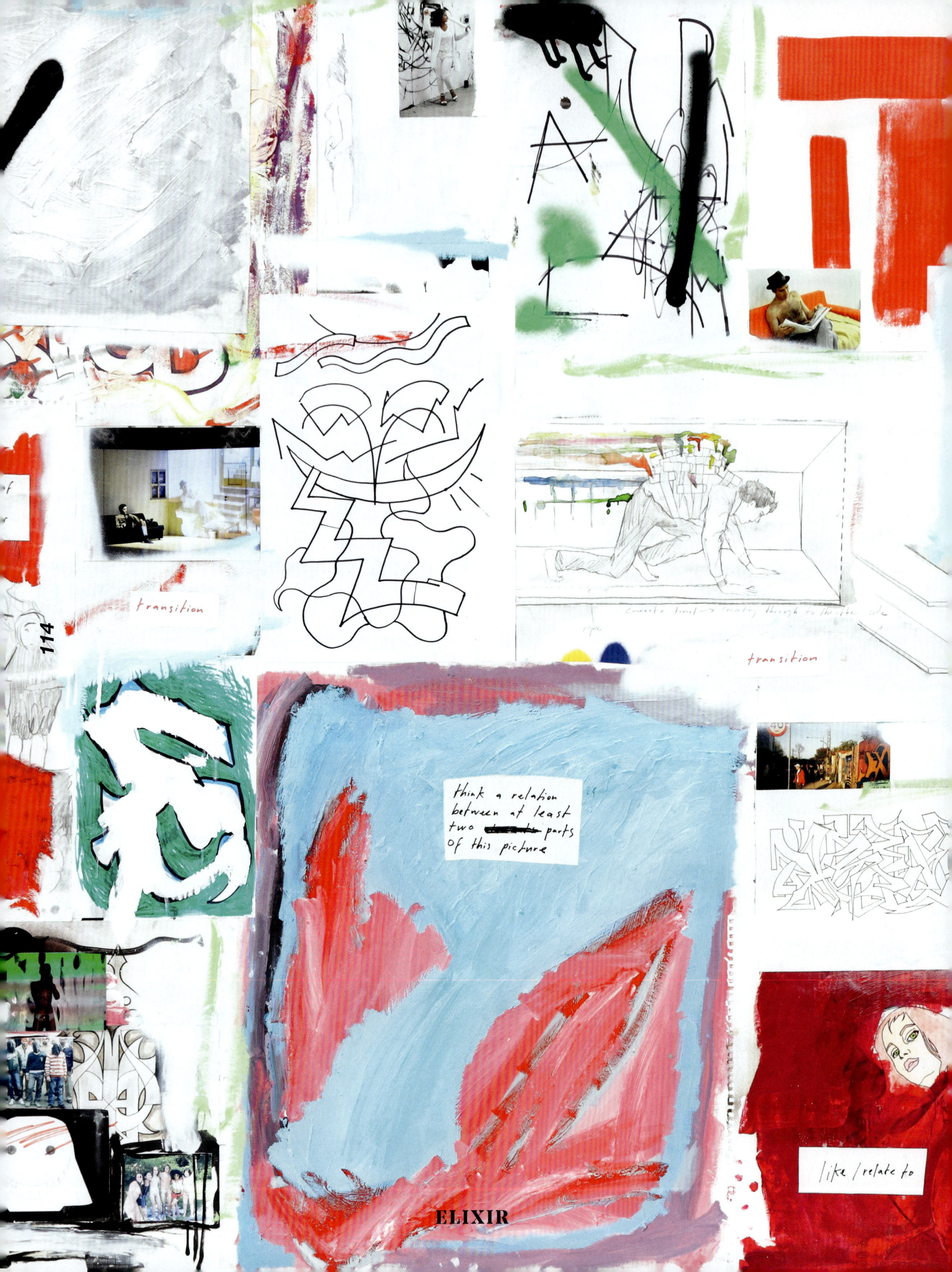
transition
transition
think a relation between at least two parts of this picture
like / relate to

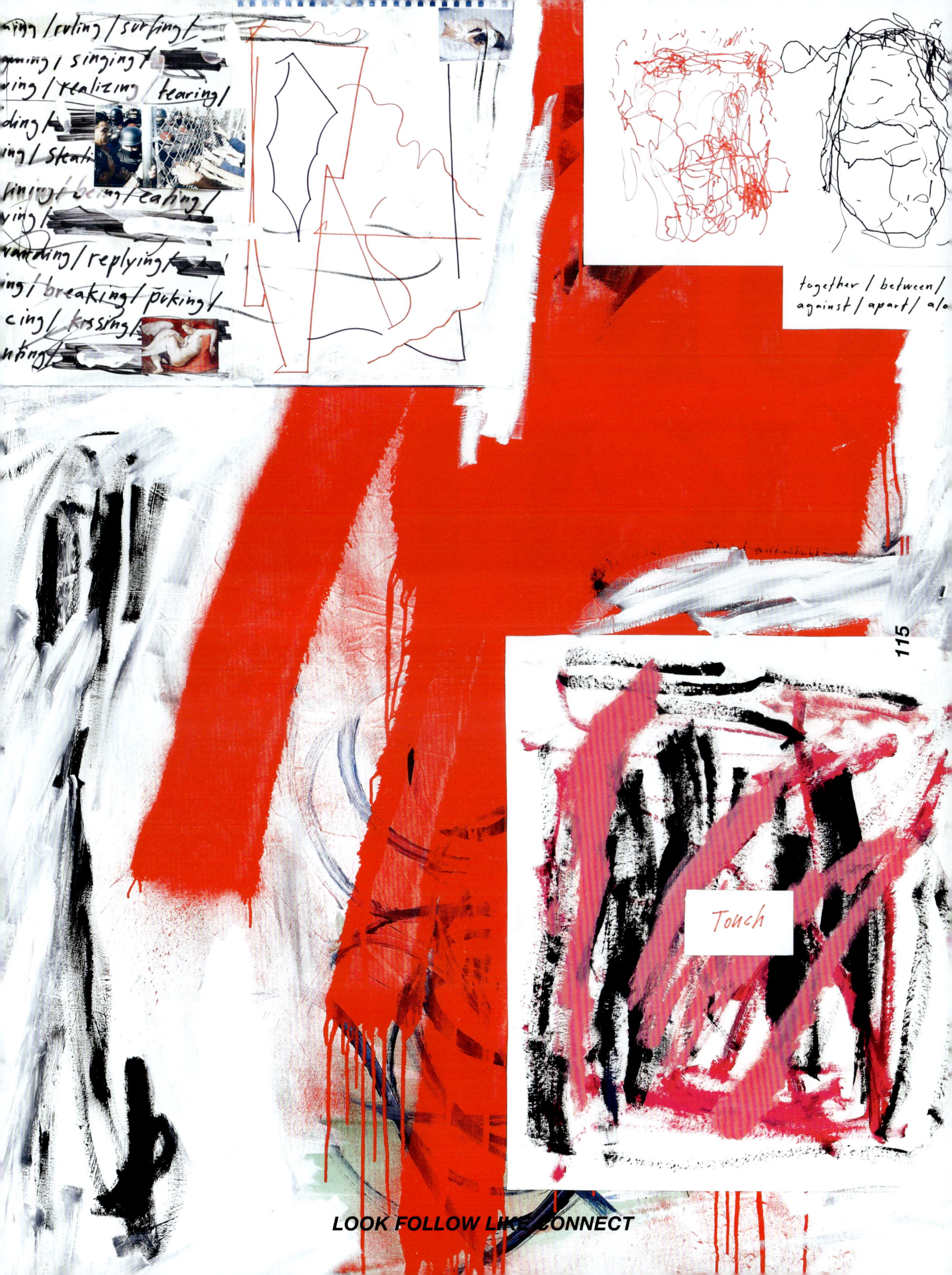

LOOK FOLLOW LIKE CONNECT

OPENIN
OPENIN
(KARE
SCHI

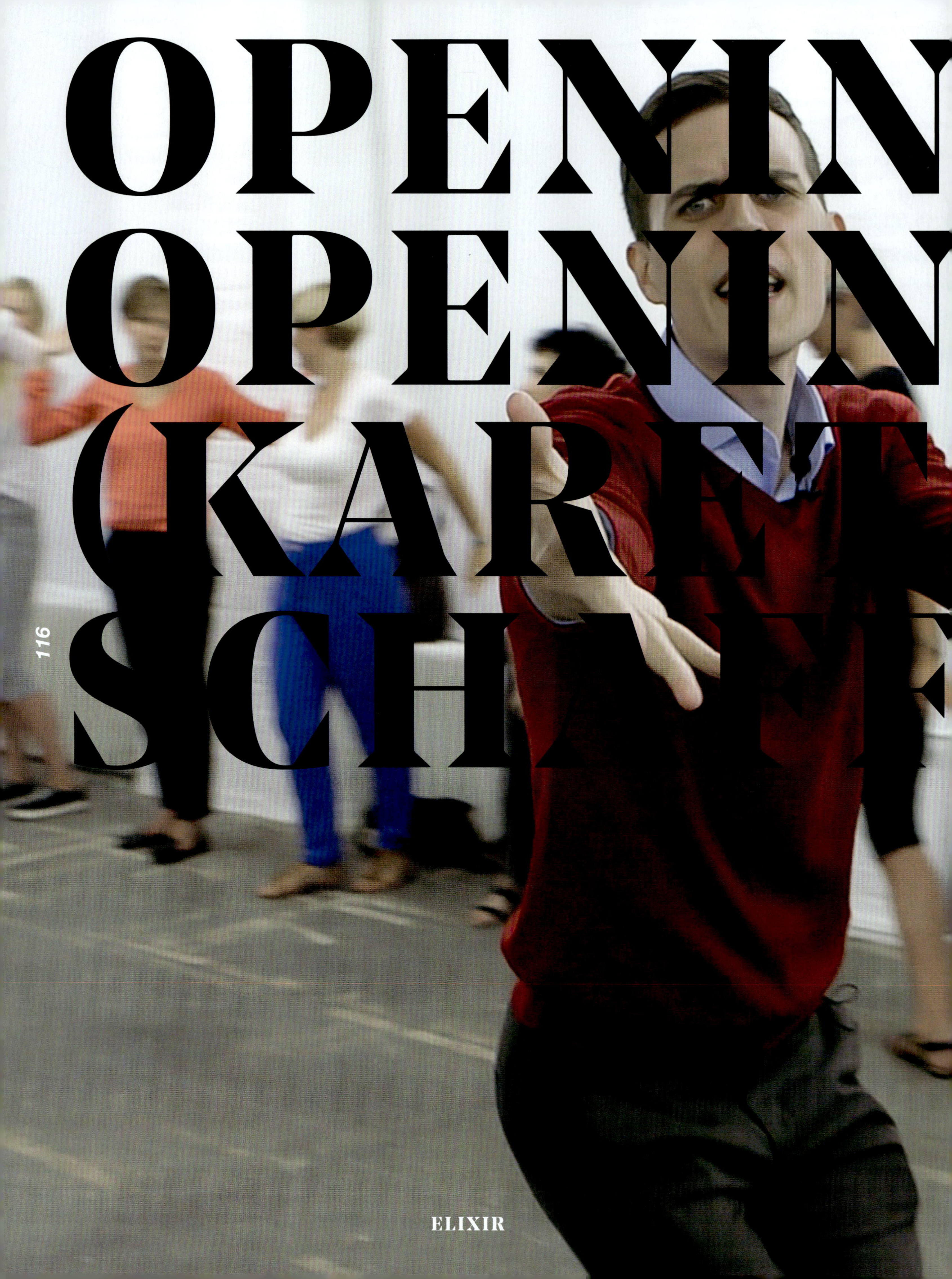

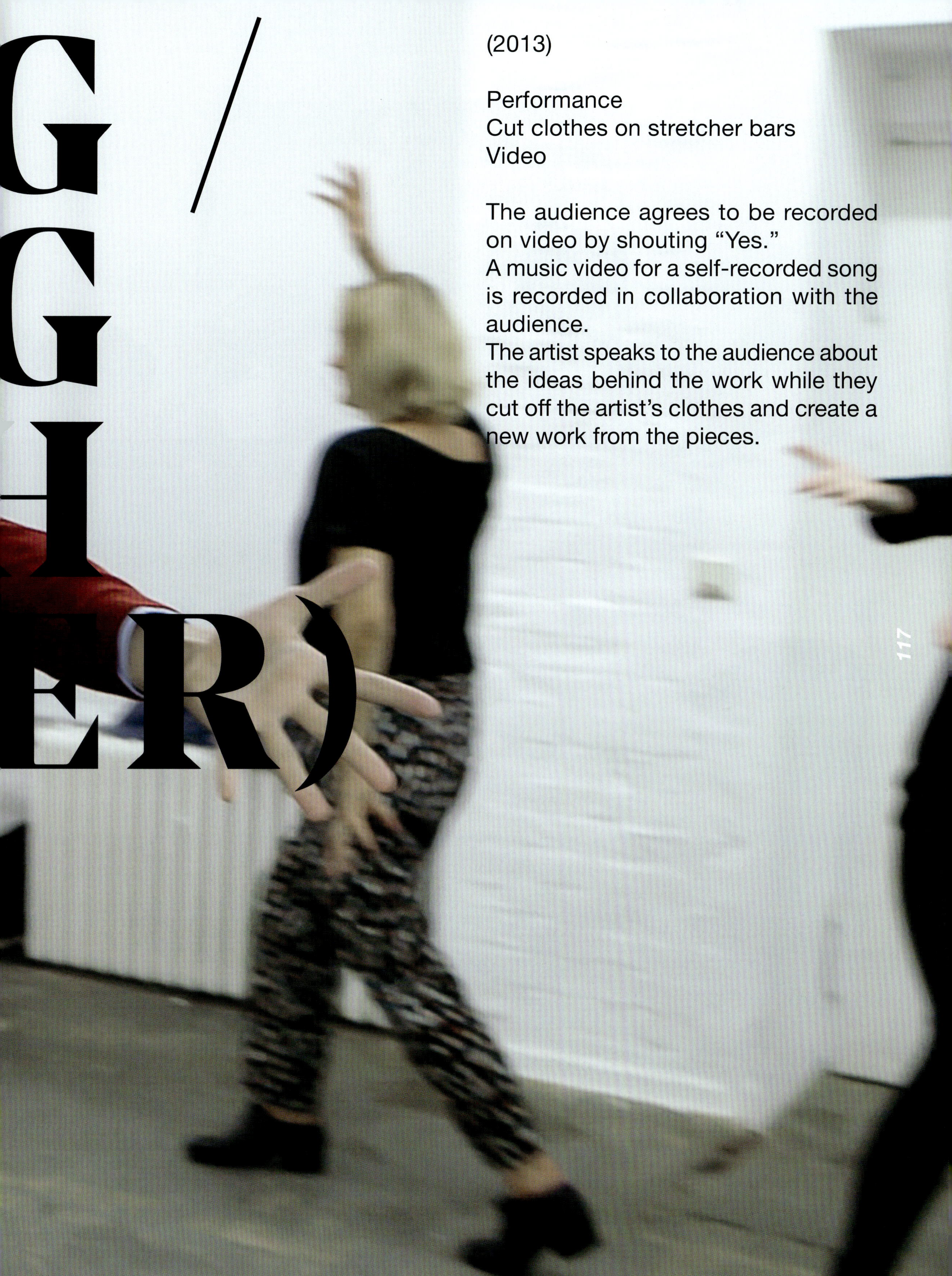

(2013)

Performance
Cut clothes on stretcher bars
Video

The audience agrees to be recorded on video by shouting "Yes."
A music video for a self-recorded song is recorded in collaboration with the audience.
The artist speaks to the audience about the ideas behind the work while they cut off the artist's clothes and create a new work from the pieces.

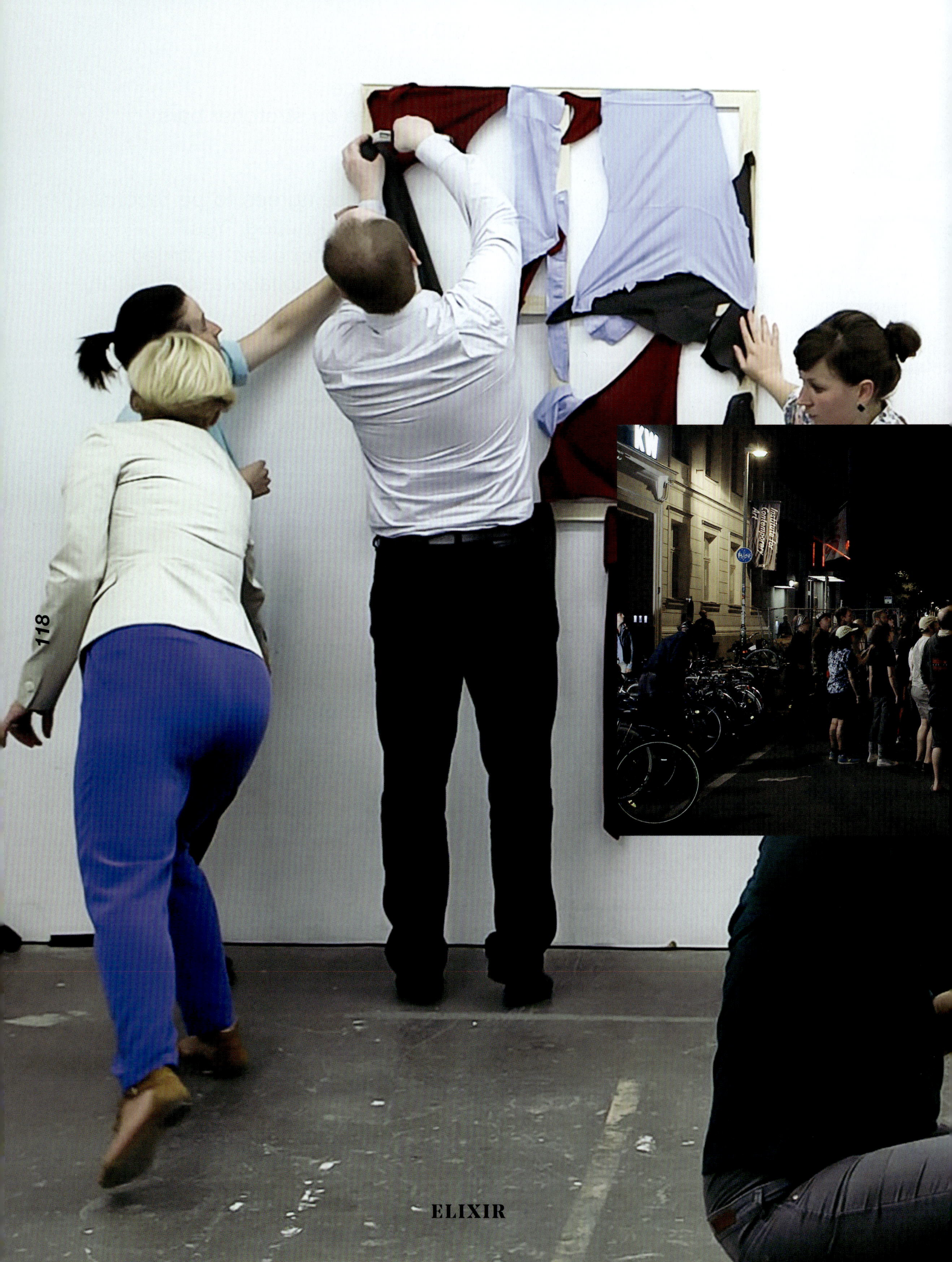
KW
Institute for Contemporary Art

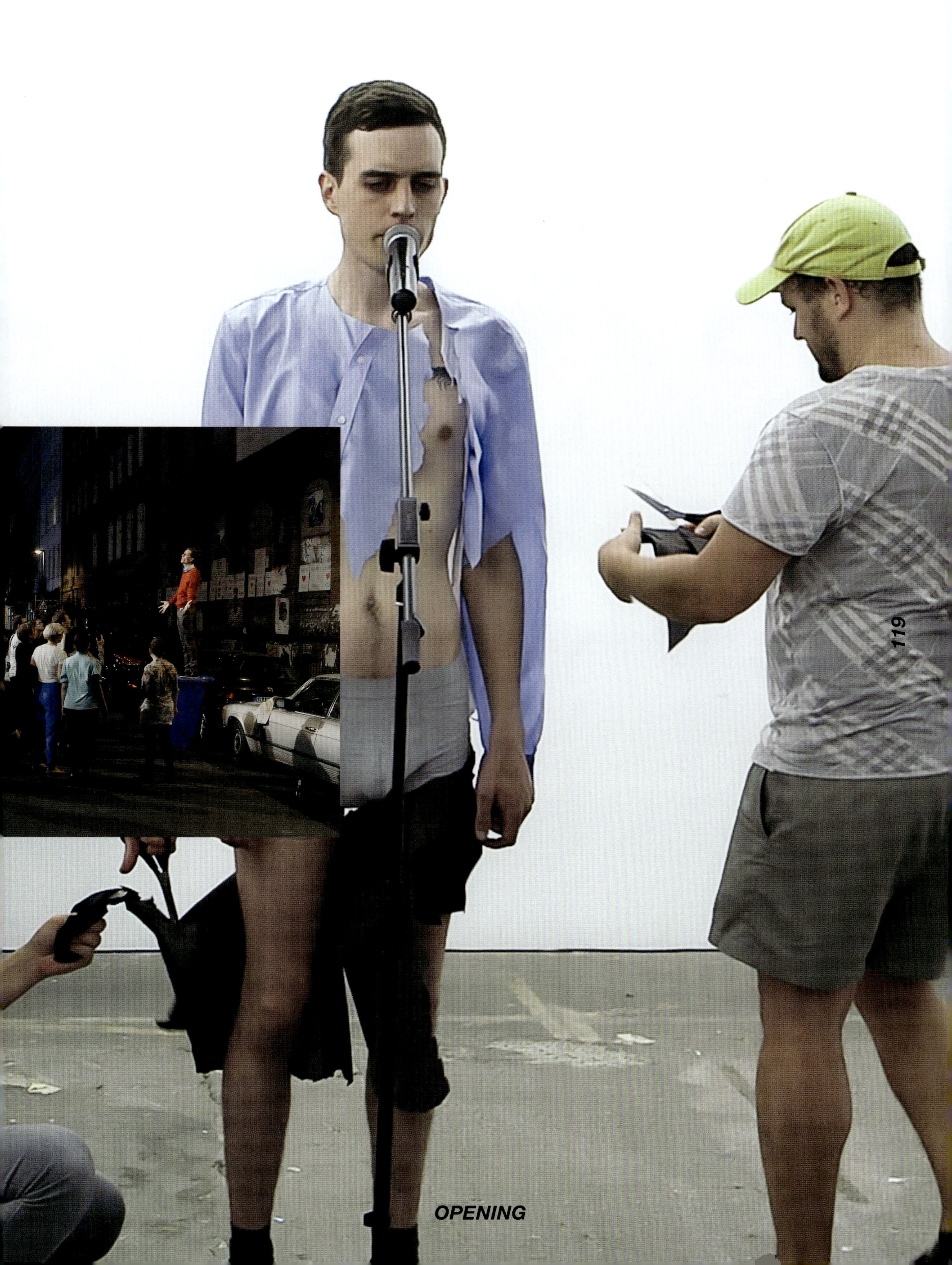

OPENING

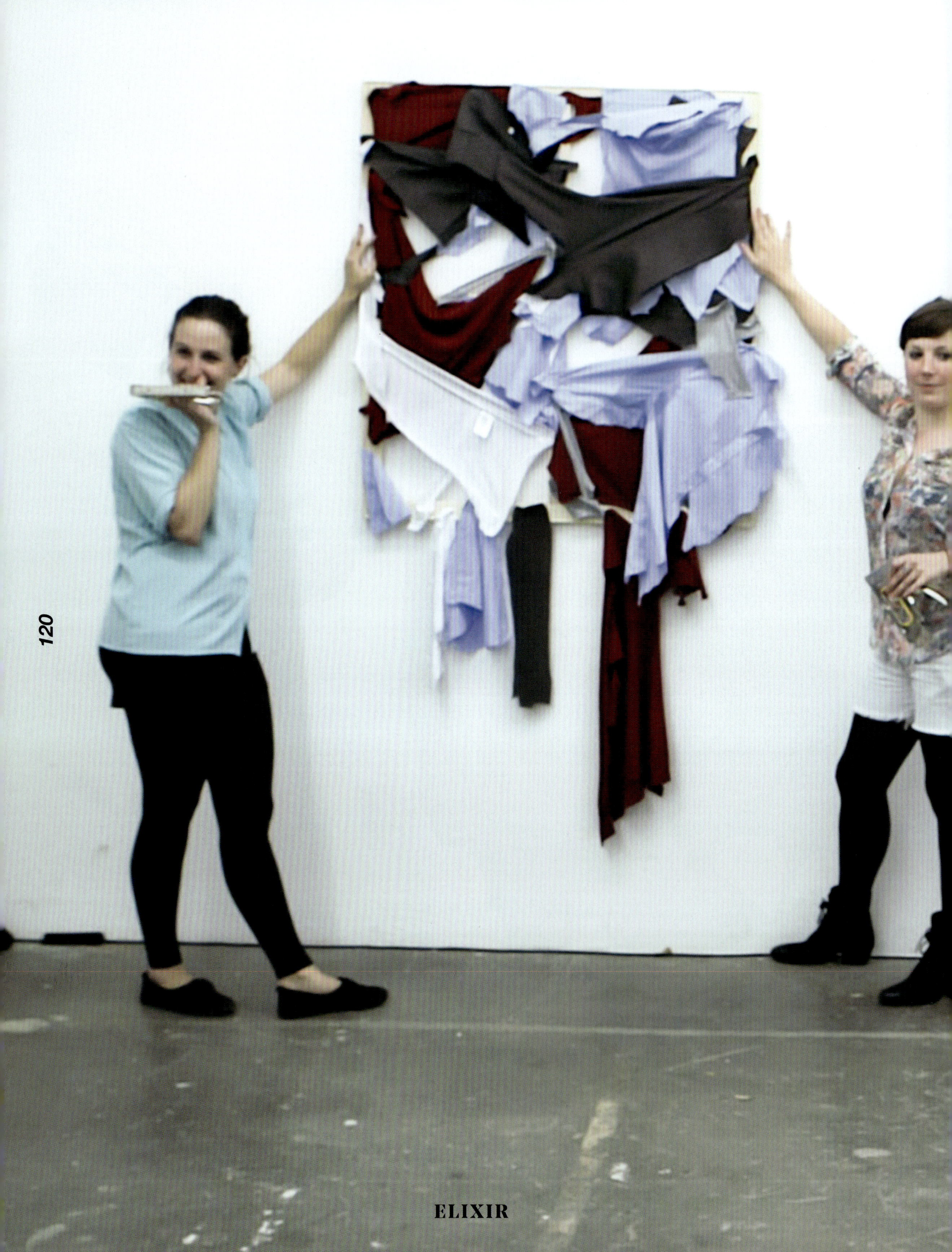

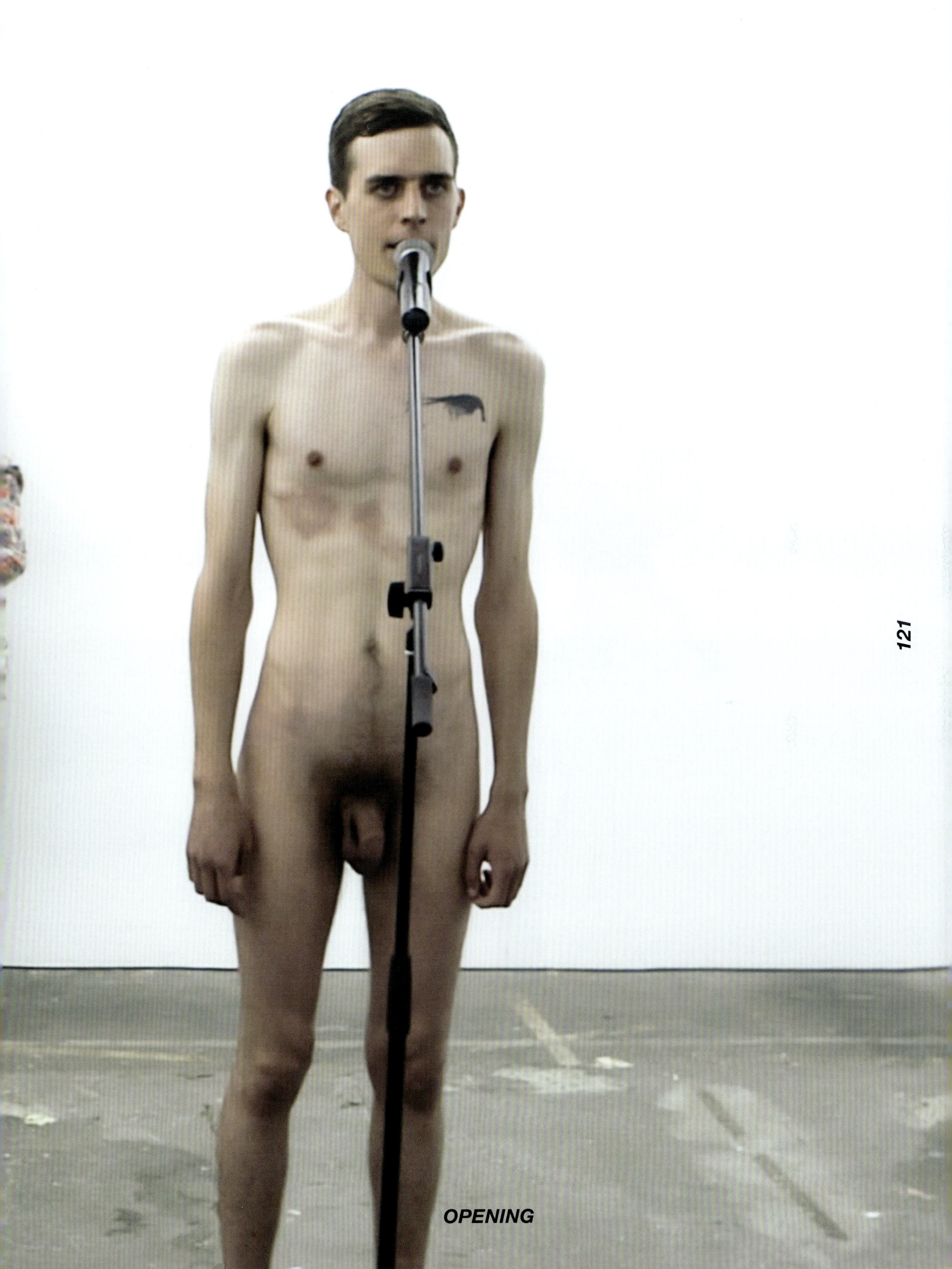

OPENING

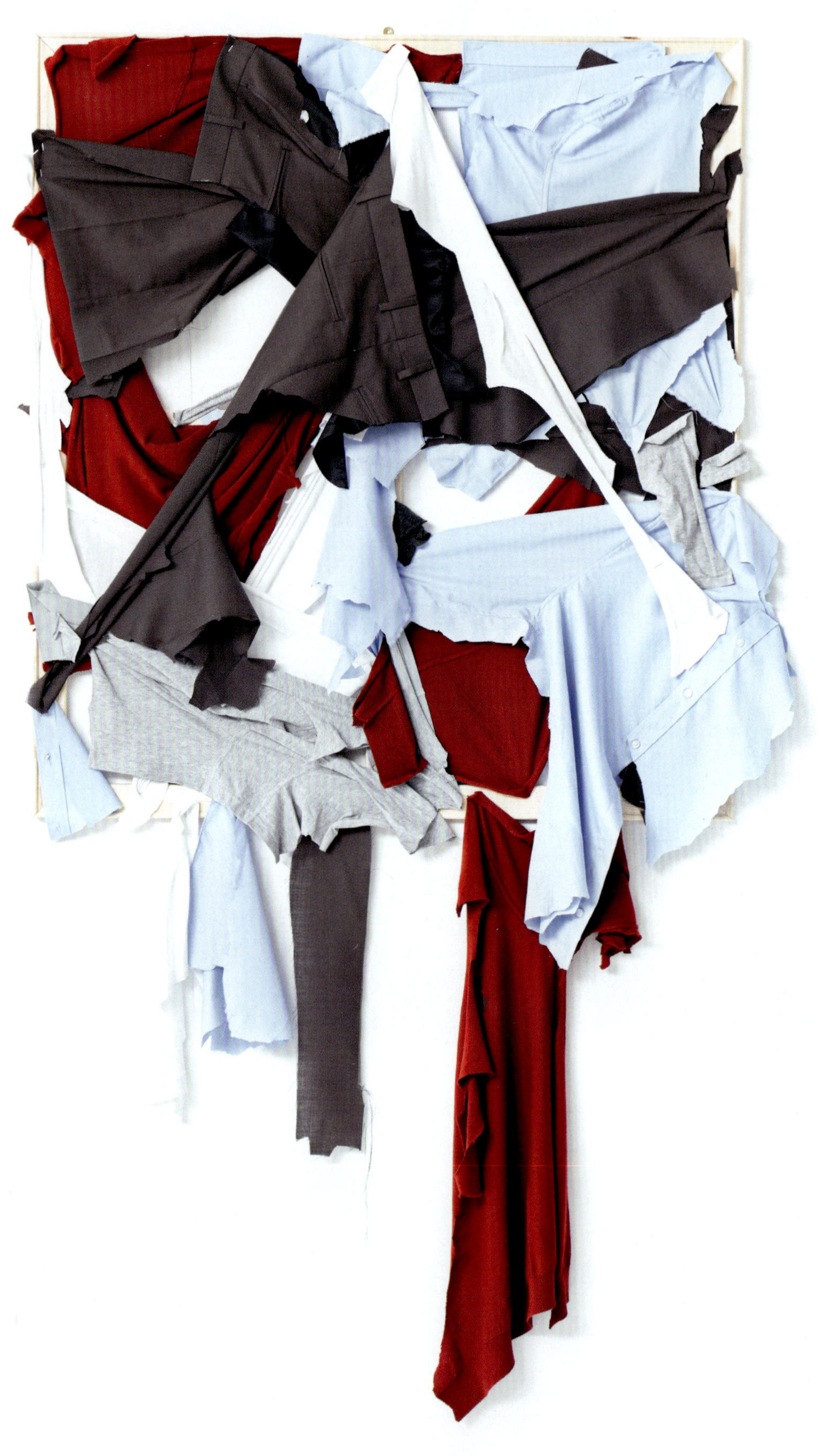

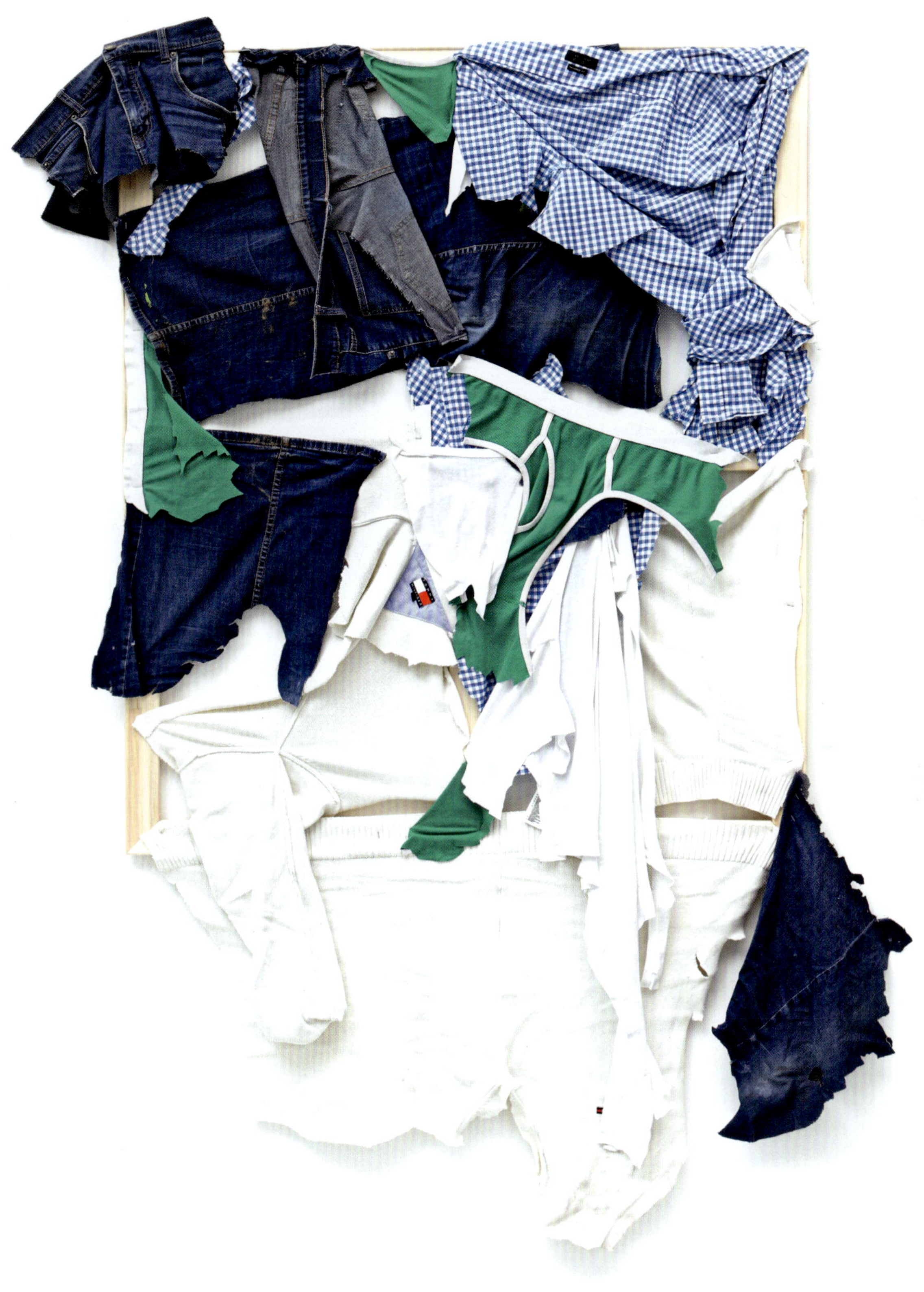

OPENING

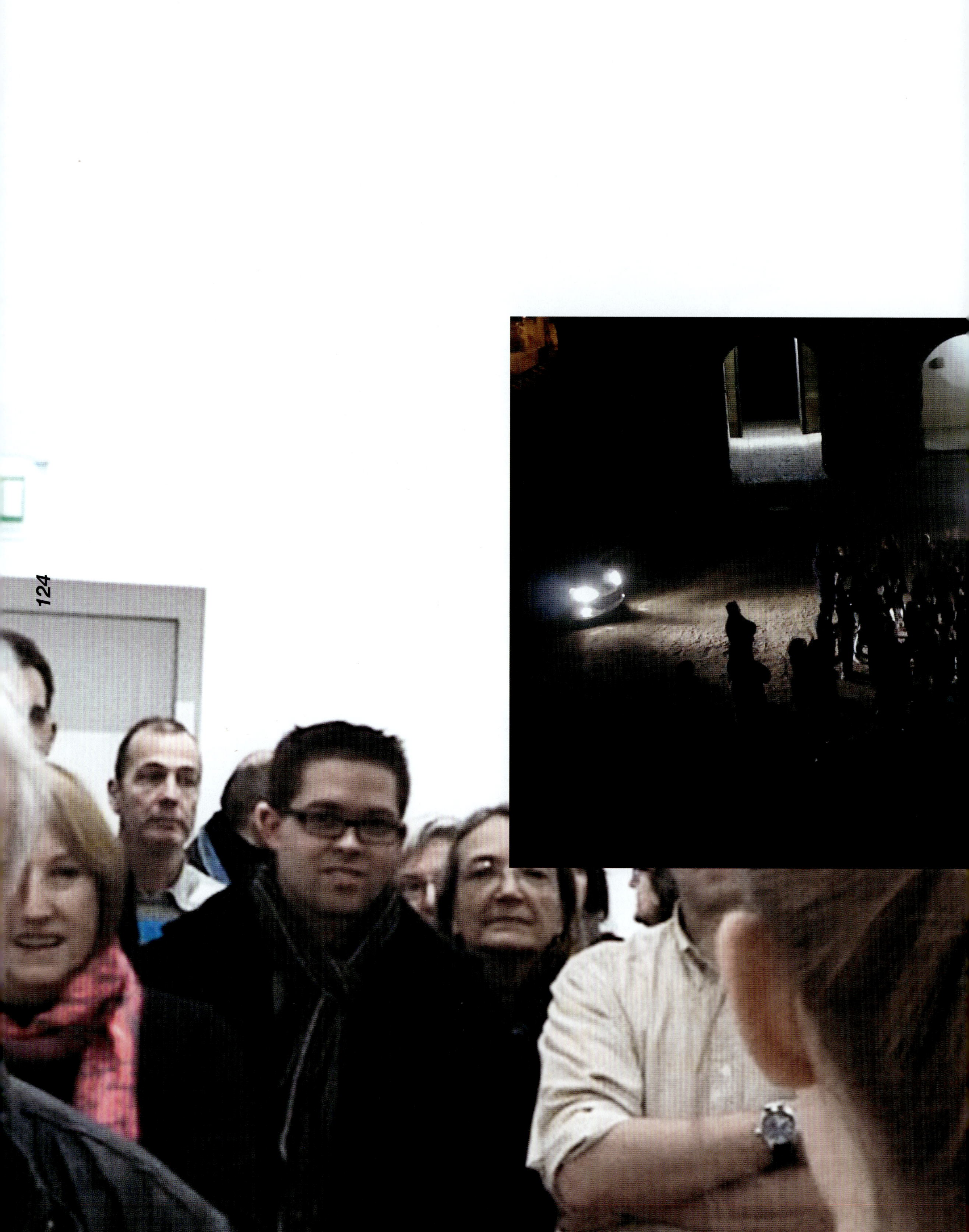

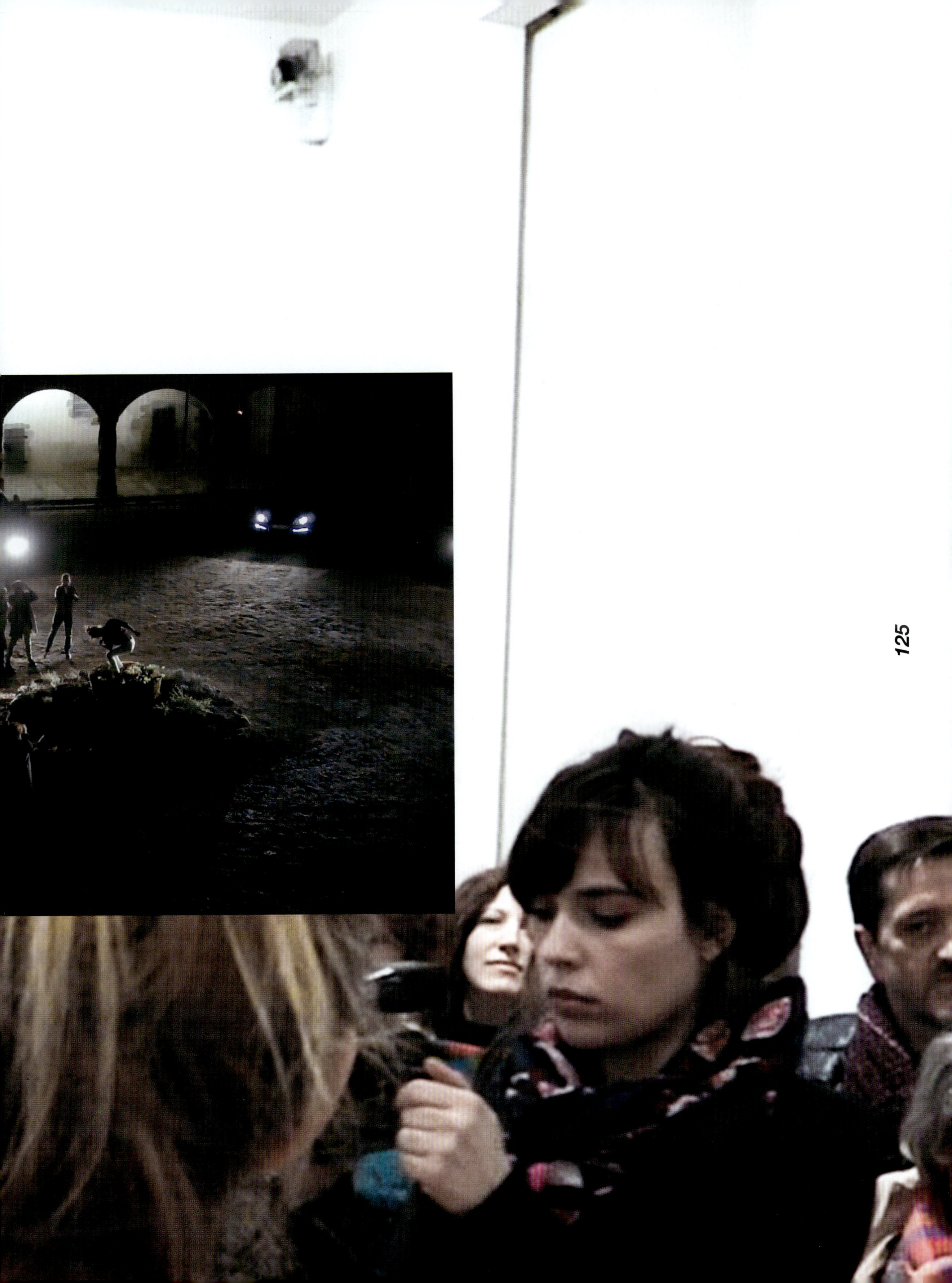

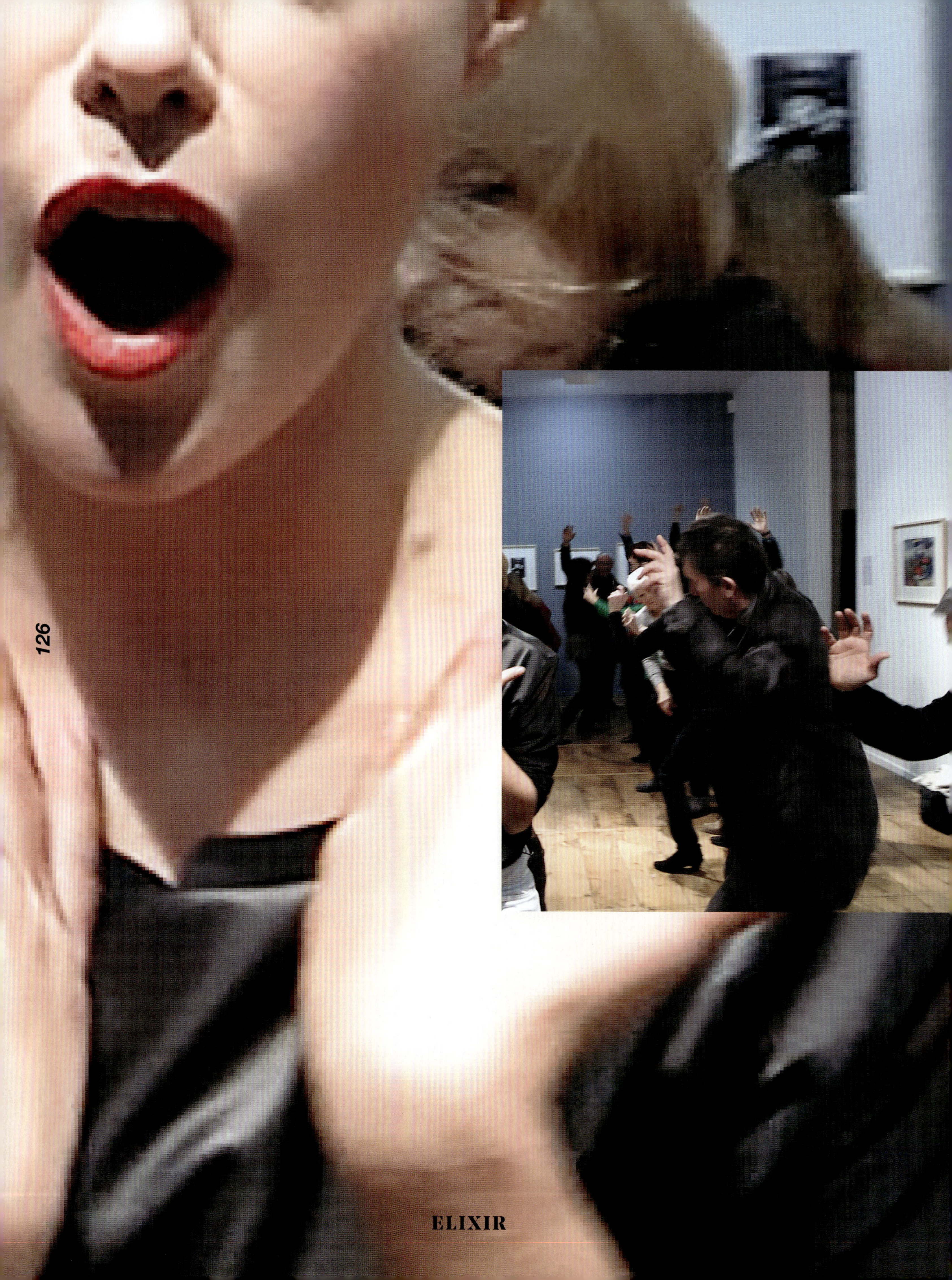

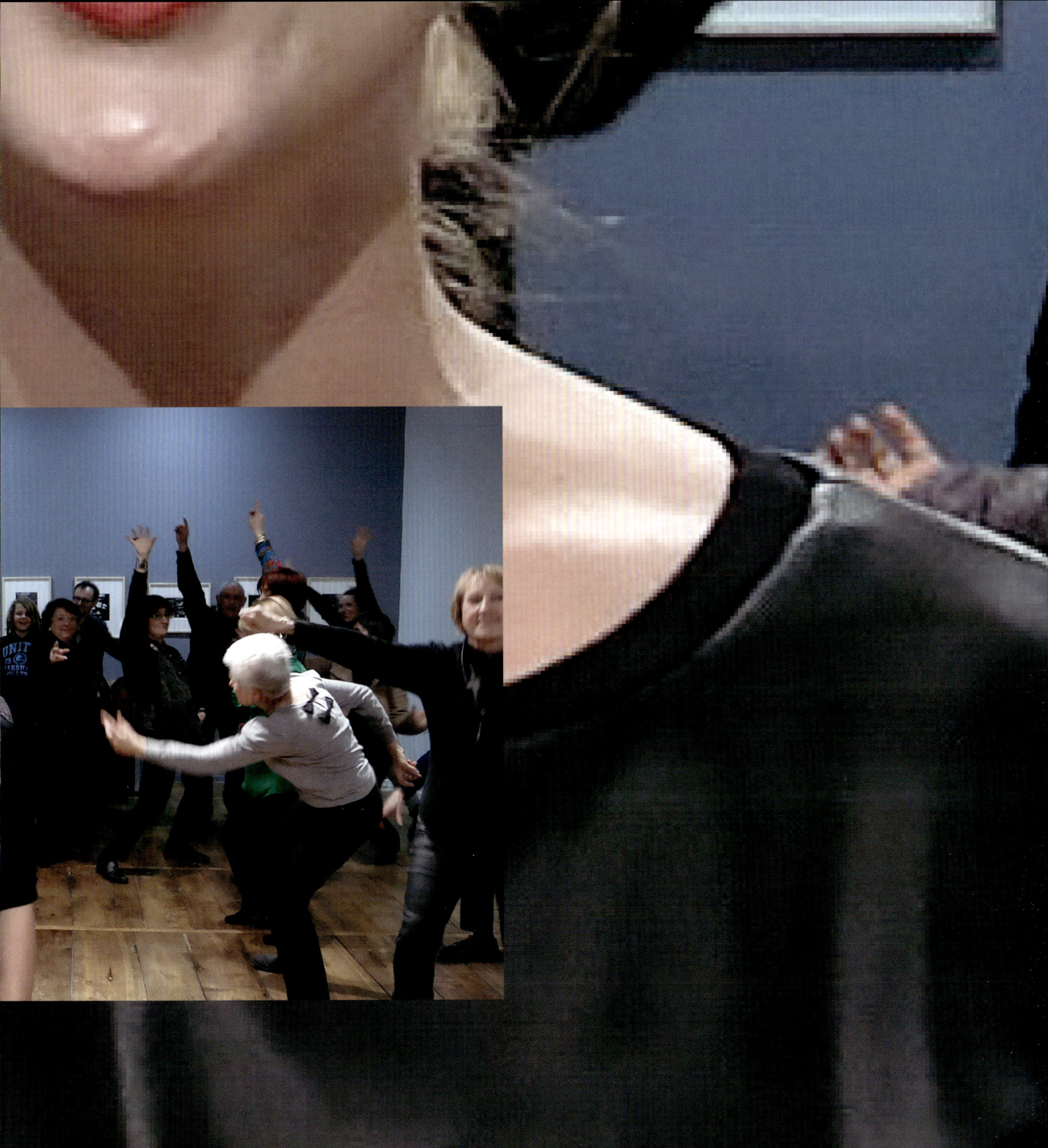

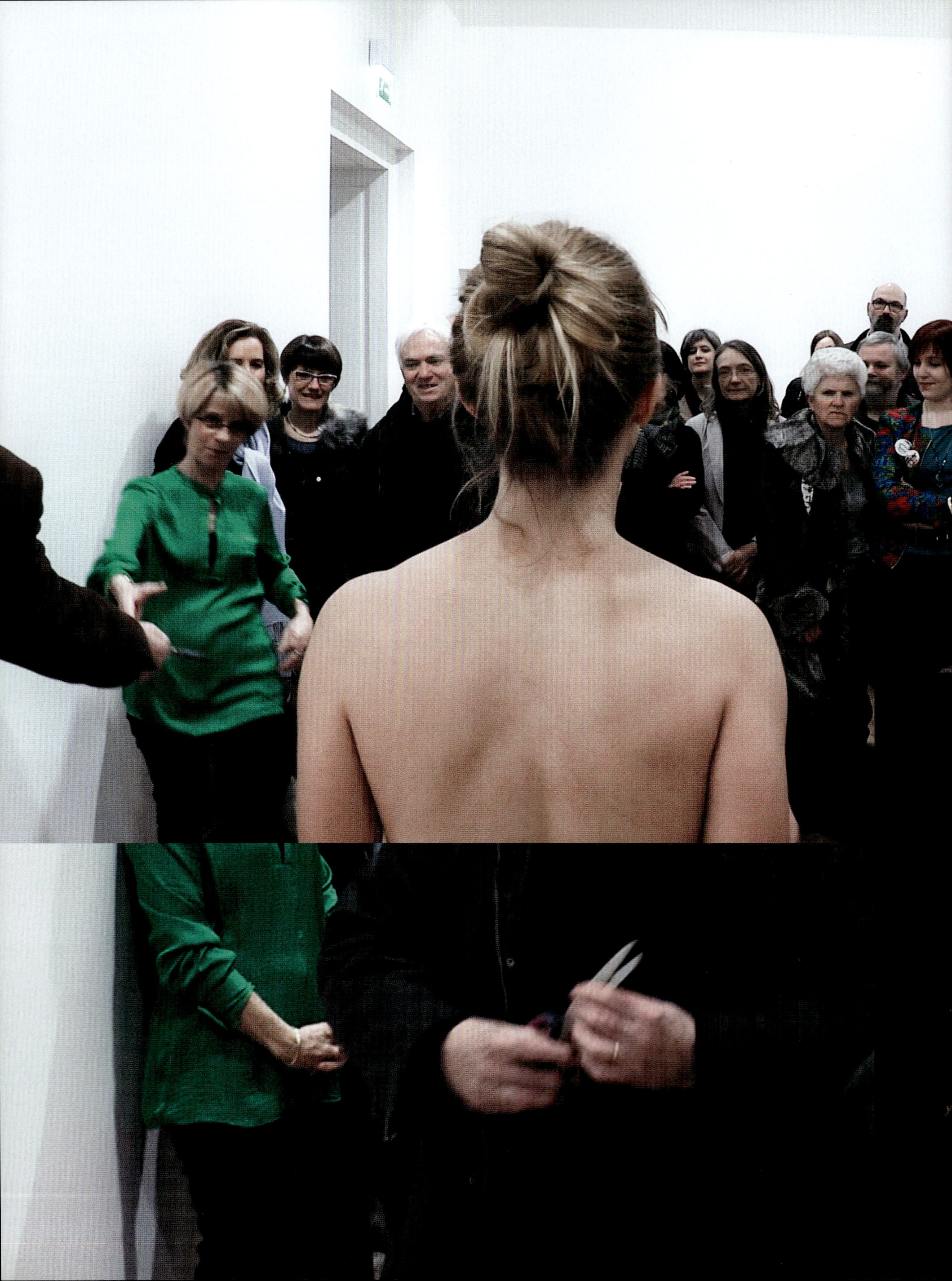

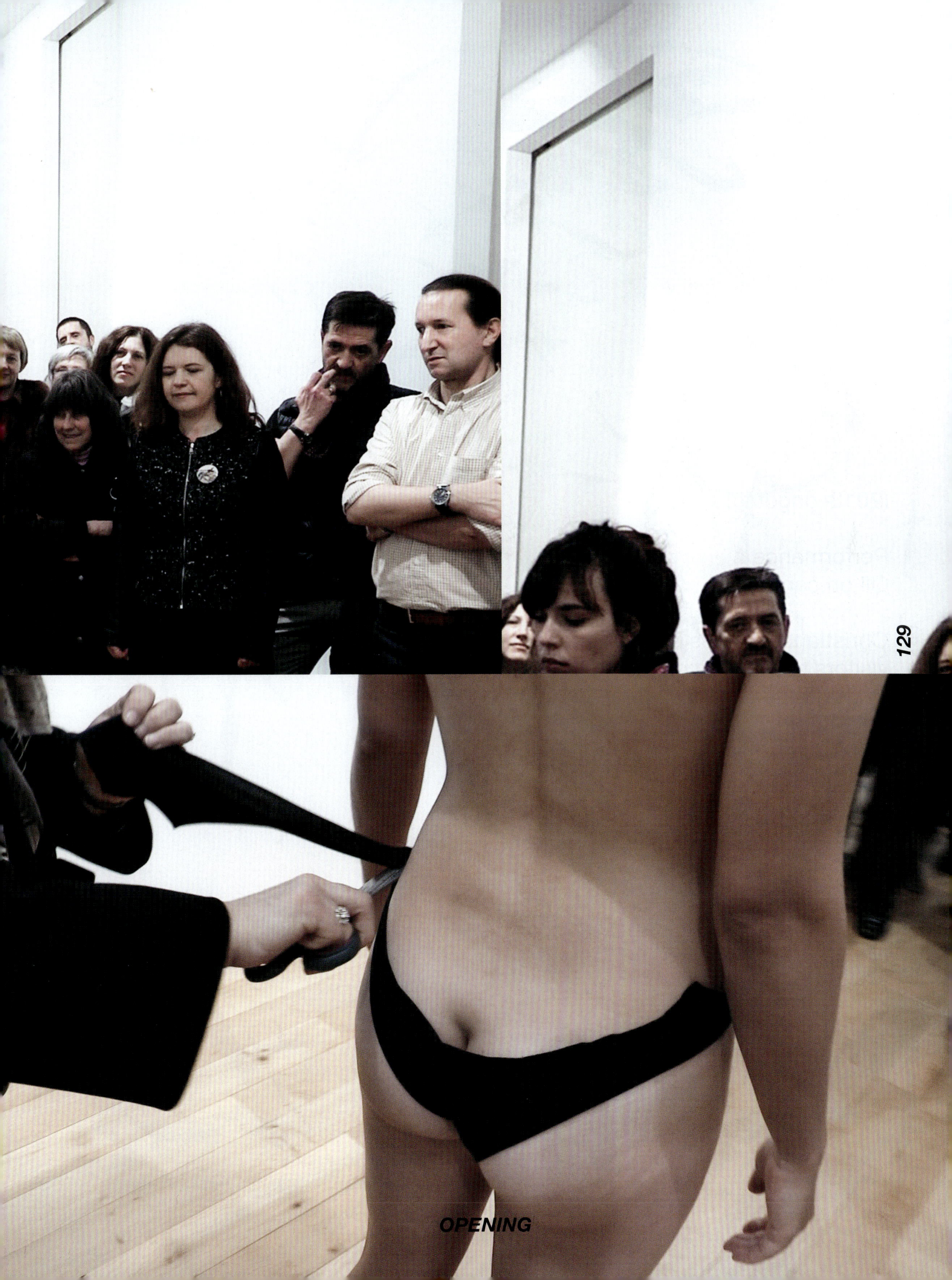

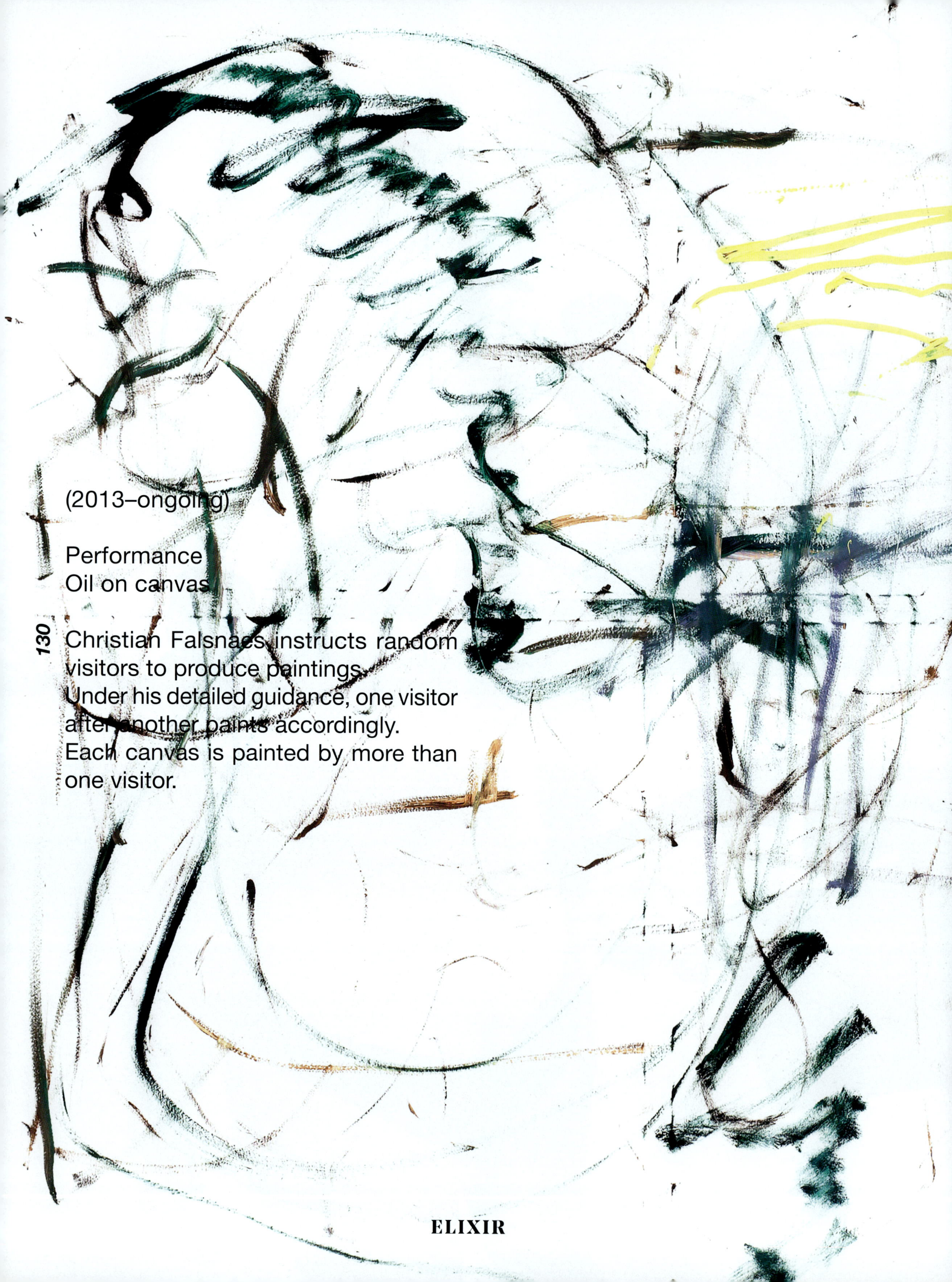

(2013–ongoing)

Performance
Oil on canvas

Christian Falsnaes instructs random visitors to produce paintings. Under his detailed guidance, one visitor after another paints accordingly. Each canvas is painted by more than one visitor.

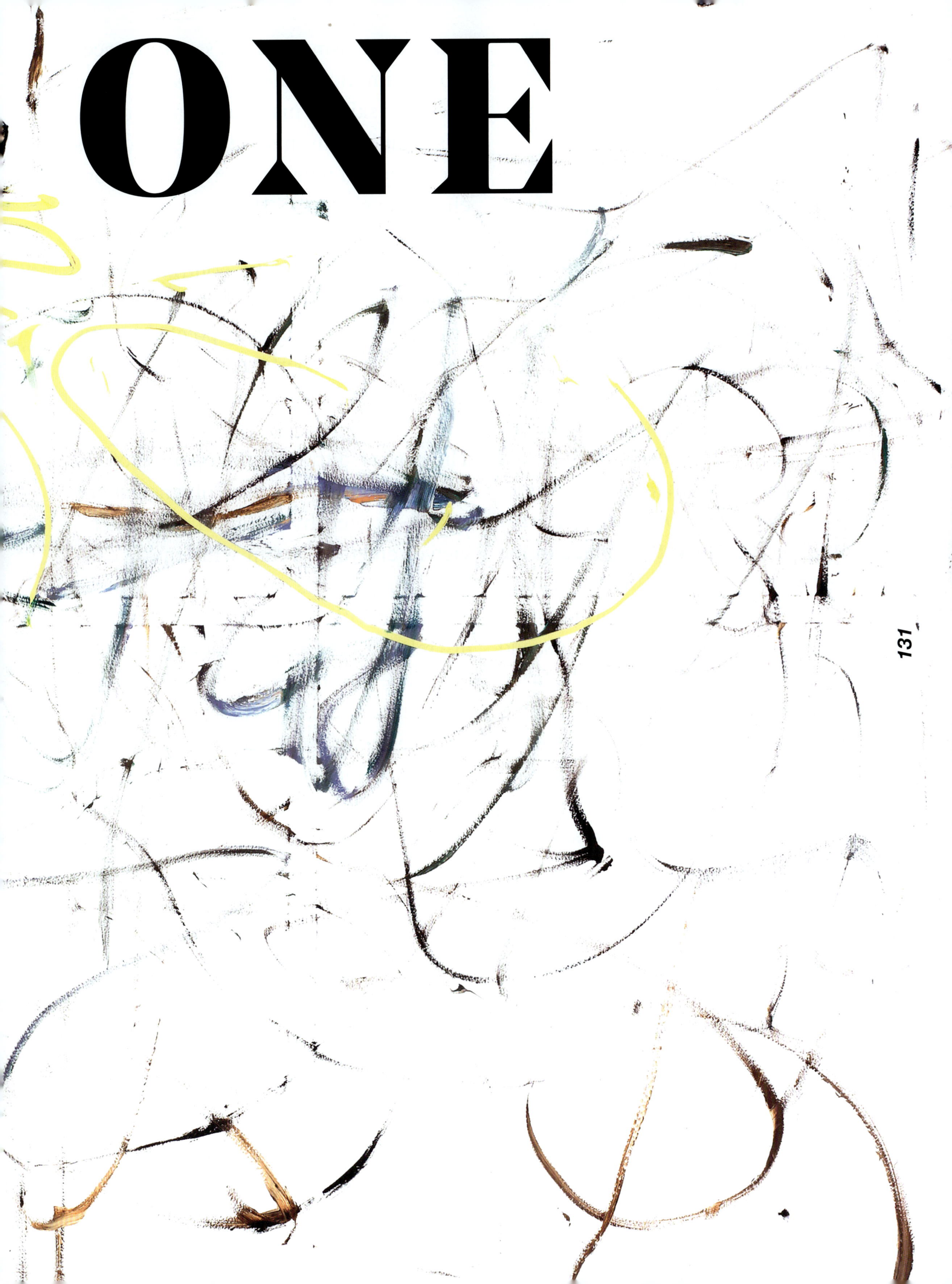
ONE

CHRISTIAN FALSNAES — MISLEADING ART

Text by Noemi Smolik

In a way, his performances are pretty cruel. This meanness, which sometimes pushes the limits of what is bearable, makes for the uniqueness of Christian Falsnaes's performances. But what does "mean" mean? This question becomes immediately clear when viewing the performance with the telling title *Männliches Auftreten als Folge gesellschaftlicher Machtverhältnisse zwischen Künstler und Publikum [Male Behavior as a Result of Societal Power Relations between Artist and Audience]*, which took place in the Bonner Kunstverein in 2013. Falsnaes invited representatives of the art industry, including curators, critics, collectors, and members of the art-interested public to the Kunstverein's space, where he animated them like a professional talk master to actions like yelling, dancing, or clapping their hands. This event can be viewed as a video, and it is surprising to see how individuals who are familiar with the traps of contemporary art let themselves get carried away by the effects of group dynamics. Pretty mean, what happens there.

The absurdity of the behavior of the participants of the event in Bonn not only raises questions of power, control, and seduction, but also about what the audience expects from a contemporary artist and to what extent it is ready to follow him without criticism. Falsnaes's performances closely implicate the participants in the event by skillful manipulation. For him, it is all about this involvement, which has been credited with a rather emancipatory character since the 1960s, even though some performances, such as those of Josef Beuys—and this is the contradiction—were quite authoritarian in character. Art critic Jan Verwoert already pointed out this paradox. In his performances, Falsnaes grabs it with his own hands.

This was also true for the opening of his exhibition in 2014 in the Cologne gallery DREI, curated by Oriane Durand. The viewer entered a room with empty canvases hung on the walls, where Falsnaes conversed with the visitors slowly arriving in a relaxed atmosphere. Suddenly, he took paint tubes and brushes, which were on the floor, and asked them to paint the canvases. They hesitantly began, constantly urged on by Falsnaes, and soon also by the audience, to follow the instructions. The atmosphere intensified, became euphoric, the screens began to fill; what remained were painted canvases, soiled floors, paint marks on the walls, and empty tubes on the floor. Whoever entered the space after the opening encountered canvases painted in the style of American Abstract Expressionists, accompanied acoustically by recordings of the performance.

The performance was entitled *One*, alluding to the relationship between the individual and the group, a basic theme of modern art. In modernity, an artwork is taken as the expression of an individual, who is not only juxtaposed to the group, but often also creates a conflict with different groups. Falsnaes inverts this; he has a communal piece created, thereby negating the individual, and gives the work the ironic title *One*.

But, it is not that easy. Falsnaes is the one who initiates, even manipulates his performances like a talk master. In a way, he is the individual who drives the group. He himself conceives of the participants of his performances as his artistic material, which he seeks to shape. The point for him is to explore his power as an artist and as an individual over the audience. Power, authority, seduction, and control on the one hand, and the dissolution of the individual in a cleverly manipulated group on the other, are therefore the themes that he seeks to make us conscious of with his performances. And this often happens quite ruthlessly.

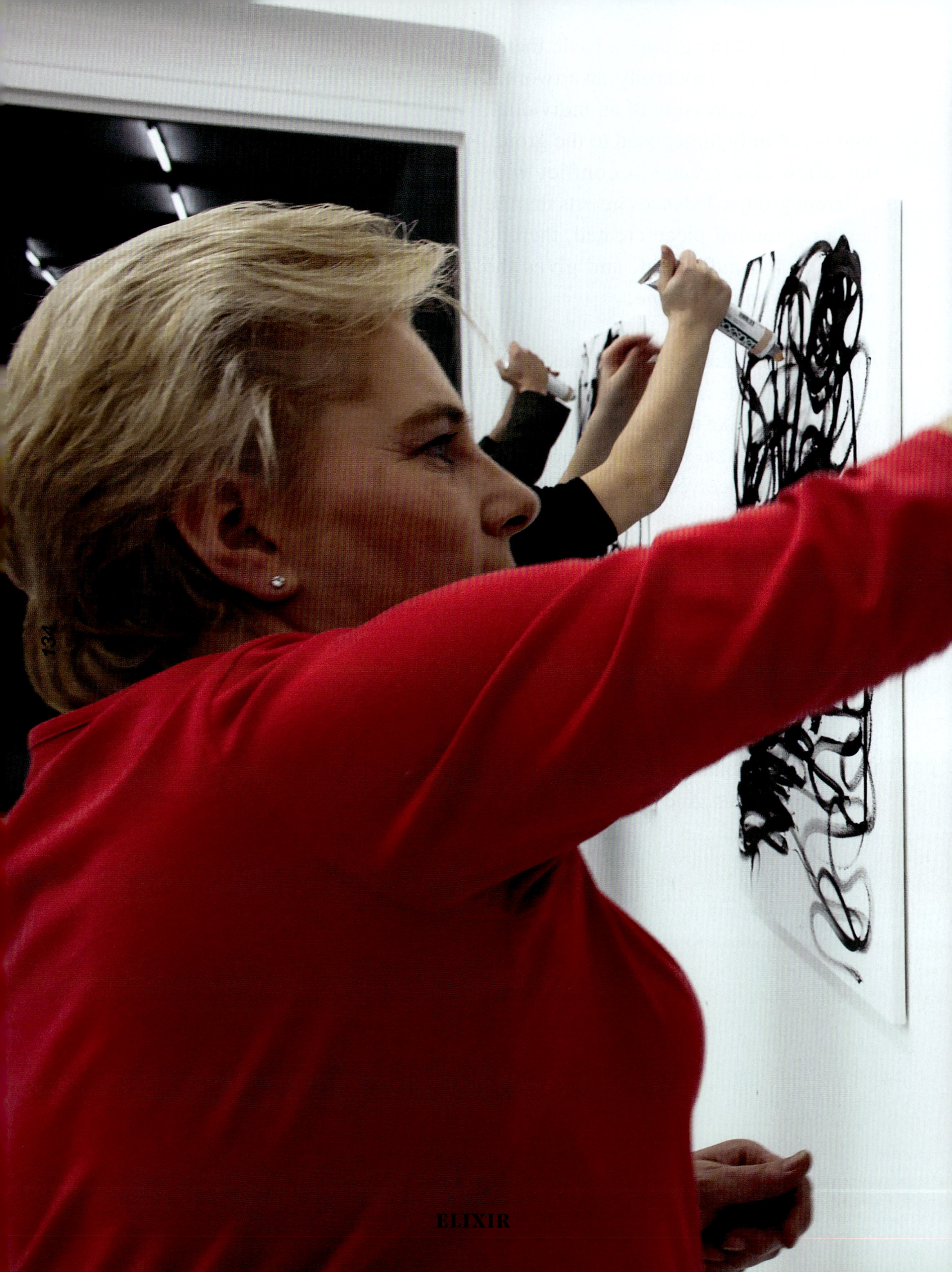

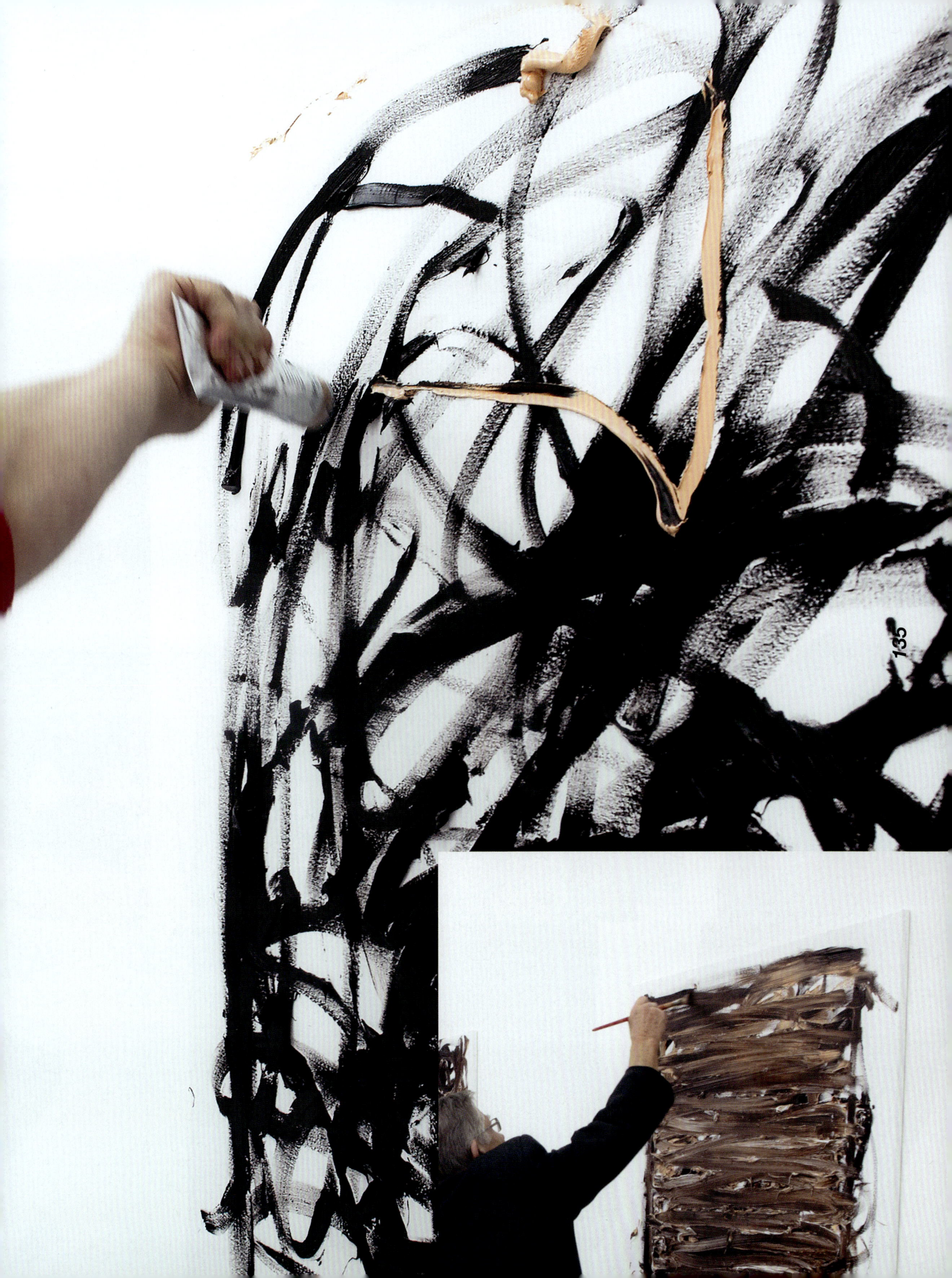

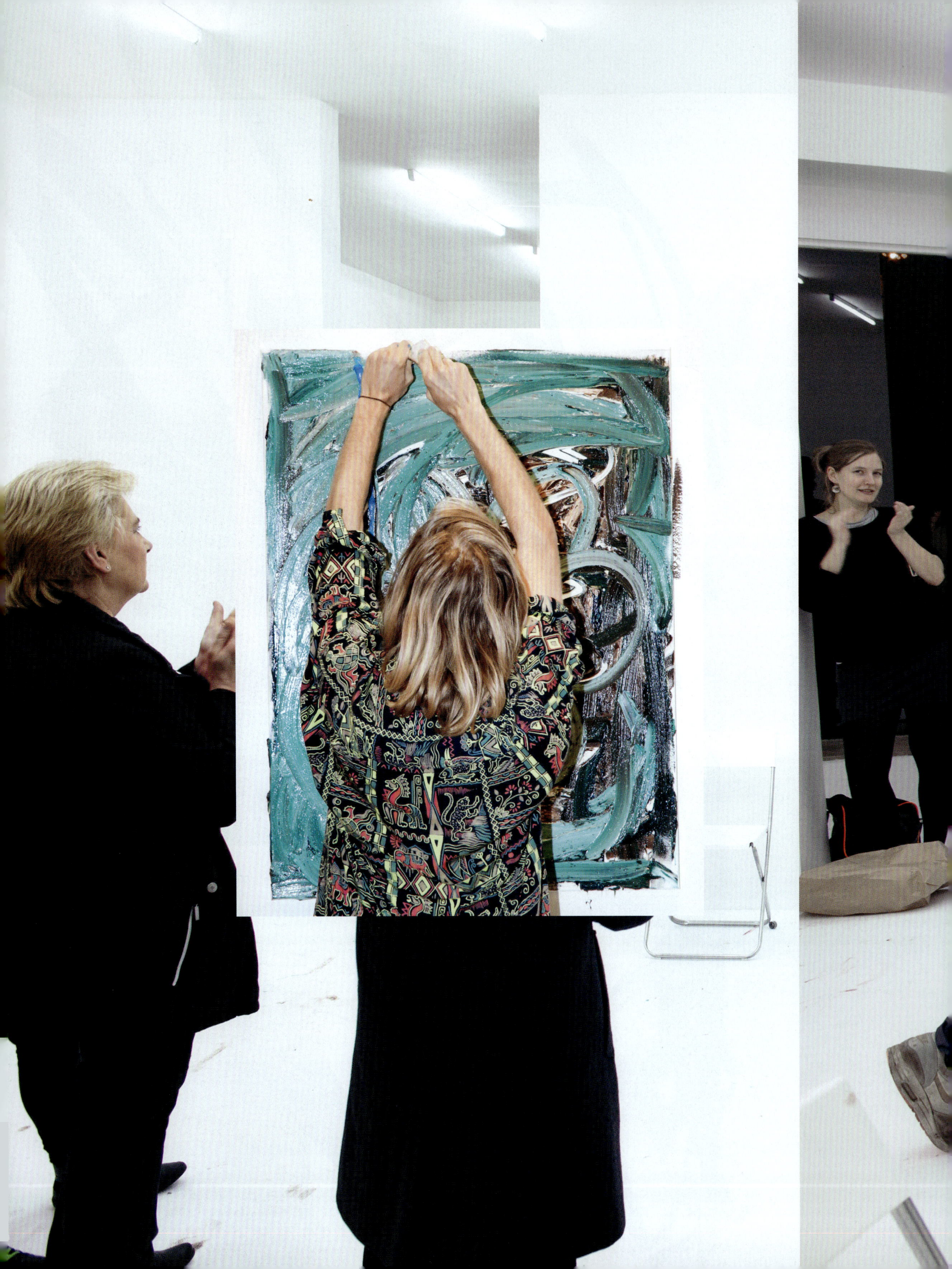

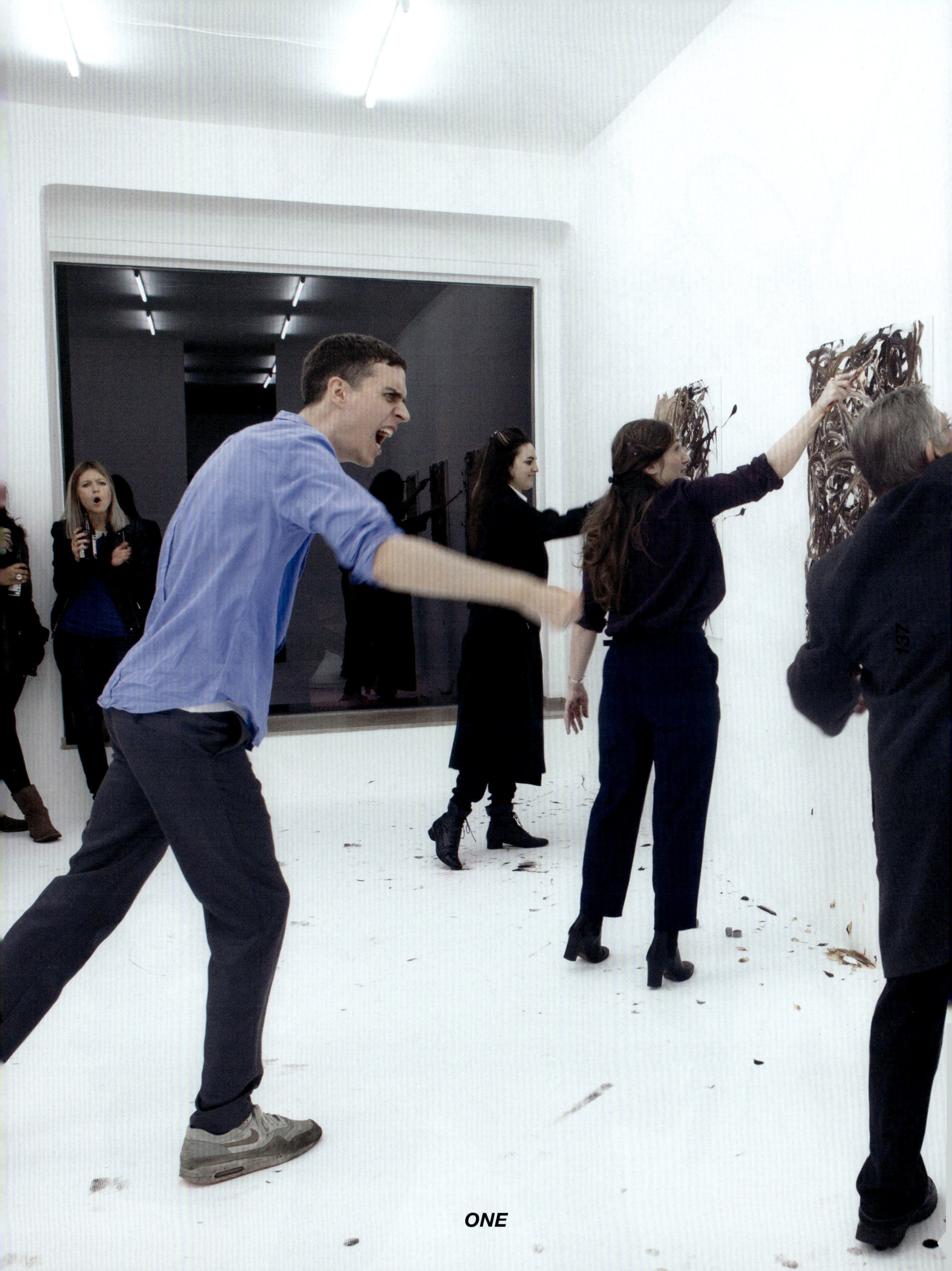

ONE

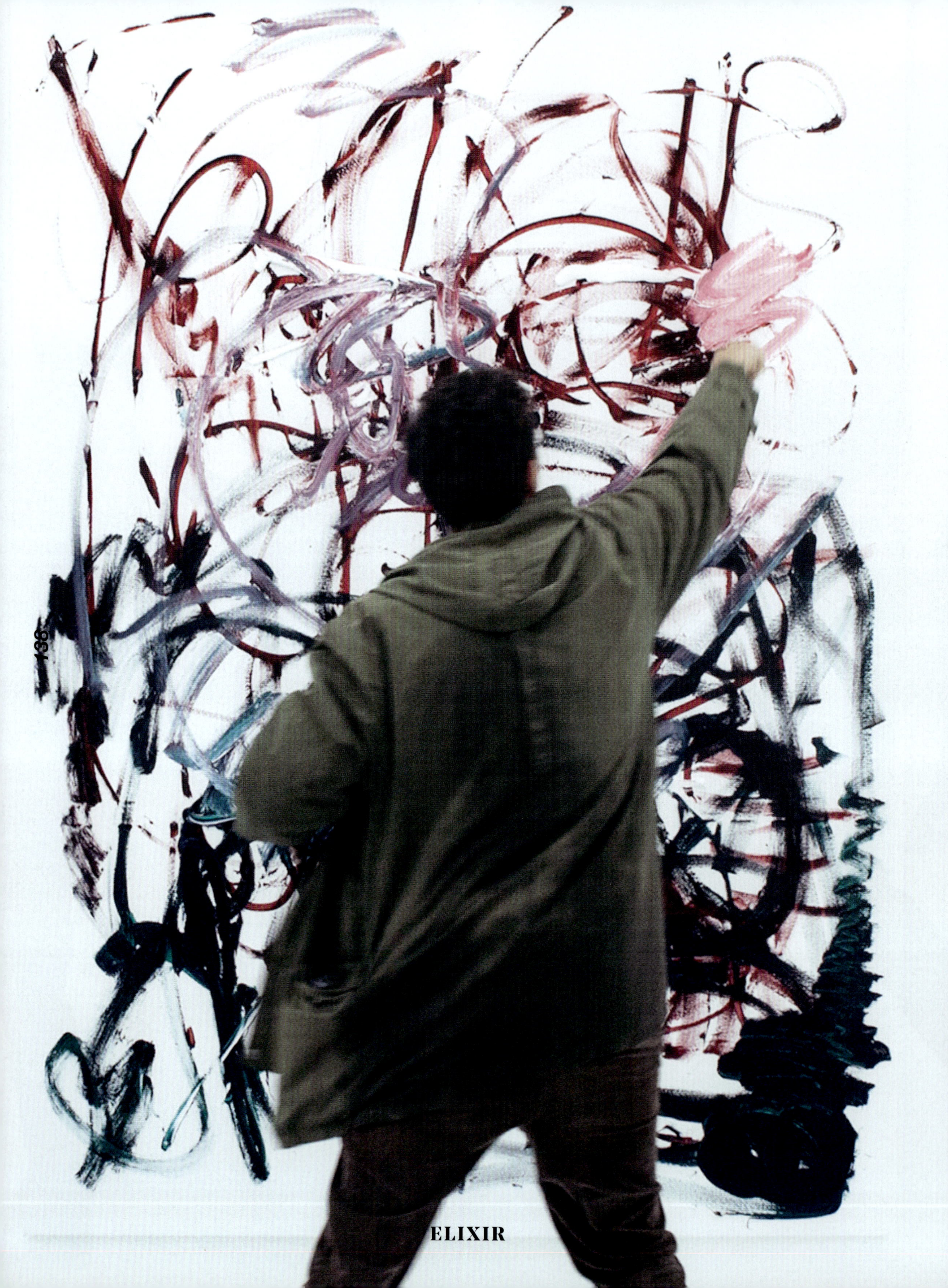

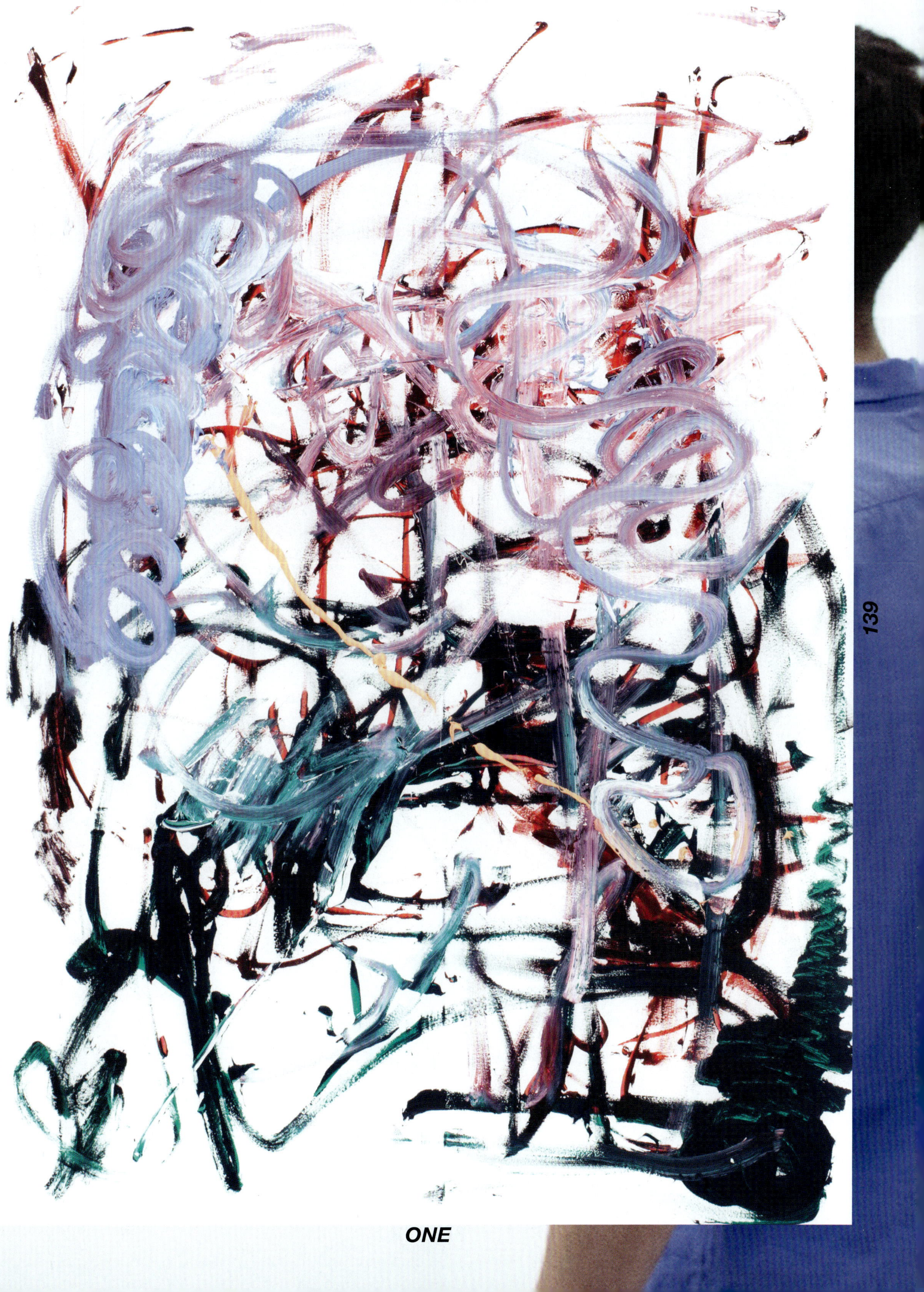

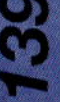

ONE

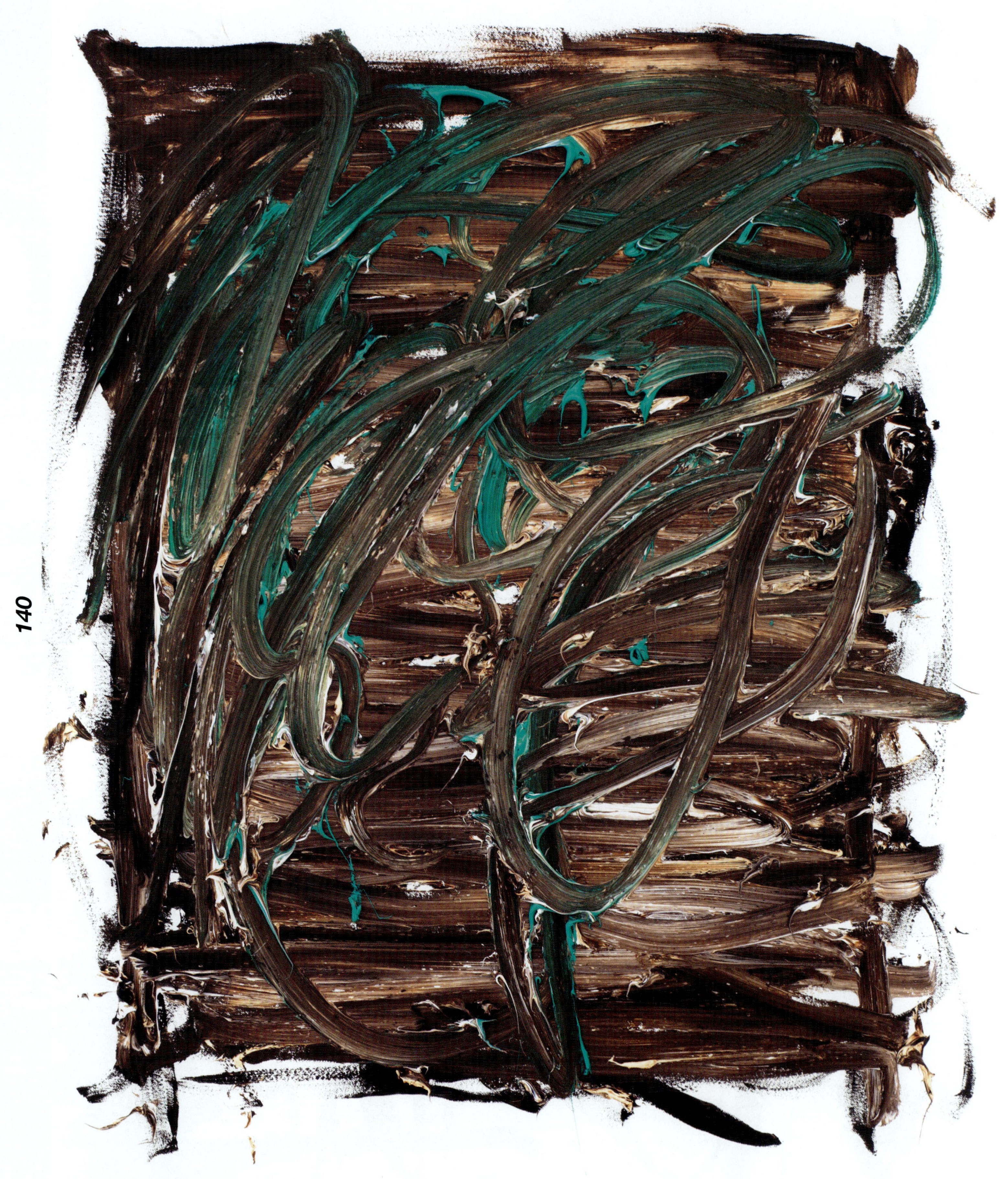

ELIXIR

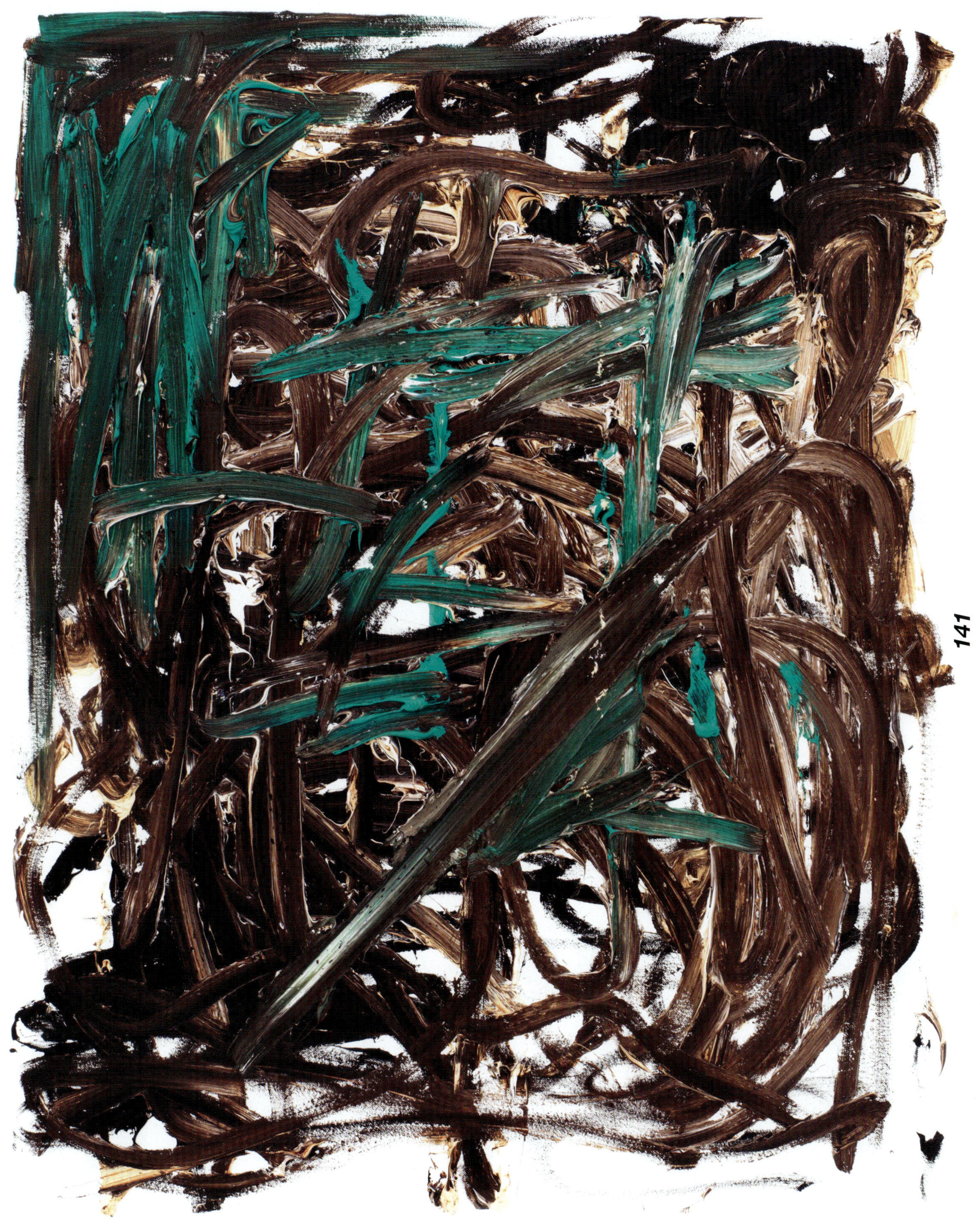

ONE

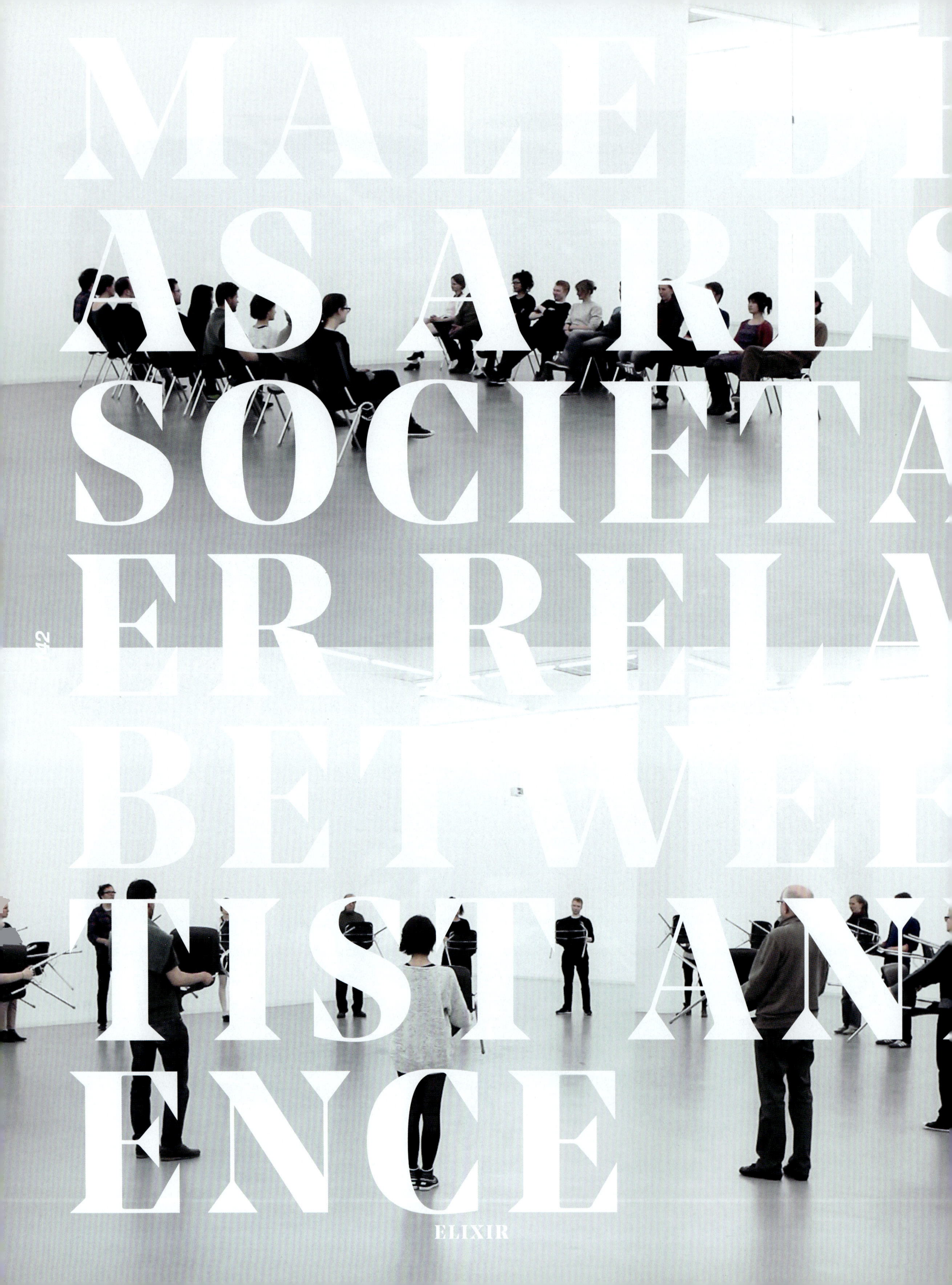

MALE
AS ARES
SOCIETA
ER RELA
BETWEE
TIST AN
ENCE

ULT OF
L POW–
TIONS

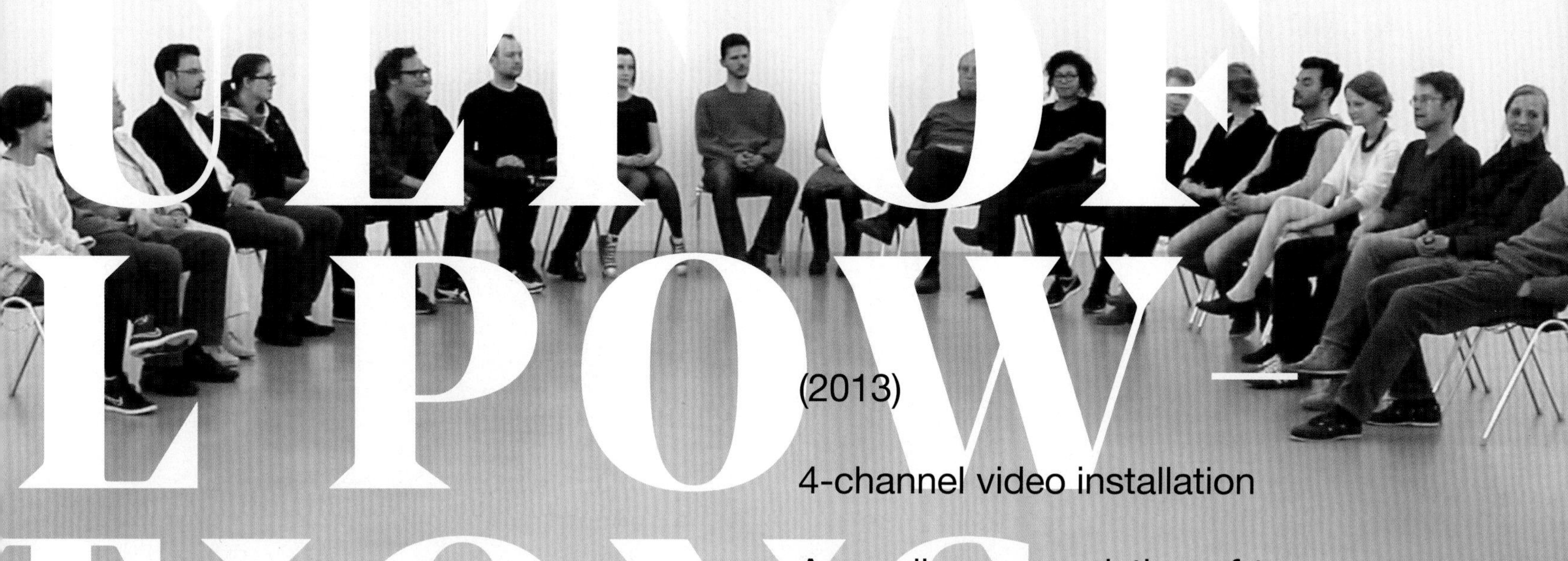

(2013)

4-channel video installation

An audience consisting of ten women and ten men are led through four different performances.
In each performance, Christian Falsnaes takes a different position of authority (teacher, commander, star, aggressor), leading to four different types of audience behavior.
All four performances are recorded on video.

D AUDI–

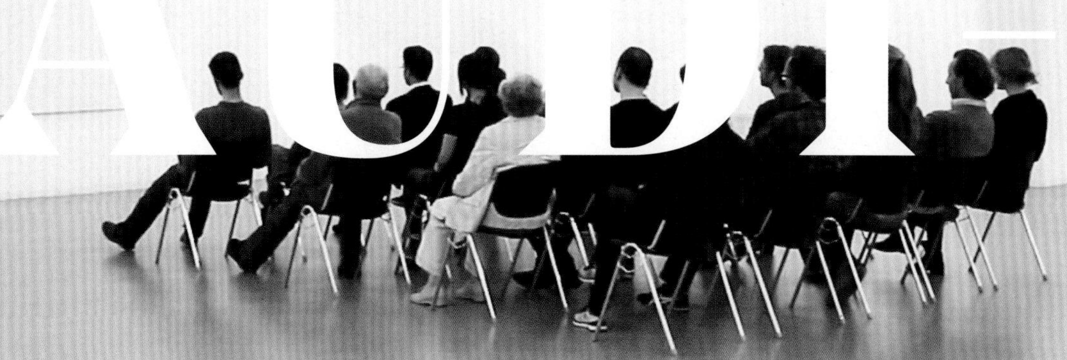

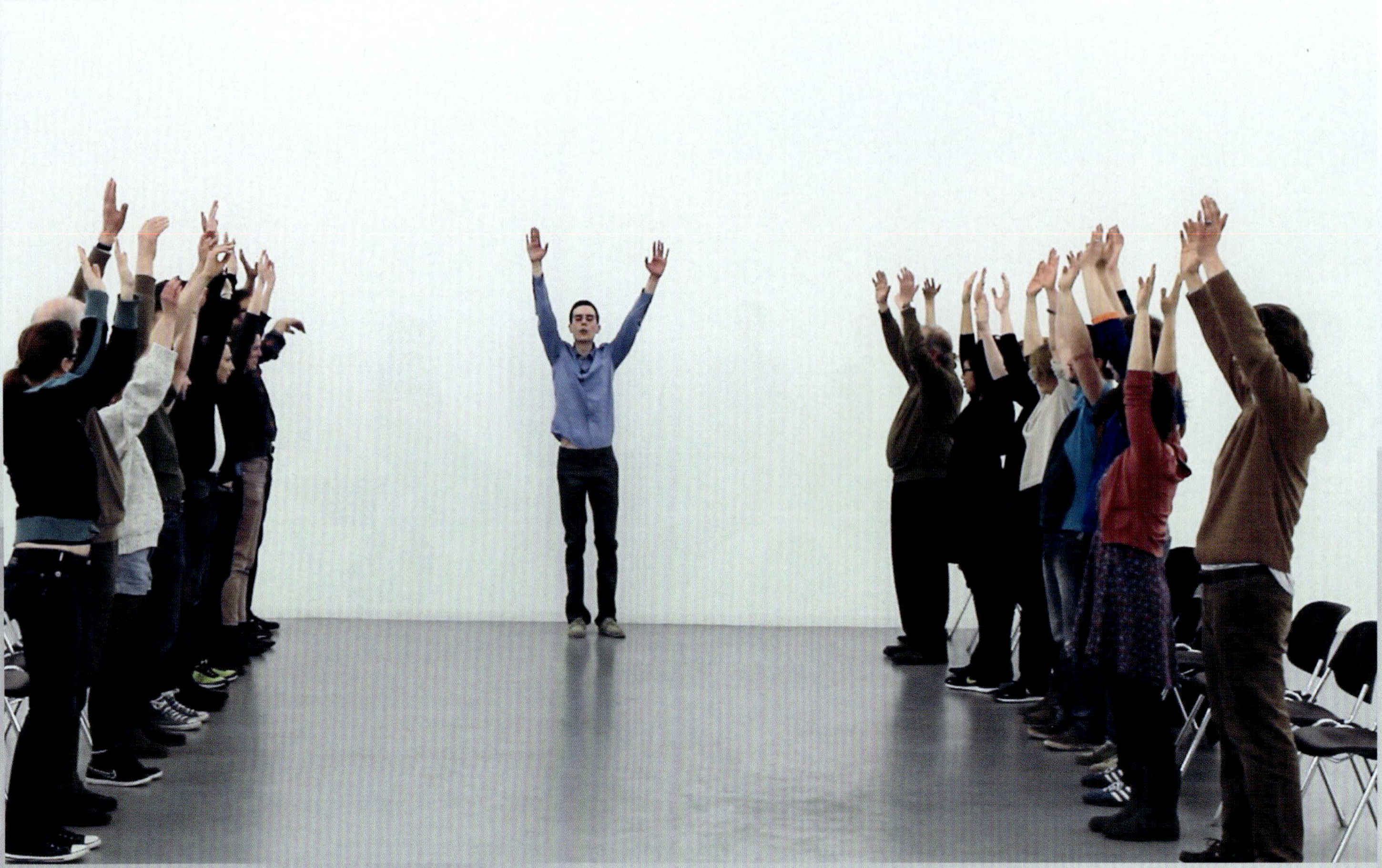

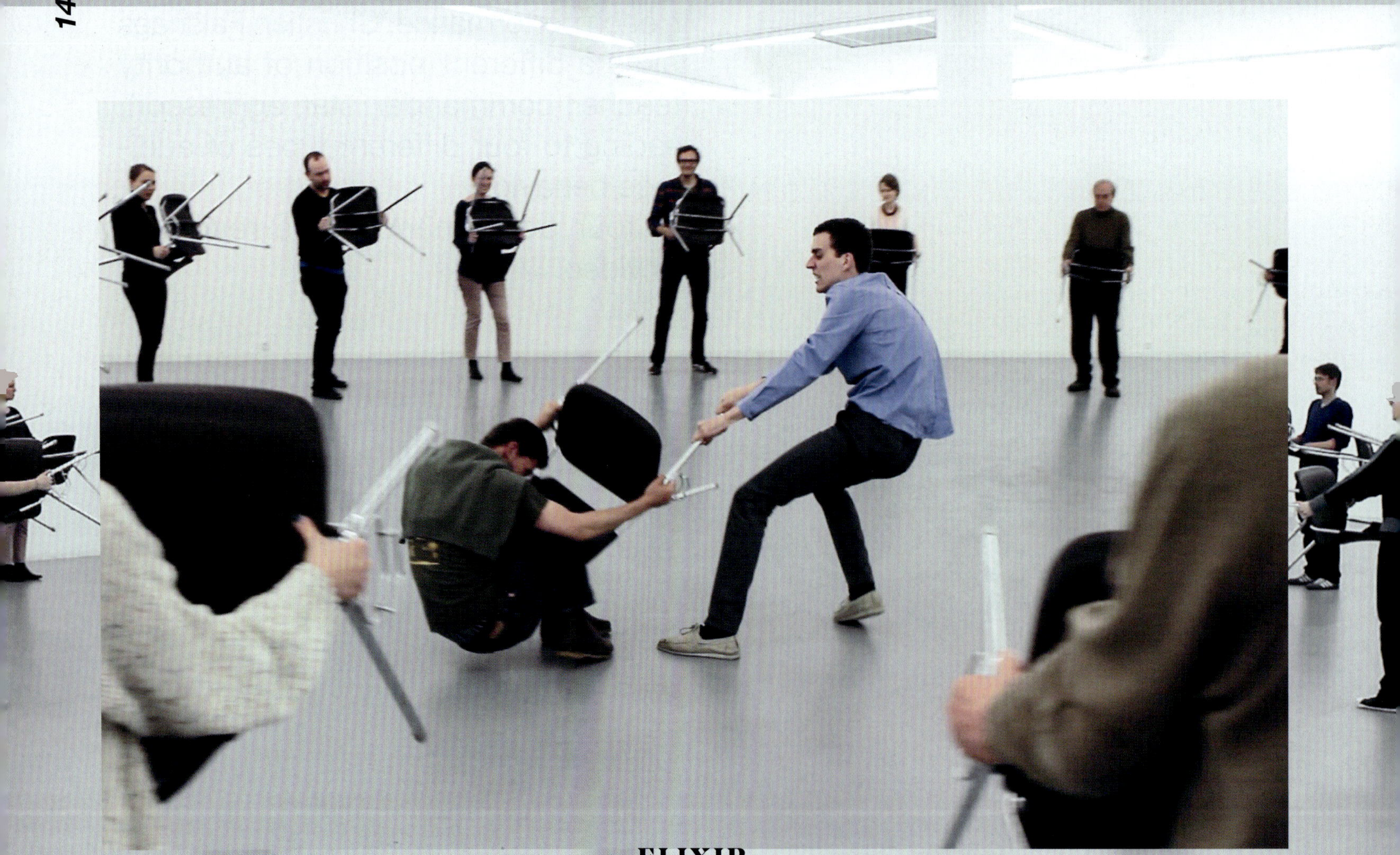

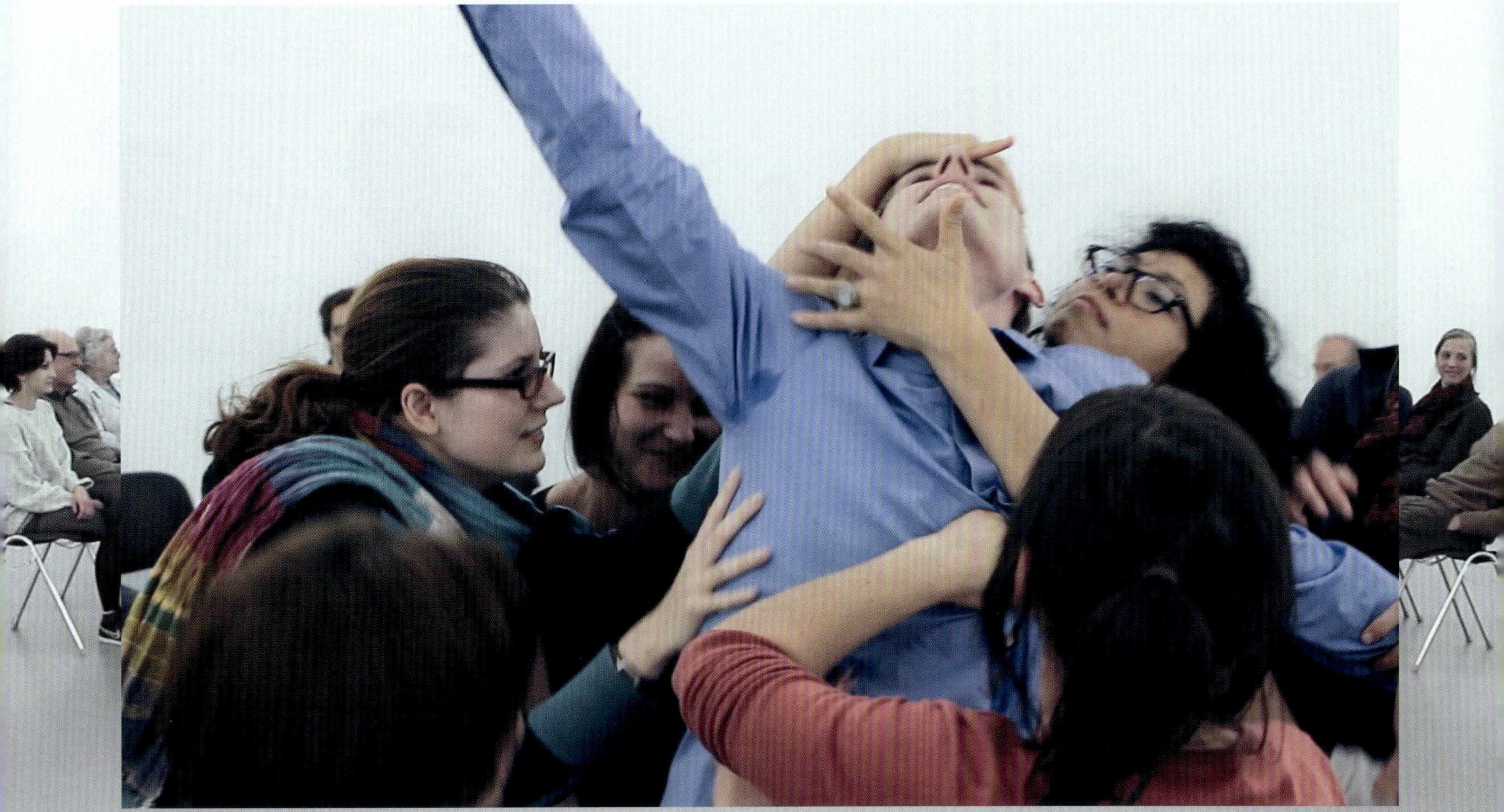

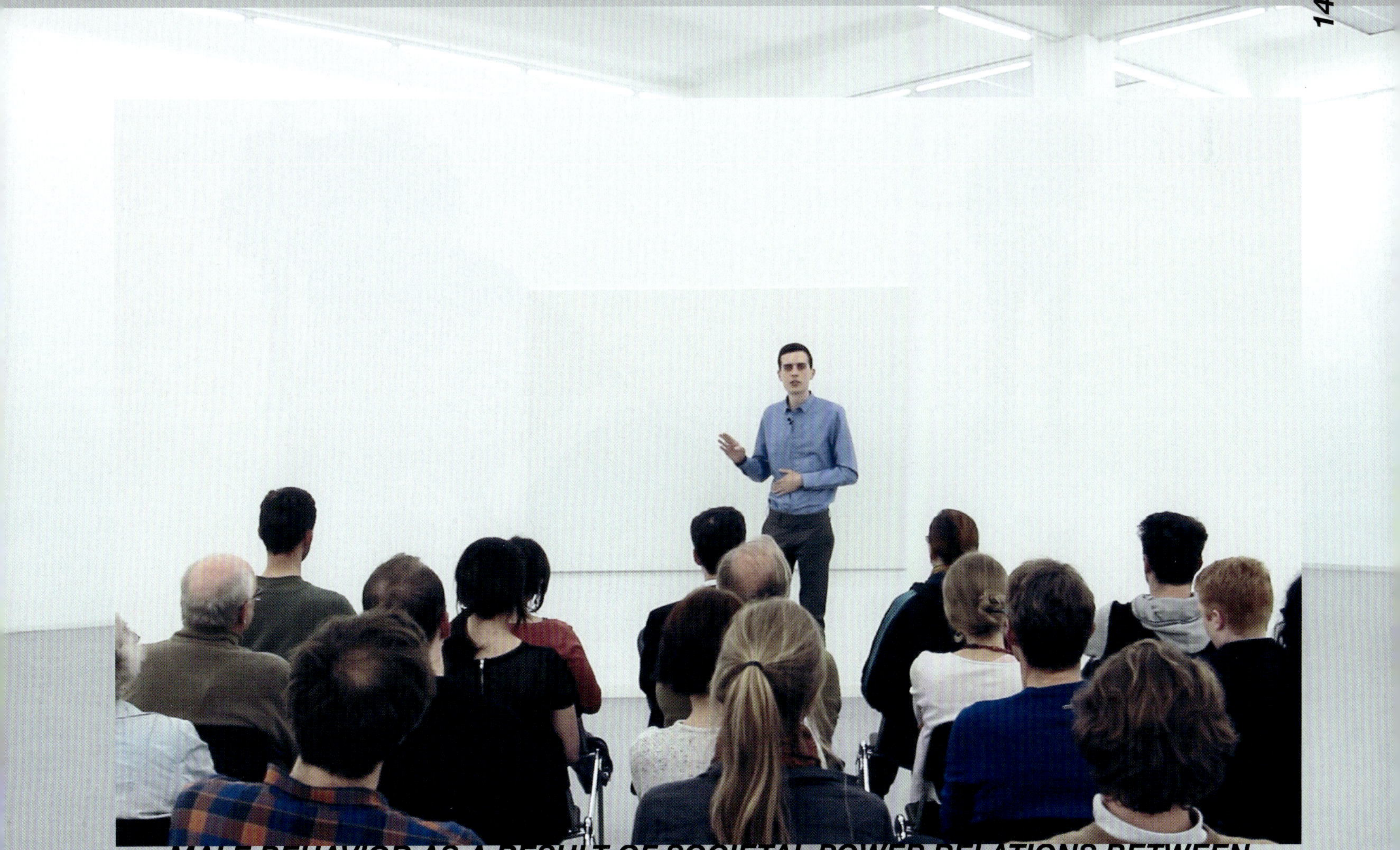

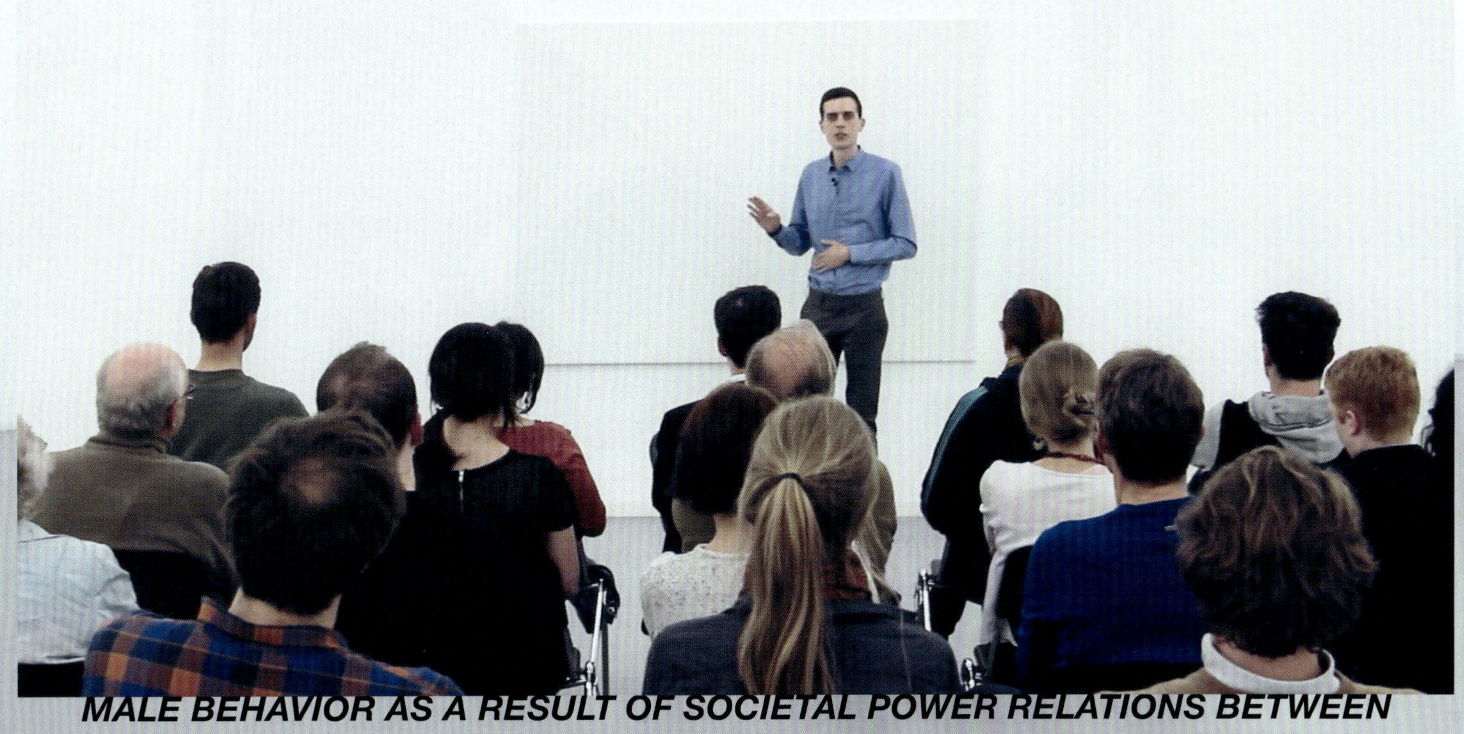

MALE BEHAVIOR AS A RESULT OF SOCIETAL POWER RELATIONS BETWEEN ARTIST AND AUDIENCE

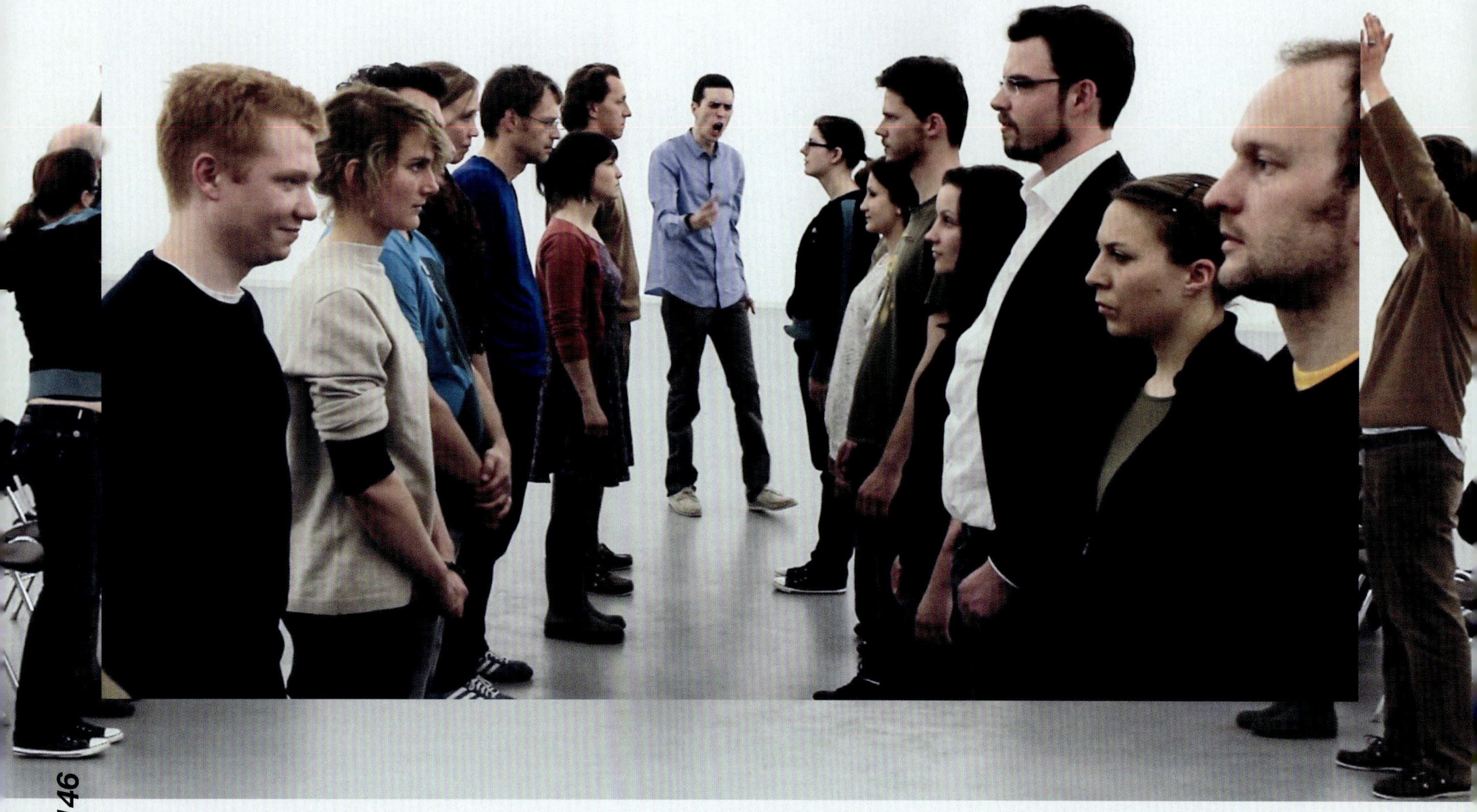

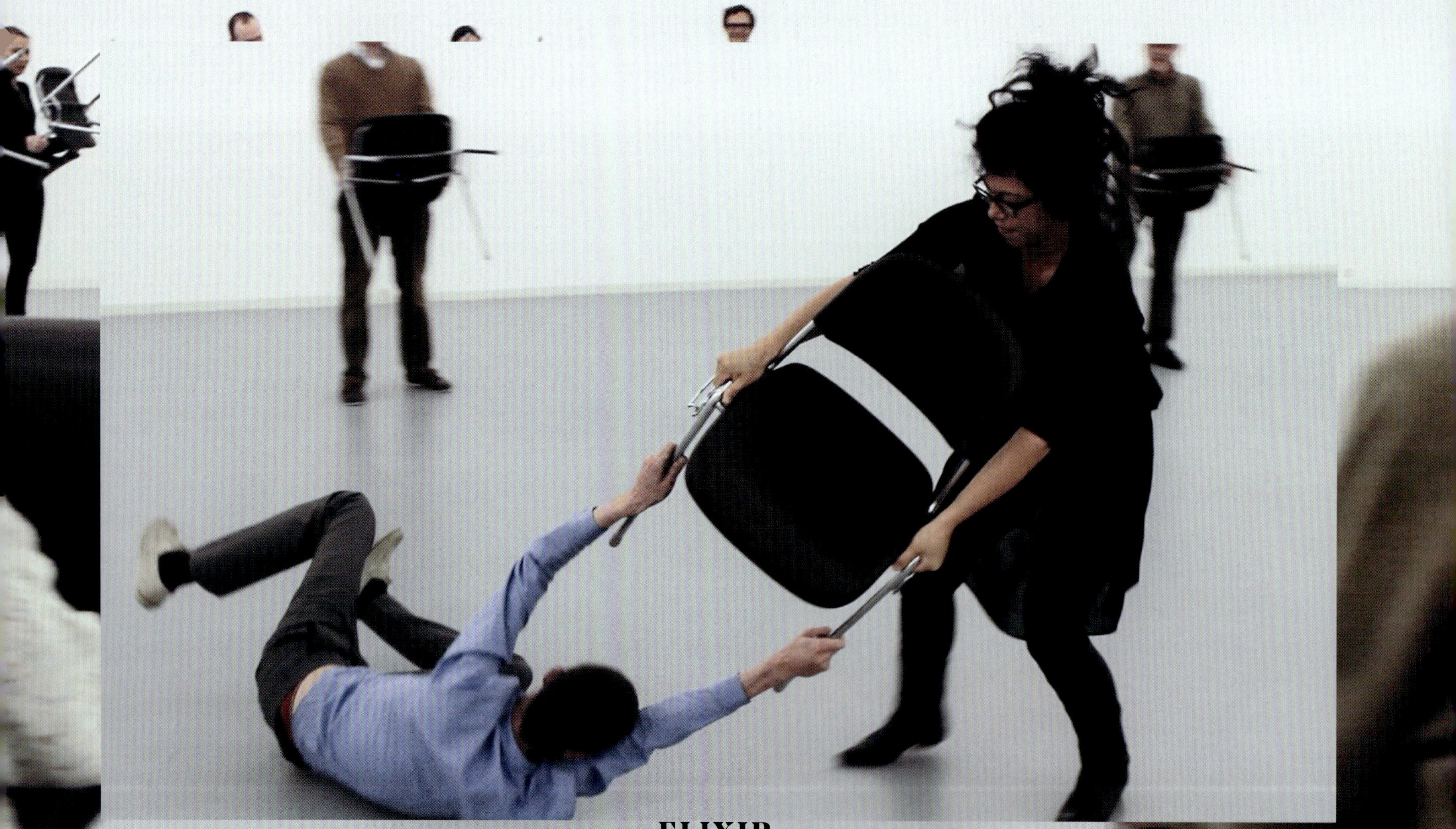

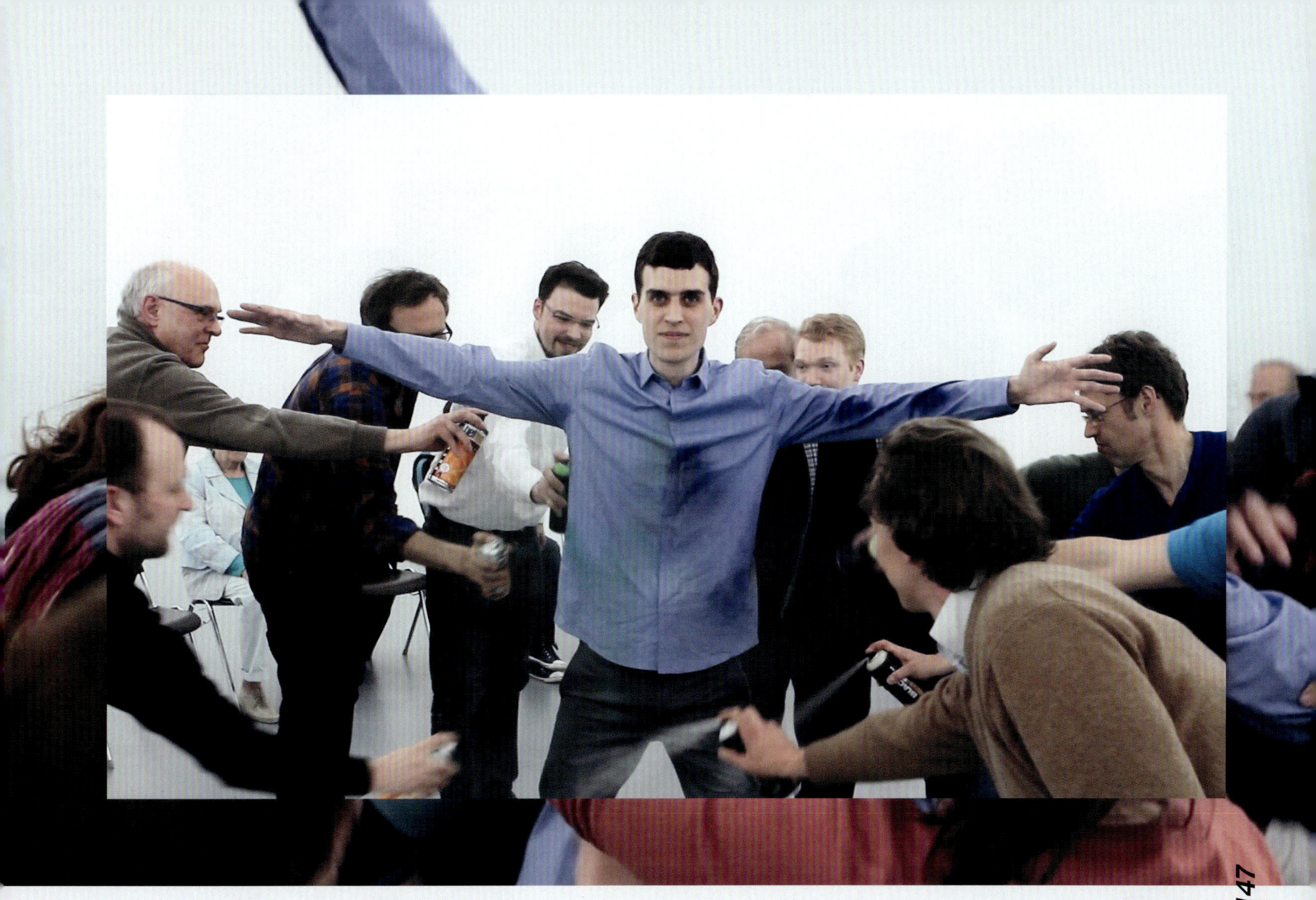

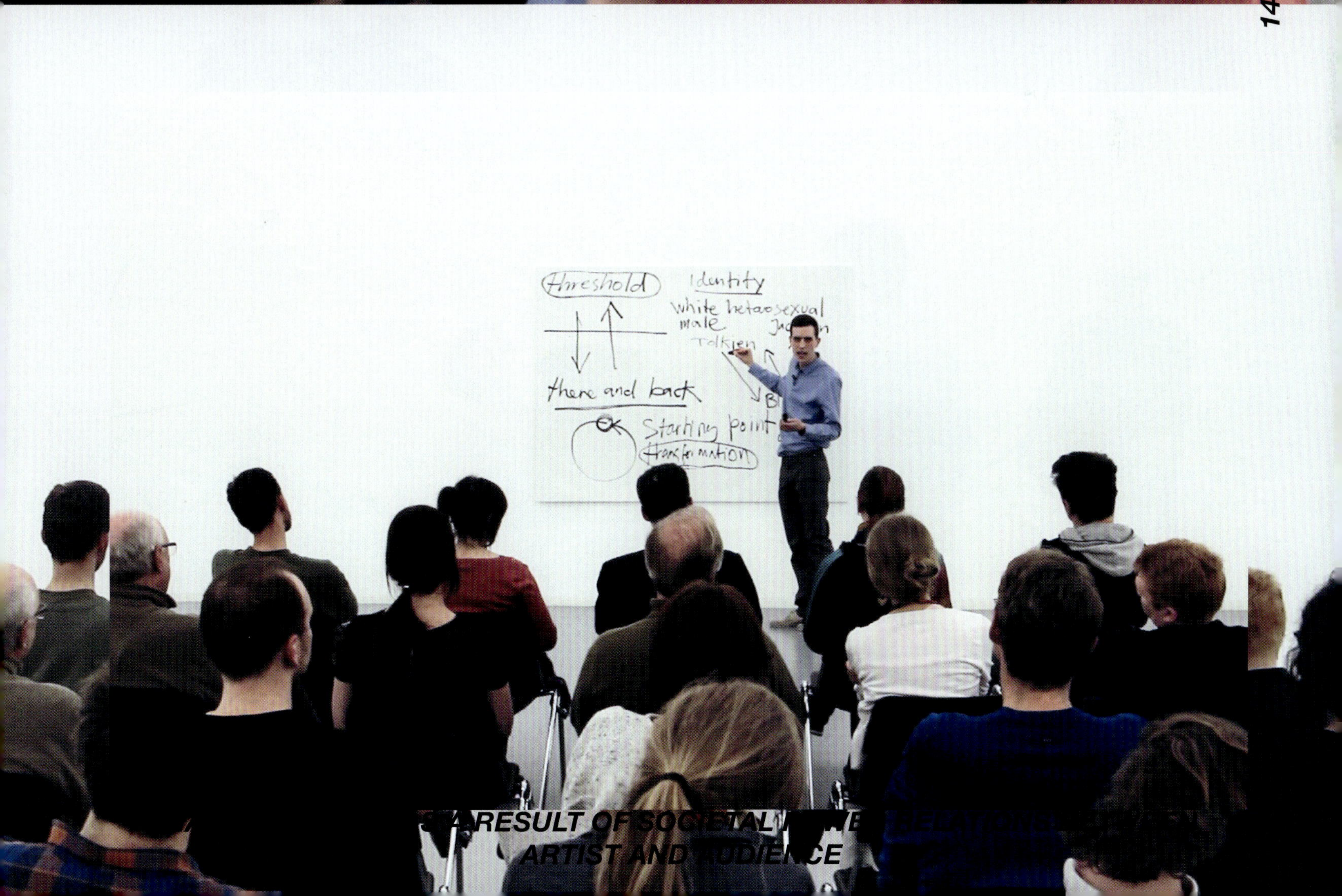

SA RESULT OF SOCIETAL

ARTIST AND AUDIENCE

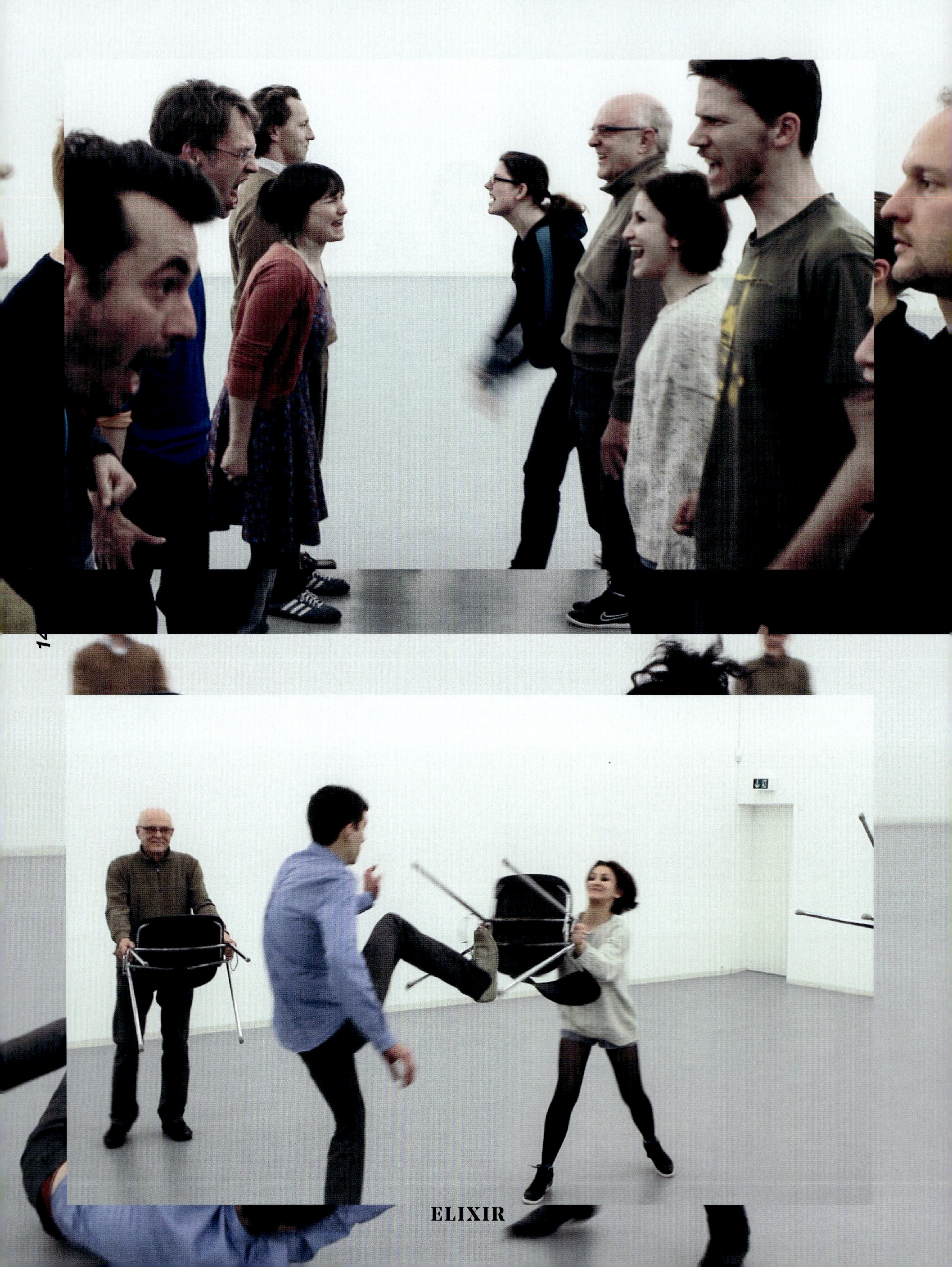

ELIXIR

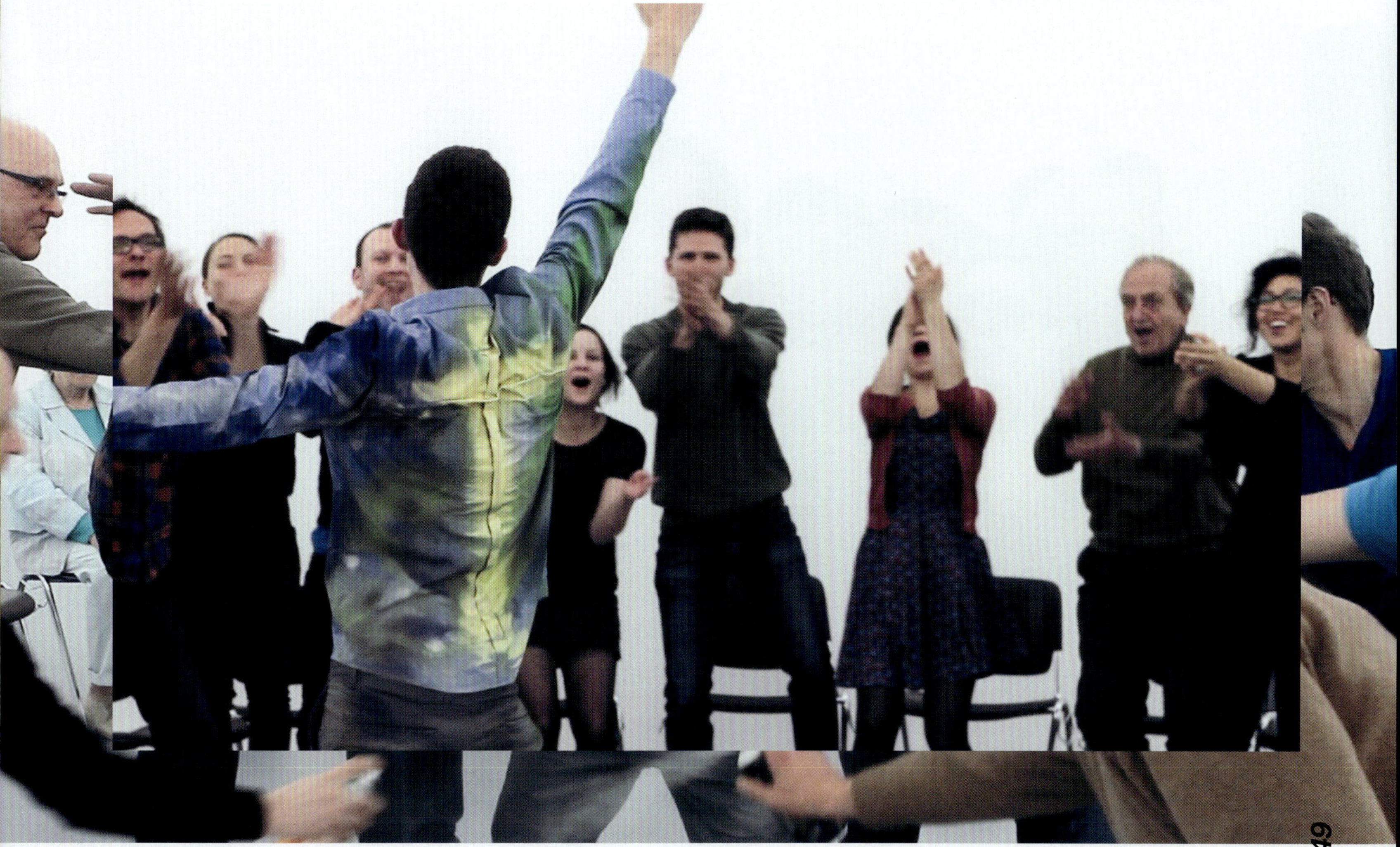

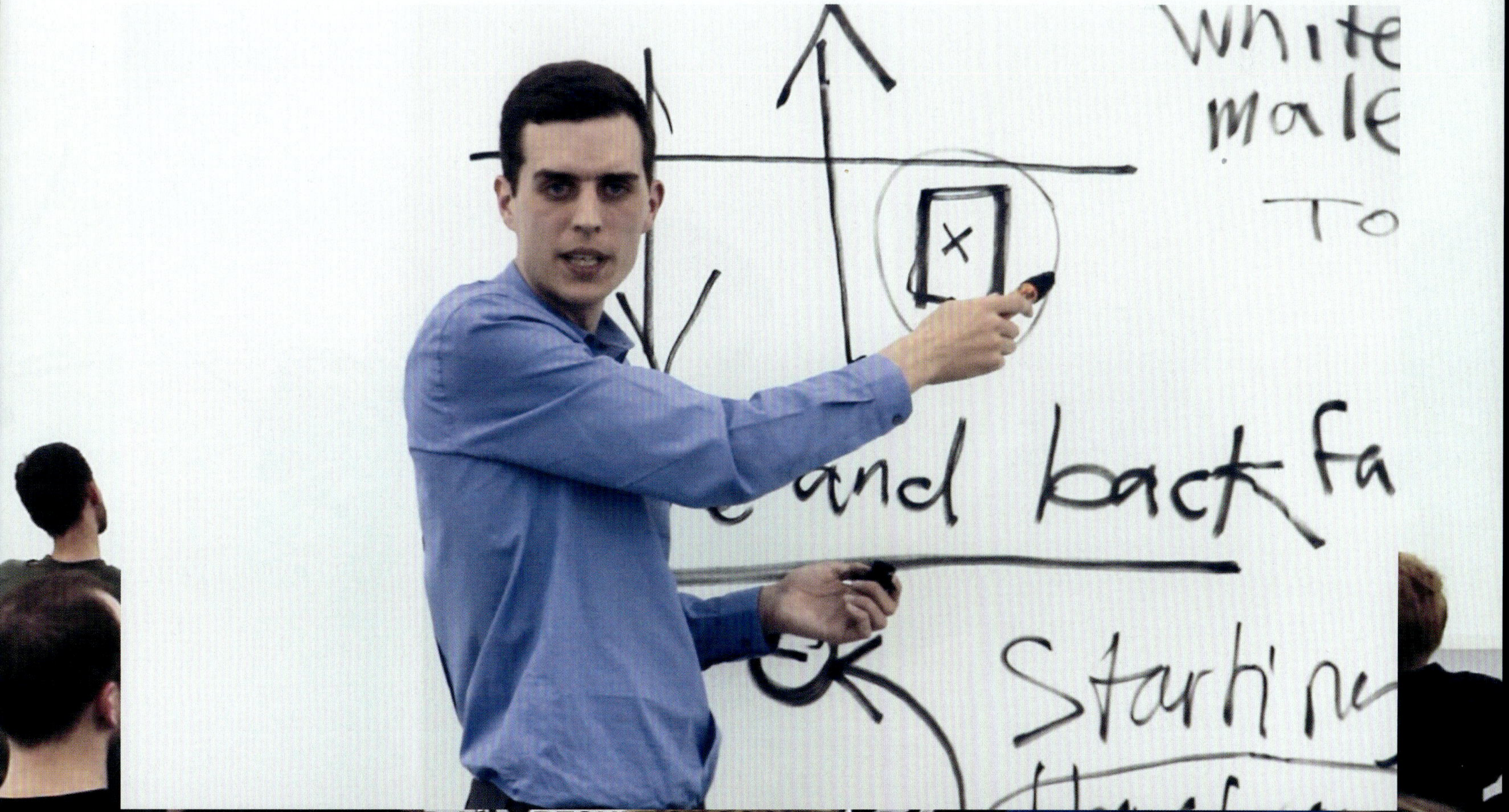

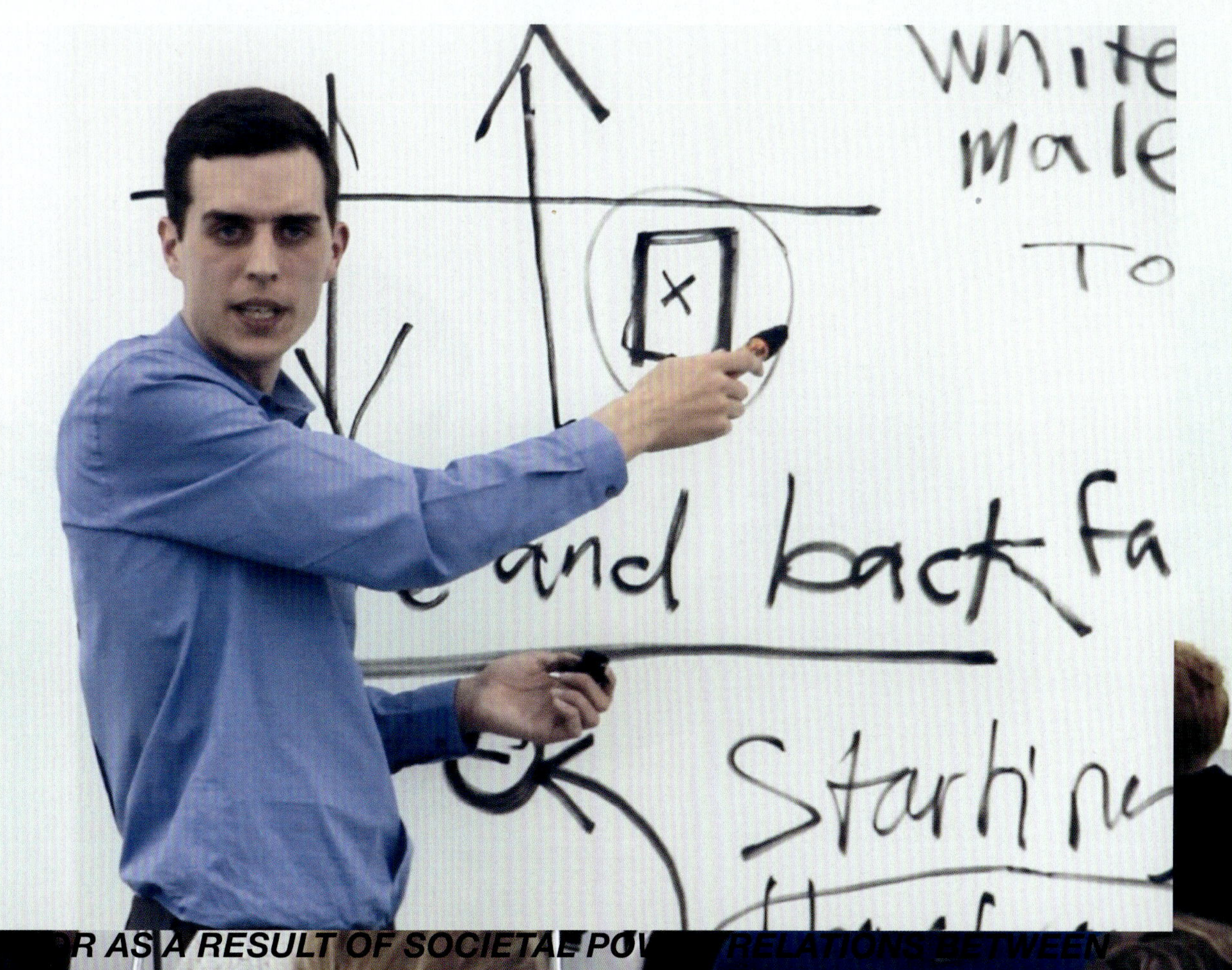

R AS A RESULT OF SOCIETAL POW RELATIONS BETWEEN
ARTIST AND AUDIENC

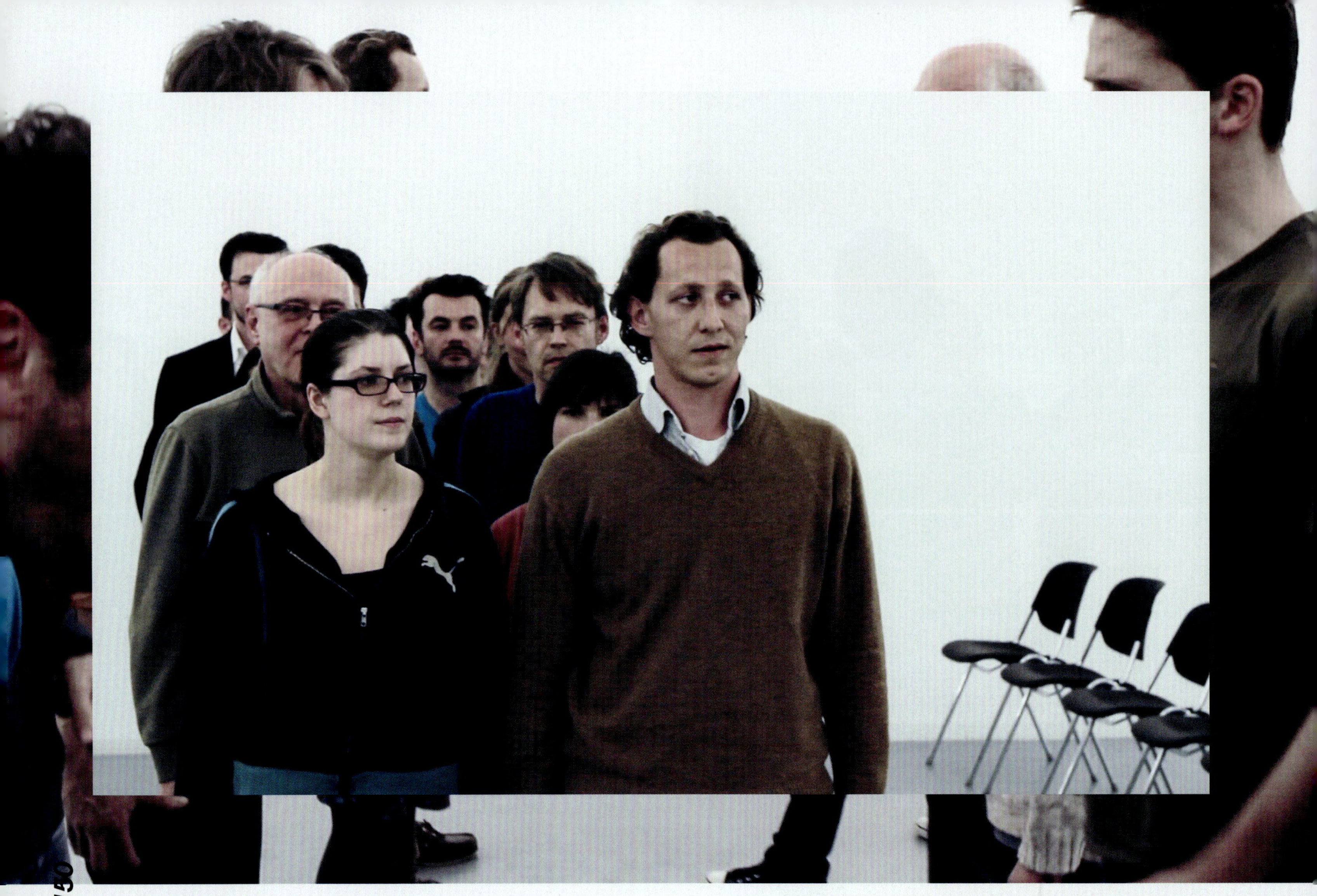

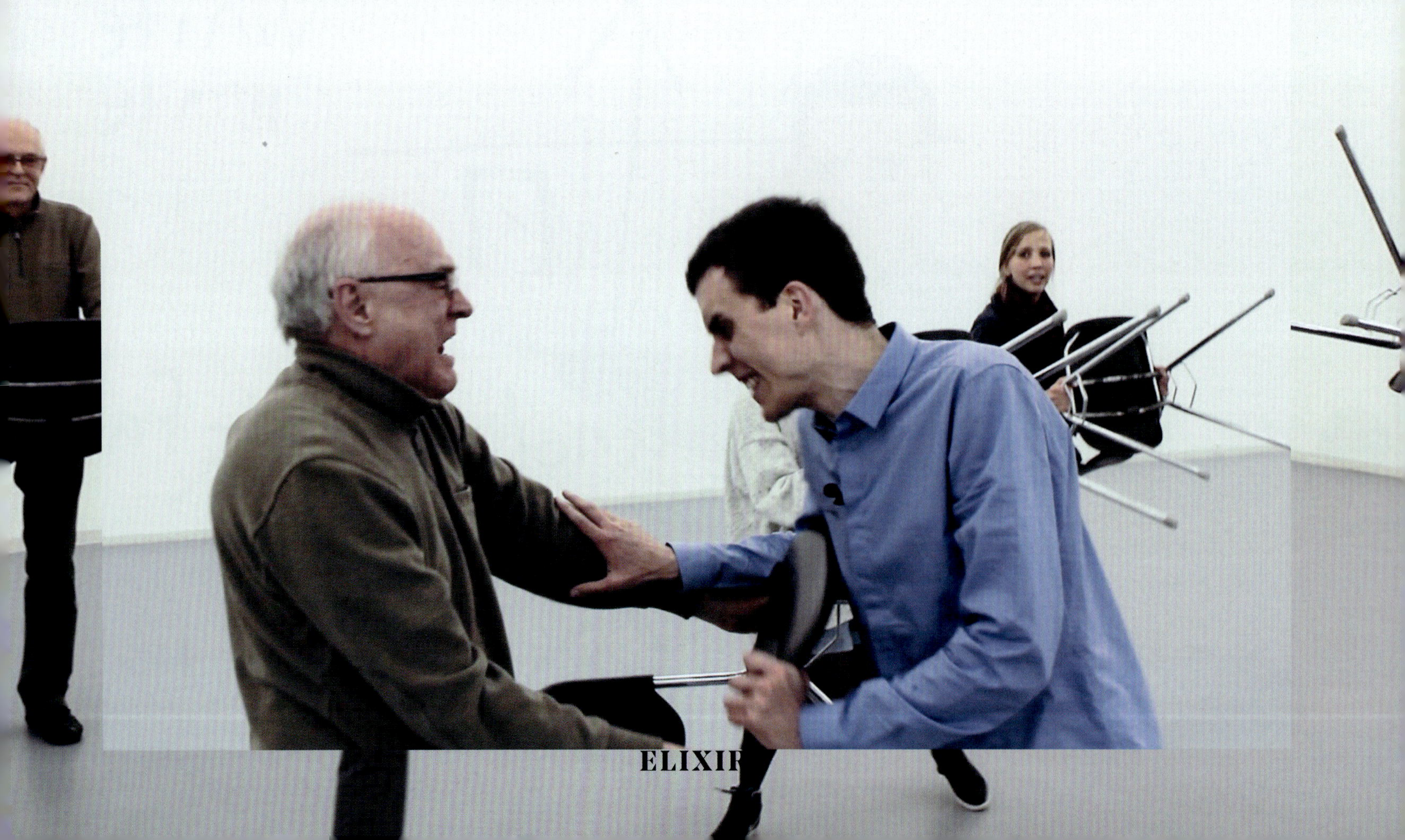

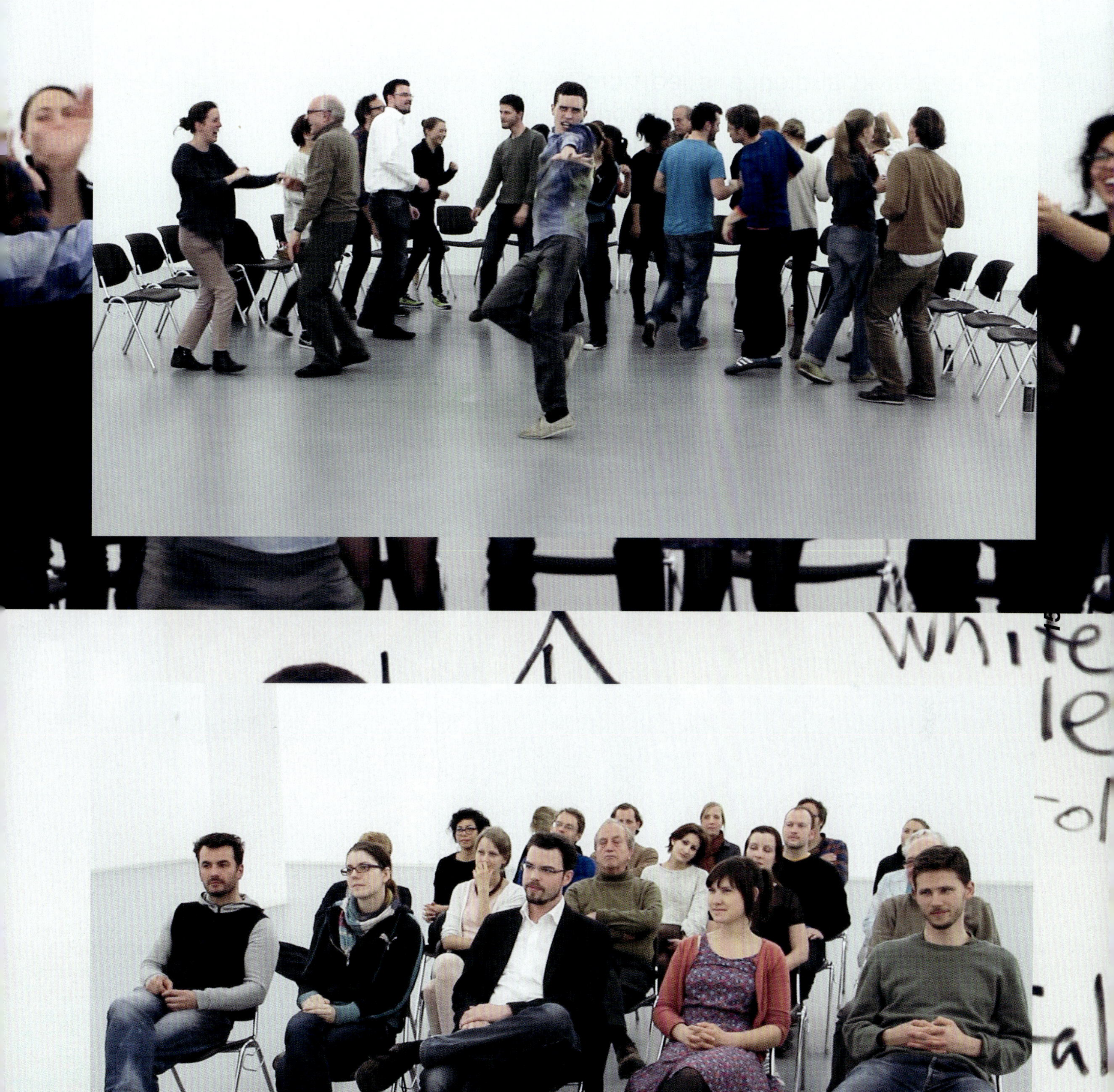

MALE BEHAVIOR AS A RESULT OF SOCIETAL POWER RELATIONS BETWEEN ARTIST AND AUDIENCE

(2012)

Performance
Video

An unprepared audience is led from initial reservation to a state of euphoria and celebration revolving around the artist as the center of attention.
The performance is recorded on video.

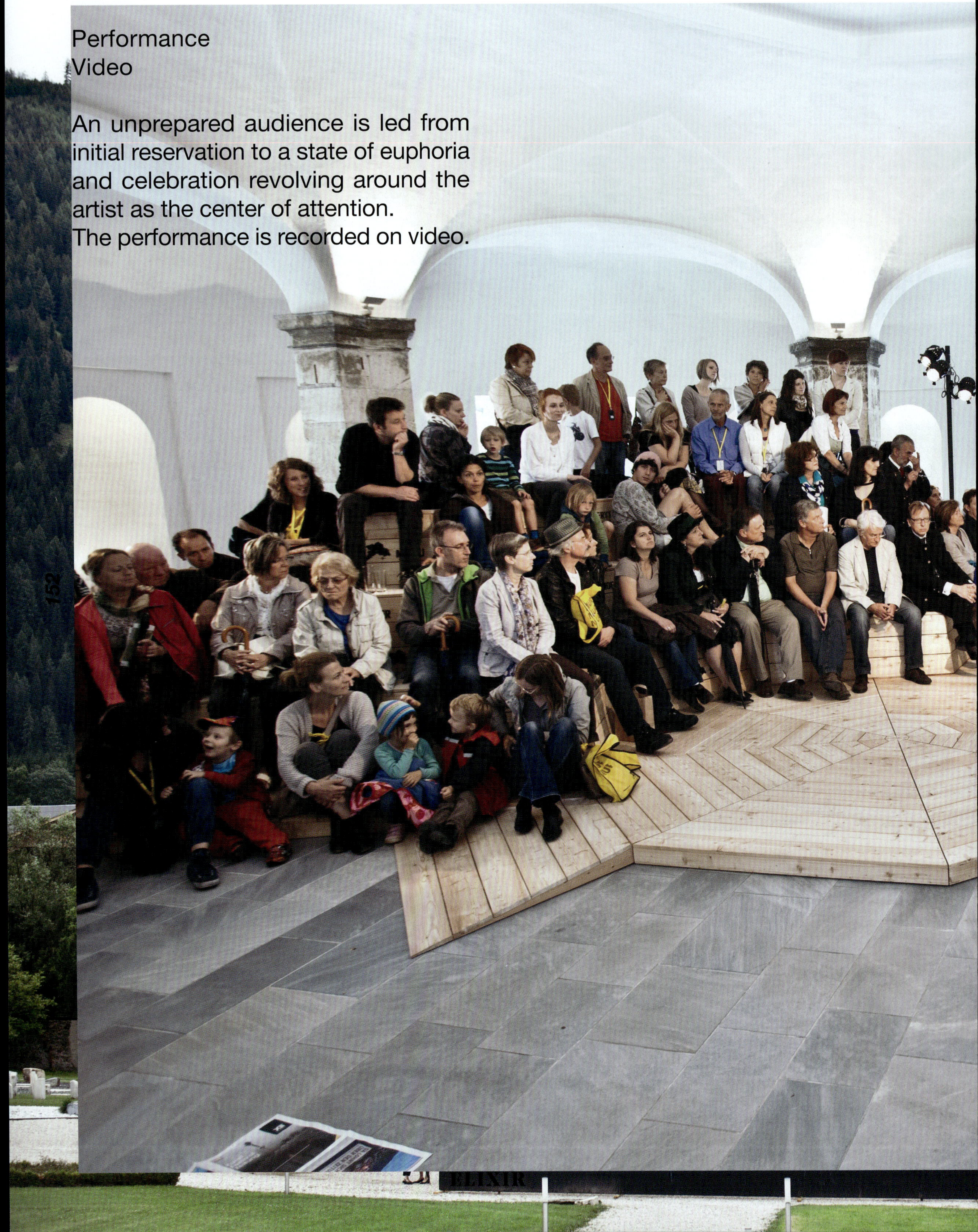

INFLU–
ENCE

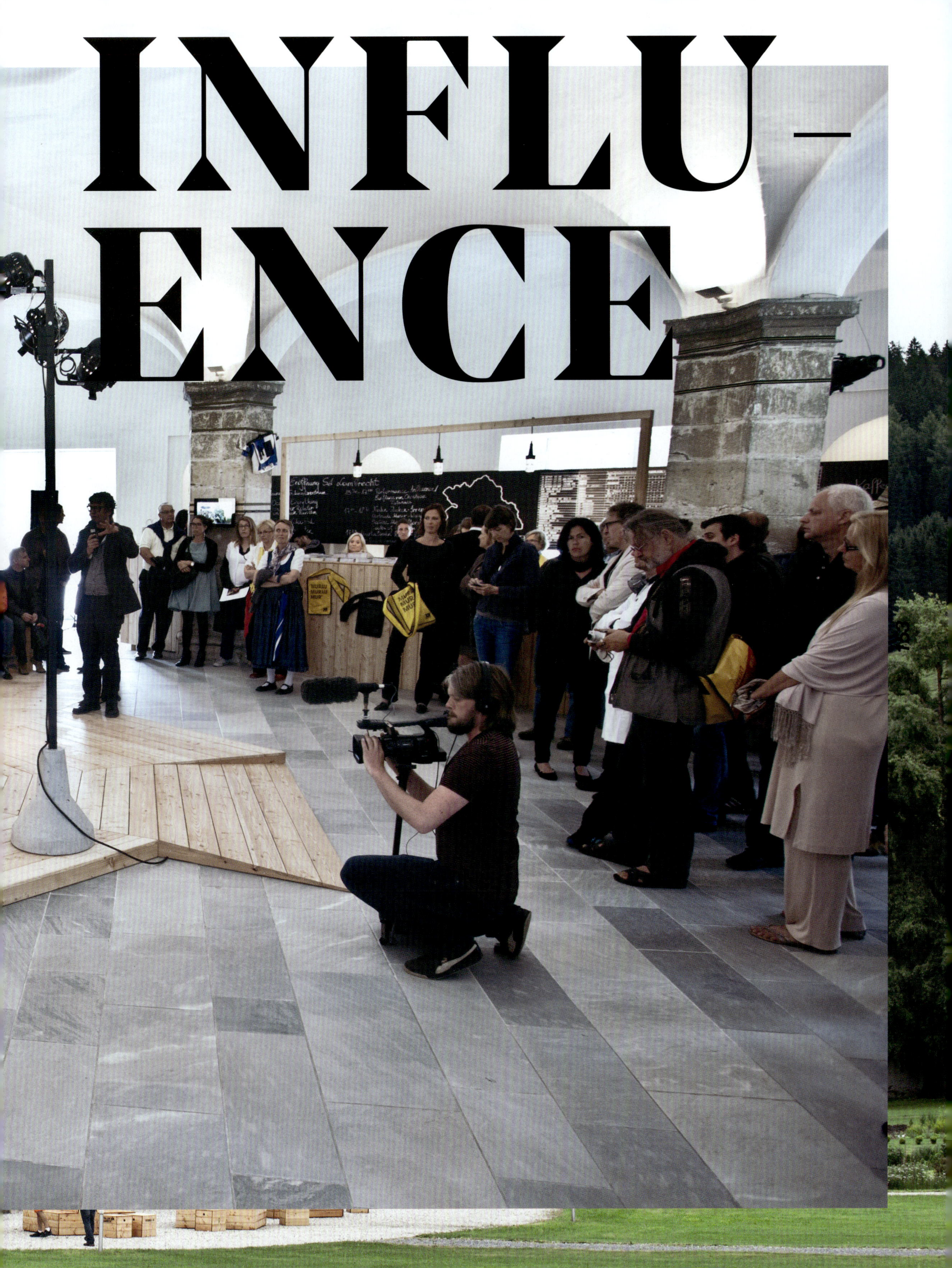

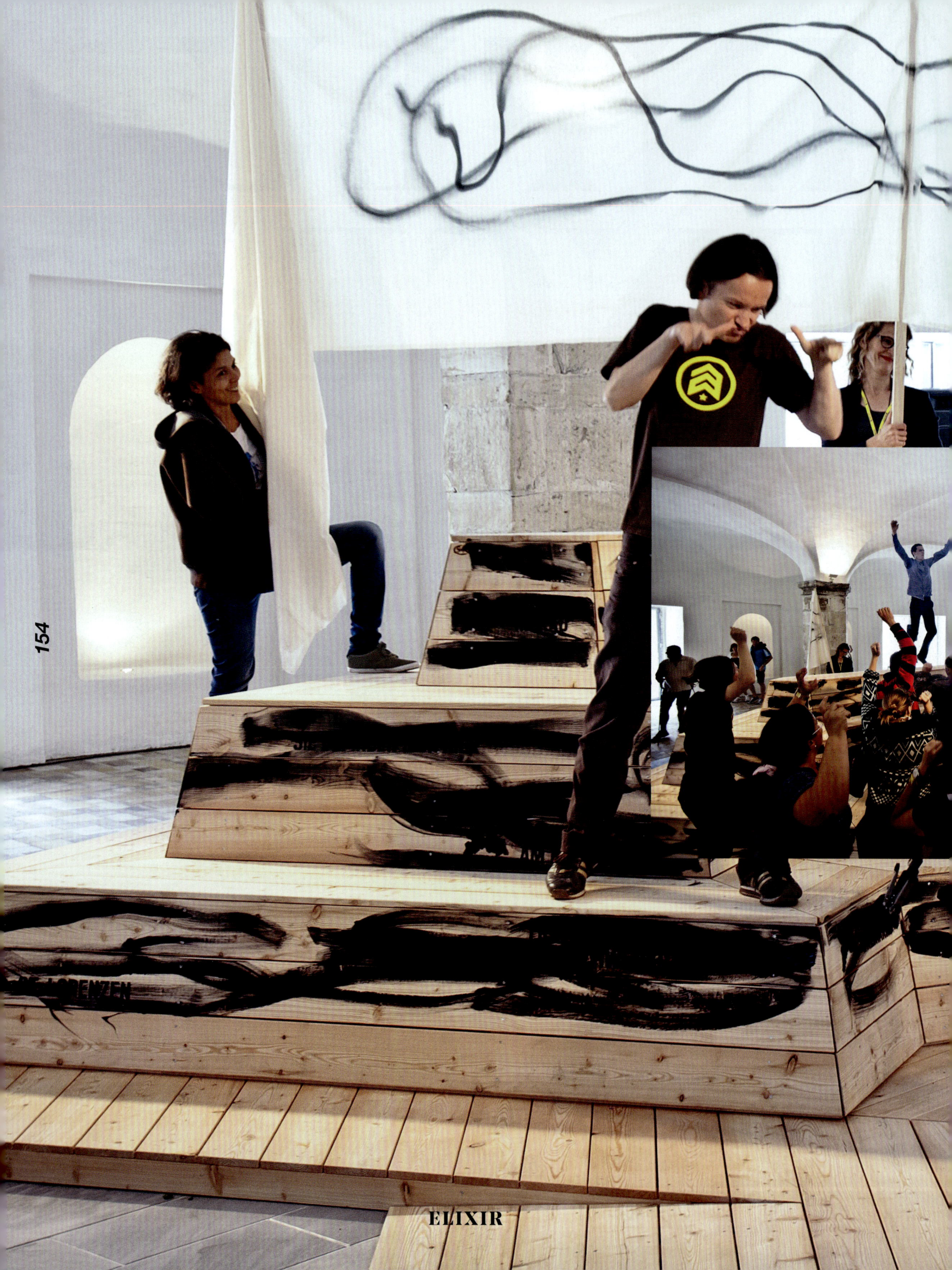

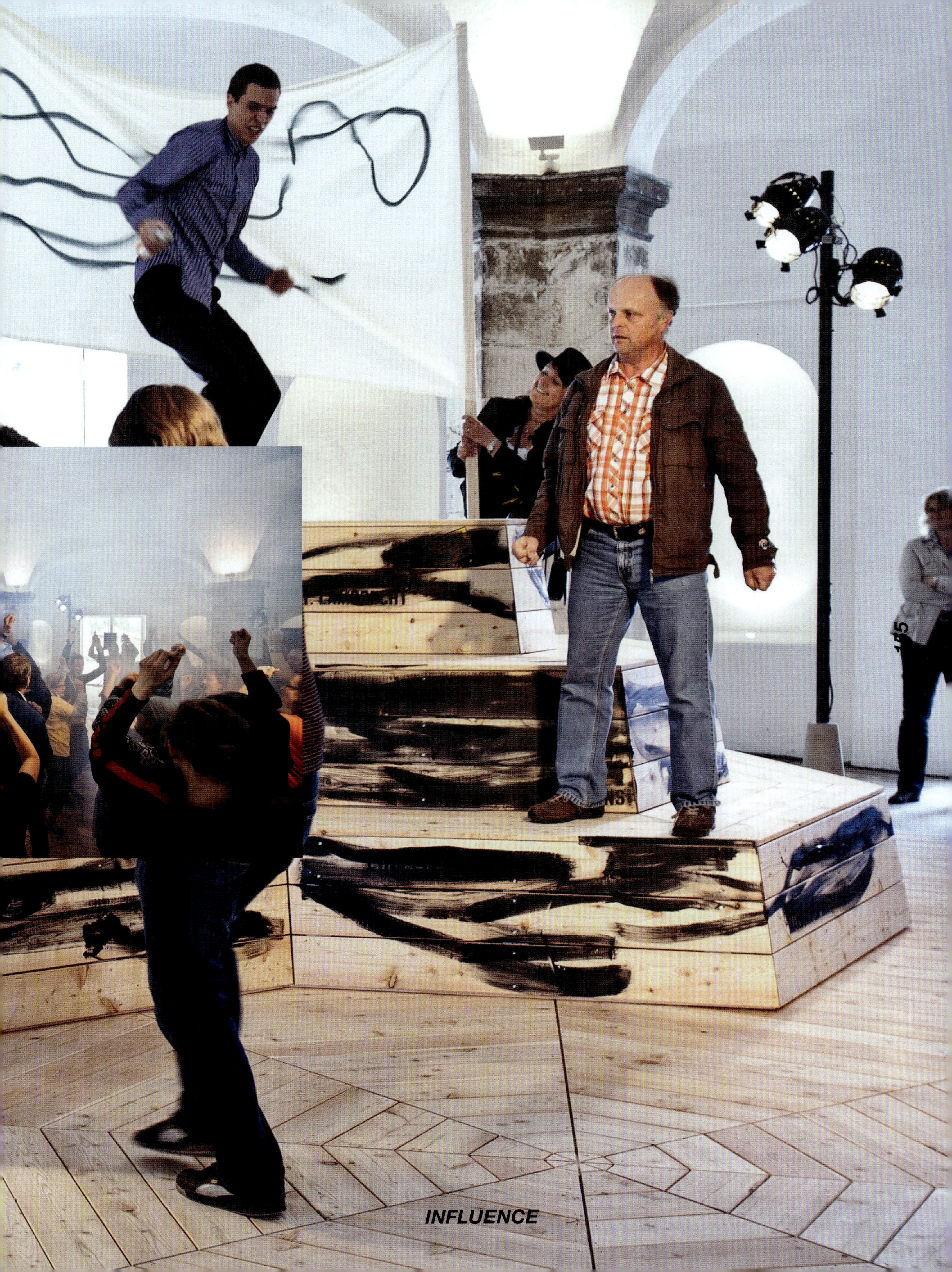

INFLUENCE

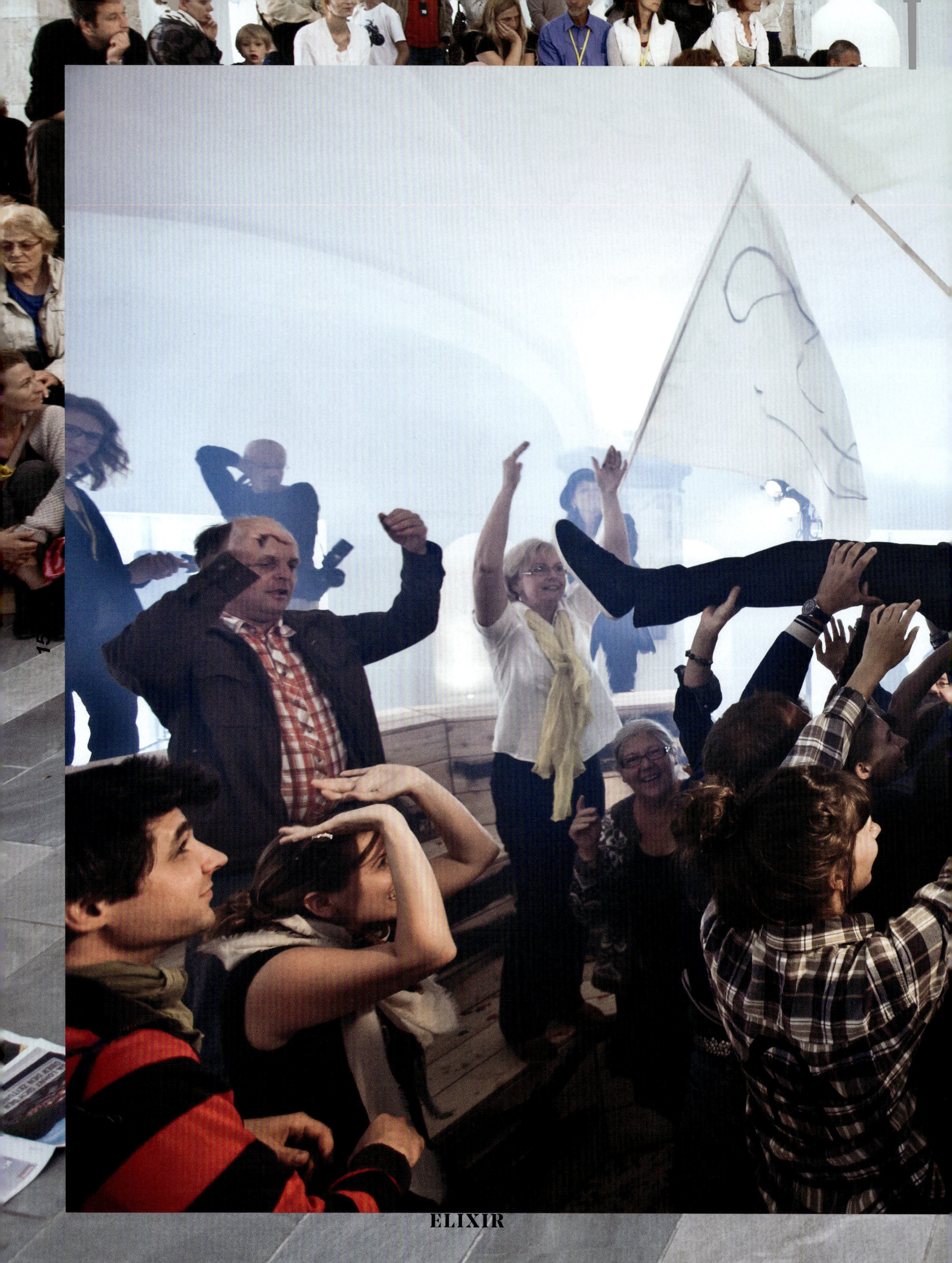

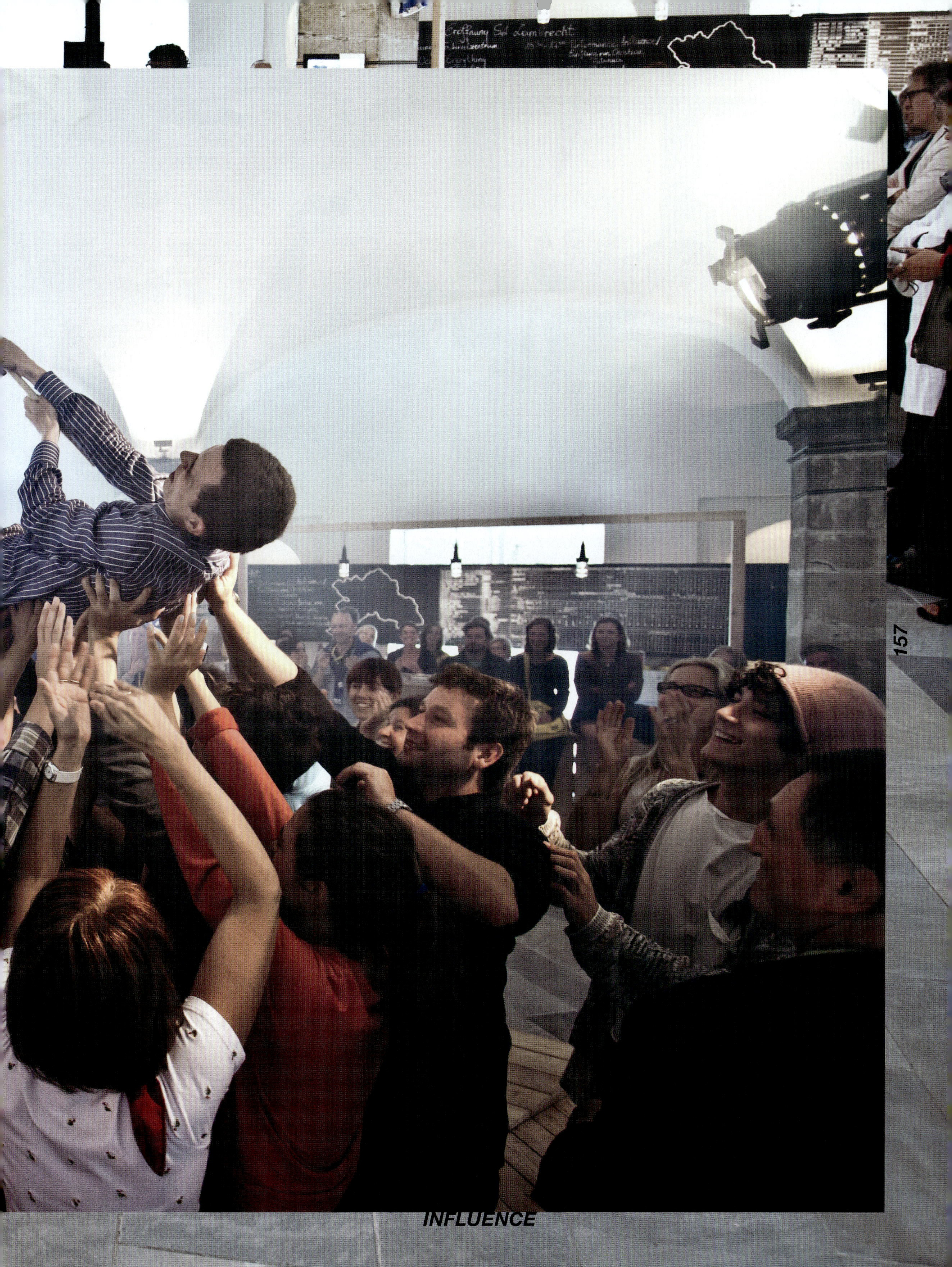

INFLUENCE

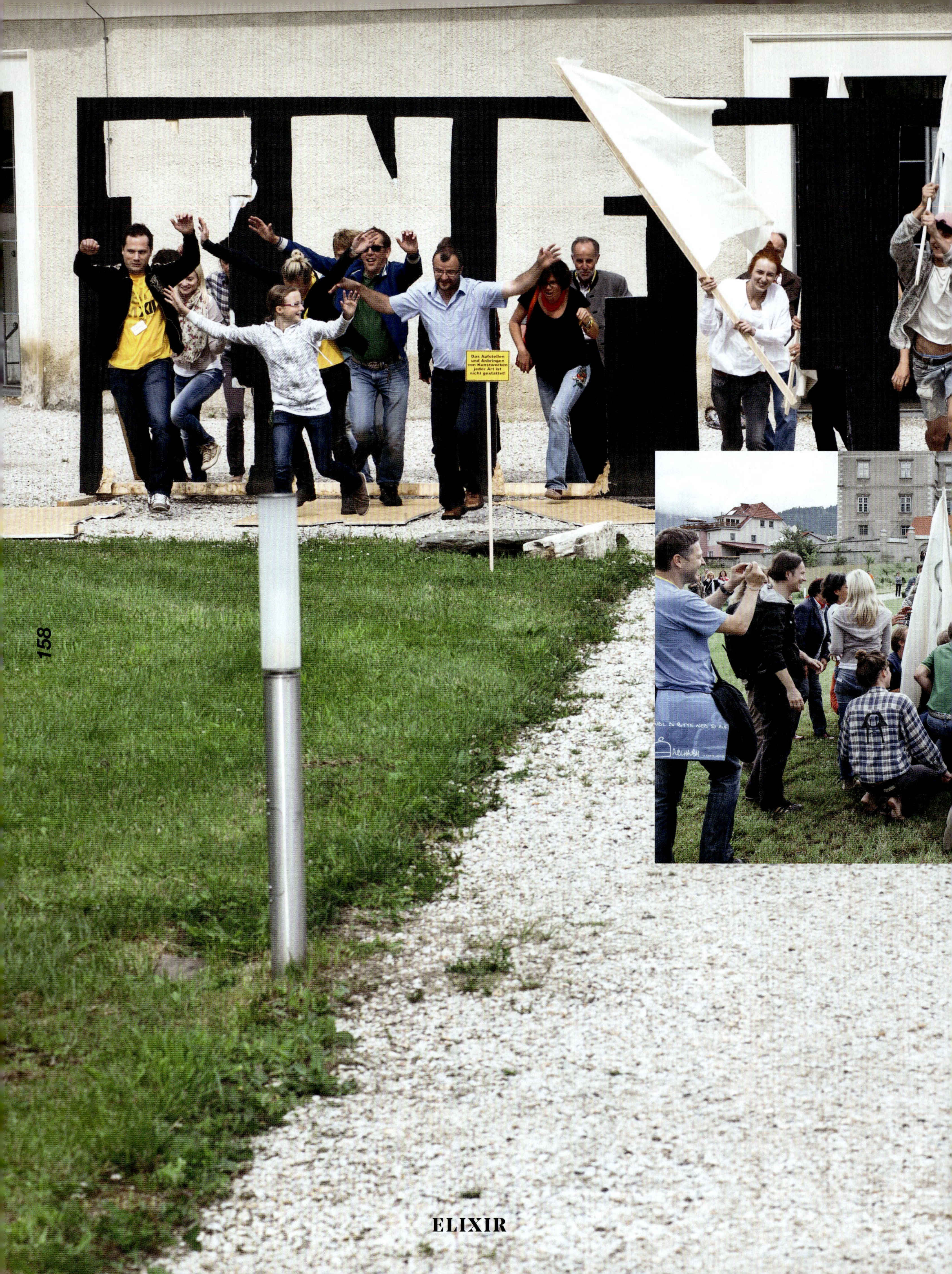
Das Aufstellen
und Anbringen
von Kunstwerken
jeder Art ist
nicht gestattet!

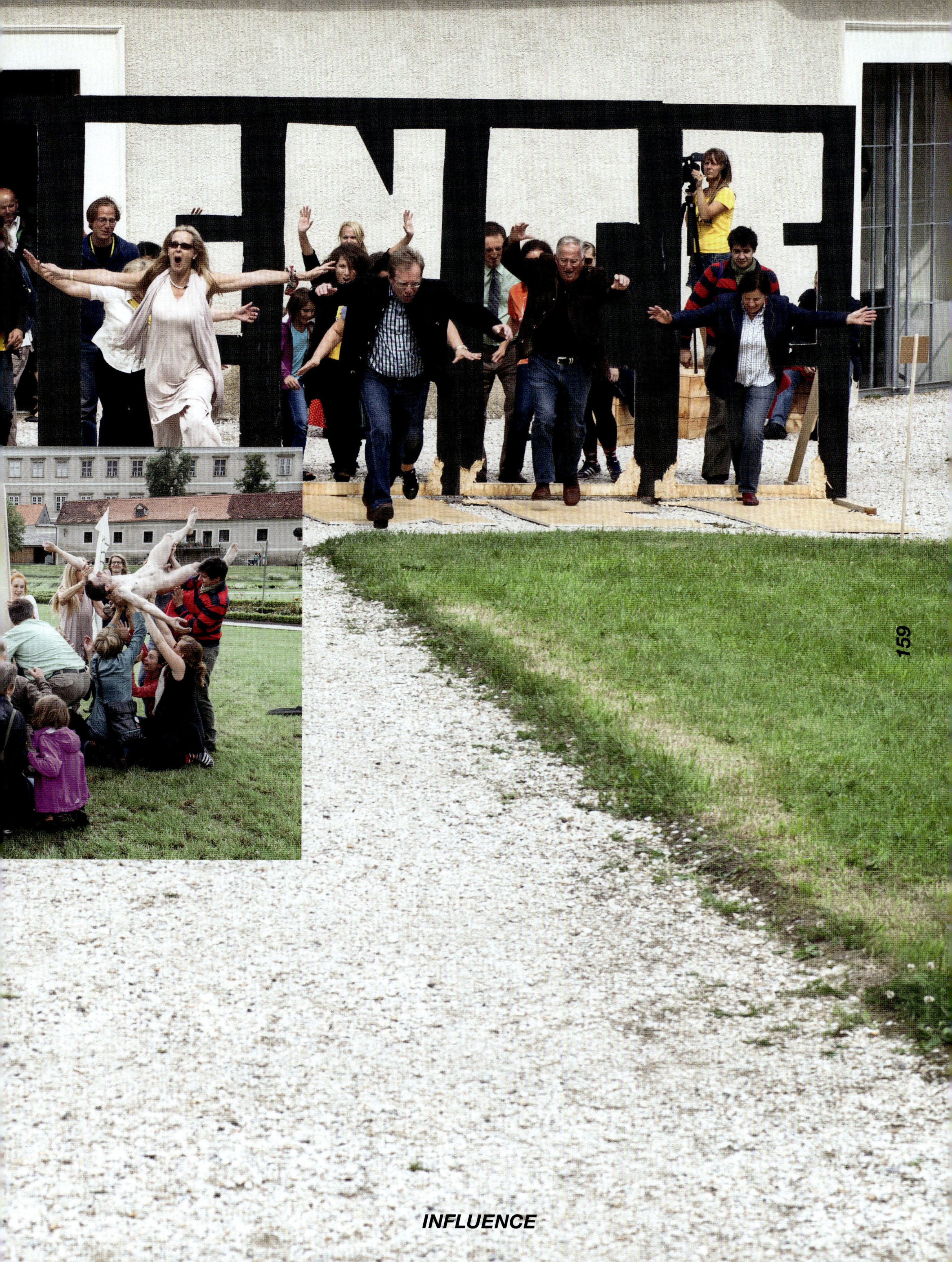

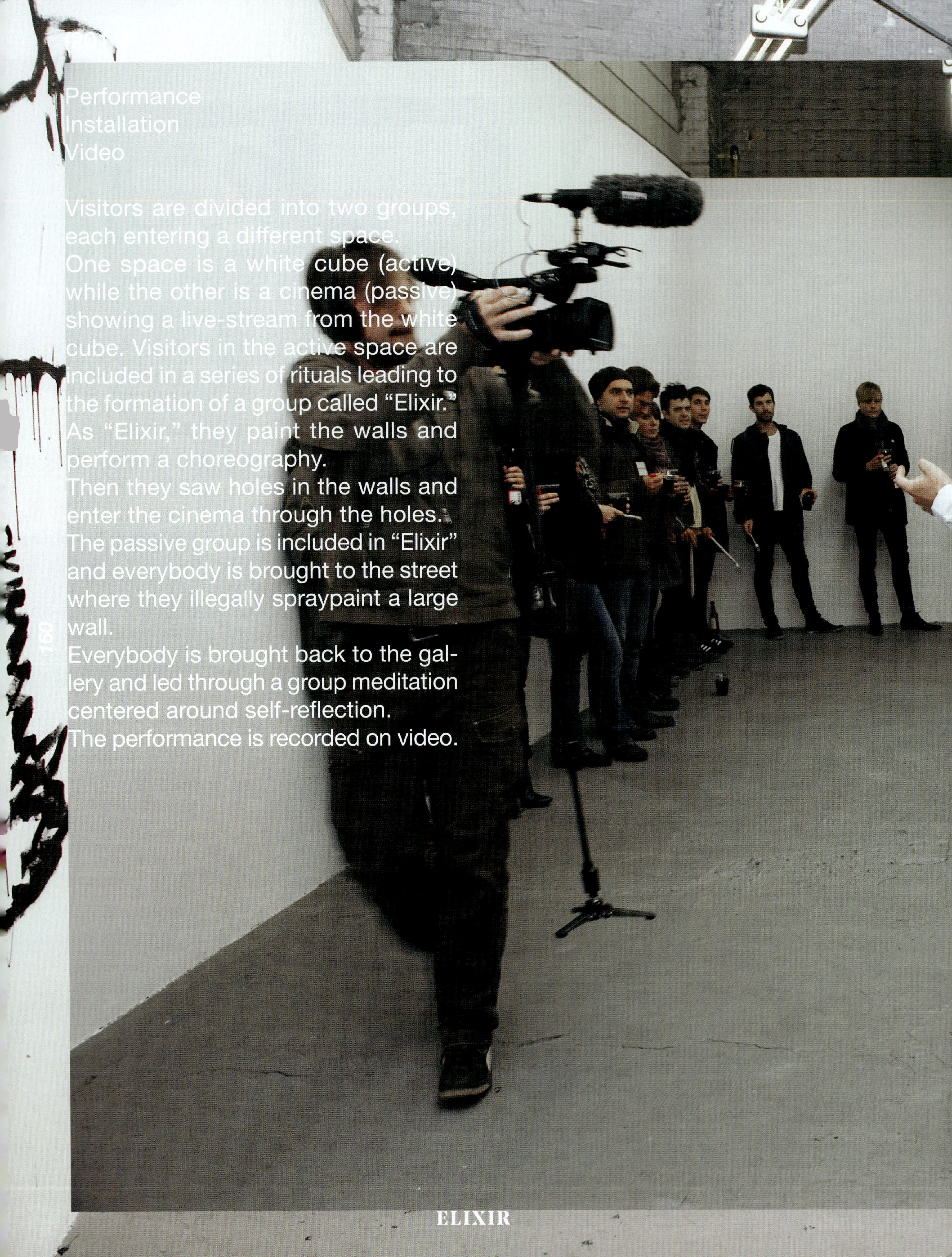

Performance
Installation
Video

Visitors are divided into two groups, each entering a different space.
One space is a white cube (active) while the other is a cinema (passive) showing a live-stream from the white cube. Visitors in the active space are included in a series of rituals leading to the formation of a group called “Elixir.”
As “Elixir,” they paint the walls and perform a choreography.
Then they saw holes in the walls and enter the cinema through the holes.
The passive group is included in “Elixir” and everybody is brought to the street where they illegally spraypaint a large wall.
Everybody is brought back to the gallery and led through a group meditation centered around self-reflection.
The performance is recorded on video.

ELIXIR

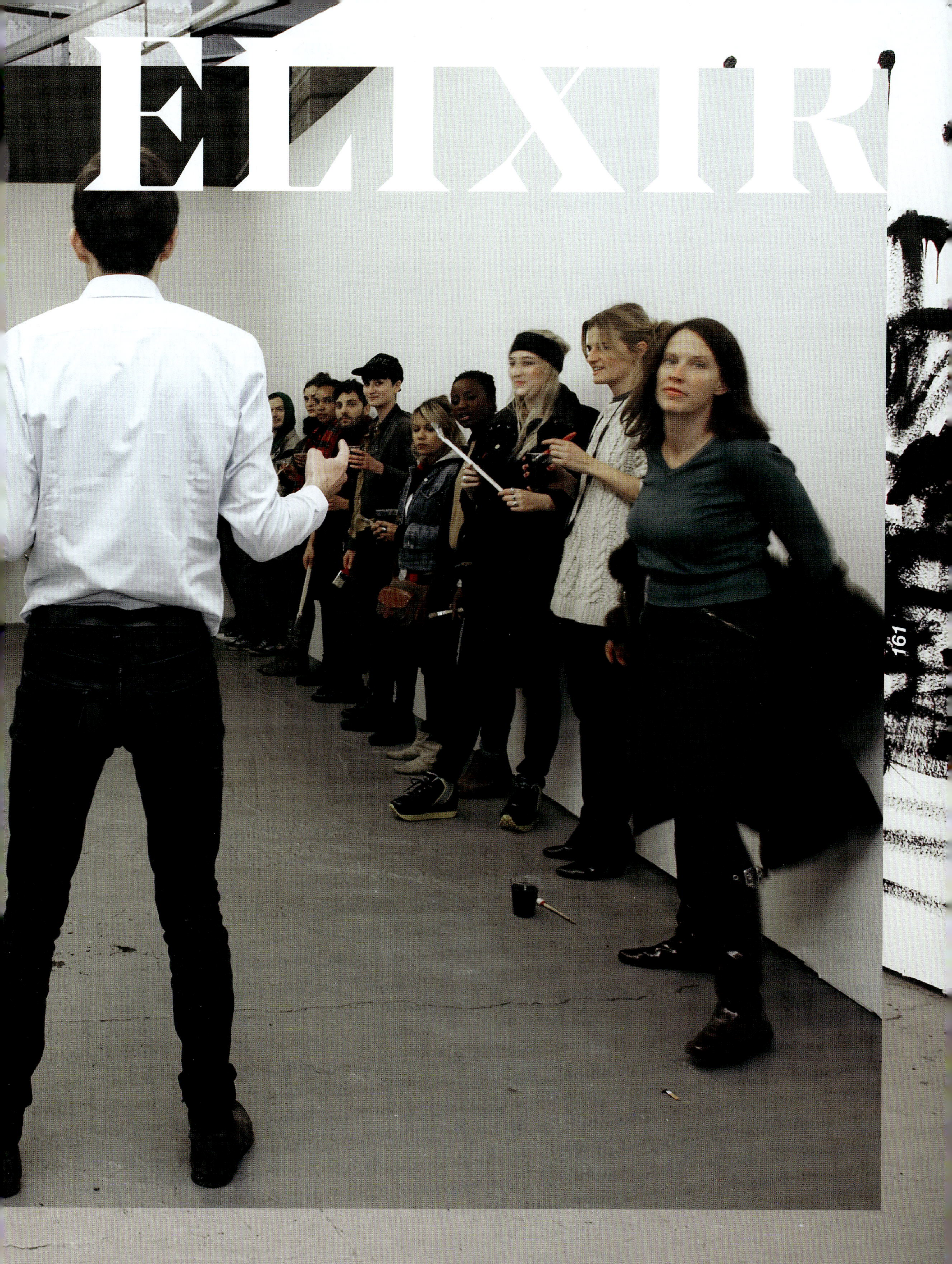
ELIXIR

ELIXIR (2011)

Text by Carson Chan

Though I wasn't there in person, I will always remember a quote from photographs I've seen of Christian Falsnaes's 2008 performance, *Rational Animal*. In a museum, Christian is sitting at a desk in a suit, which he'll be taking off before long. Projected on a screen behind the artist are the words: A good reason is one that looks like one. It's a phrase that I've turned over in my mind many times, particularly when thinking about Christian's work. (Did he write it? Who cares.) To give reason a physical semblance—a *look*—is a perplexing thought. How something looks is an effect; Reason is the cause. The phrase throws both "good" and "reason," or perhaps "the good" and "the reasonable," into question. More interesting is that by qualifying a cause with its visual manifestation, by claiming that the better concept is also better looking, the phrase inverts the relationship between a thing and its representation. The representation, it seems, precedes the thing.

I was in the audience of *ELIXIR* (2011). Christian had built a wall bisecting his gallery in Berlin, PSM, down the middle. Attendees were placed on either side: about a dozen on one side, an empty white room, and everyone else was seated on benches watching a live-feed projection of the chosen few, with Christian among them. At some point, Christian, in a button down shirt, begins to rally the group. He paces around, his voice raised. "We're going to take a journey," he tells them, and to journey together, they needed to "feel as a group." "We are: Elixir," and at that moment, they had a name—they became a community, if only by chance of proximity and by name. They were given black paint and told to paint whatever they liked on the walls. Christian narrated the group into formation. "This is the moment you have been waiting for. Right now! Right here! We are Elixir!" The artist led the group in synchronized fist pumps, chants, and group hugs. Pointing at the wall dividing the gallery, he shouted, "This wall prevents us from growing, from living our true potential, and from having hope for the future!" He gave out handsaws and instructed the group to cut holes in the wall. As the blade came through, what I saw on the live feed, what was second-hand, suddenly became first-hand experience. They all came through the wall to where we were seated, Christian passed cans of spray paint around as members of Elixir were instructed to nail the cut out fragments of the wall onto a wooden frame. "Everyone of you," he yelled out at us on the benches, "go one after another and write the name," pointing at the recomposed fragments. And one after another, people got up and sprayed "ELIXIR" on this new surface, christening a gathering of people who's purpose earlier in the night was little more than to mill around with beer at a gallery opening. (In protest to being commanded, I wrote "FUCK YOU" instead.) By now, Christian was singing over a piano accompaniment ("Joy is to win what you love…"), everyone was led in cheers, and then by force of assembly, they followed the artist out of the gallery, into the night and onto the streets, where they shouted out their new name in unison as they sprayed it on a wall. The audience became a faction of a purposeless movement, a force without a cause other than the self-propelling drive of a communal identity called *ELIXIR*. It had no internal reason for being, but it looked like it did.

An elixir is nothing if not the manifestation of belief, as well as its test. It is a magic potion, relying on faith, not knowledge, for its ability to work. In Plato's *Ion*, Socrates and an actor named Ion agree that an actor's ability to deliver beautifully written lines is not a skill, but "a divine power" moving through him, "like the power in the stone which Euripides calls a magnet." Through divine power, moving from the poet, to the actor, to the audience, and so forth, like a chain of magnetized rings, the actor is rendered a segment of this chain: an "interpreter of interpreters." In a sense, there is no original moment for us mortals. Any work of art is a mere vehicle for conveying the divine. The logical progression of cause and effect we find important for mundane matters is irrelevant here. As suggested by *Rational Animal*, an effect can indeed come before its cause if we see it connected to a longer chain of events.

What is the difference between the *ELIXIR* group acting like a community under Christian's instruction, and actually being one? Can a community arise out of *acting* like a community? Can a purpose emerge from *acting* like a purpose exists? Was the group merely the cast in Christian's theater, or did they cast themselves into new roles? My mind drifts as I ponder this, and I remember Mari Lending's writing on nineteenth and twentieth-century plaster cast collections. The cast of a sculpture is not merely a copy of an original, not merely a representation, but an original occupying its own space and time. In Proust's *Swann's Way*, Lending has observed the narrator's disappointment after a long-awaited visit to a medieval church he had seen previously as a plaster cast fragment in a museum in Paris. The original church was anticipated to be even more striking than the admired cast, but alas, it turned out to be "nothing but its own shape in stone." Here, the copy exceeded the original.

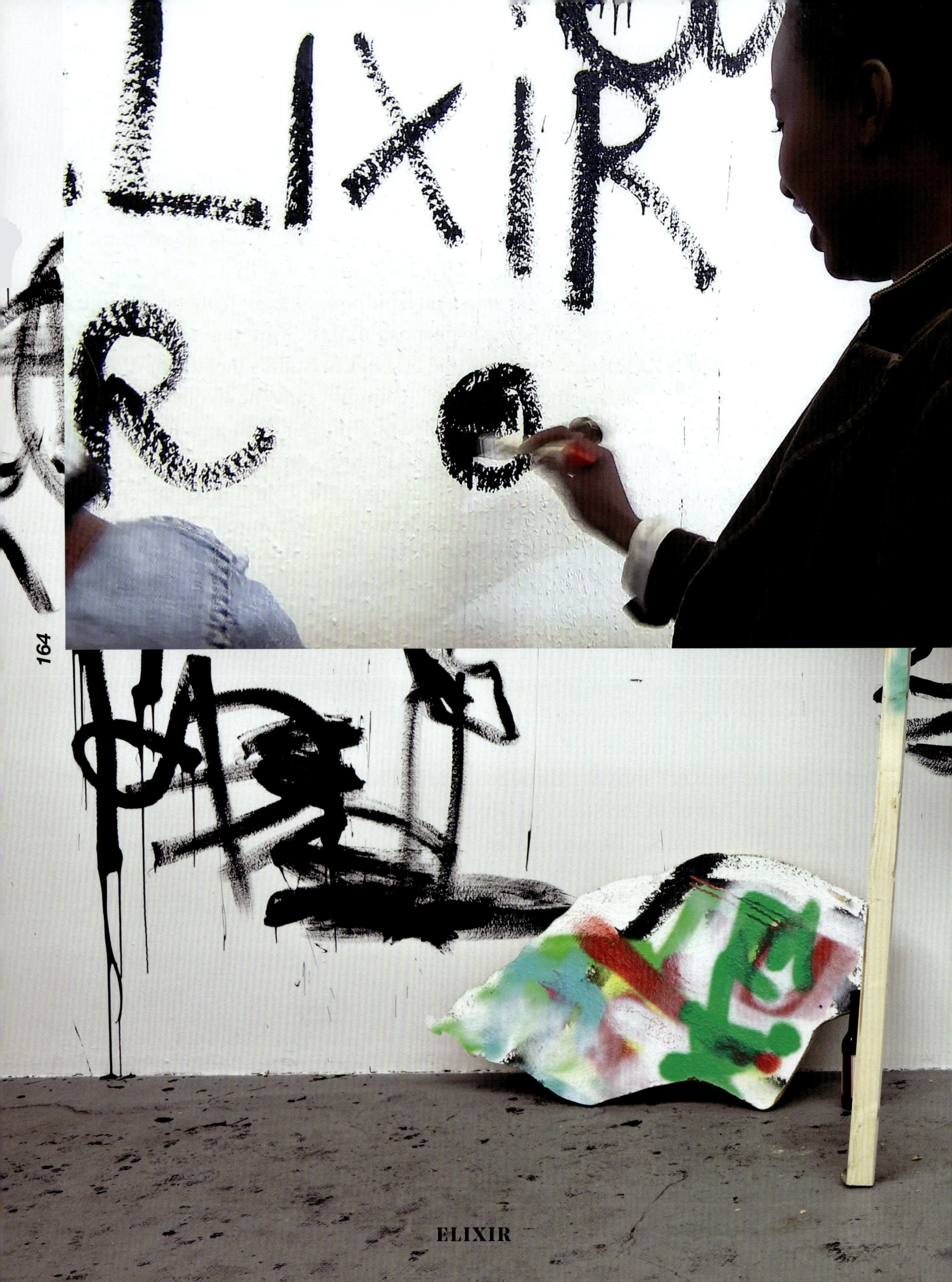
LIXIR

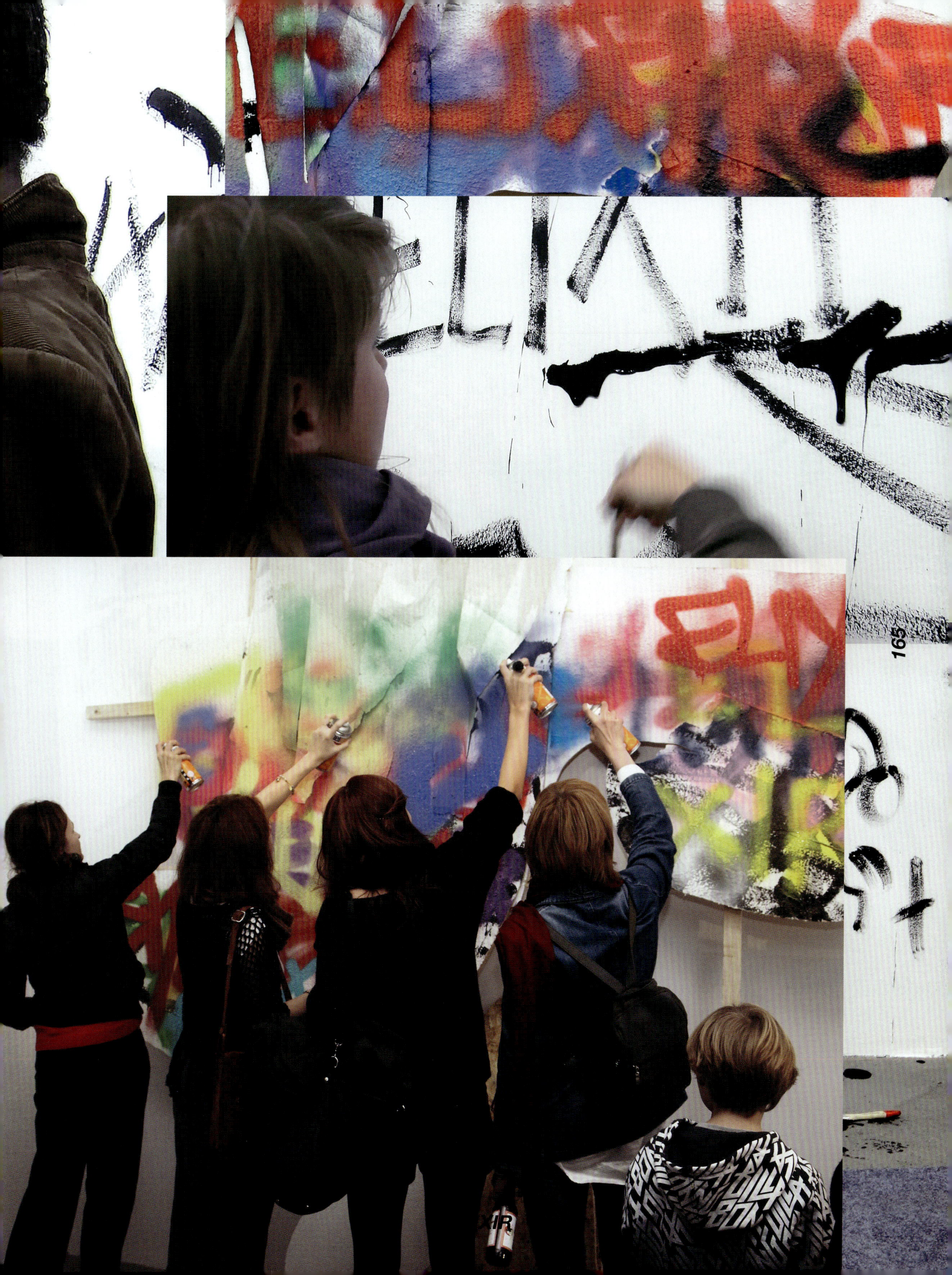

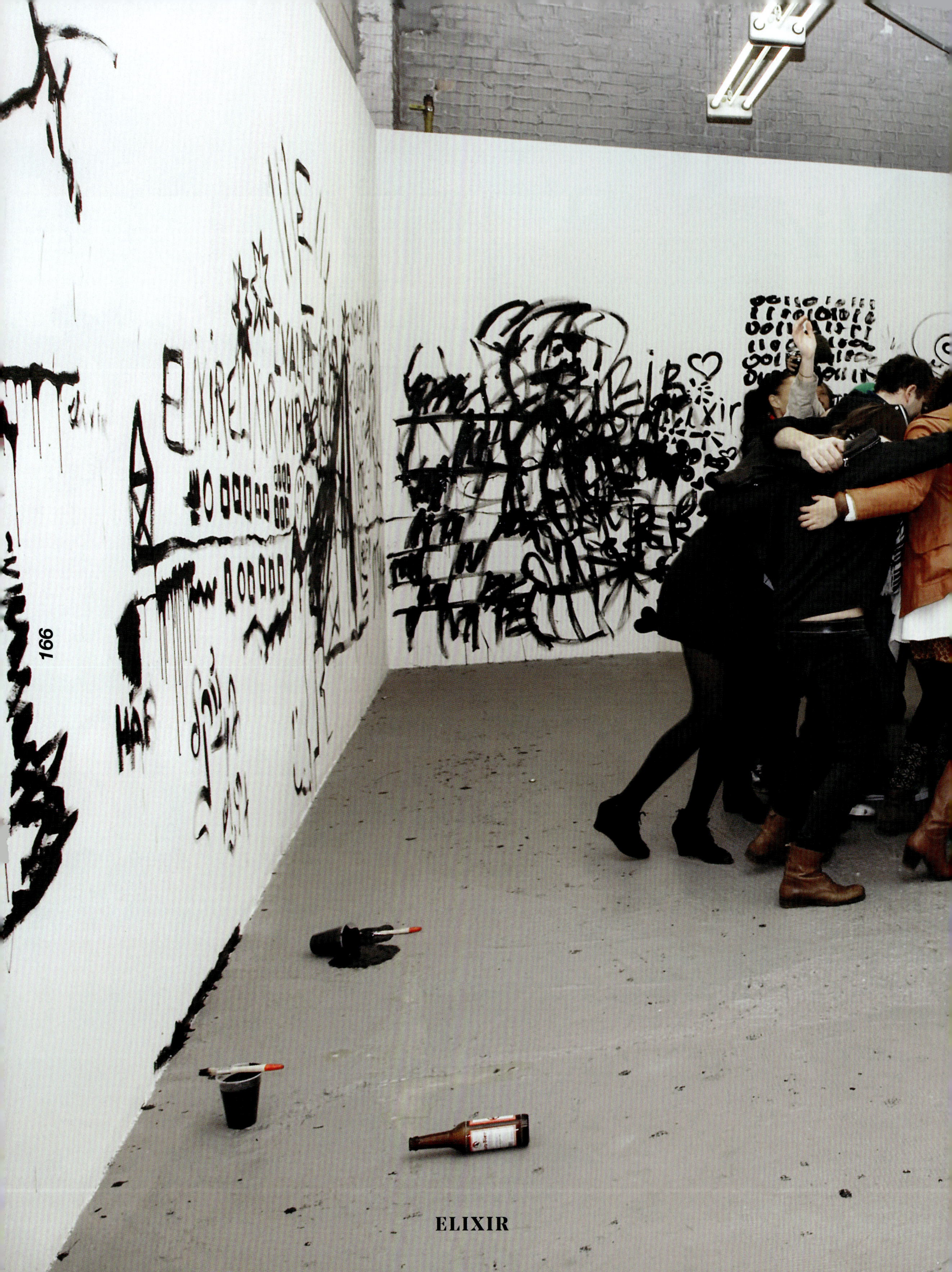

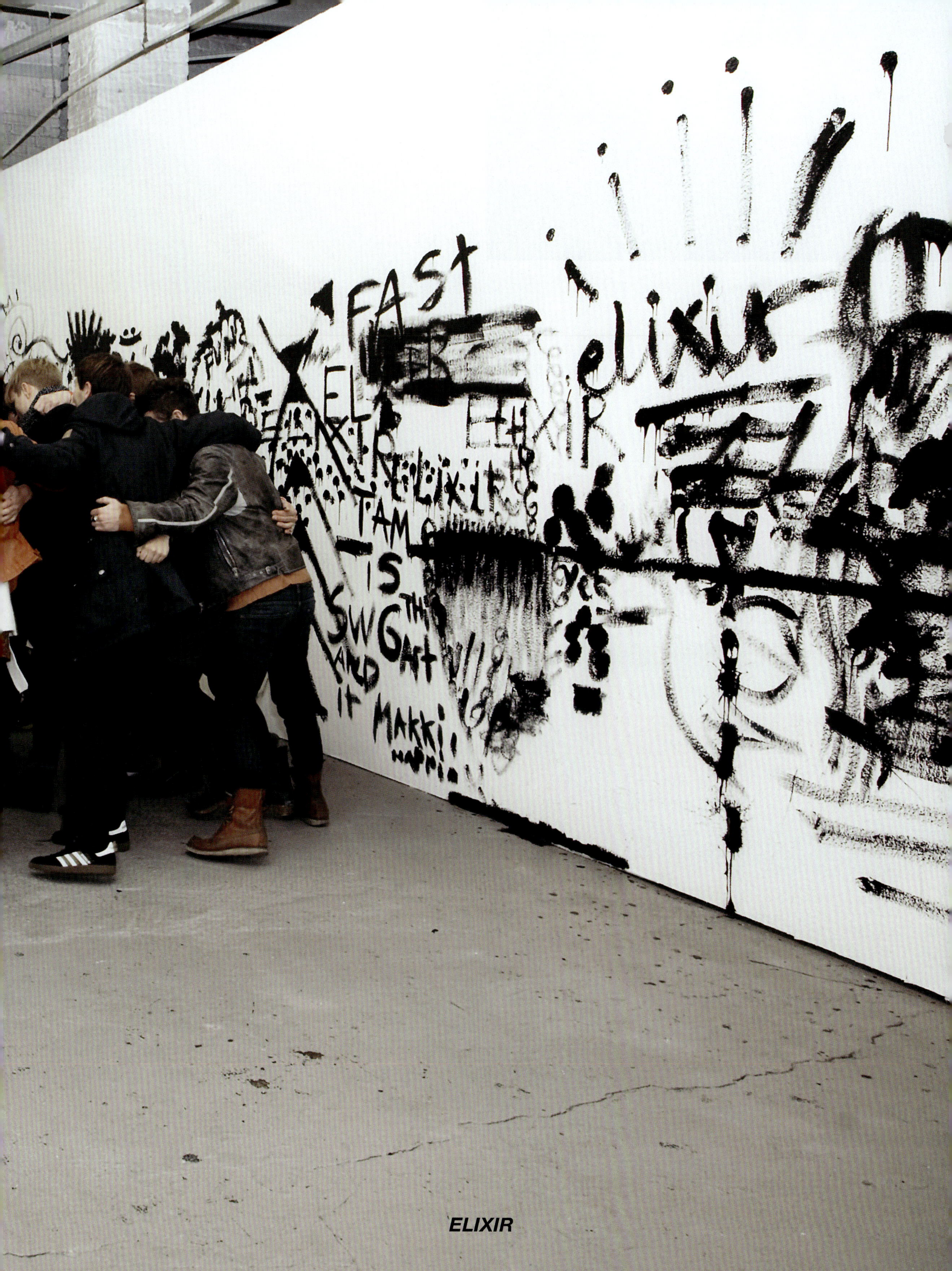

ELIXIR

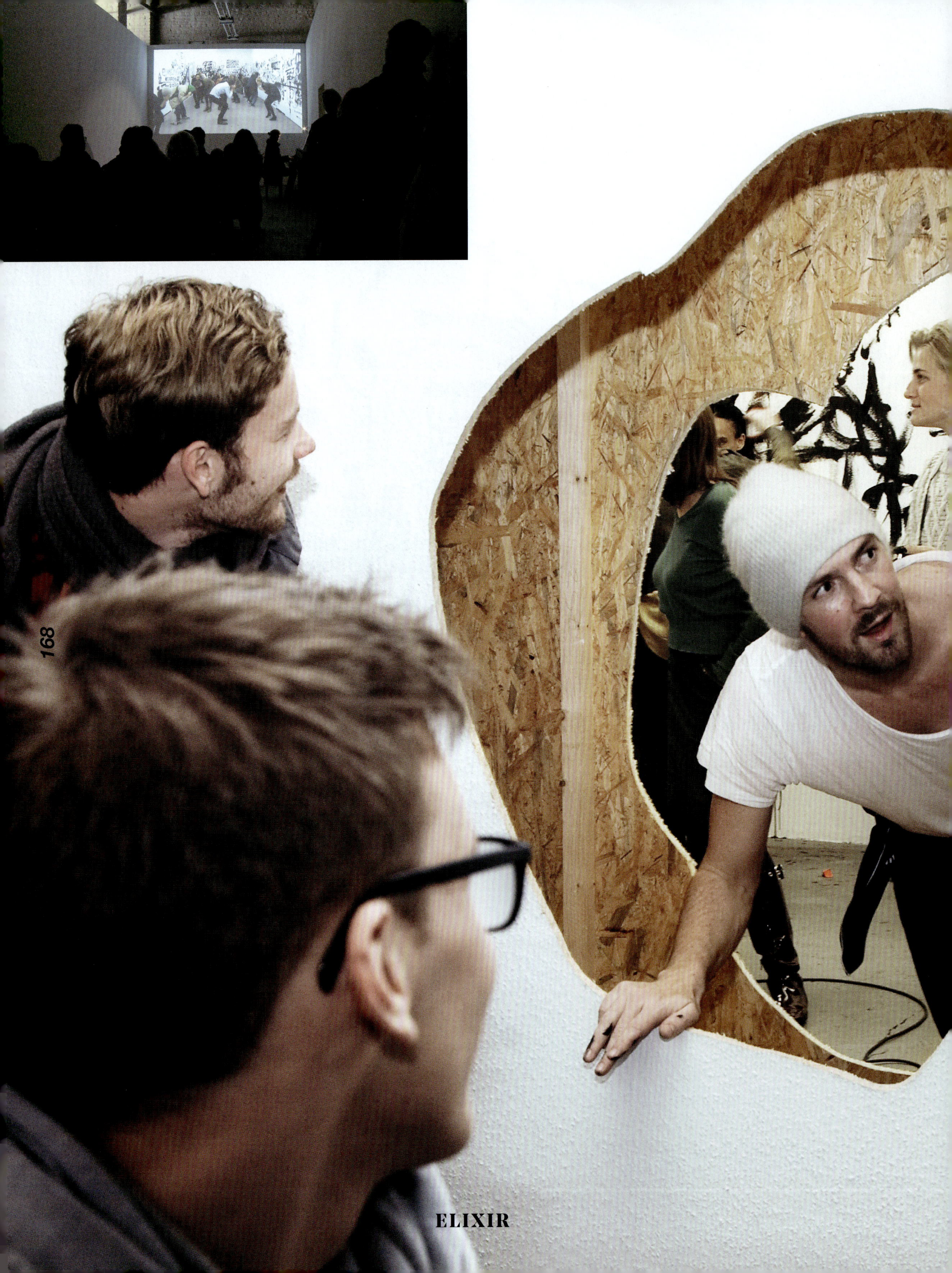

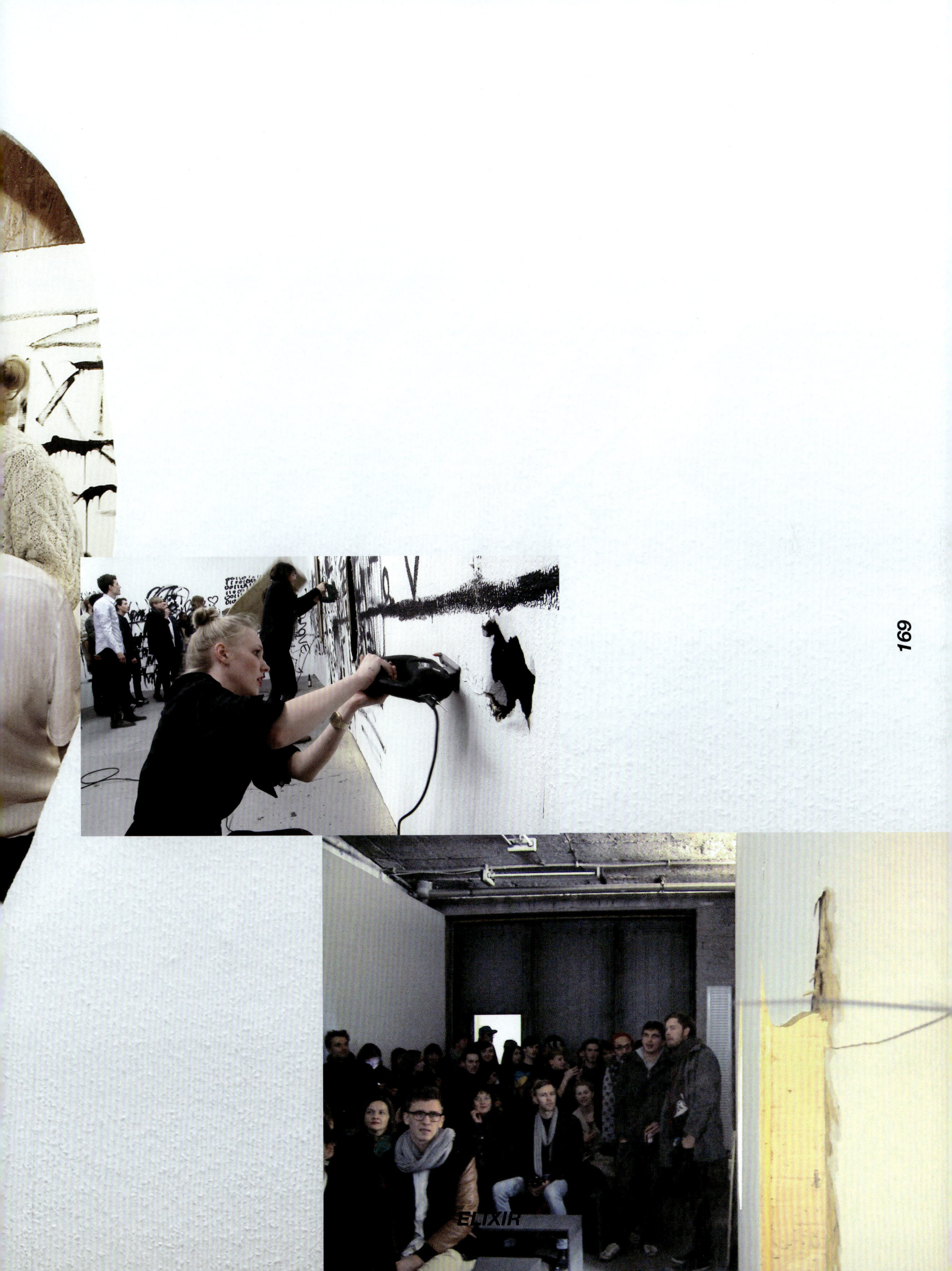
ELIXIR

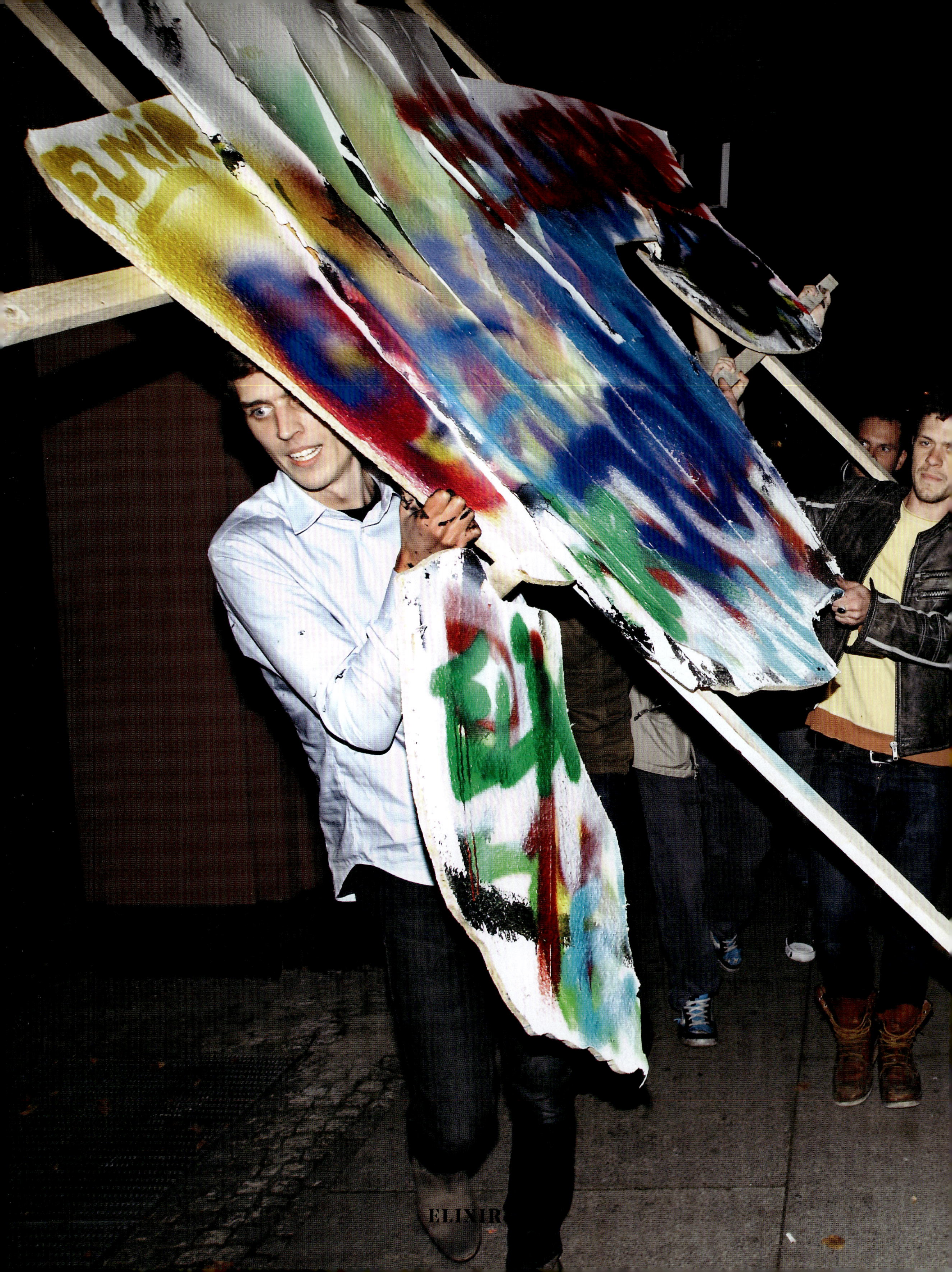

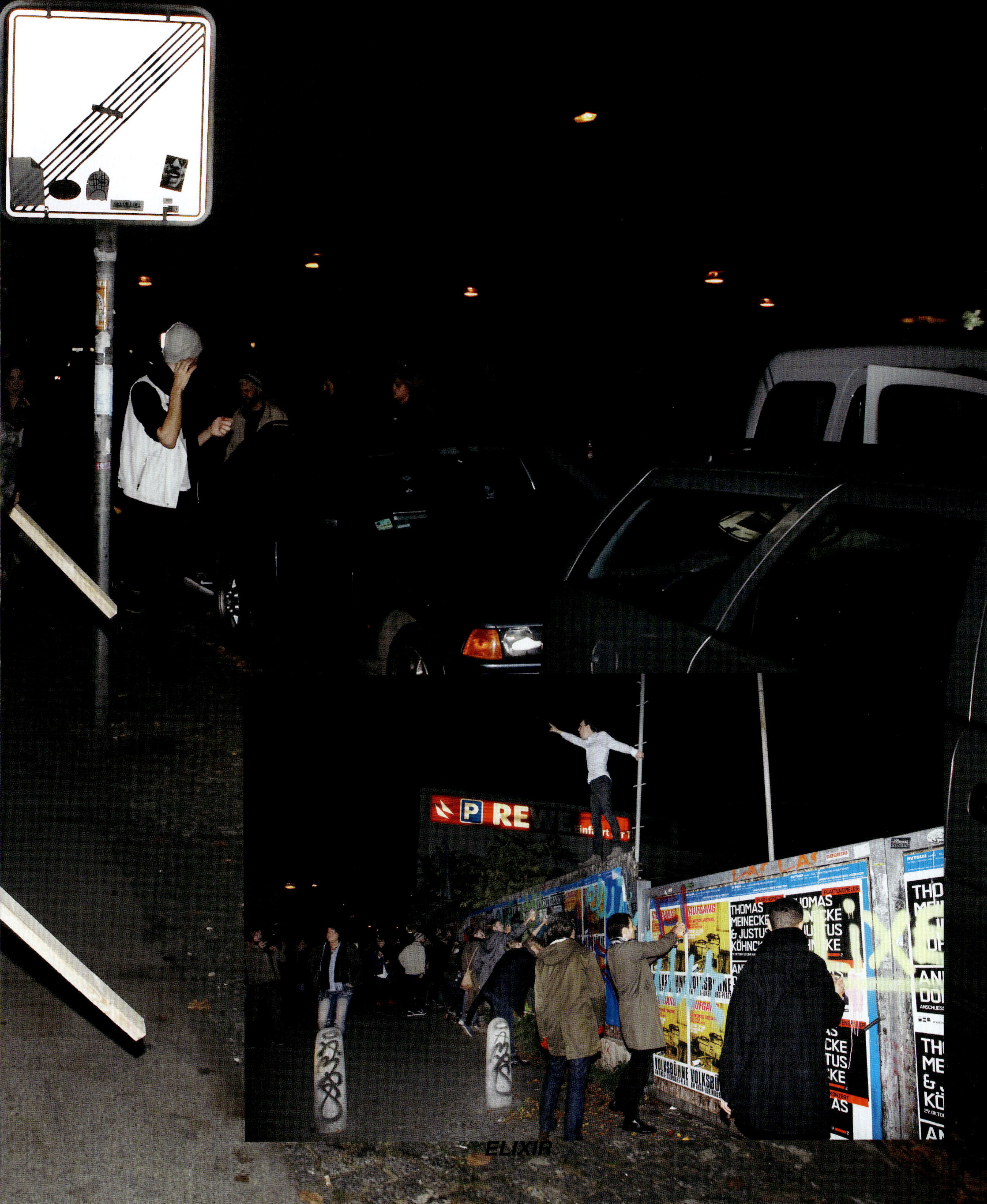
P REWE
THOMAS MEINECKE & JUSTUS KÖHNCKE
AUFGANG
VOLKSBÜHNE
ELIXIR

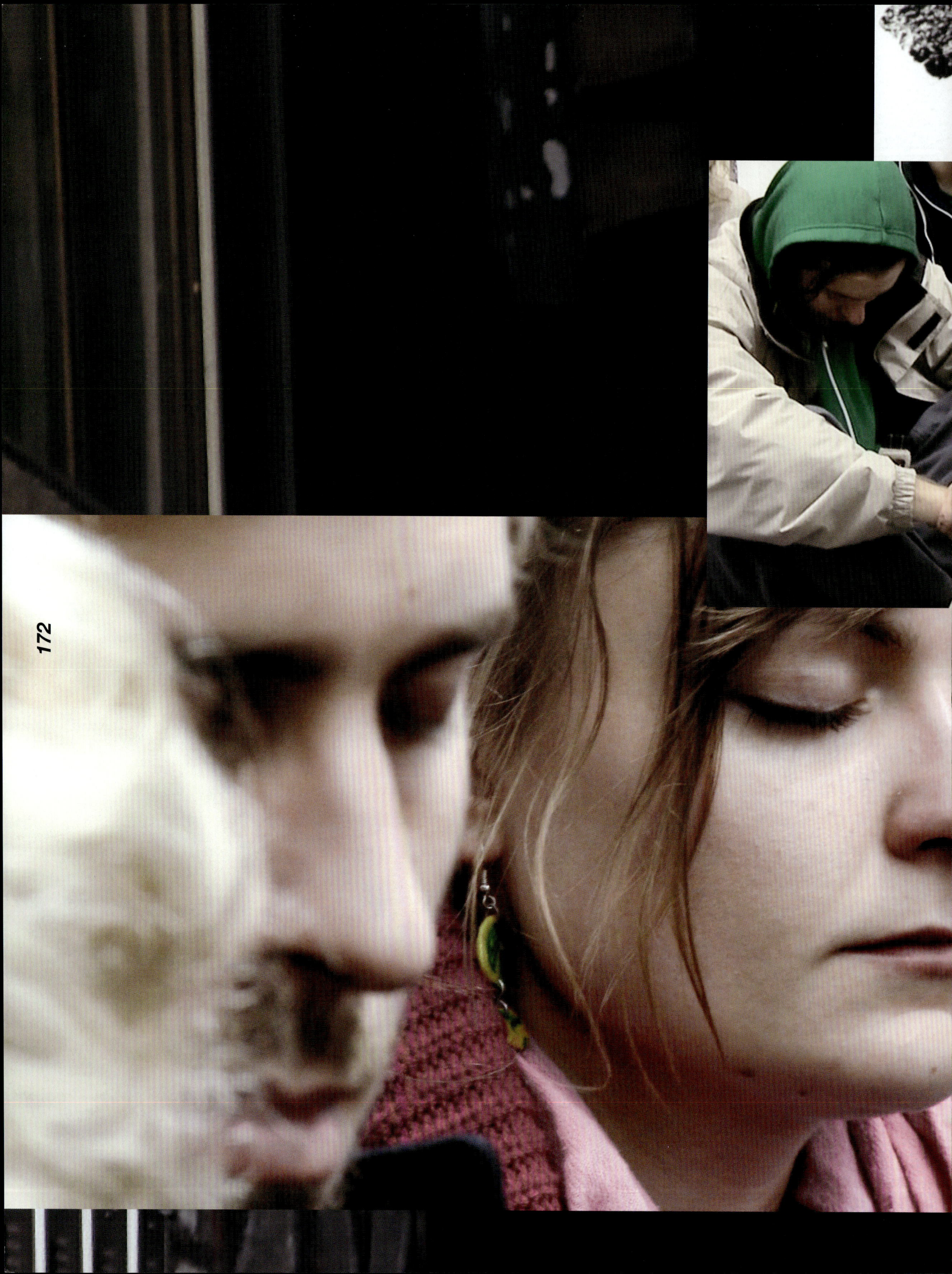

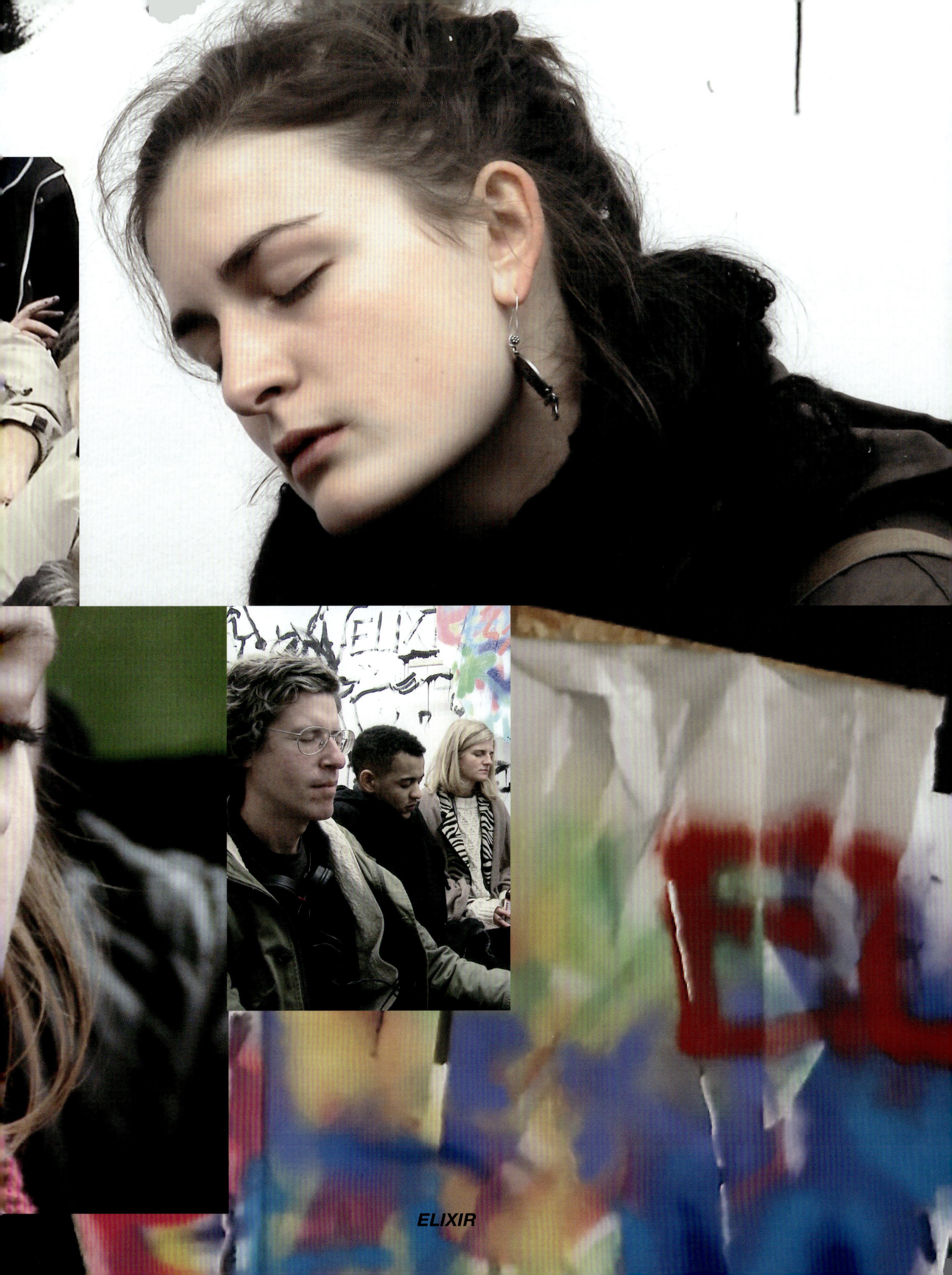

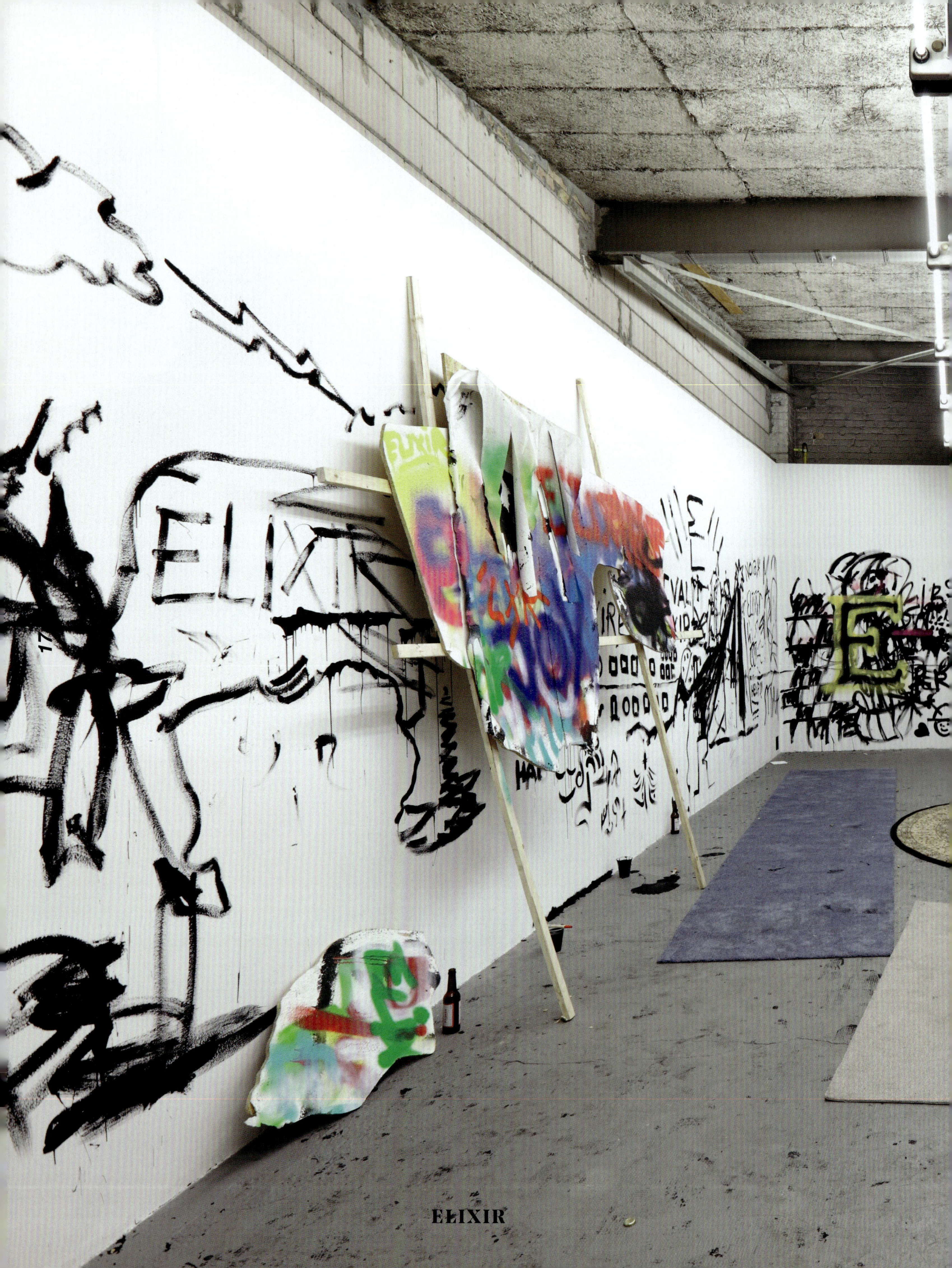
ELIXIR

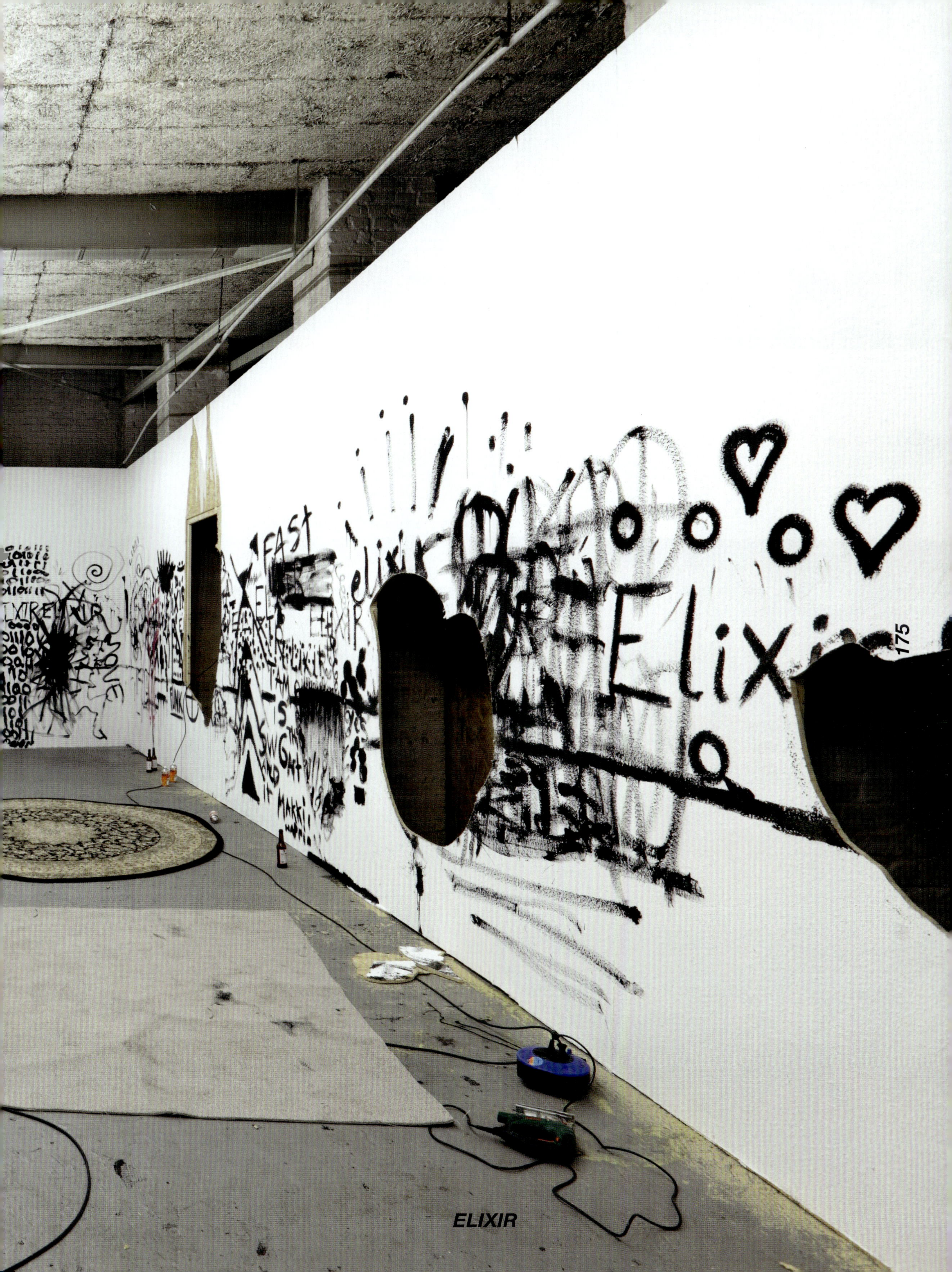

ELIXIR

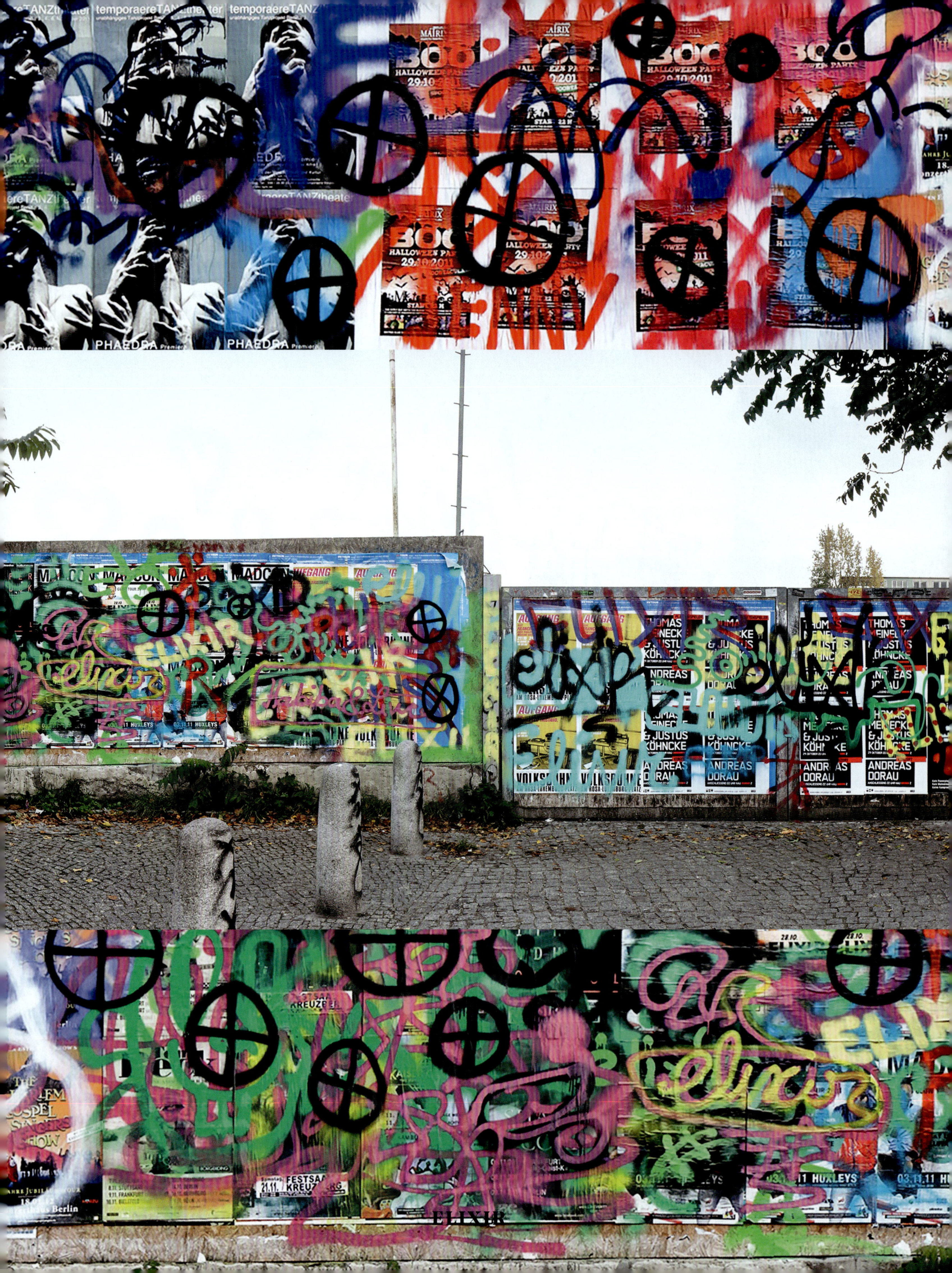
temporaereTANZtheater
PHAEDRA Premiere
BOO
HALLOWEEN PARTY
29.10.2011
MADCON
THOMAS MEINECKE & JUSTUS KÖHNCKE
ANDREAS DORAU
03.11.11 HUXLEYS
ELIXIR
FESTSAAL KREUZBERG
ELIXIR

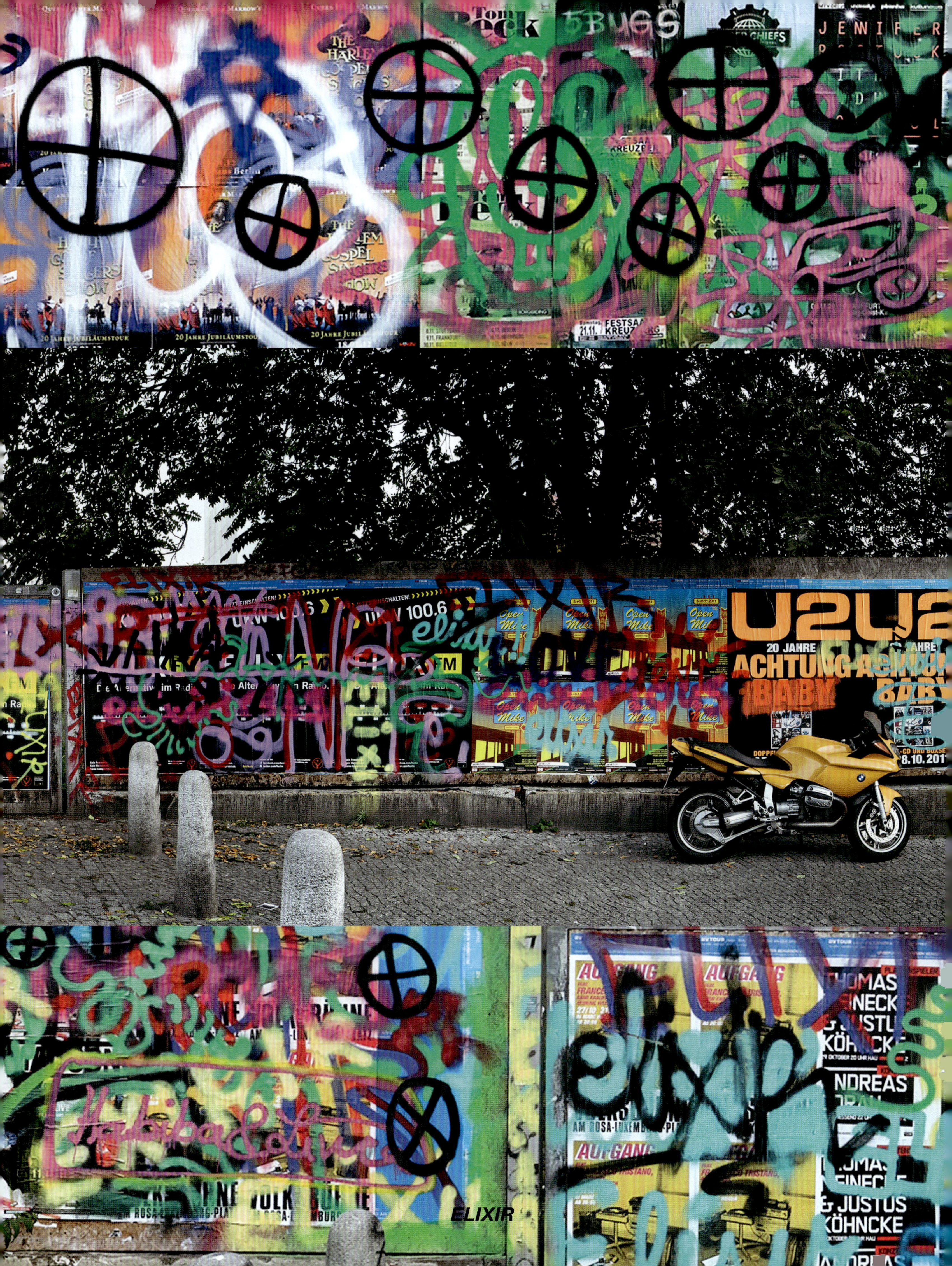
5BUGS
JENIFER
20 JAHRE JUBILÄUMSTOUR
UKW 100,6
Open Mike
U2U2
20 JAHRE
ACHTUNG BABY
8.10.201
AUFGANG
THOMAS
JUSTUS
KÖHNCKE
NDREAS
AM ROSA-LUXEMBURG-PLATZ
ELIXIR

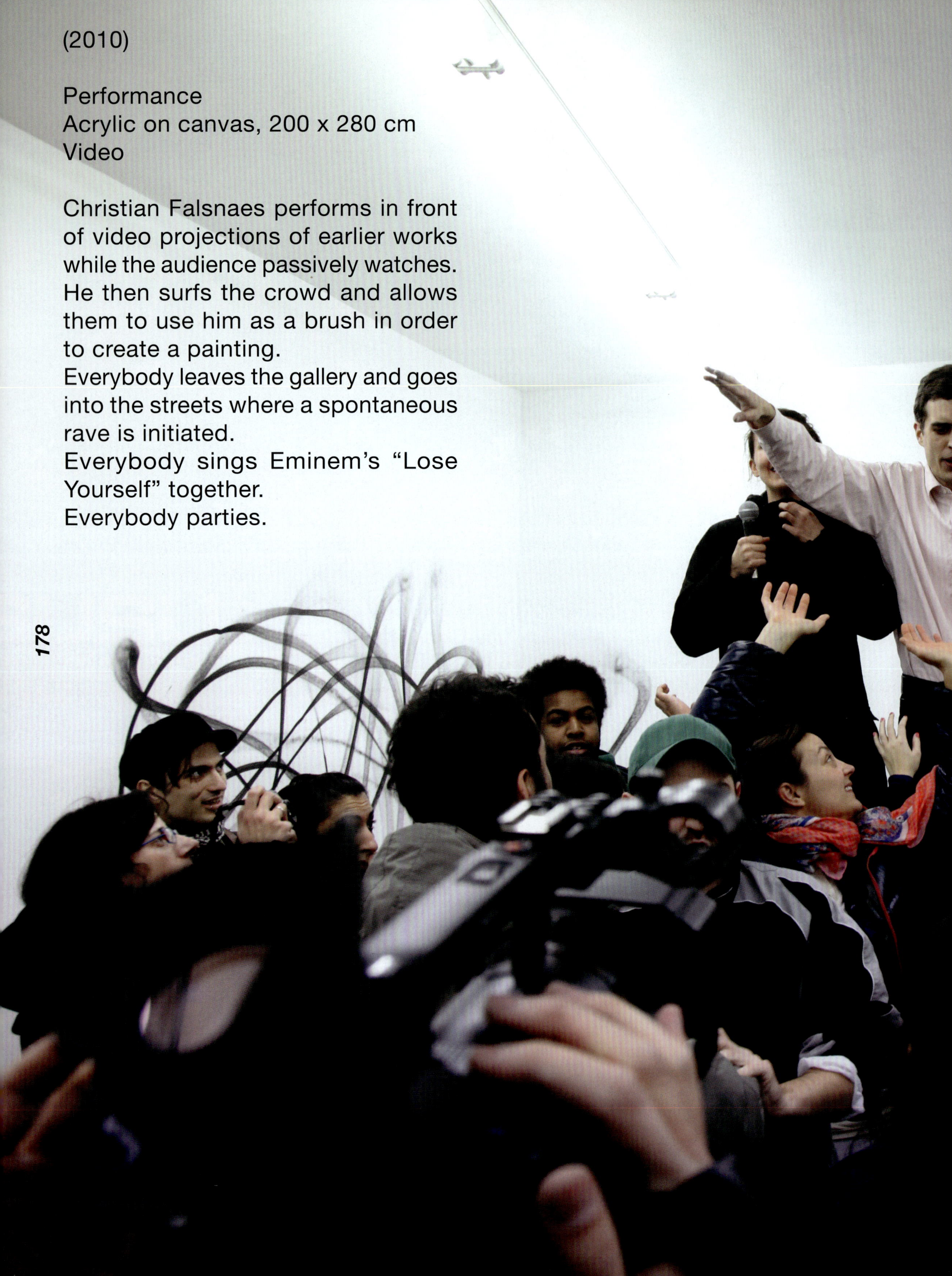

(2010)

Performance
Acrylic on canvas, 200 x 280 cm
Video

Christian Falsnaes performs in front of video projections of earlier works while the audience passively watches. He then surfs the crowd and allows them to use him as a brush in order to create a painting.
Everybody leaves the gallery and goes into the streets where a spontaneous rave is initiated.
Everybody sings Eminem's "Lose Yourself" together.
Everybody parties.

EXIST–
ING
THINGS

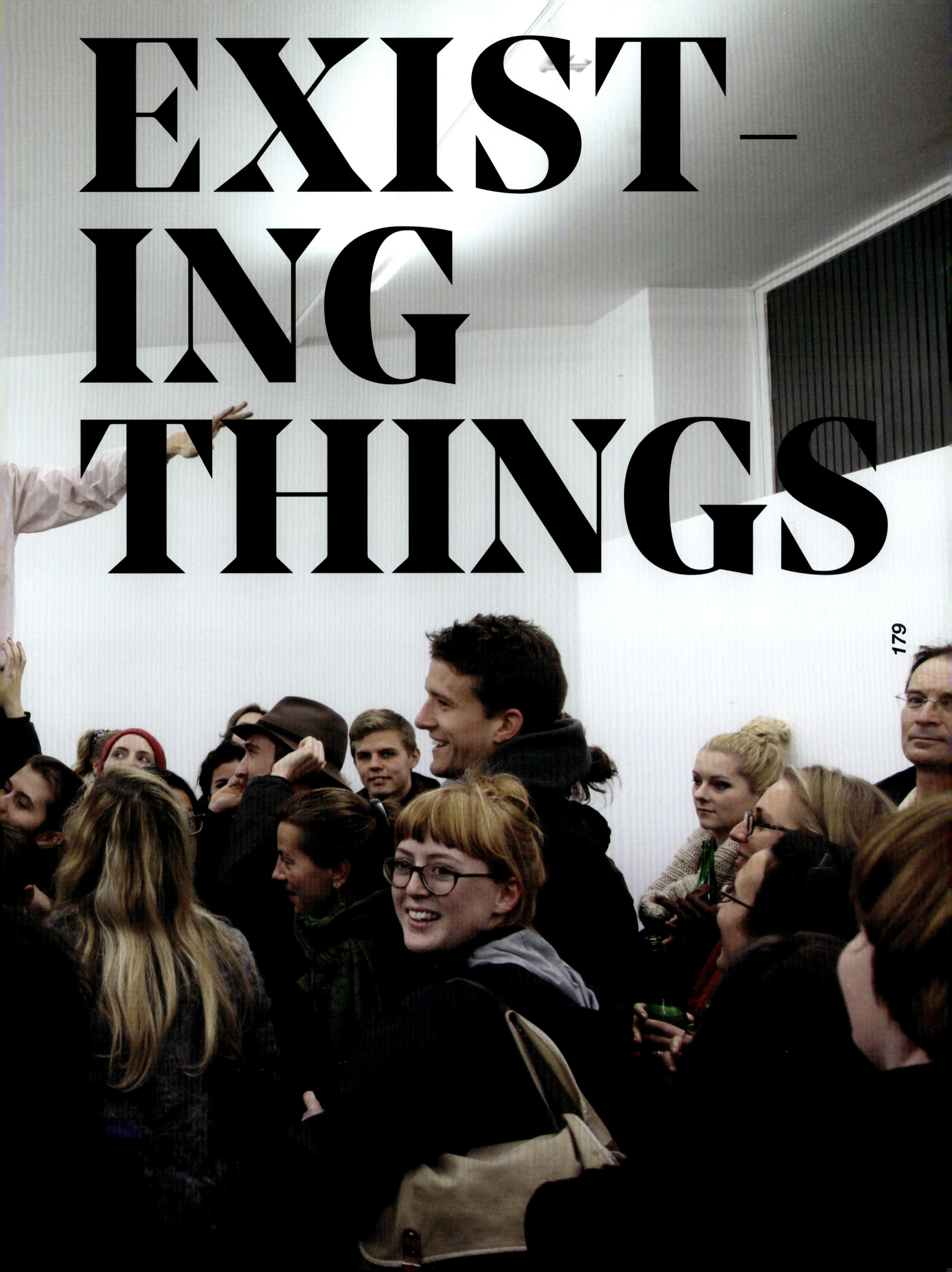

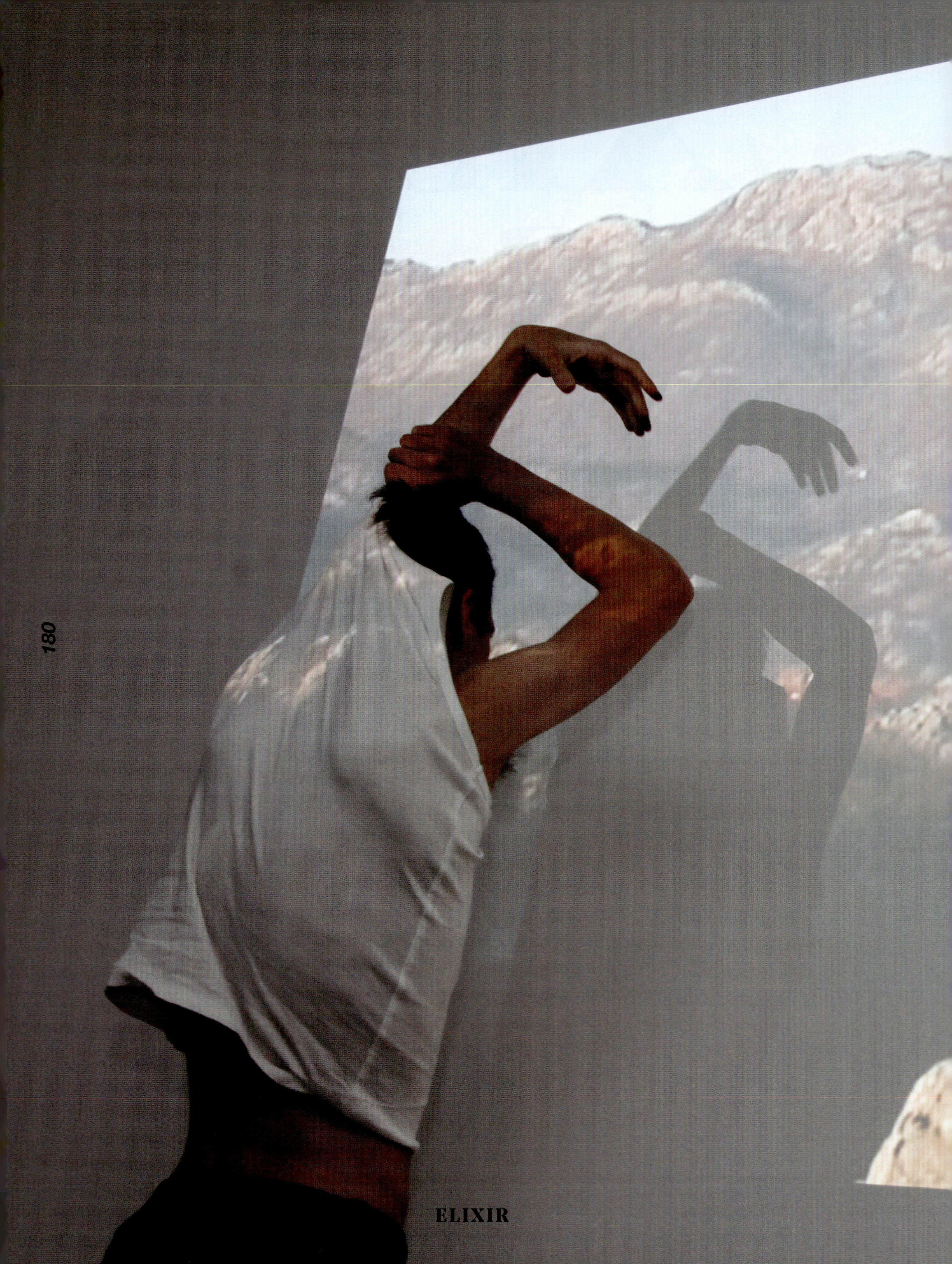

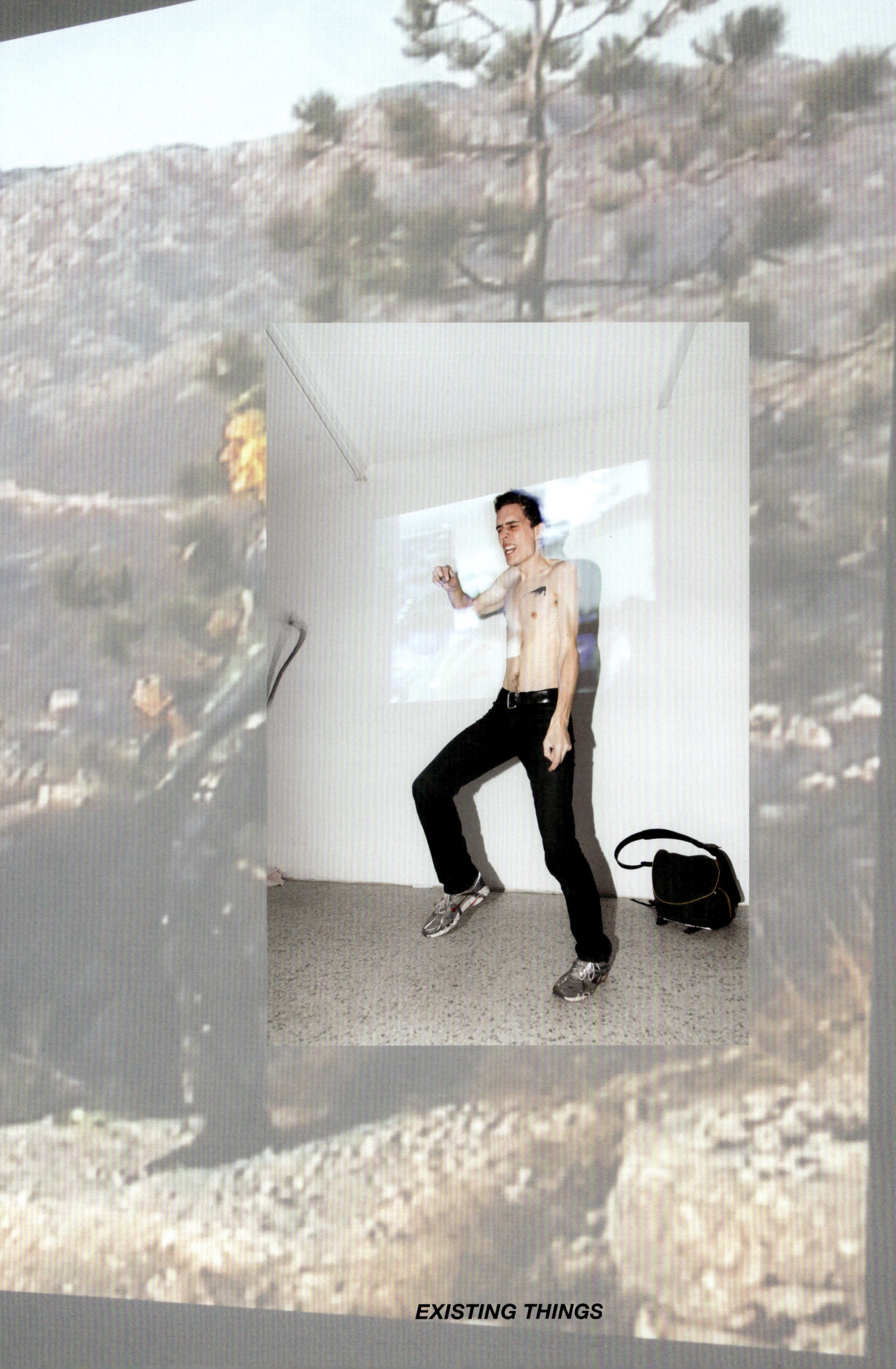

EXISTING THINGS

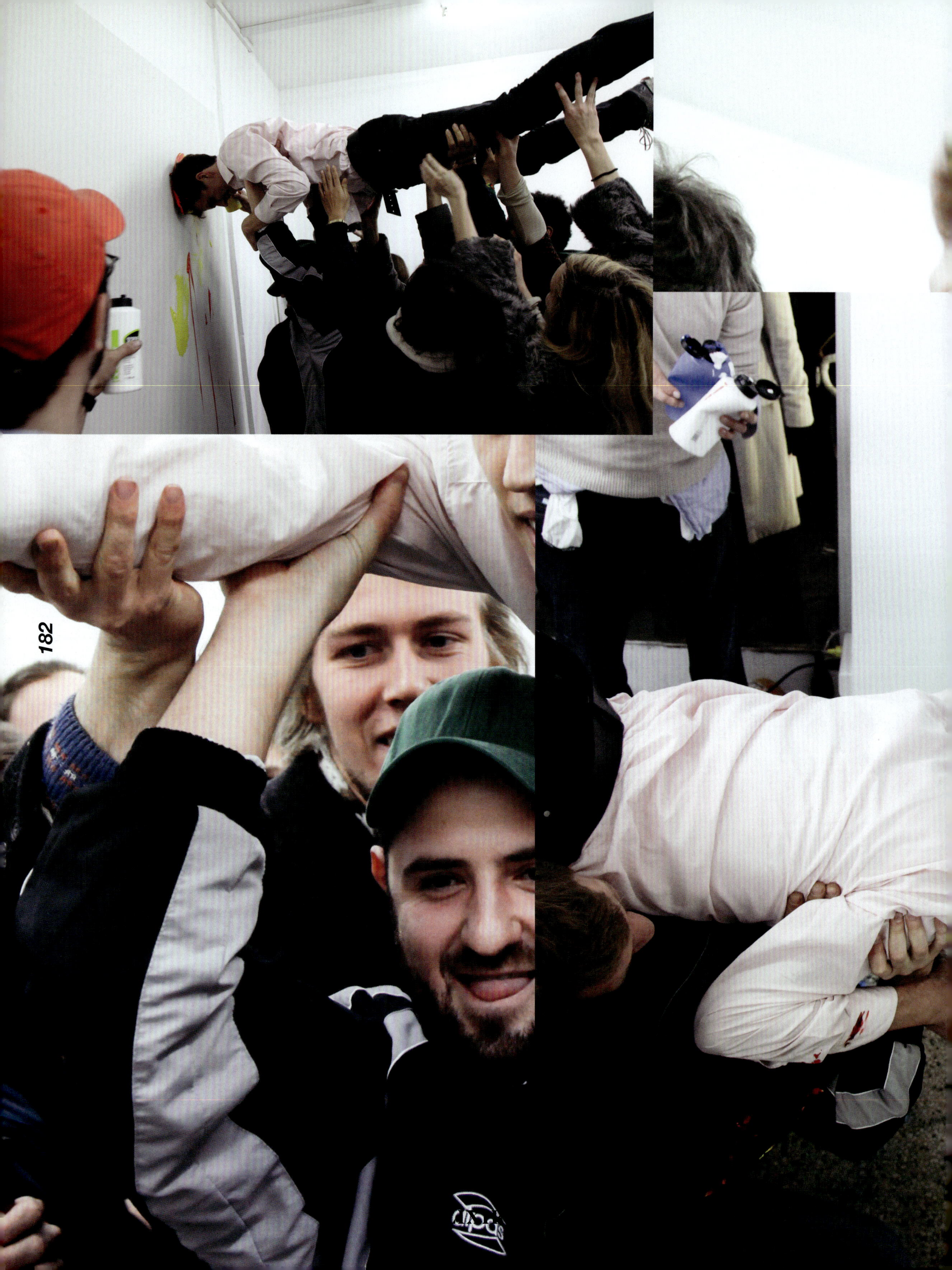

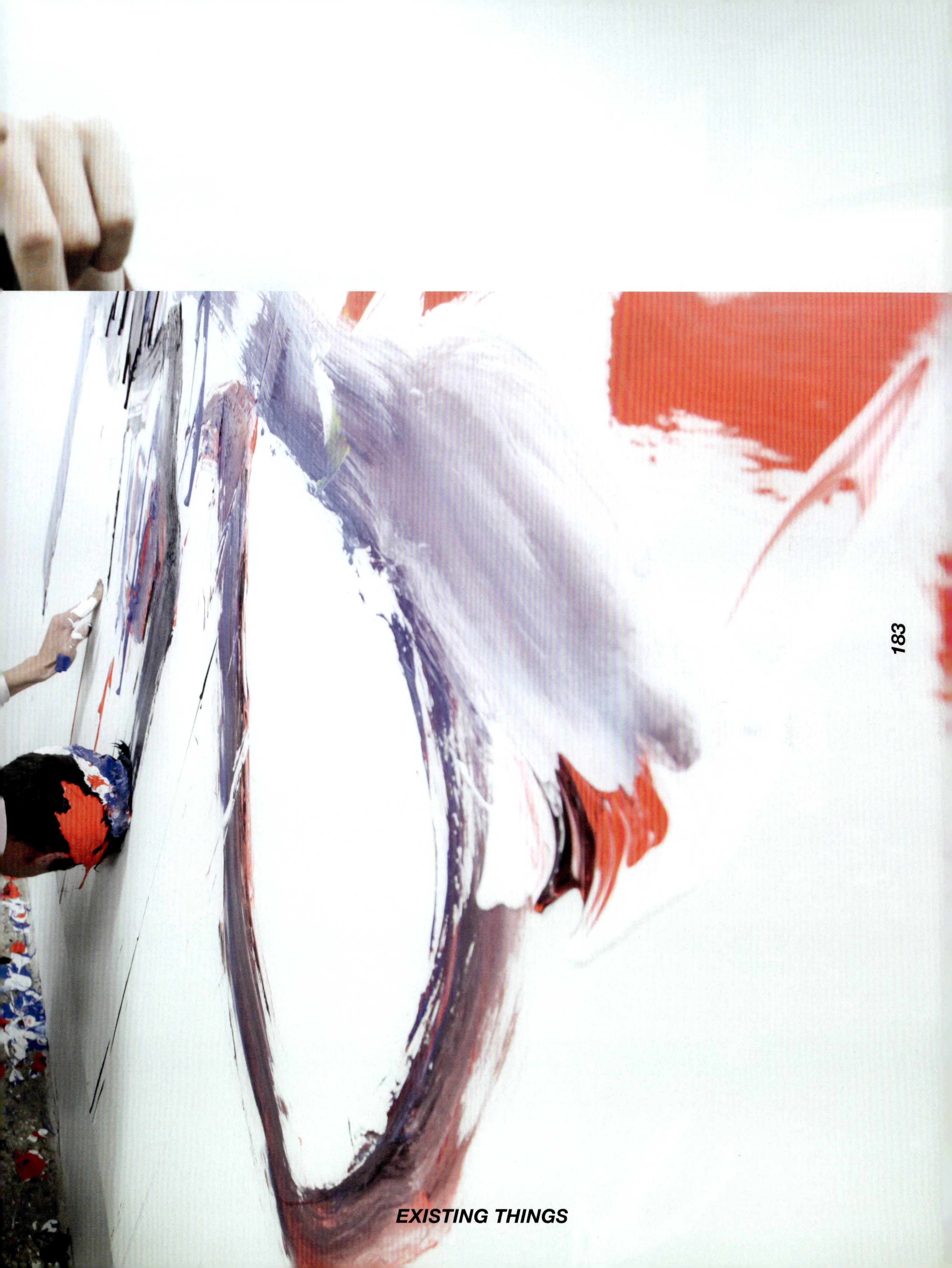

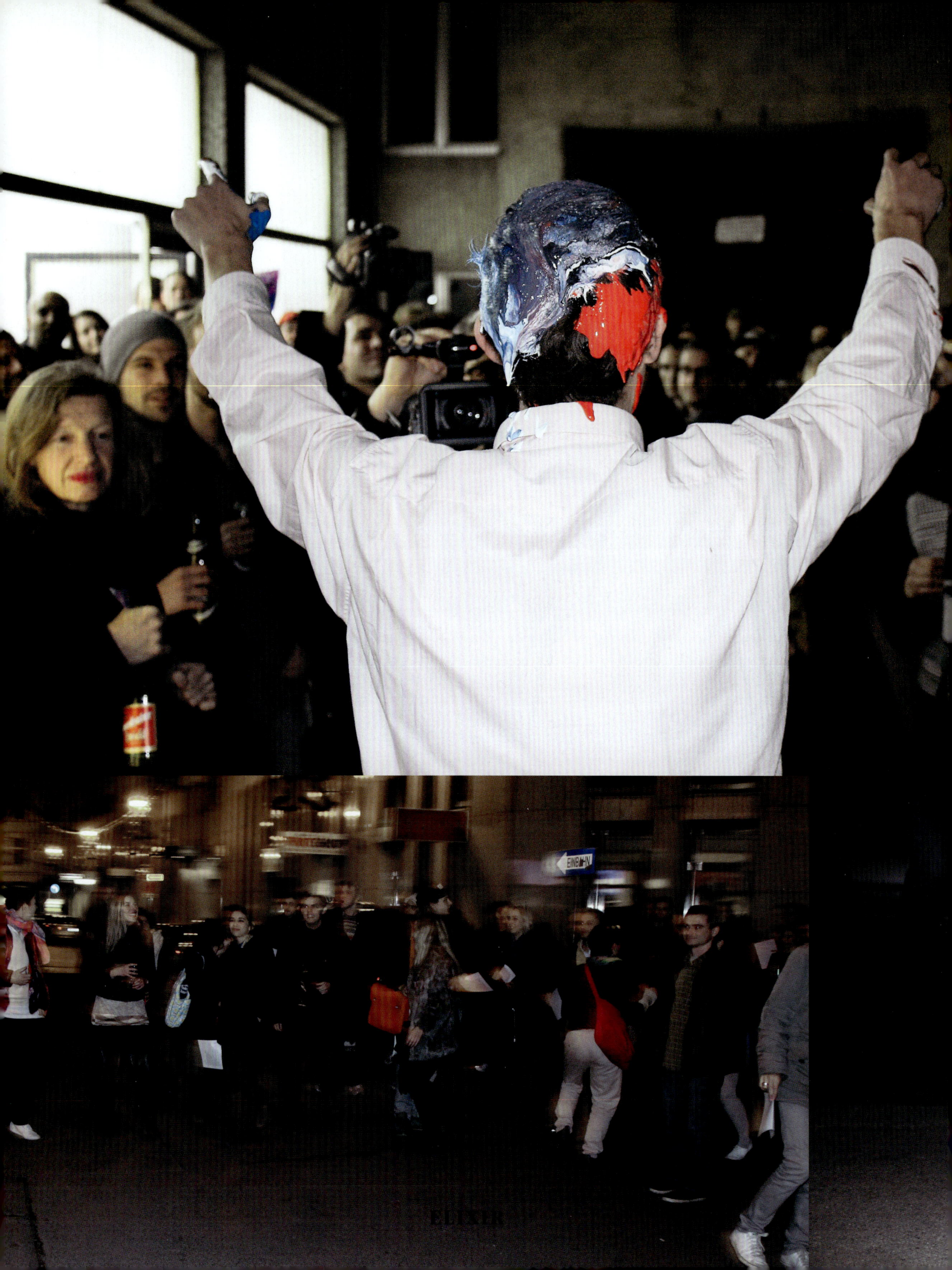
EINBAHN

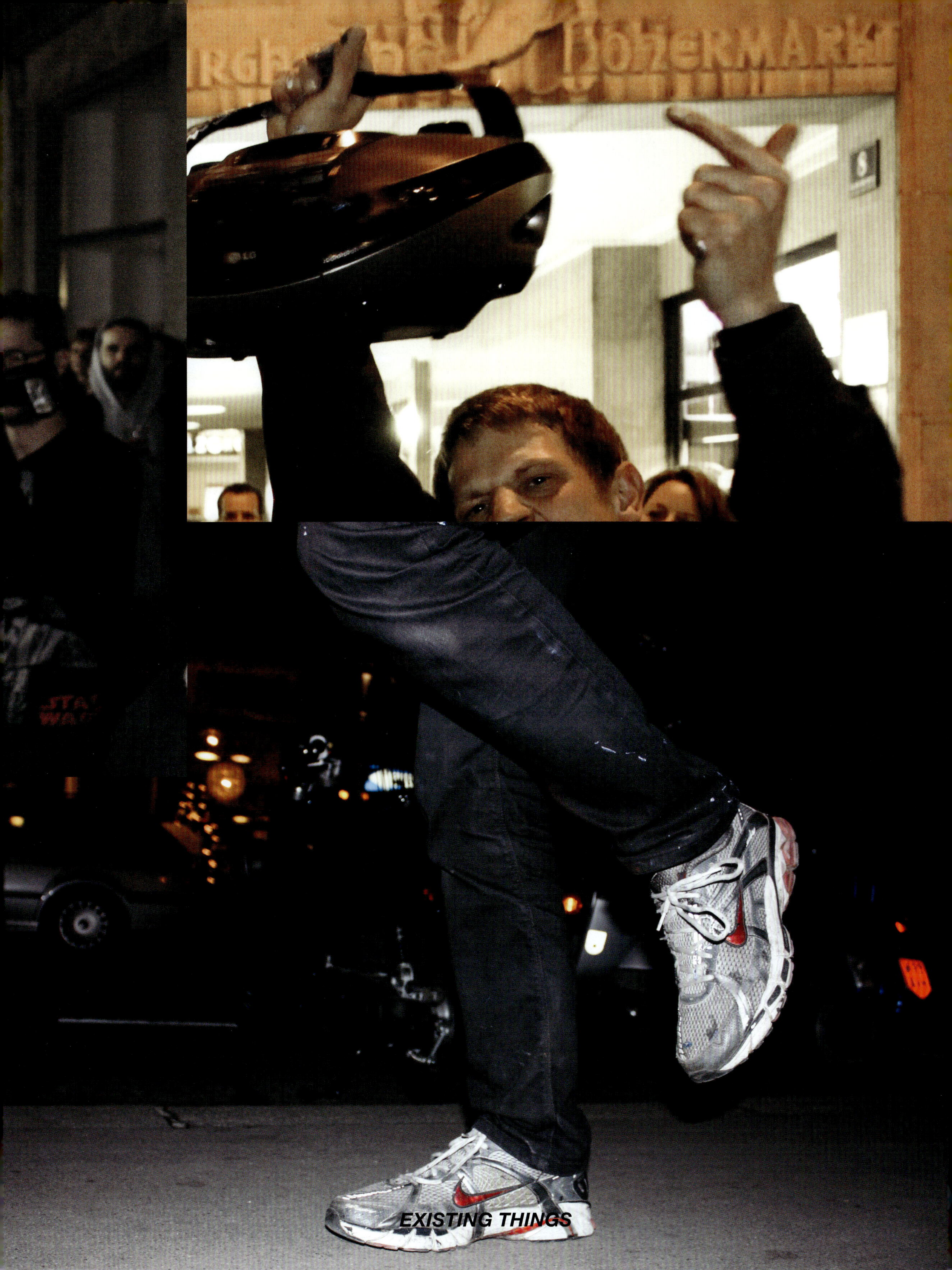

EXISTING THINGS

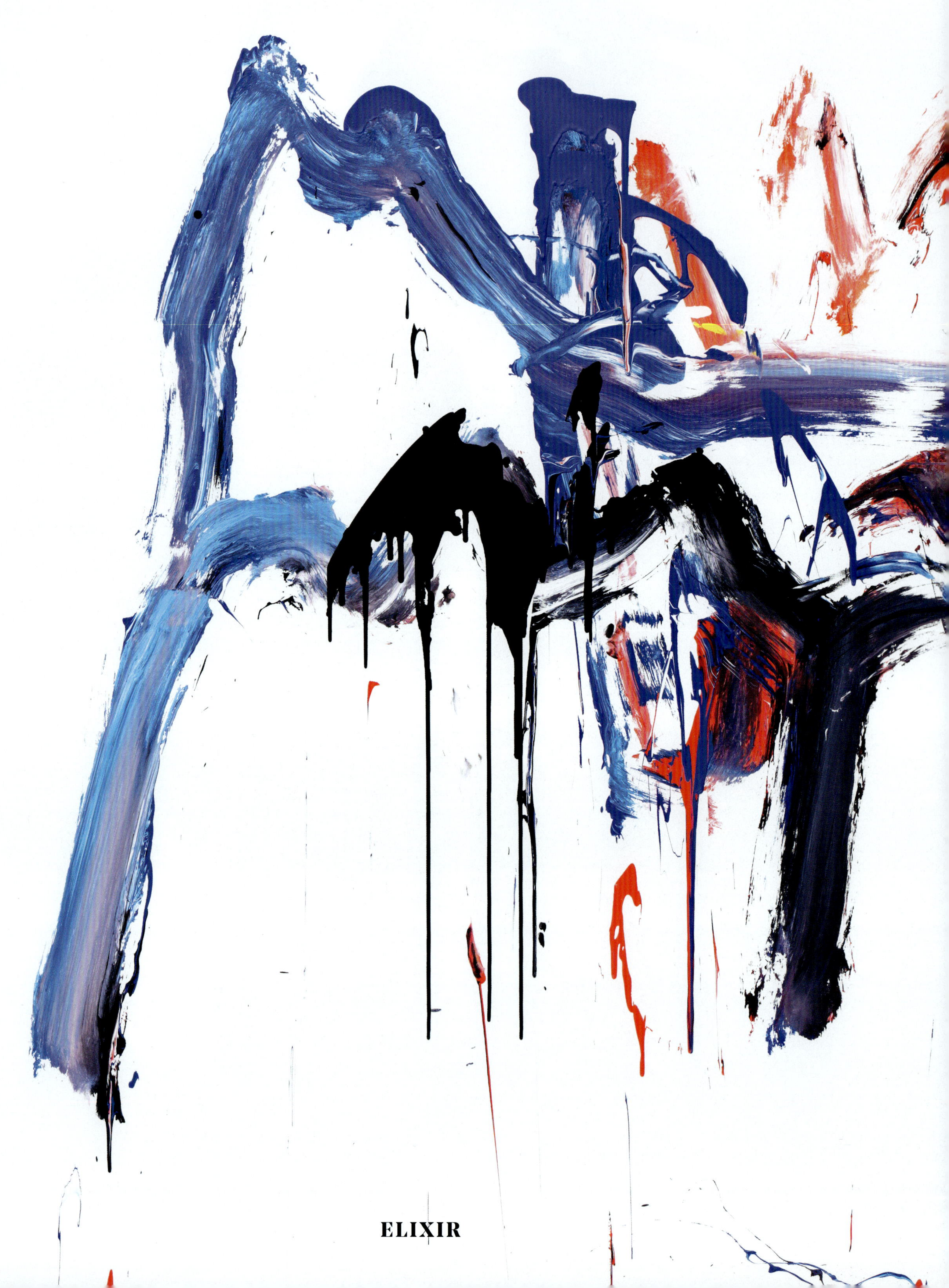

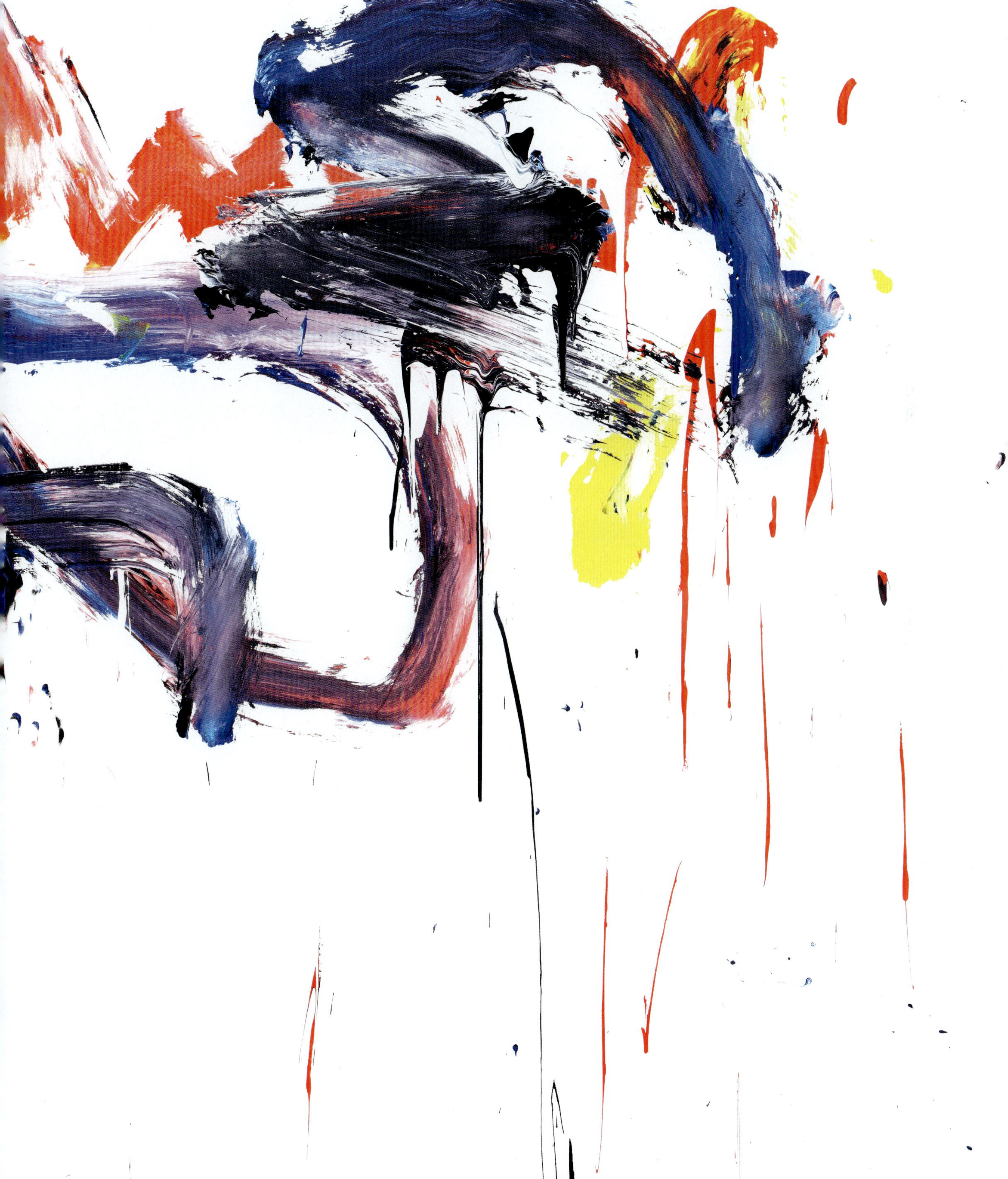

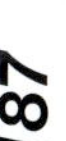

Performance
Installation
Video

The exhibition space is turned into a set. A camera team is present at the opening. The audience is included in the production of a video work loosely following the steps of the "hero's journey" as described by Joseph Campbell. The final video is installed in the space.

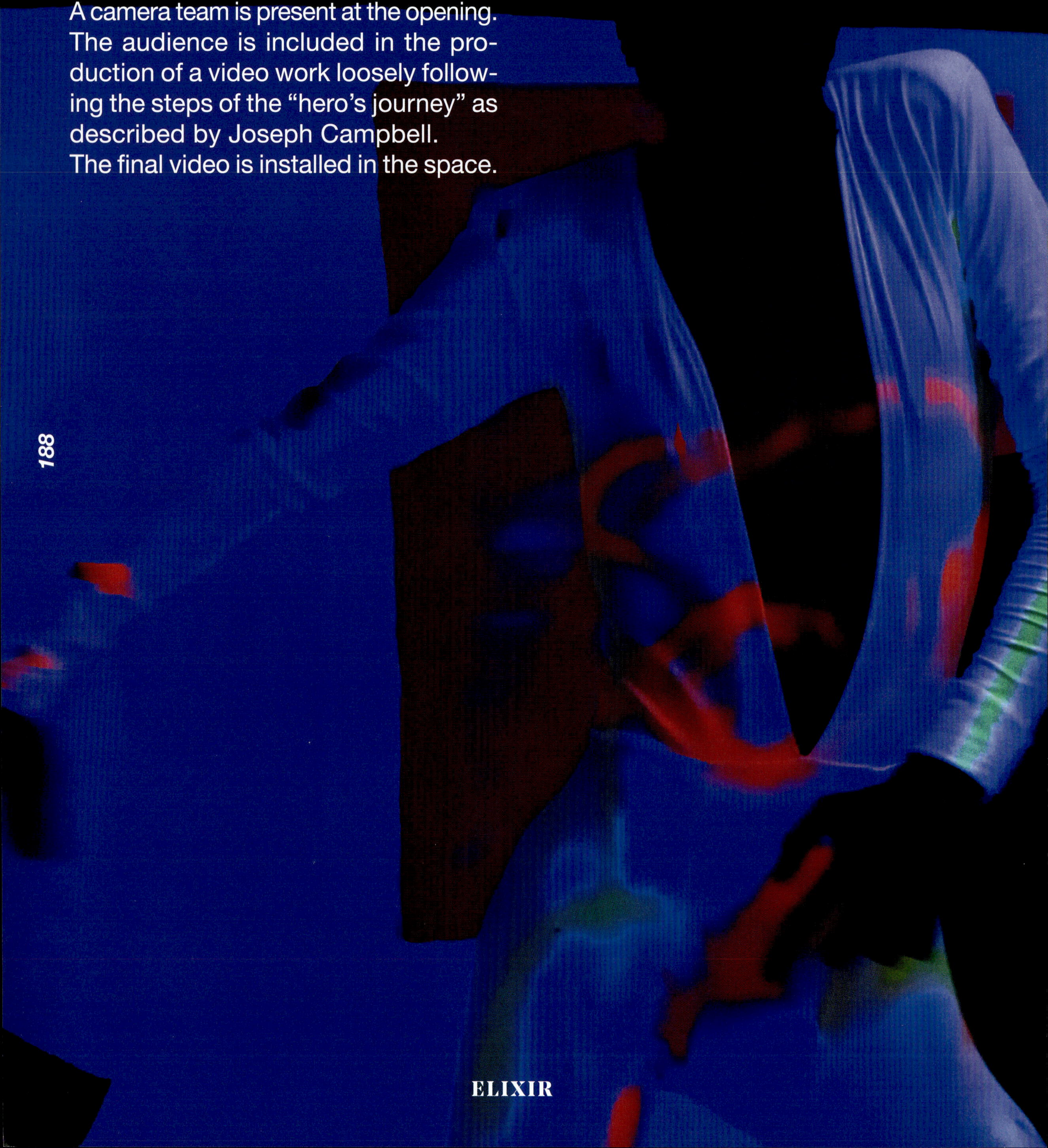

ELIXIR

THERE AND BACK

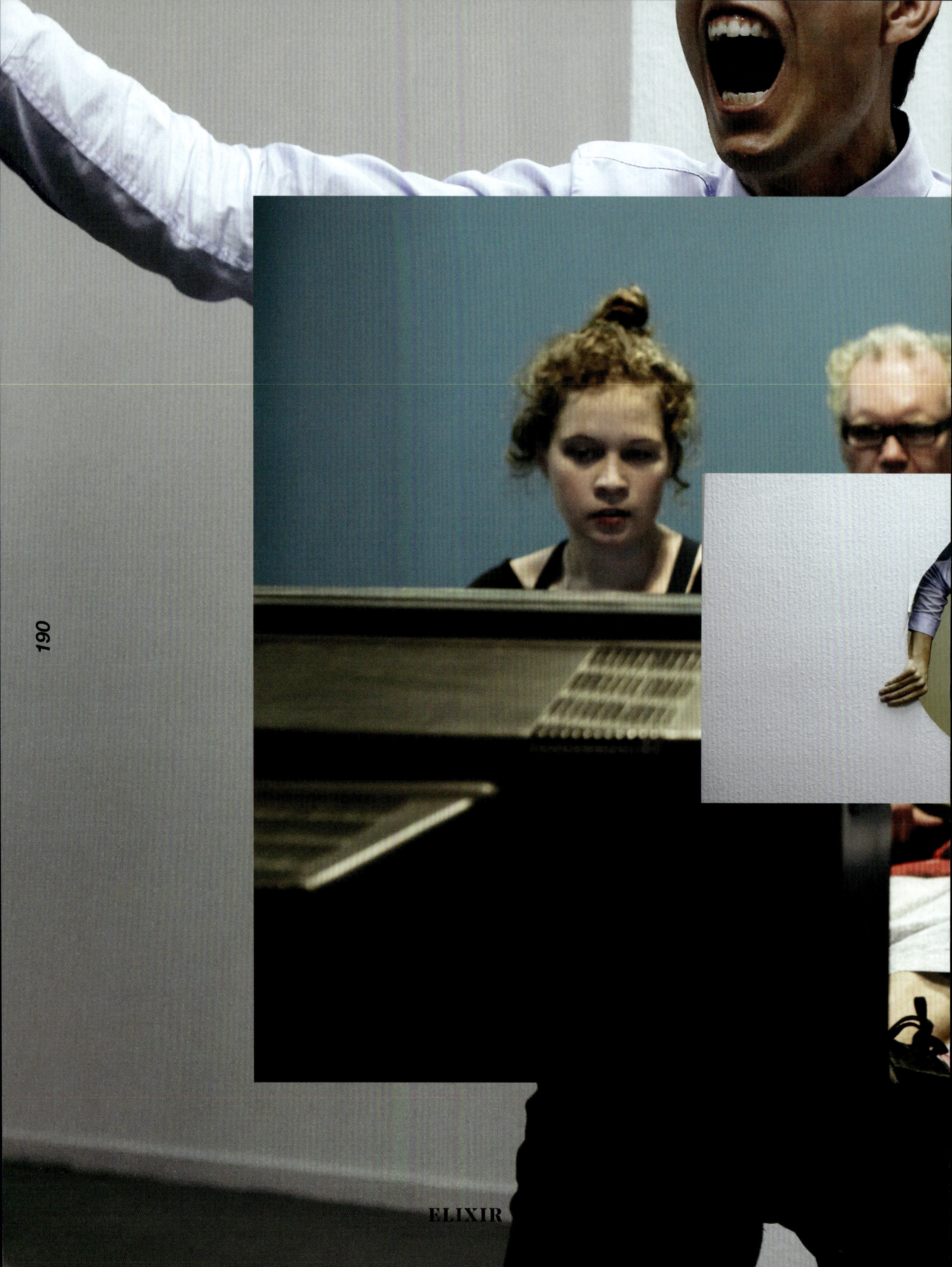

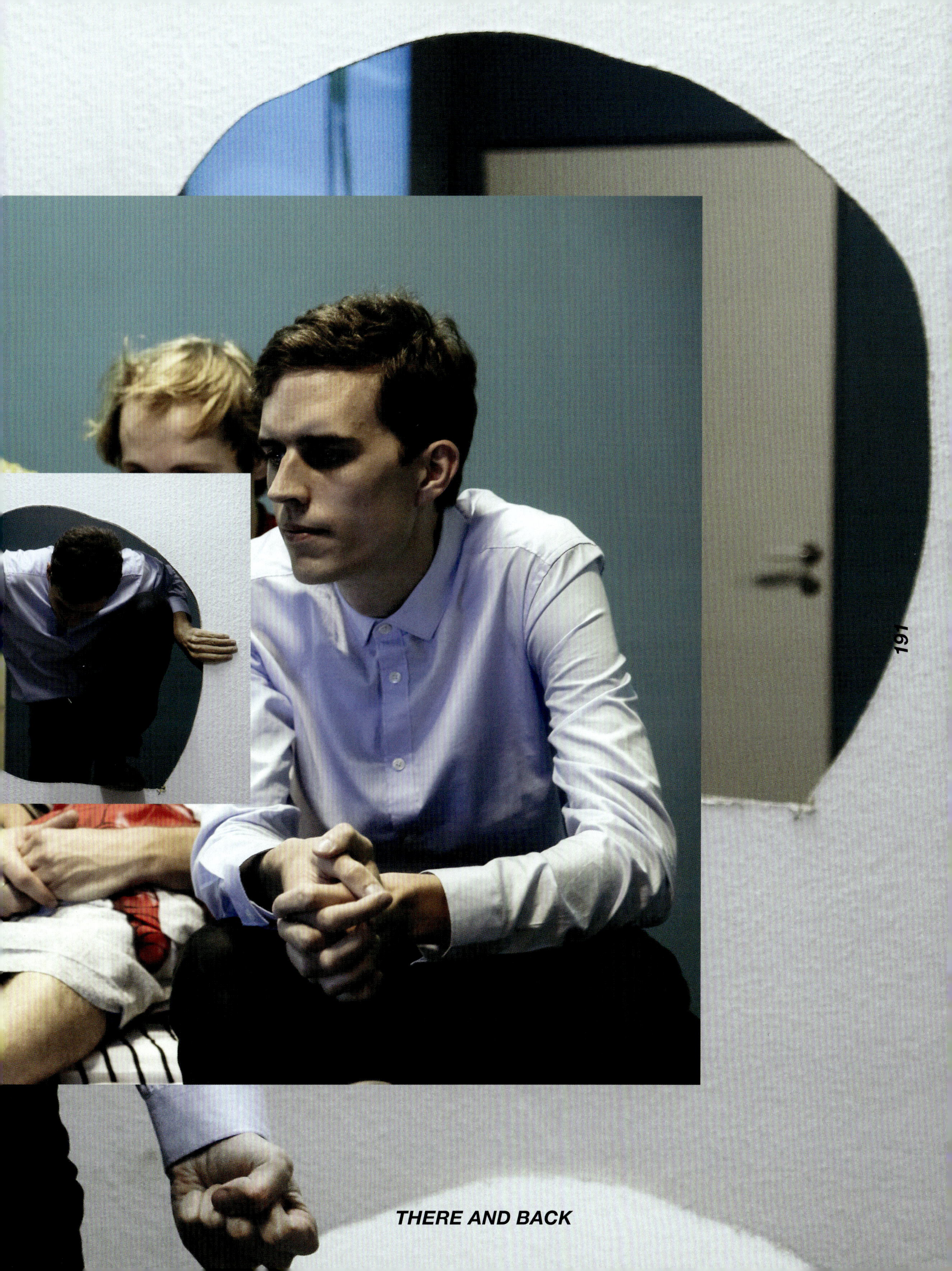

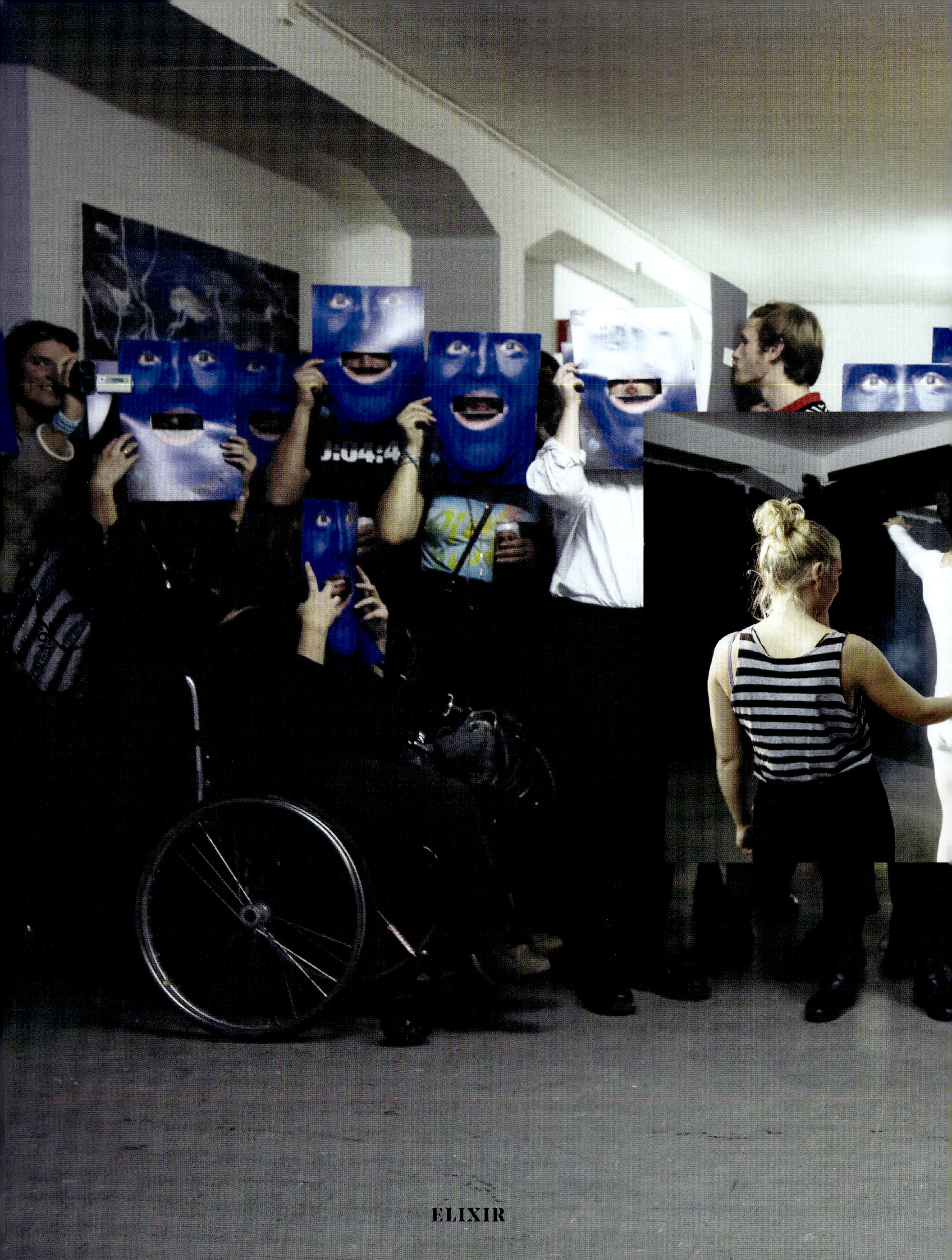

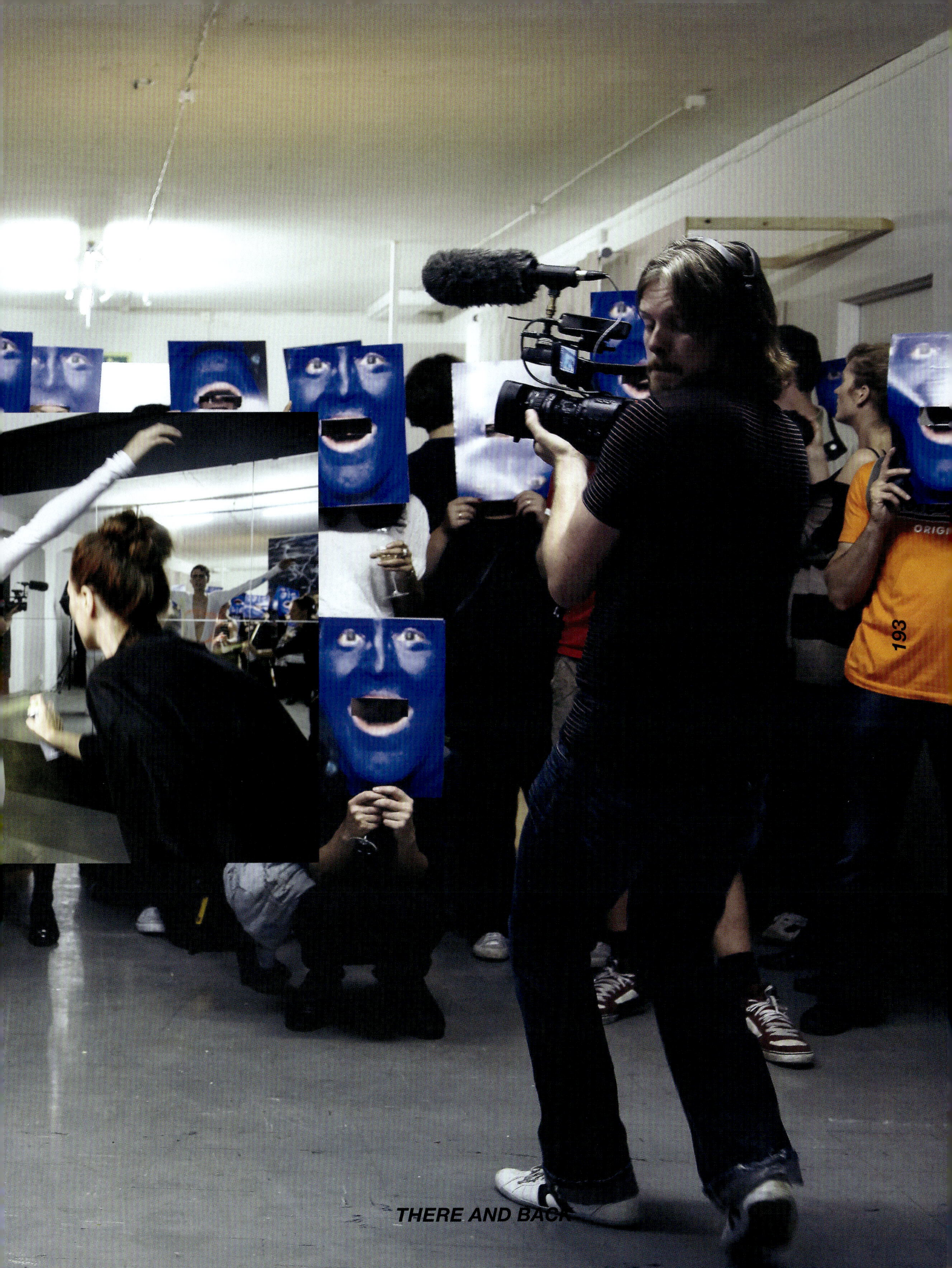

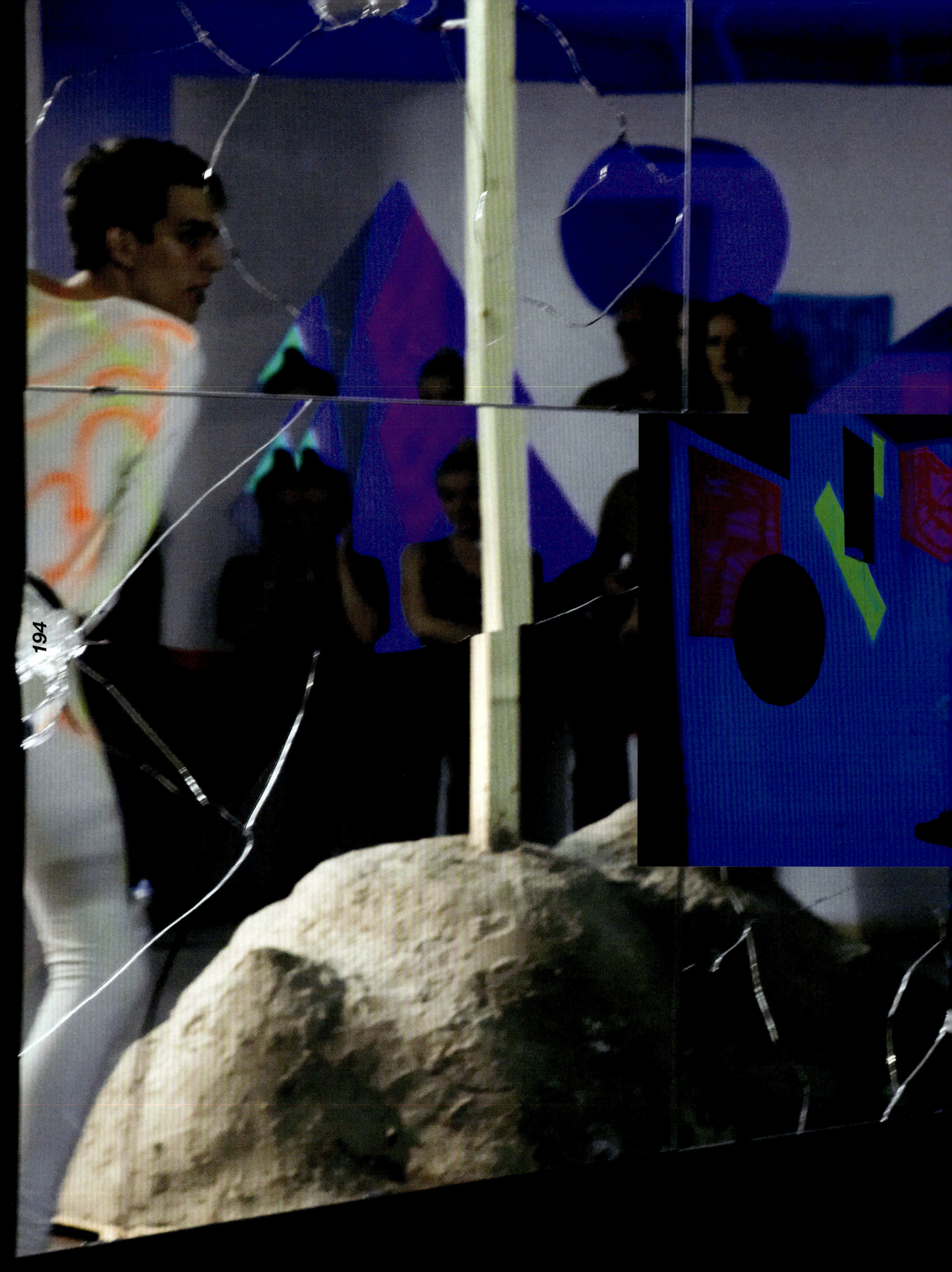

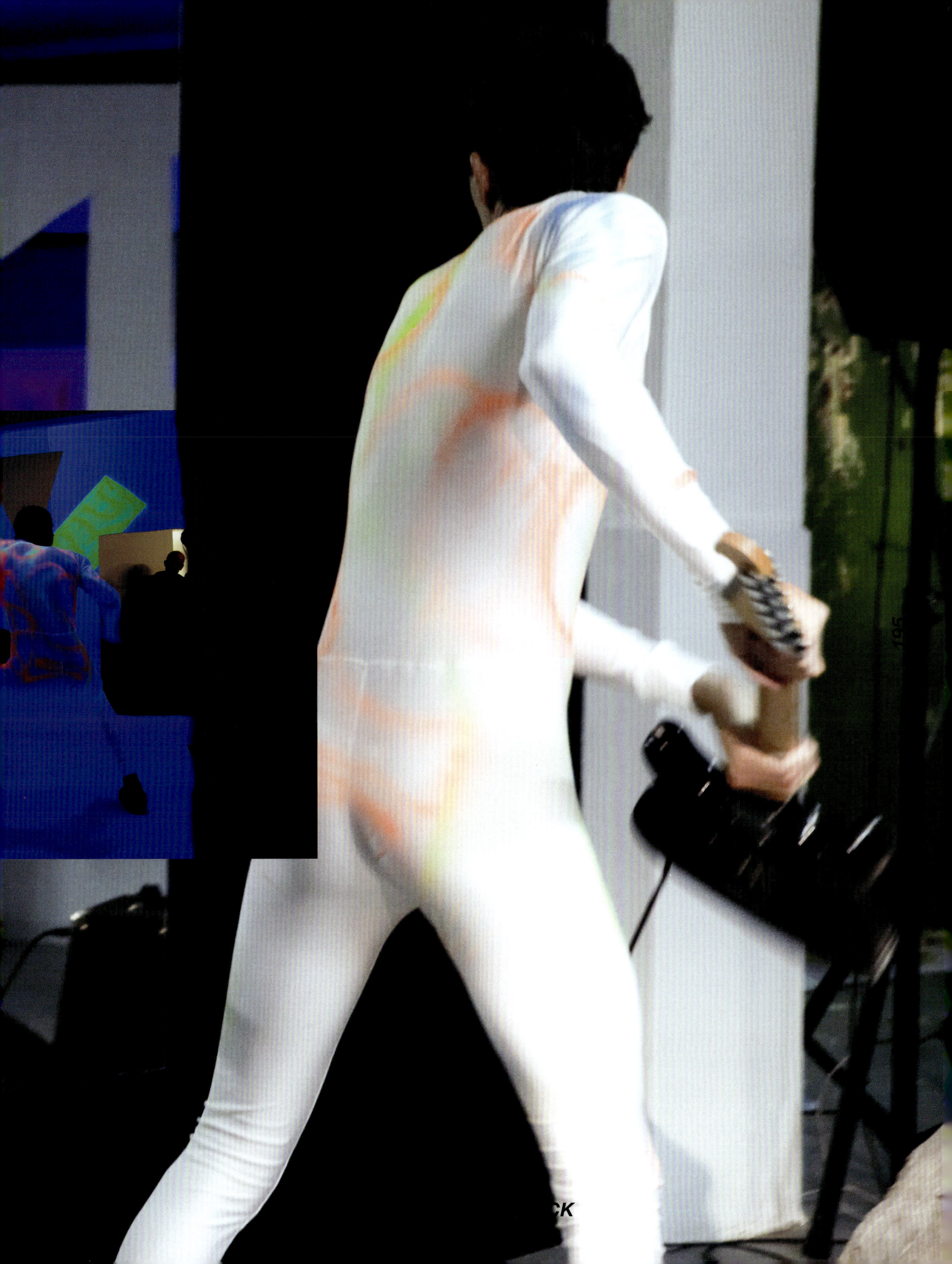

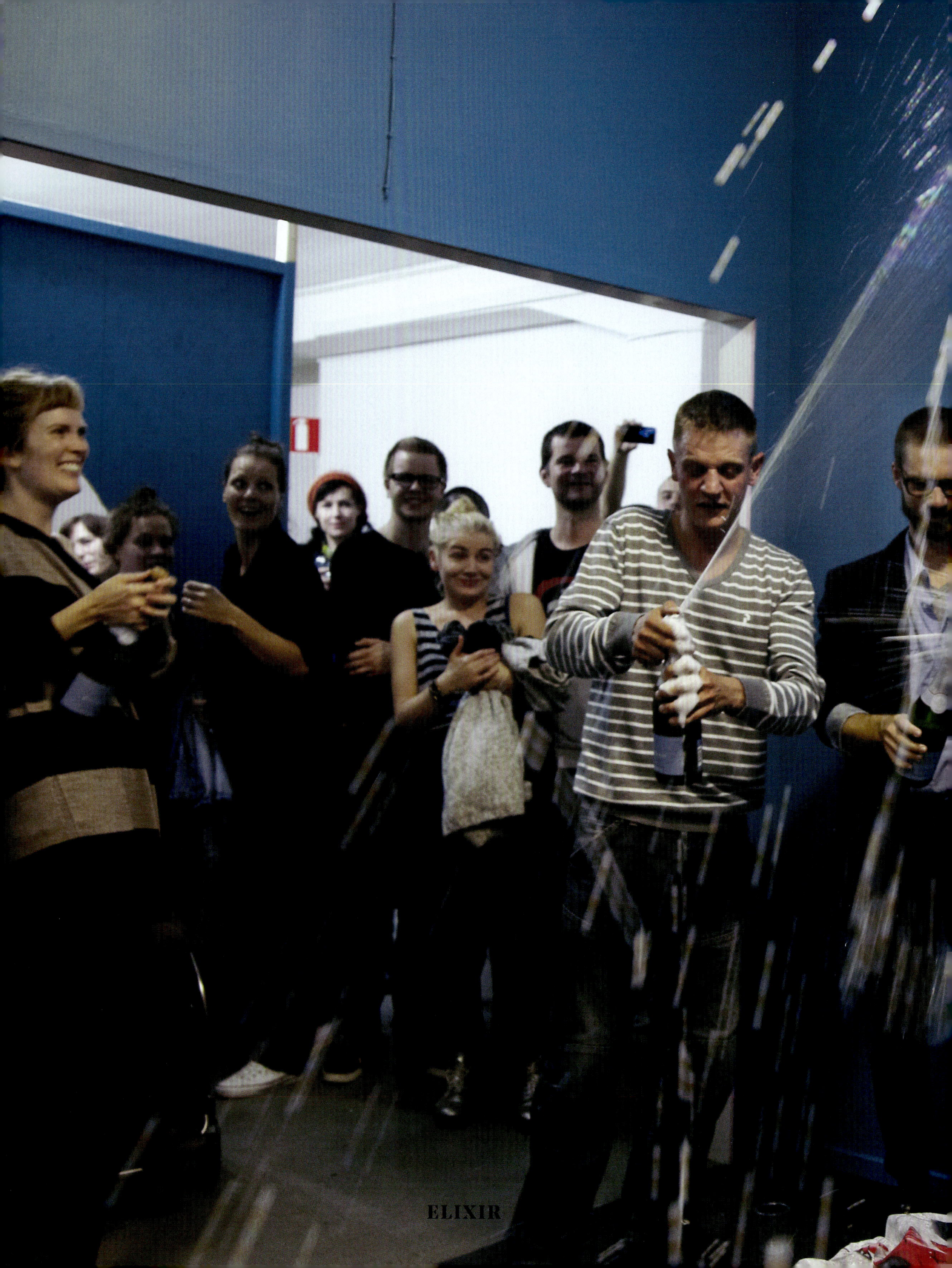

ELIXIR

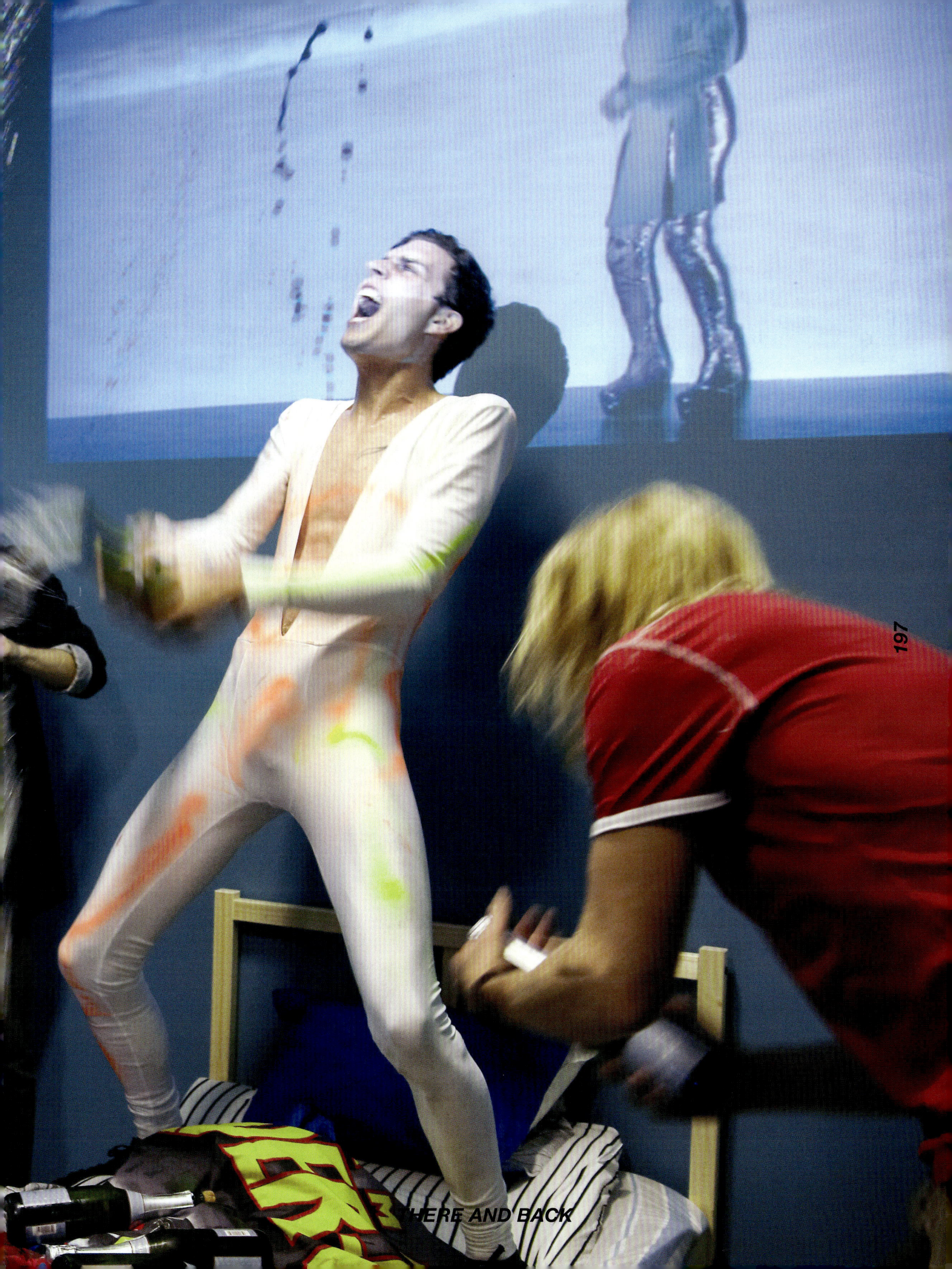

Index

INSIDE COVER
Opening, 2013
cut clothes on stretcher bars, 100 x 80 cm
The Collection Juan & Patricia Vergez, Buenos Aires

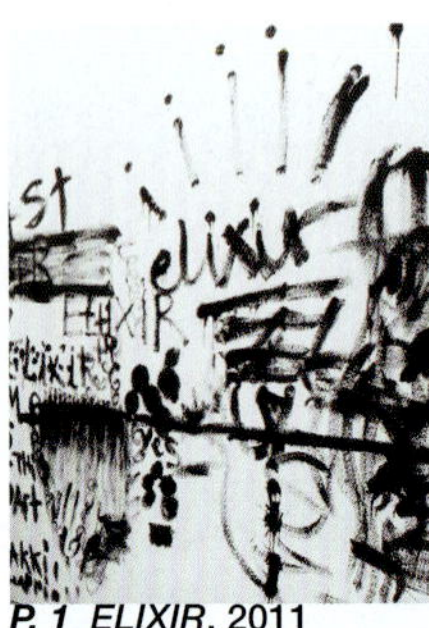

P. 1 ELIXIR, 2011
installation view (detail), PSM, Berlin
Photo: Hans-Georg Gaul
Courtesy of the artist and PSM, Berlin

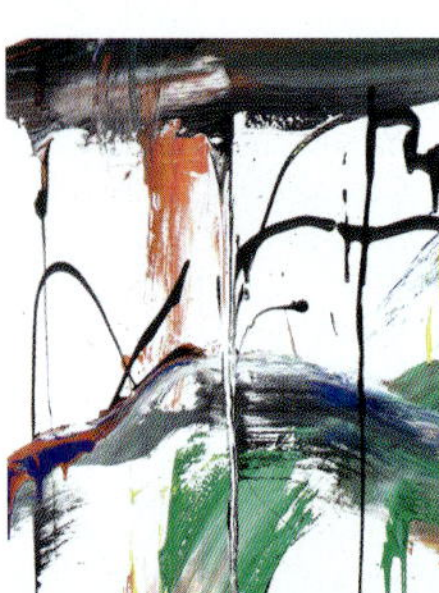

P. 2 Existing Things, 2011
acrylic on canvas, 200 x 280 cm
Private collection, London

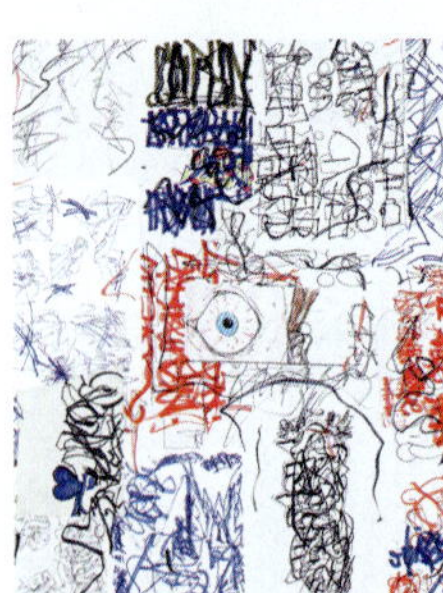

P. 3 All of Us, 2016
mixed media on canvas, 160 x 120 cm
Courtesy of the artist and PSM, Berlin

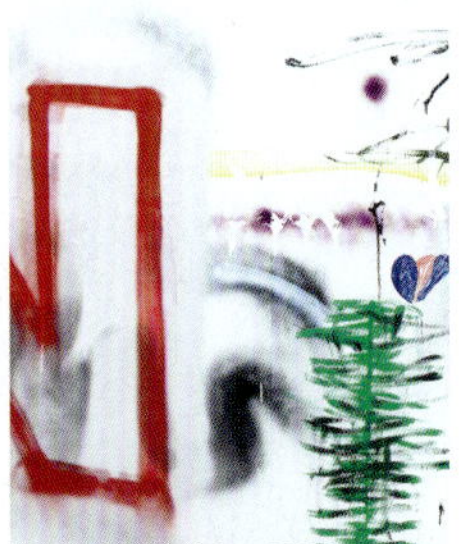

P. 4 Available, 2015
installation view (detail), Kunstverein Braunschweig
Photo: Stefan Stark
Courtesy of the artist and PSM, Berlin

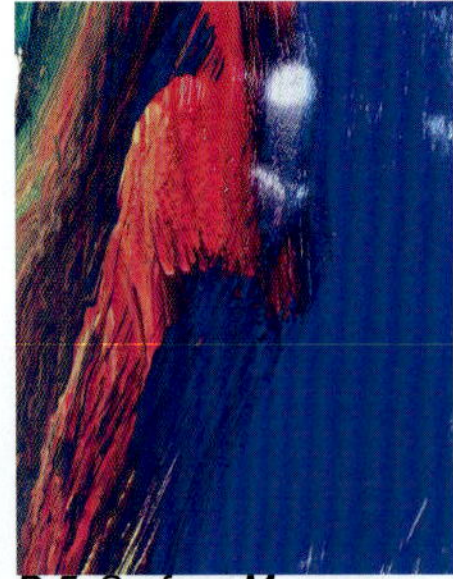

P. 5 Surface Memory, 2010
acrylic on canvas, 80 x 60 cm
Courtesy of Juan Vergez, Switzerland

MOVING IMAGES

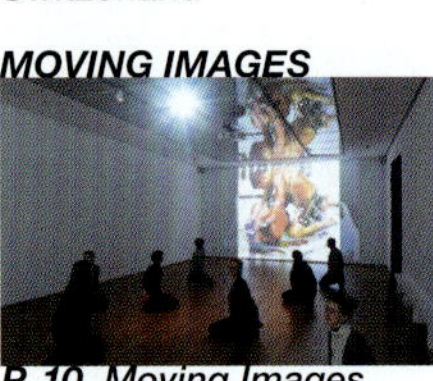

P. 10 Moving Images, 2015
installation view, Hamburger Bahnhof – Museum für Gegenwart, Berlin
Photo: David von Becker
Courtesy of the artist and PSM, Berlin

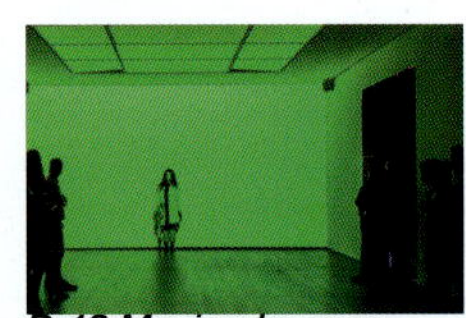

P. 12 Moving Images, 2015
installation view, Hamburger Bahnhof – Museum für Gegenwart, Berlin
Photo: David von Becker
Courtesy of the artist and PSM, Berlin

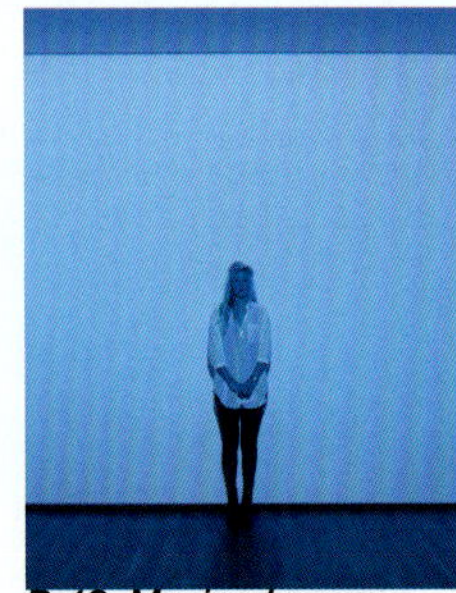

P. 13 Moving Images, 2015
installation view, Hamburger Bahnhof – Museum für Gegenwart, Berlin
Photo: David von Becker
Courtesy of the artist and PSM, Berlin

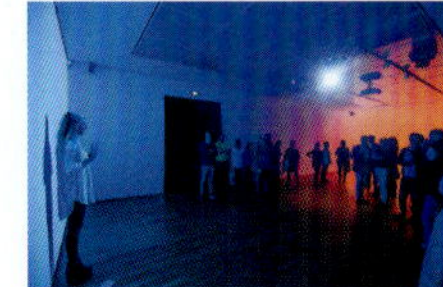

P. 14 Moving Images, 2015
installation view, Hamburger Bahnhof – Museum für Gegenwart, Berlin
Photo: David von Becker
Courtesy of the artist and PSM, Berlin

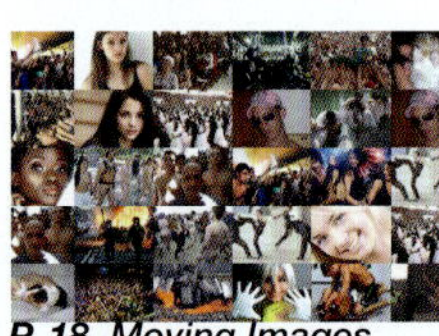

P. 18 Moving Images, 2015
video stills
Courtesy of the artist and PSM, Berlin

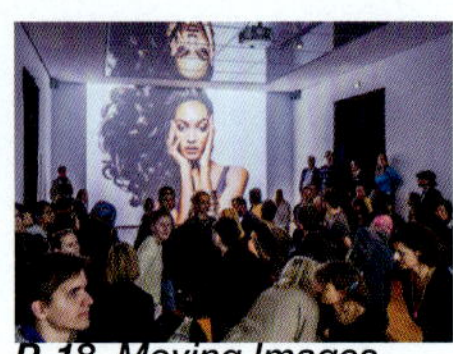

P. 18 Moving Images, 2015
installation view, Hamburger Bahnhof – Museum für Gegenwart, Berlin
Photo: David von Becker
Courtesy of the artist and PSM, Berlin

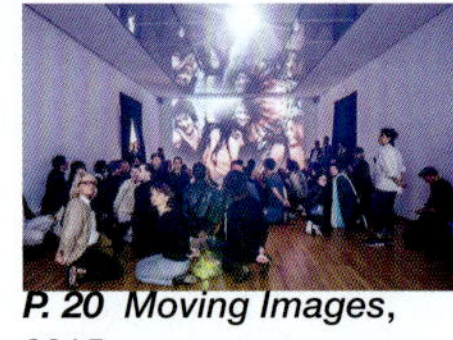

P. 20 Moving Images, 2015
installation view, Hamburger Bahnhof – Museum für Gegenwart, Berlin
Photo: David von Becker
Courtesy of the artist and PSM, Berlin

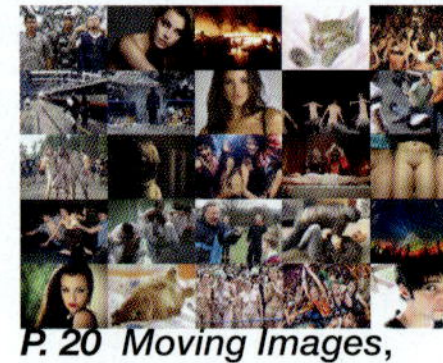

P. 20 Moving Images, 2015
video stills
Courtesy of the artist and PSM, Berlin

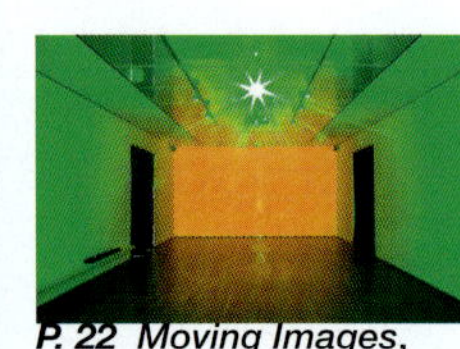

P. 22 Moving Images, 2015
installation view, Hamburger Bahnhof – Museum für Gegenwart, Berlin
Photo: David von Becker
Courtesy of the artist and PSM, Berlin

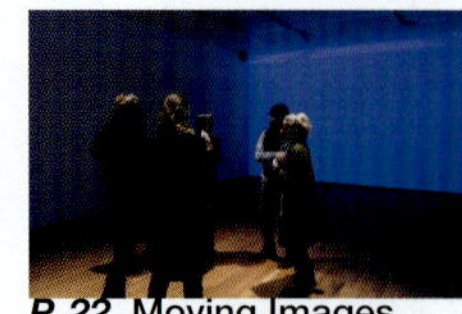

P. 22 Moving Images, 2015
installation view, Hamburger Bahnhof – Museum für Gegenwart, Berlin
Photo: David von Becker
Courtesy of the artist and PSM, Berlin

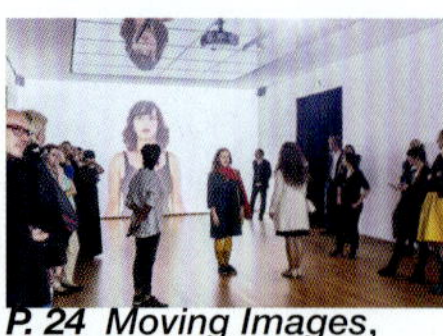

P. 24 Moving Images, 2015
installation view, Hamburger Bahnhof – Museum für Gegenwart, Berlin
Photo: David von Becker
Courtesy of the artist and PSM, Berlin

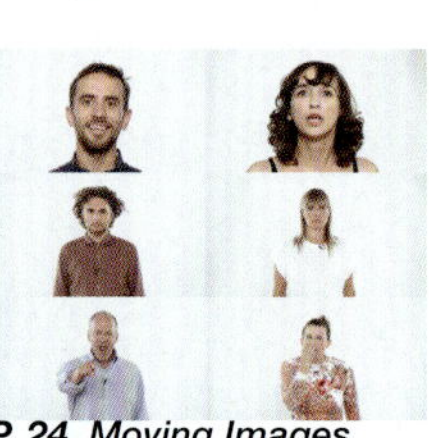

P. 24 Moving Images, 2015
video stills
Courtesy of the artist and PSM, Berlin

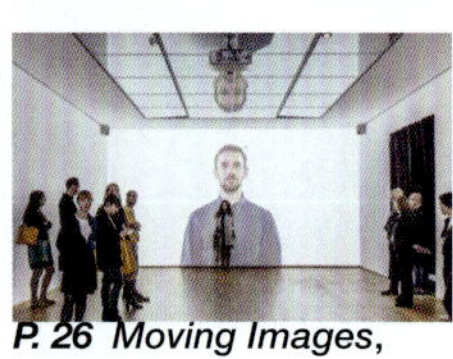

P. 26 Moving Images, 2015
installation view, Hamburger Bahnhof – Museum für Gegenwart, Berlin
Photo: David von Becker
Courtesy of the artist and PSM, Berlin

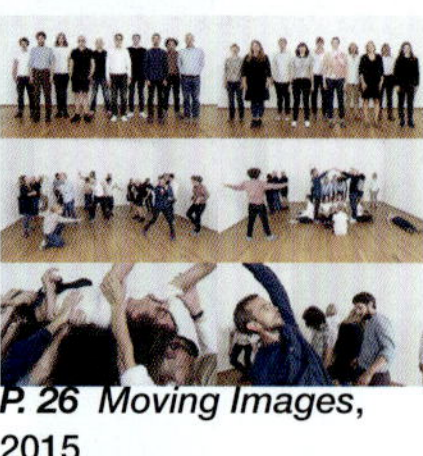

P. 26 Moving Images, 2015
video stills
Courtesy of the artist and PSM, Berlin

A GOOD REASON IS ONE THAT LOOKS LIKE ONE

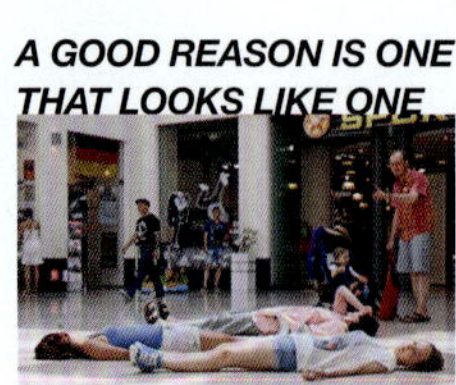

P. 28 A Good Reason Is One That Looks Like One, 2015
Postgalerie Karlsruhe as a part of the ZKM exhibition GLOBALE
Photo: ONUK
Courtesy of the artist and PSM, Berlin

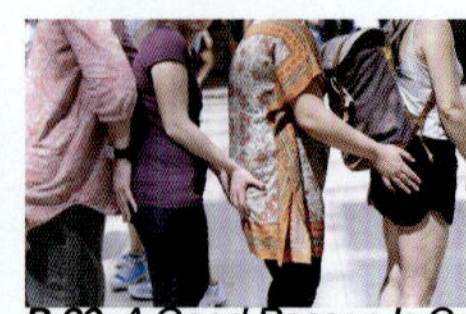

P. 30 A Good Reason Is One That Looks Like One, 2015
Postgalerie Karlsruhe as a part of the ZKM exhibition GLOBALE
Photo: ONUK
Courtesy of the artist and PSM, Berlin

P. 30 A Good Reason Is One That Looks Like One, 2015
Postgalerie Karlsruhe as a part of the ZKM exhibition GLOBALE
Photo: ONUK
Courtesy of the artist and PSM, Berlin

P. 31 A Good Reason Is One That Looks Like One, 2015
Postgalerie Karlsruhe as a part of the ZKM exhibition GLOBALE
Photo: ONUK
Courtesy of the artist and PSM, Berlin

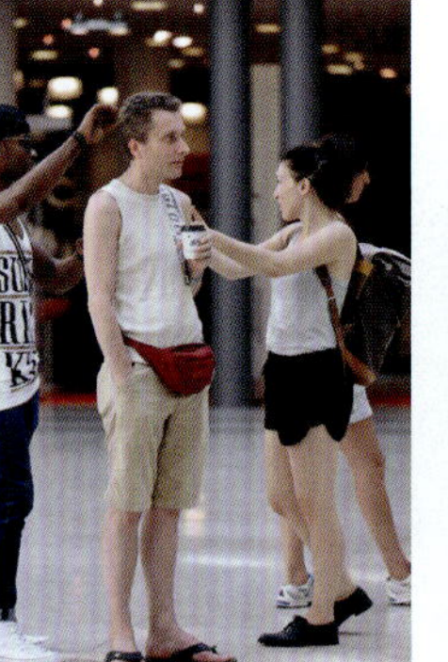

P. 32 A Good Reason Is One That Looks Like One, 2015
Postgalerie Karlsruhe as a part of the ZKM exhibition GLOBALE
Photo: ONUK
Courtesy of the artist and PSM, Berlin

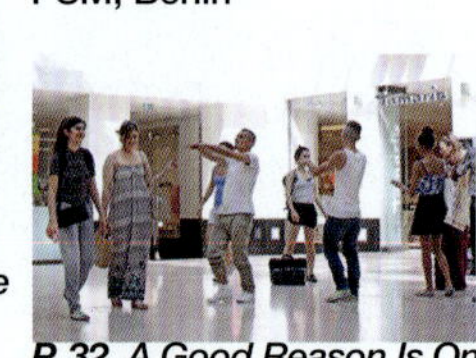

P. 32 A Good Reason Is One That Looks Like One, 2015
Postgalerie Karlsruhe as a part of the ZKM exhibition GLOBALE
Photo: ONUK
Courtesy of the artist and PSM, Berlin

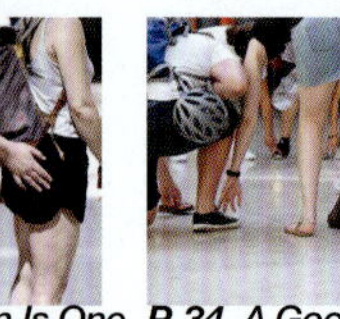

P. 34 A Good Reason Is One That Looks Like One, 2015
Postgalerie Karlsruhe as a part of the ZKM exhibition GLOBALE
Photo: ONUK
Courtesy of the artist and PSM, Berlin

FRONT

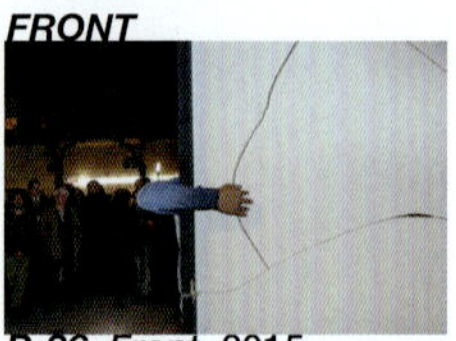

P. 36 Front, 2015
performance, Kunsthalle Wien
Photo: esel.at
Courtesy of the artist and PSM, Berlin

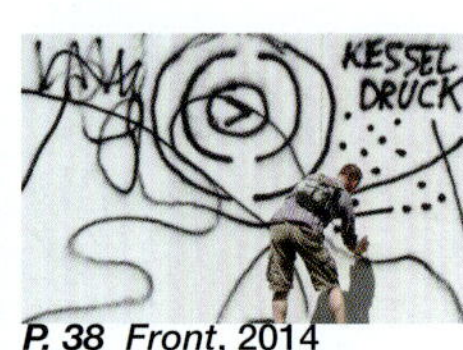

P. 38 Front, 2014
performance, Sennestadt, Bielefeld
Photo: Peter Händel
Courtesy of the artist and PSM, Berlin

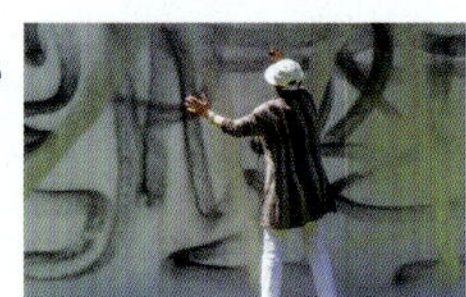

P. 38 Front, 2014
performance, Sennestadt, Bielefeld
Photo: Peter Händel
Courtesy of the artist and PSM, Berlin

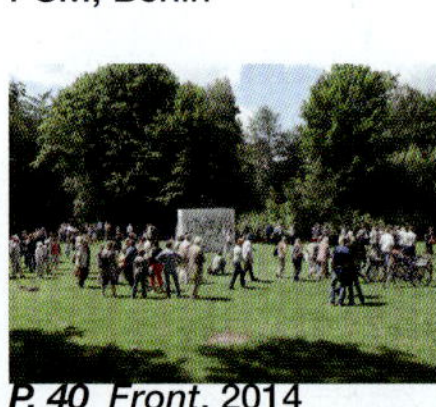

P. 40 Front, 2014
performance, Sennestadt, Bielefeld
Photo: Philipp Ottendörfer
Courtesy of the artist and PSM, Berlin

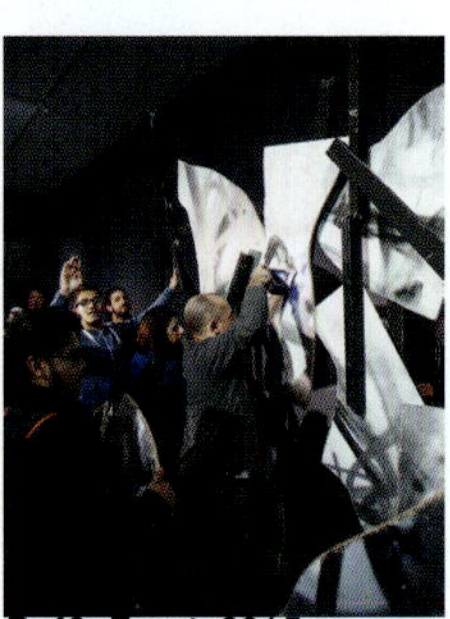

P. 40 Front, 2015
performance, Kunsthalle Wien
Photo: esel.at
Courtesy of the artist and PSM, Berlin

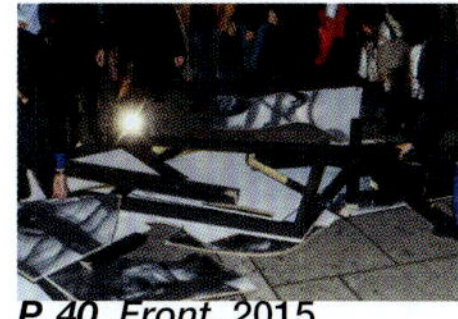
P. 40 Front, 2015
performance, Kunsthalle Wien
Photo: esel.at
Courtesy of the artist and PSM, Berlin

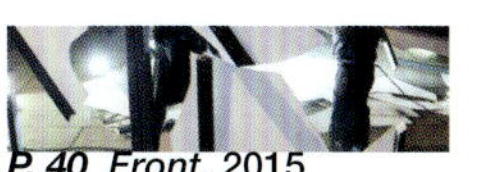
P. 40 Front, 2015
performance, Kunsthalle Wien
Photo: esel.at
Courtesy of the artist and PSM, Berlin

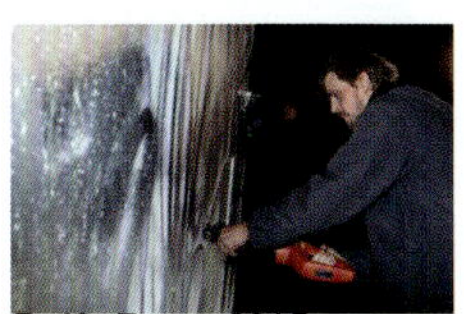
P. 42 Front, 2015
performance, Kunsthalle Wien
Photo: esel.at
Courtesy of the artist and PSM, Berlin

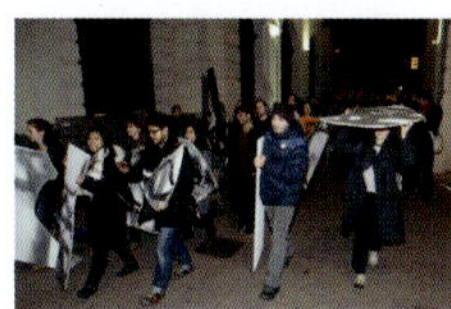
P. 42 Front, 2015
performance, Kunsthalle Wien
Photo: esel.at
Courtesy of the artist and PSM, Berlin

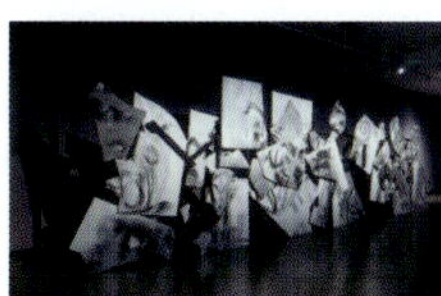
P. 44 Front, 2015
installation view, Political Populism, Kunsthalle Wien
Photo: Jorit Aust
Courtesy of the artist and PSM, Berlin

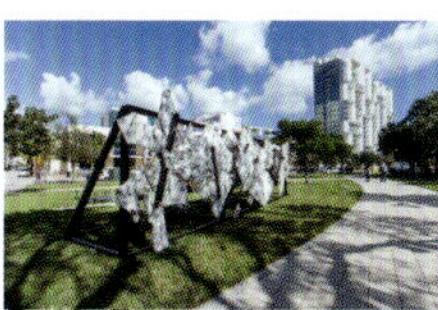
P. 46 Front, 2014
installation view, Public, Art Basel Miami Beach
Photo: Silvia Ros
Courtesy of the artist and PSM, Berlin

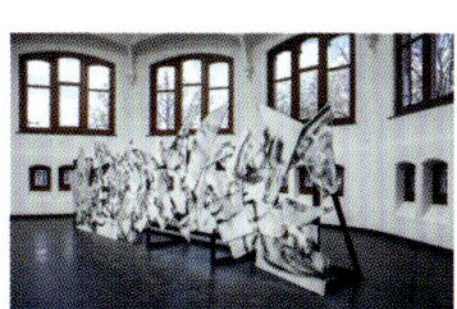
P. 48 Front (Kareth Schaffer), 2015
installation view, KIOSK, Ghent
Photo: Tom Callemin
Courtesy of the artist and PSM, Berlin

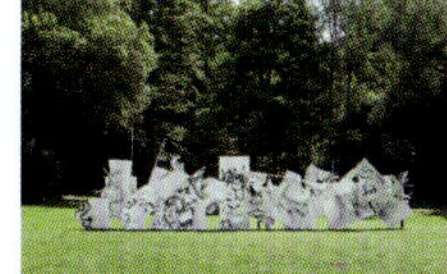
P. 50 Front, 2014
installation view, Vor Ort – Kunstprojekt Sennestadt
Photo: Philipp Ottendörfer
Courtesy of the artist and PSM, Berlin

AVAILABLE

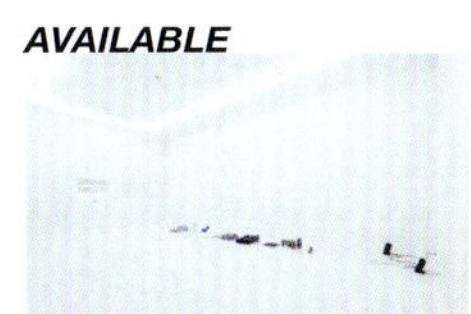
P. 52 Available, 2015
installation view, Kunstverein Braunschweig
Photo: Stefan Stark
Courtesy of the artist and PSM, Berlin

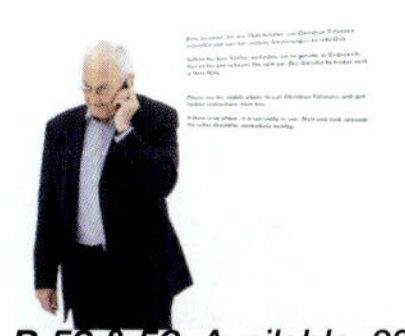
P. 52 & 56 Available, 2015
installation view, Kunstverein Braunschweig
Photo: Stefan Stark
Courtesy of the artist and PSM, Berlin

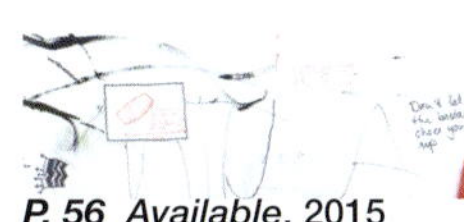
P. 56 Available, 2015
installation view, Kunstverein Braunschweig
Photo: Stefan Stark
Courtesy of the artist and PSM, Berlin

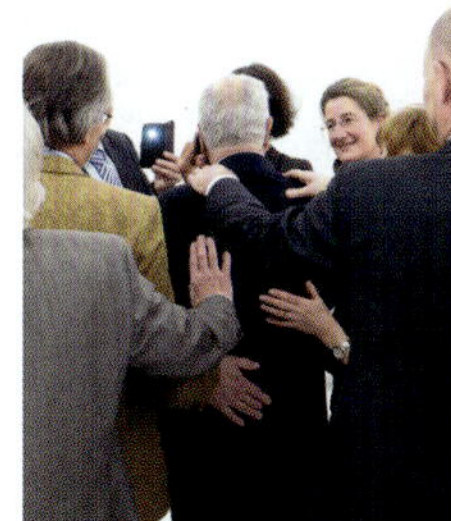
P. 57 Available, 2015
installation view, Kunstverein Braunschweig
Photo: Stefan Stark
Courtesy of the artist and PSM, Berlin

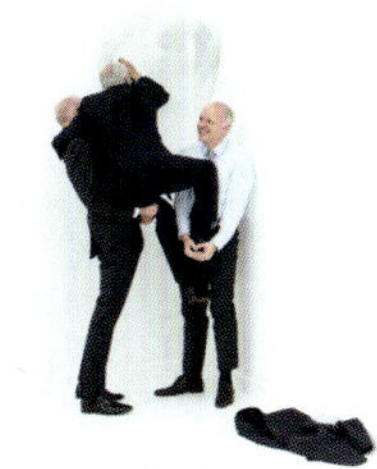
P. 58 Available, 2015
installation view, Kunstverein Braunschweig
Photo: Stefan Stark
Courtesy of the artist and PSM, Berlin

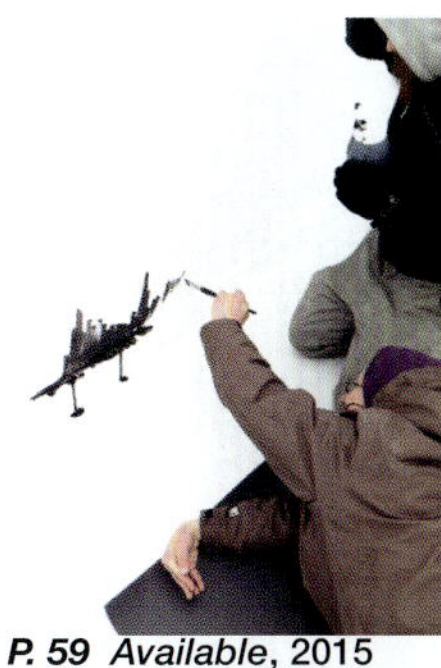
P. 59 Available, 2015
installation view, Kunstverein Braunschweig
Photo: Stefan Stark
Courtesy of the artist and PSM, Berlin

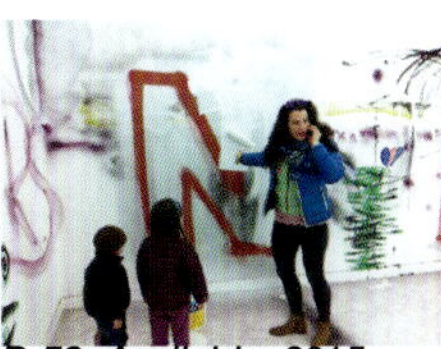
P. 59 Available, 2015
installation view, Kunstverein Braunschweig
Photo: sent by Email by visitor
Courtesy of the artist and PSM, Berlin

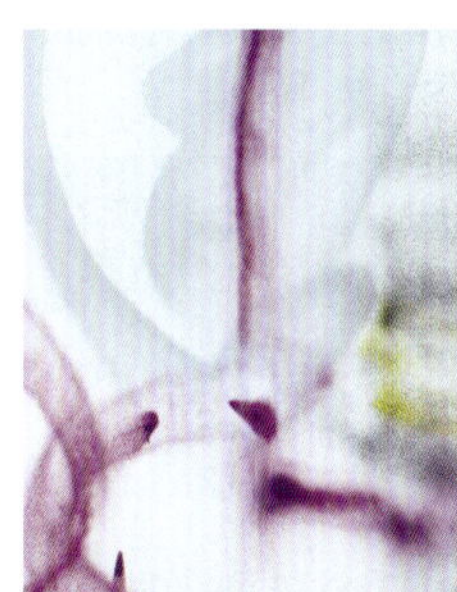
P. 59 Available, 2015
installation view, Kunstverein Braunschweig
Photo: Stefan Stark
Courtesy of the artist and PSM, Berlin

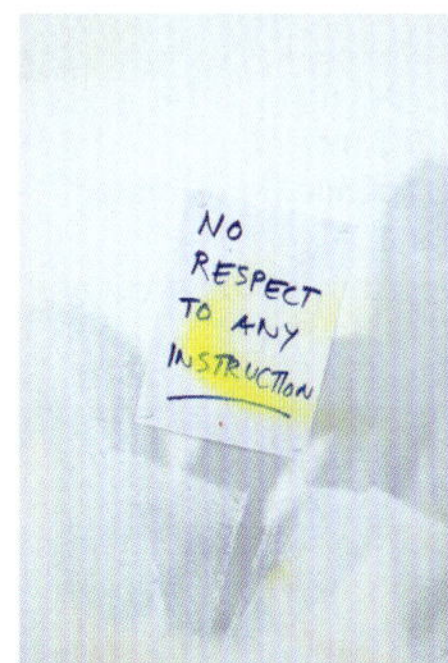

P. 59 Available, 2015
installation view, Kunstverein Braunschweig
Photo: Stefan Stark
Courtesy of the artist and PSM, Berlin

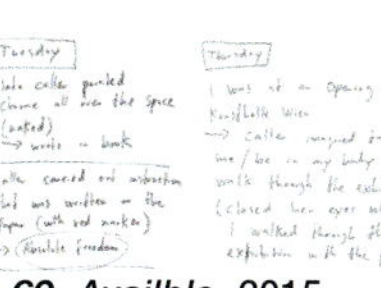
P. 60 Availble, 2015
Scan from Christian Falsnaes' exhibition diary.
Courtesy of the artist and PSM, Berlin

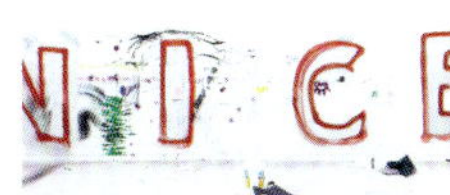
P. 62 Available, 2015
installation view, Kunstverein Braunschweig
Photo: Stefan Stark
Courtesy of the artist and PSM, Berlin

JUSTIFIED BELEIFS

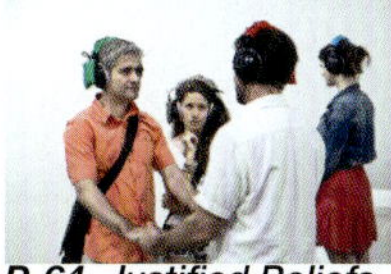
P. 64 Justified Beliefs, 2014
installation view, Art Basel Statements with PSM, Berlin
Photo: Kostas Maros
Courtesy of the artist and PSM, Berlin / Private collection, London

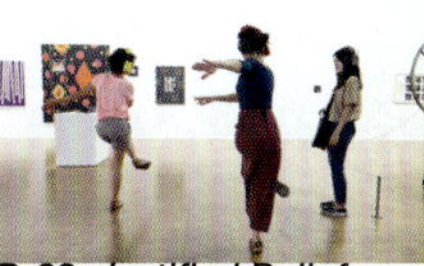
P. 66 Justified Beliefs, 2014
installation view, Centre Pompidou, Paris, 2015
Image Courtesy of Centre Pompidou.
Photo: Hervé Véronèse
Courtesy of the artist and PSM, Berlin / Private collection, London

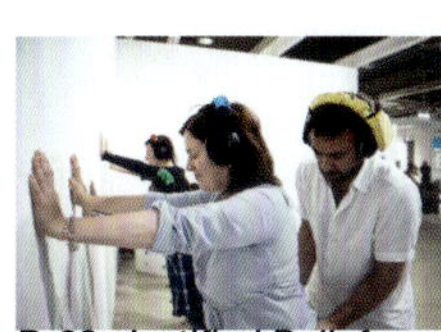
P. 66 Justified Beliefs, 2014
installation view, Art Basel Statements with PSM, Berlin
Photo: Kostas Maros
Courtesy of the artist and PSM, Berlin / Private collection, London

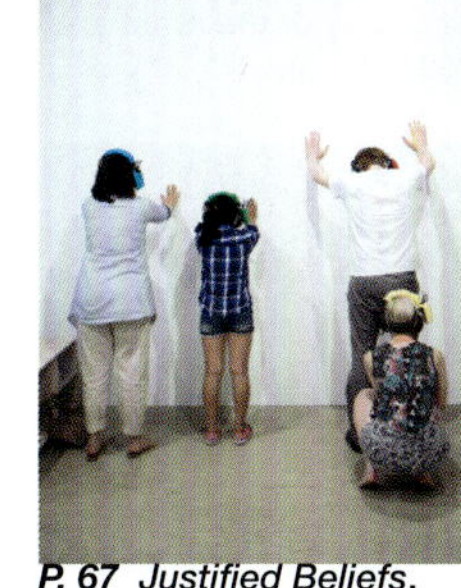
P. 67 Justified Beliefs, 2014
installation view, Art Basel Statements with PSM, Berlin
Photo: Kostas Maros
Courtesy of the artist and PSM, Berlin / Private collection, London

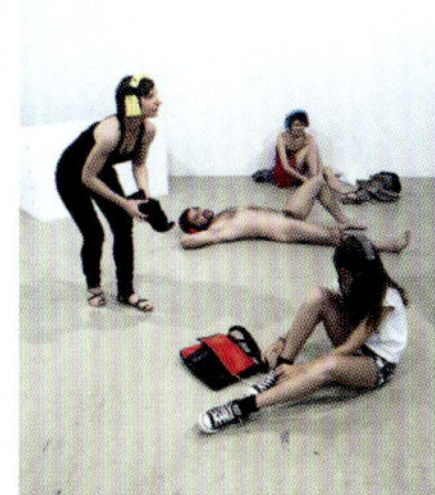
P. 68 Justified Beliefs, 2014
installation view, Art Basel Statements with PSM, Berlin
Photo: Kostas Maros
Courtesy of the artist and PSM, Berlin / Private collection, London

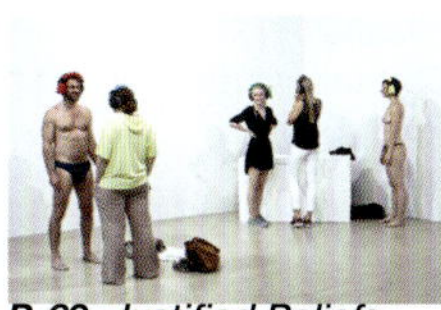
P. 69 Justified Beliefs, 2014
installation view, Art Basel Statements with PSM, Berlin
Photo: Kostas Maros
Courtesy of the artist and PSM, Berlin / Private collection, London

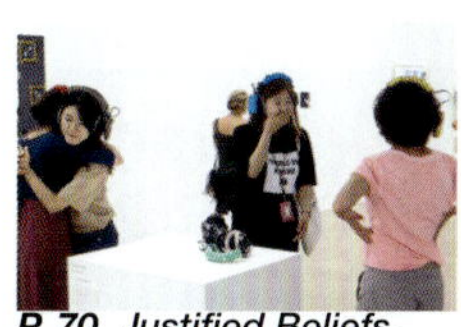
P. 70 Justified Beliefs, 2014
installation view, Centre Pompidou, Paris, 2015
Image Courtesy of Centre Pompidou. Photo: Hervé Véronèse
Courtesy of the artist and PSM, Berlin / Private collection, London

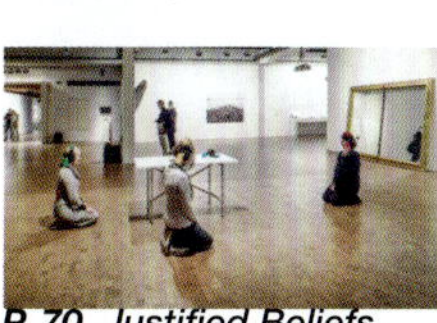
P. 70 Justified Beliefs, 2014
installation view, Akademie der Künste, Berlin
Photo: Roman März
Courtesy of the artist and PSM, Berlin / Private collection, London

SURFACE MEMORY

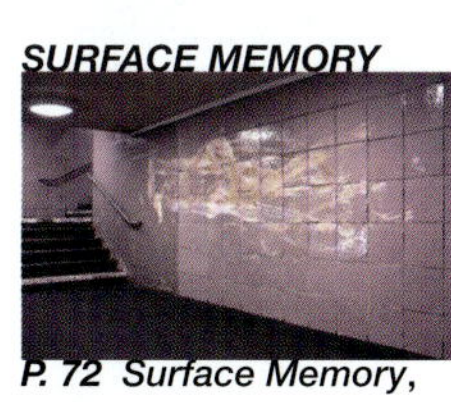
P. 72 Surface Memory, 2015
acrylic on surface in public space
Photo: Christian Falsnaes
Courtesy of the Collection Juan and Patricia Vergez, Buenos Aires

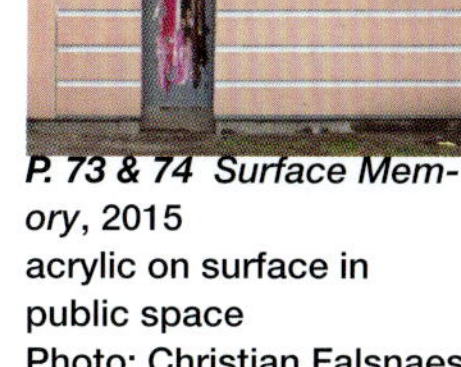
P. 73 & 74 Surface Memory, 2015
acrylic on surface in public space
Photo: Christian Falsnaes
Courtesy of Peter Eiff, Berlin

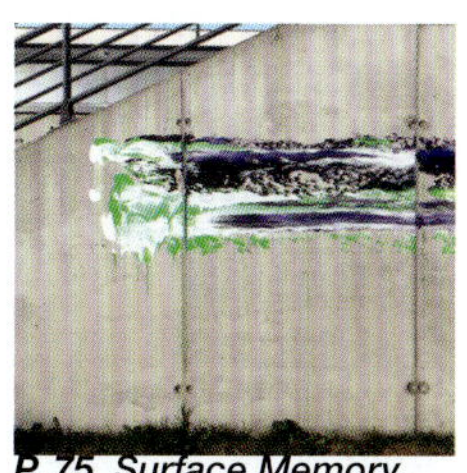
P. 75 Surface Memory, 2015
acrylic on surface in public space
Photo: Christian Falsnaes
Private Collection, Berlin

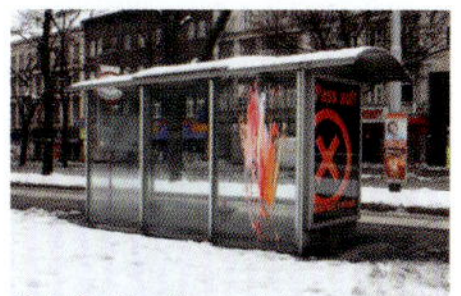
P. 76 Surface Memory, 2010
acrylic on surface in public space
Photo: Christian Falsnaes
Private collection, Vienna

P. 76 Surface Memory, 2010
acrylic on canvas, 80 x 60 cm
Private collection, Vienna

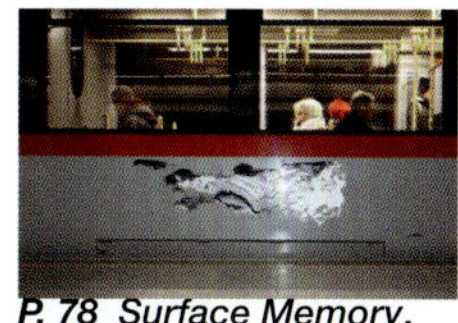
P. 78 Surface Memory, 2012
oil on surface in public space
Photo: Christian Falsnaes
Courtesy of the artist and PSM, Berlin

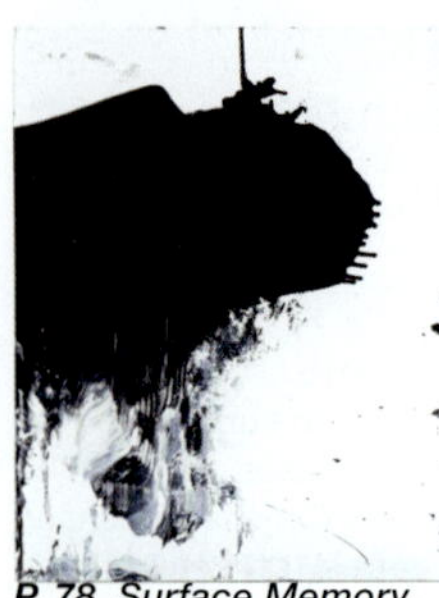
P. 78 Surface Memory, 2010
oil on canvas, 110 x 90 cm
Courtesy of the artist and PSM, Berlin

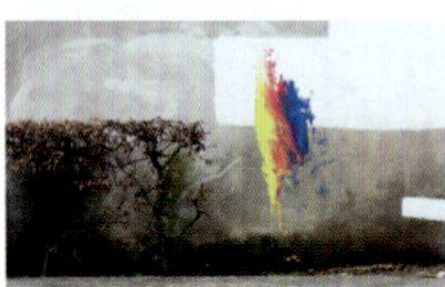
P. 80 Surface Memory, 2010
acrylic on surface in public space
Photo: Christian Falsnaes
Collection of Juan Vergez, Switzerland

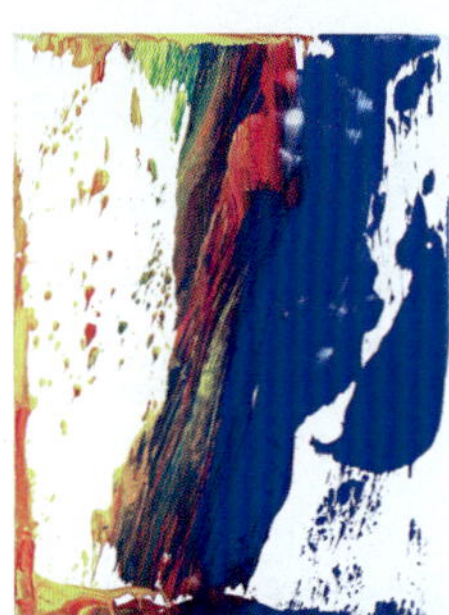
P. 80 Surface Memory, 2010
acrylic on canvas, 80 x 60 cm
Collection of Juan Vergez, Switzerland

THE TITLE IS YOUR NAME

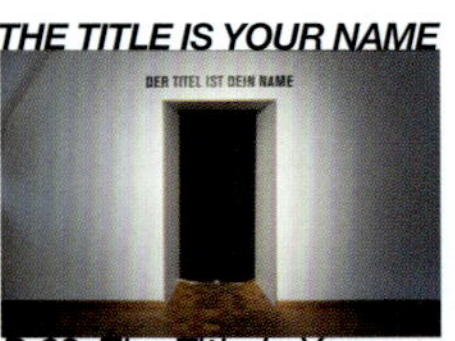

P. 82 The Title Is Your Name, 2015
installation view, Bielefelder Kunstverein
Photo: Philipp Ottendörfer
Courtesy of the artist and PSM, Berlin

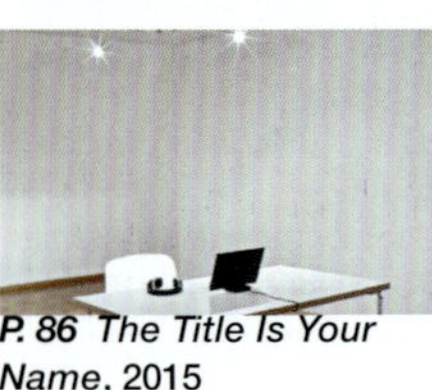
P. 86 The Title Is Your Name, 2015
installation view, Bielefelder Kunstverein
Photo: Philipp Ottendörfer
Courtesy of the artist and PSM, Berlin

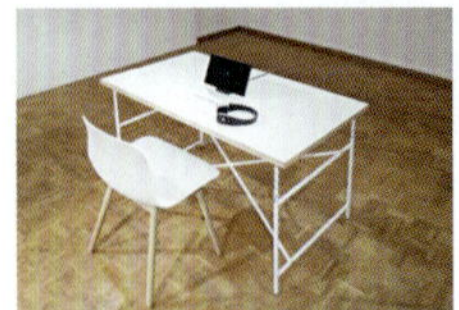
P. 86 The Title Is Your Name, 2015
installation view, Bielefelder Kunstverein
Photo: Philipp Ottendörfer
Courtesy of the artist and PSM, Berlin

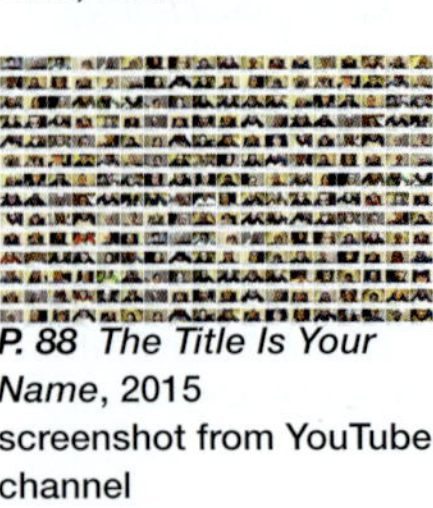
P. 88 The Title Is Your Name, 2015
screenshot from YouTube channel
Courtesy of the artist and PSM, Berlin

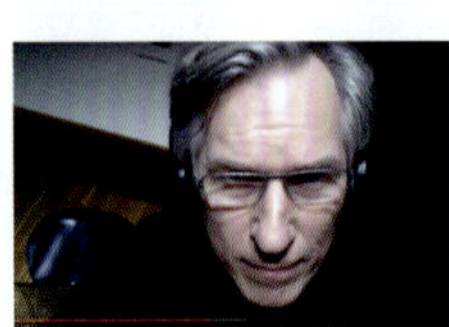
P. 90 The Title Is Your Name, 2015
screenshot from YouTube channel
Courtesy of the artist and PSM, Berlin

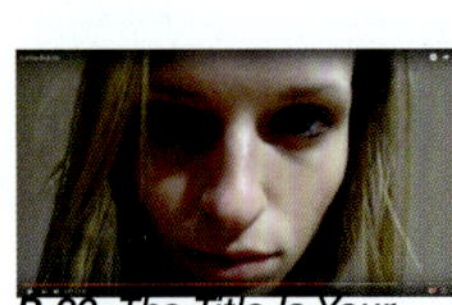
P. 90 The Title Is Your Name, 2015
screenshot from YouTube channel
Courtesy of the artist and PSM, Berlin

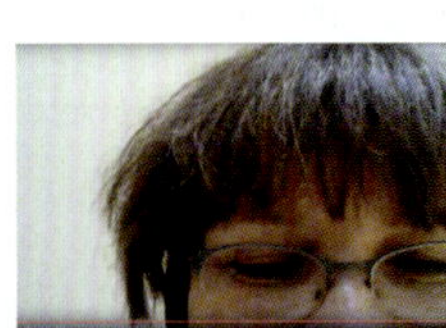
P. 92 The Title Is Your Name, 2015
screenshot from YouTube channel
Courtesy of the artist and PSM, Berlin

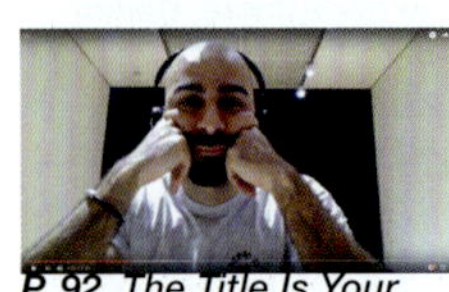
P. 92 The Title Is Your Name, 2015
screenshot from YouTube channel
Courtesy of the artist and PSM, Berlin

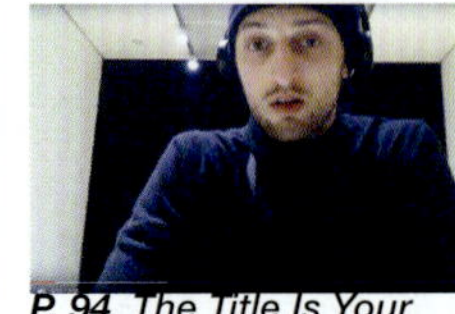
P. 94 The Title Is Your Name, 2015
screenshot from YouTube channel
Courtesy of the artist and PSM, Berlin

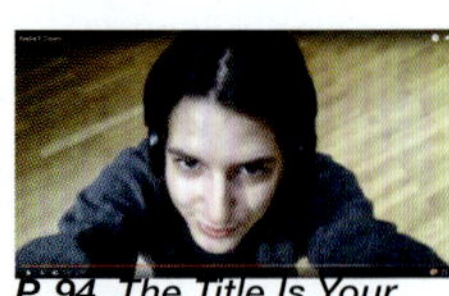
P. 94 The Title Is Your Name, 2015
screenshot from YouTube channel
Courtesy of the artist and PSM, Berlin

RISE

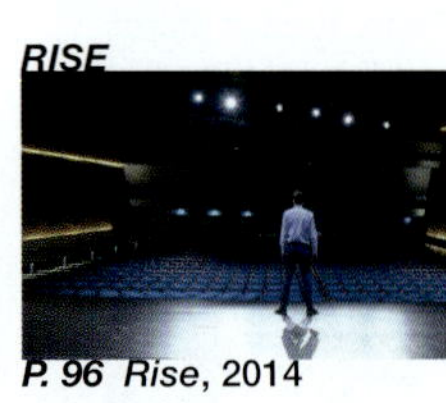
P. 96 Rise, 2014
video still
Akademie der Künste, Berlin
Courtesy of the artist and PSM, Berlin

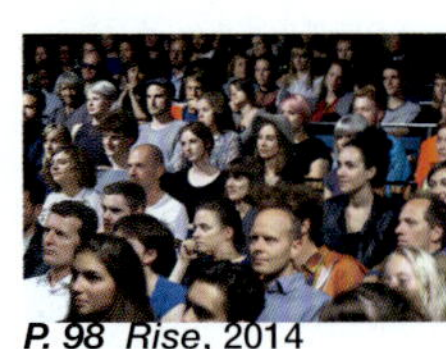
P. 98 Rise, 2014
video still
Akademie der Künste, Berlin
Courtesy of the artist and PSM, Berlin

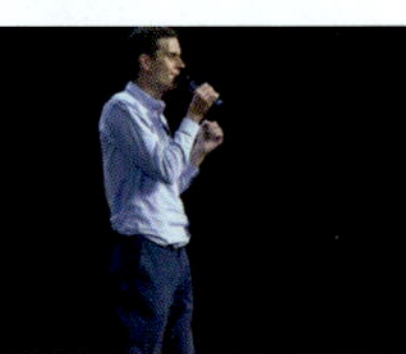
P.98 Rise, 2014
video still
Akademie der Künste, Berlin
Courtesy of the artist and PSM, Berlin

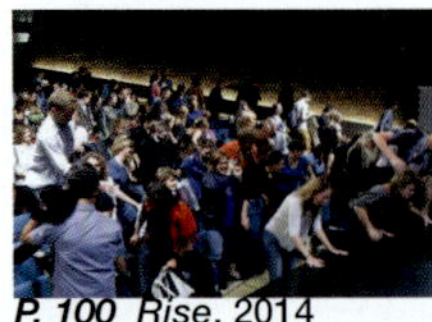
P. 100 Rise, 2014
video still
Akademie der Künste, Berlin
Courtesy of the artist and PSM, Berlin

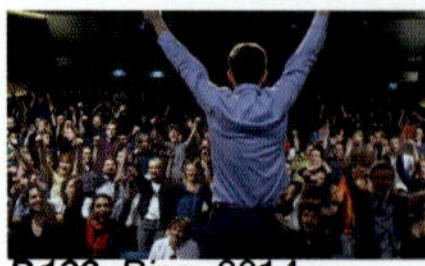
P.100 Rise, 2014
video still
Akademie der Künste, Berlin
Courtesy of the artist and PSM, Berlin

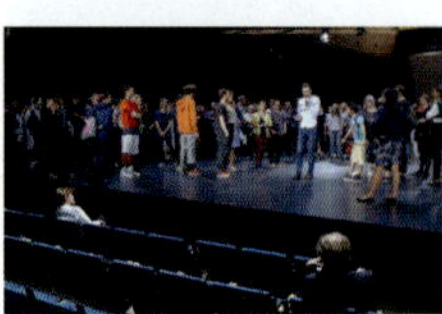
P. 102 Rise, 2014
video still
Akademie der Künste, Berlin
Courtesy of the artist and PSM, Berlin

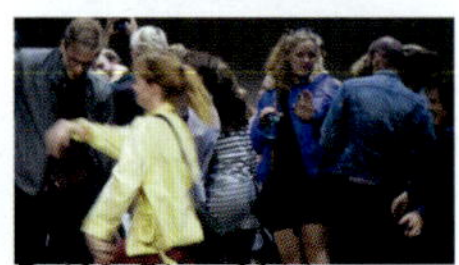
P. 102 Rise, 2014
video still
Akademie der Künste, Berlin
Courtesy of the artist and PSM, Berlin

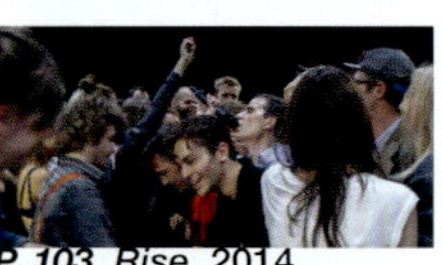
P. 103 Rise, 2014
video still
Akademie der Künste, Berlin
Courtesy of the artist and PSM, Berlin

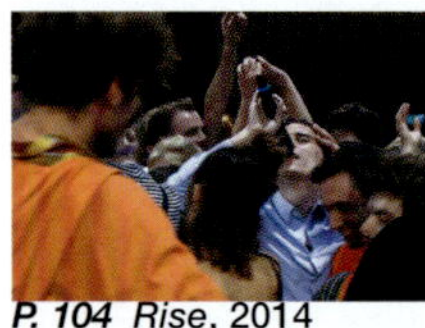
P. 104 Rise, 2014
video still
Akademie der Künste, Berlin
Courtesy of the artist and PSM, Berlin

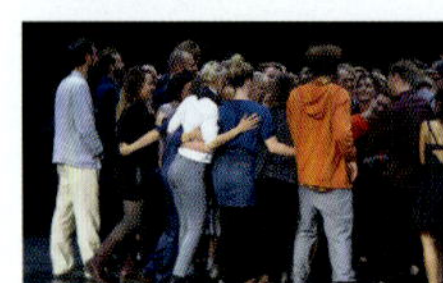
P. 104 Rise, 2014
video still
Akademie der Künste, Berlin
Courtesy of the artist and PSM, Berlin

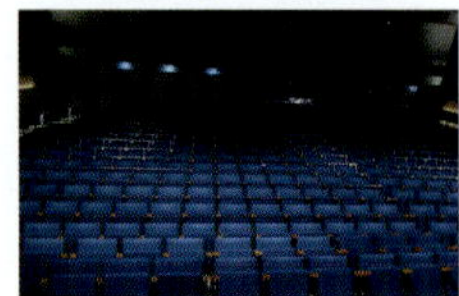
P. 106 Rise, 2014
video still
Akademie der Künste, Berlin
Courtesy of the artist and PSM, Berlin

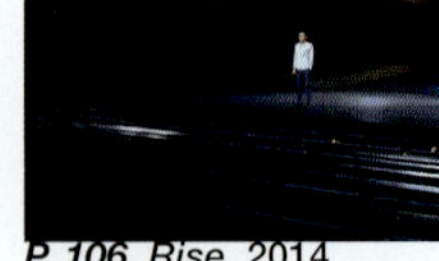
P. 106 Rise, 2014
video still
Akademie der Künste, Berlin
Courtesy of the artist and PSM, Berlin

LOOK FOLLOW LIKE CONNECT

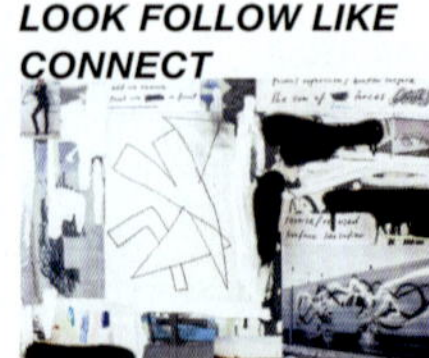
P. 108 Afterwards, 2013
mixed media behind and on glass, 70 x 100 cm
Courtesy of the artist and PSM, Berlin

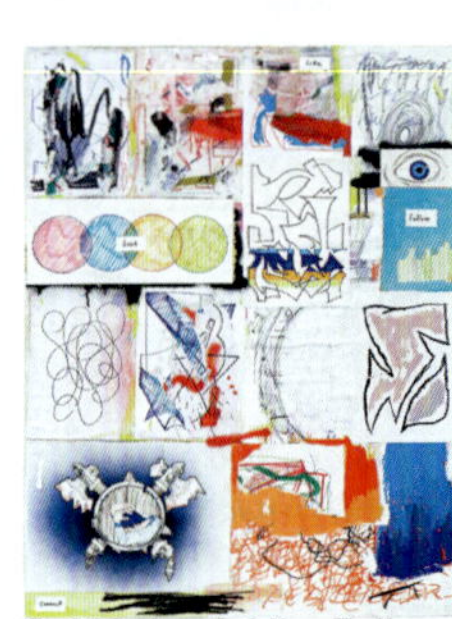
P. 110 Look Like Follow Connect, 2016
mixed media on canvas, 160 x 120 cm
Private collection, London

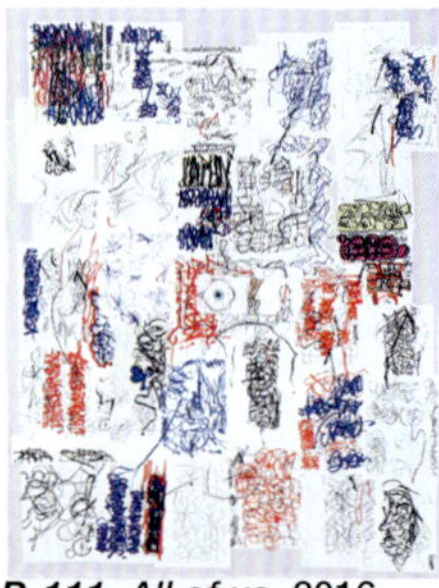
P. 111 All of us, 2016
mixed media on canvas, 160 x 120 cm
Courtesy of the artist and PSM, Berlin

P. 112 Perfect Body, 2012
mixed media behind and on glass, 73 x 53 cm
Courtesy of the artist and PSM, Berlin

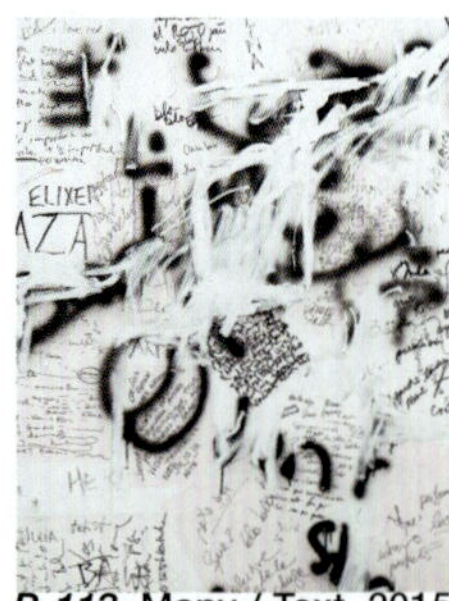
P. 113 Many / Text, 2015
mixed media on canvas, 200 x 150 cm
Courtesy of the artist and PSM, Berlin

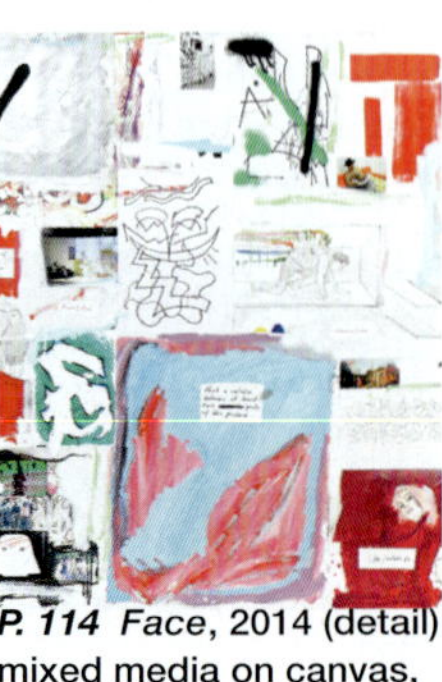
P. 114 Face, 2014 (detail)
mixed media on canvas, 150 x 200 cm
Private collection, London

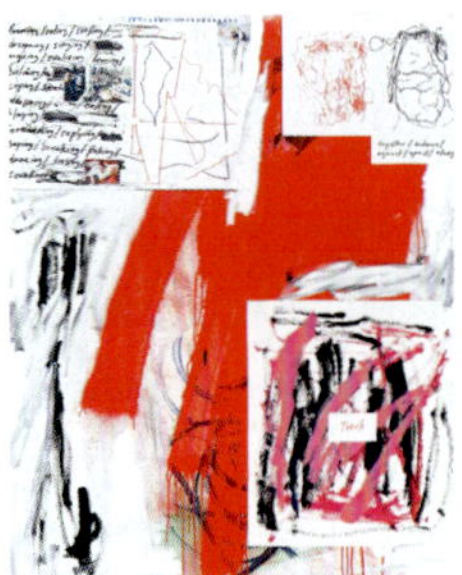
P. 115 Touch, 2014
mixed media on canvas, 150 x 110 cm
Collection of Juan and Patricia Vergez, Buenos Aires

OPENING

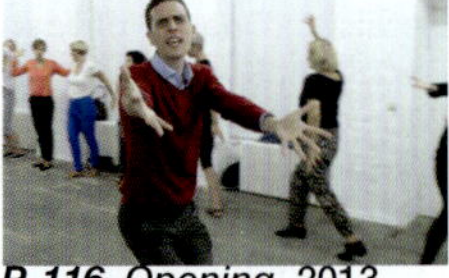
P. 116 Opening, 2013
video still
KW Institute of Contemporary Art, Berlin
Courtesy of the artist and PSM, Berlin / Collection of Juan and Patricia Vergez, Buenos Aires

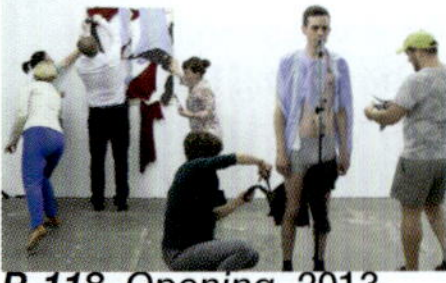
P. 118 Opening, 2013
video still
KW Institute of Contemporary Art, Berlin
Courtesy of the artist and PSM, Berlin / Collection of Juan and Patricia Vergez, Buenos Aires

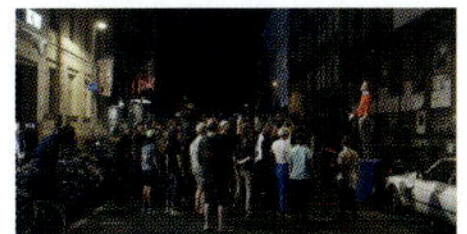
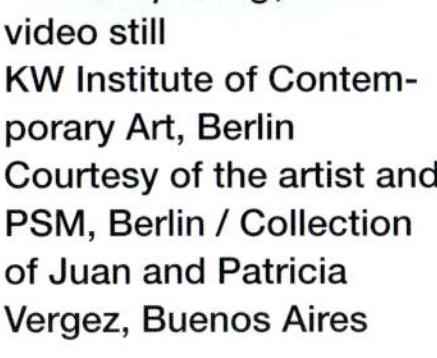

***P. 118** Opening*, 2013
video still
KW Institute of Contemporary Art, Berlin
Courtesy of the artist and PSM, Berlin / Collection of Juan and Patricia Vergez, Buenos Aires

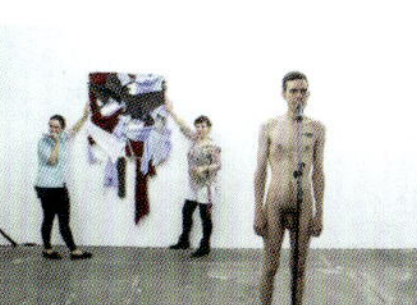

***P. 120** Opening*, 2013
video still
KW Institute of Contemporary Art, Berlin
Courtesy of the artist and PSM, Berlin / Collection of Juan and Patricia Vergez, Buenos Aires

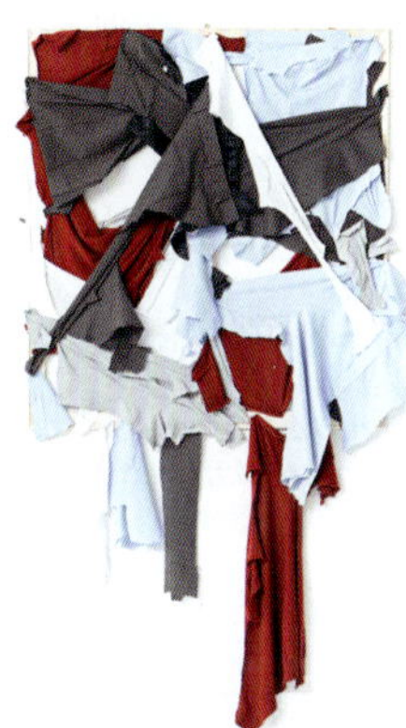

***P. 122** Opening*, 2013
cut clothes on stretcher bars, 100 x 80 cm
Collection of Juan and Patricia Vergez, Buenos Aires

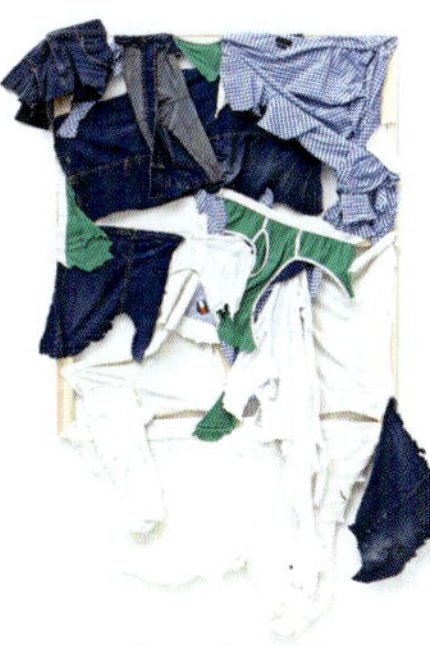

***P. 123** Opening*, 2014
cut clothes on stretcher bars, 120 x 100 cm
Courtesy of the artist and PSM, Berlin

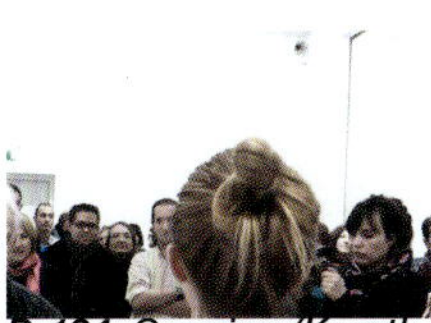

***P. 124** Opening (Kareth Schaffer)*, 2015
video still
Courtesy of the Musée départemental d'art contemporain de Rochechouart

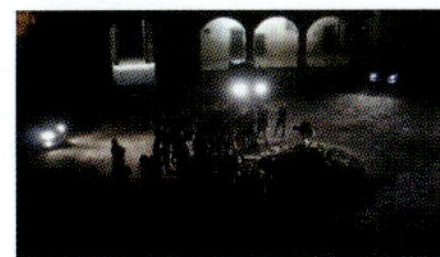

***P. 124** Opening (Kareth Schaffer)*, 2015
video still
Courtesy of the Musée départemental d'art contemporain de Rochechouart

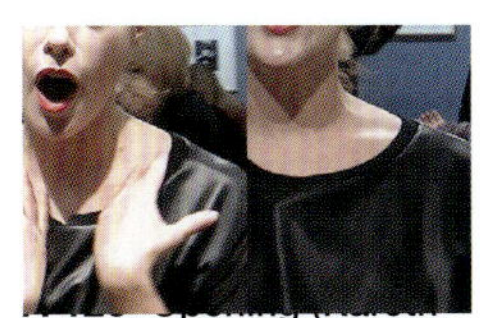

Schaffer), 2015
video stills
Courtesy of the Musée départemental d'art contemporain de Rochechouart

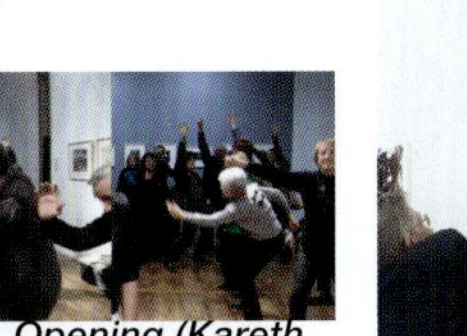

***P. 126** Opening (Kareth Schaffer)*, 2015
video still
Courtesy of the Musée départemental d'art contemporain de Rochechouart

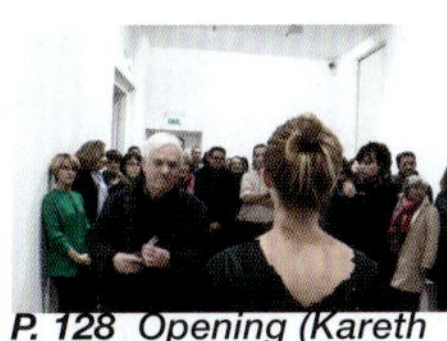

***P. 128** Opening (Kareth Schaffer)*, 2015
video still
Courtesy of the Musée départemental d'art contemporain de Rochechouart

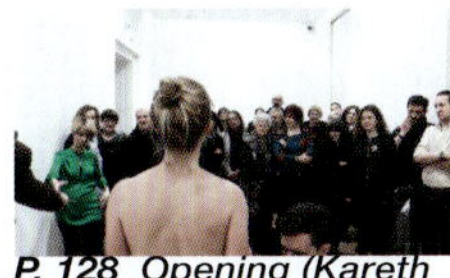

***P. 128** Opening (Kareth Schaffer)*, 2015
video still
Courtesy of the Musée départemental d'art contemporain de Rochechouart

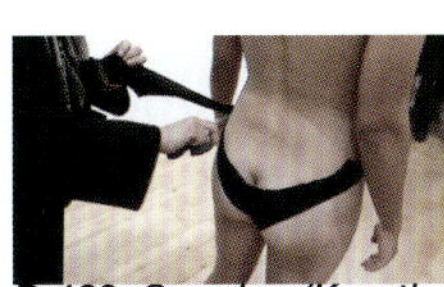

***P. 129** Opening (Kareth Schaffer)*, 2015
video still
Courtesy of the Musée départemental d'art contemporain de Rochechouart

ONE

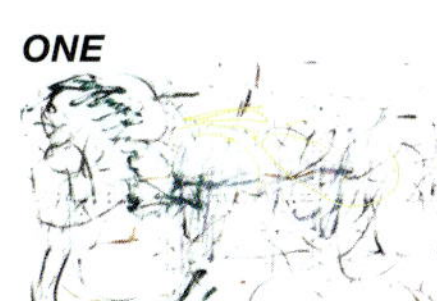

***P. 130** One*, 2013
oil on canvas, 200 x 280 cm
Private collection, London

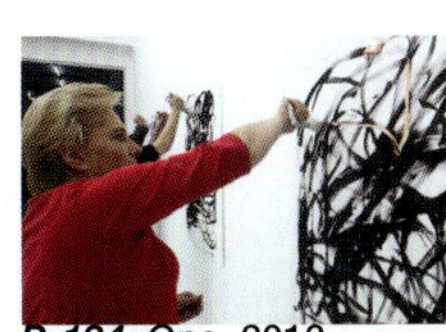

***P. 134** One*, 2013
performance, DREI, Cologne
Photo: Alwin Lay
Courtesy of the artist and PSM, Berlin

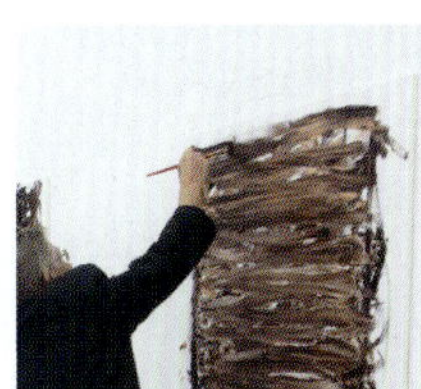

***P. 135** One*, 2013
performance, DREI, Cologne
Photo: Alwin Lay
Courtesy of the artist and PSM, Berlin

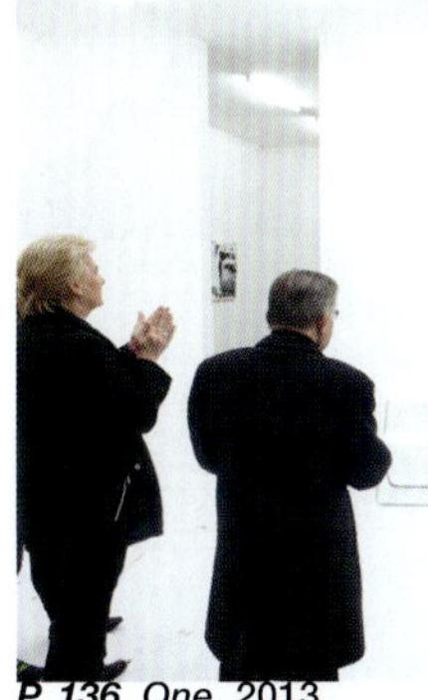

***P. 136** One*, 2013
performance, DREI, Cologne
Photo: Alwin Lay
Courtesy of the artist and PSM, Berlin

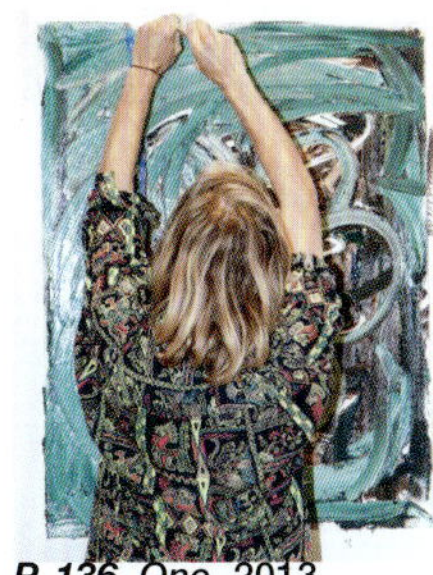

***P. 136** One*, 2013
performance, Galerie im Taxis Palais, Innsbruck
Photo: Rainar Iglar
Courtesy of the artist and PSM, Berlin

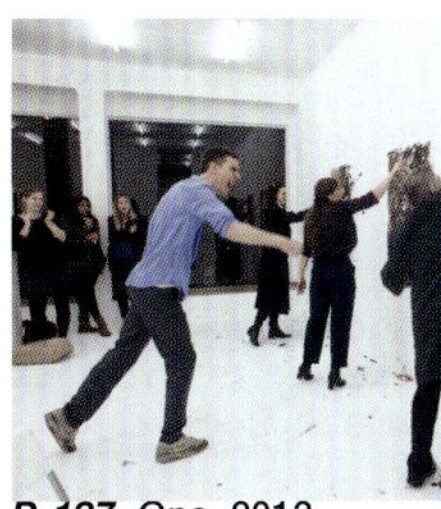

***P. 137** One*, 2013
performance, DREI, Cologne
Photo: Alwin Lay
Courtesy of the artist and PSM, Berlin

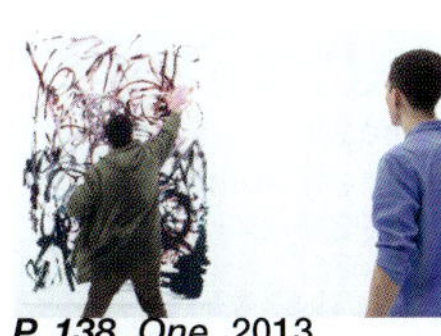

***P. 138** One*, 2013
performance, DREI, Cologne
Photo: Alwin Lay
Courtesy of the artist and PSM, Berlin

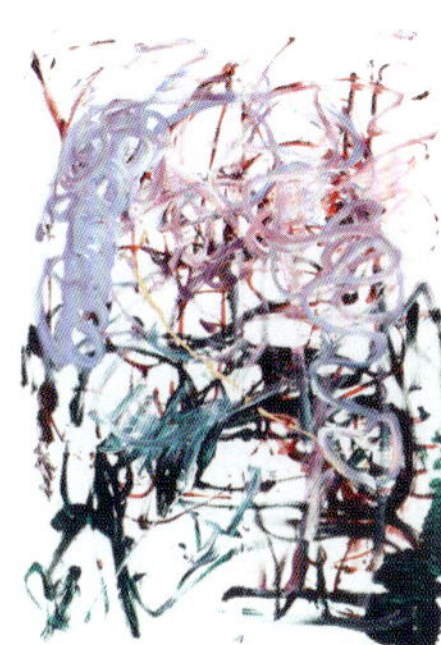

***P. 139** One*, 2013
oil on canvas, 220 x 150 cm
Courtesy of the artist and PSM, Berlin

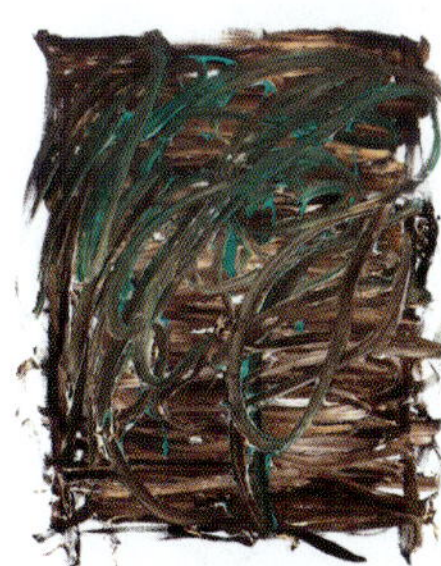

***P. 140** One*, 2013
oil on canvas, 100 x 80 cm
Courtesy of the artist and PSM, Berlin

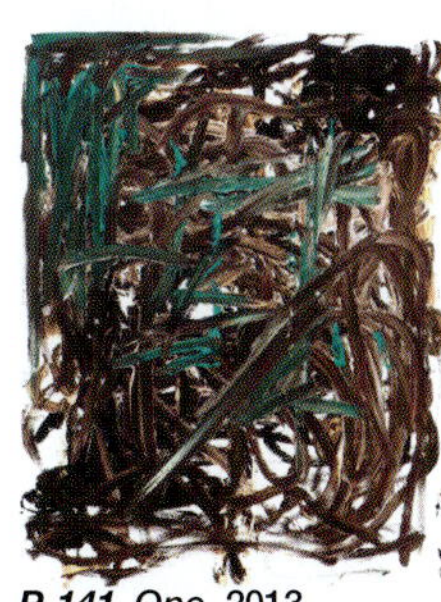

***P. 141** One*, 2013
oil on canvas, 100 x 80 cm
Courtesy of the artist and PSM, Berlin

MALE BEHAVIOR AS A RESULT OF SOCIETAL POWER RELATIONS BETWEEN ARTIST AND AUDIENCE

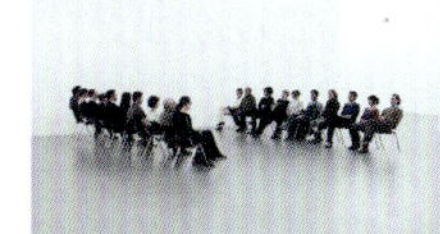
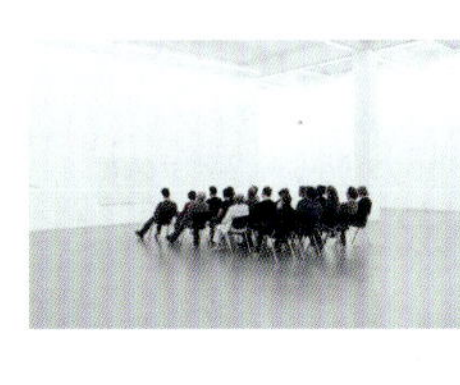
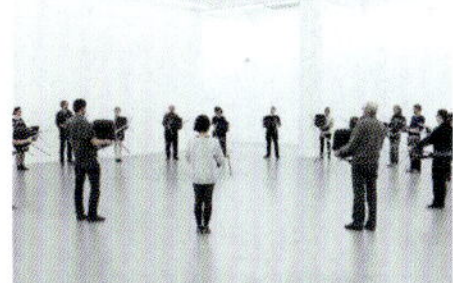
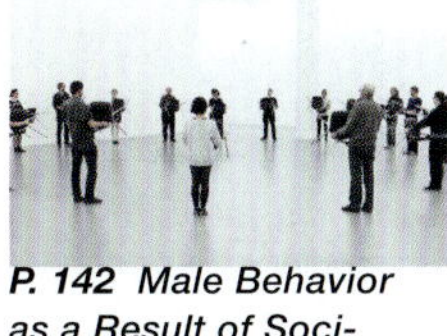

***P. 142** Male Behavior as a Result of Societal Power Relations between Artist and Audience*, 2013
video stills
Bonner Kunstverein
Courtesy of the artist and PSM, Berlin

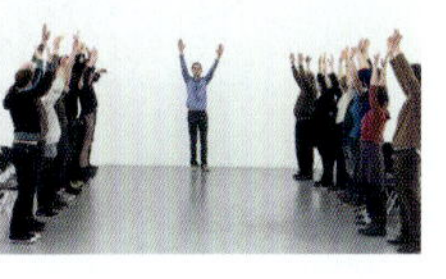
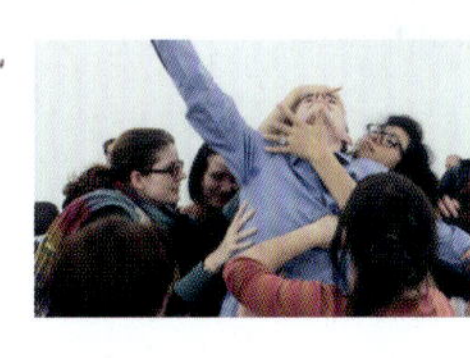
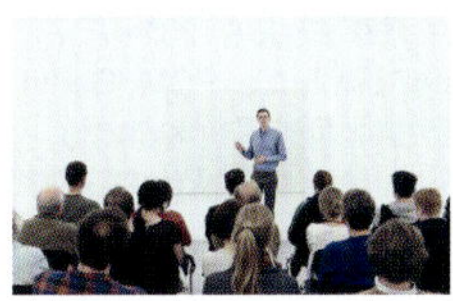
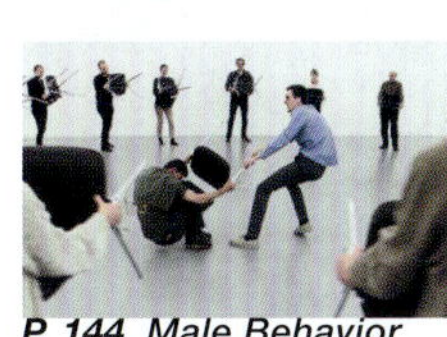

***P. 144** Male Behavior as a Result of Societal Power Relations between Artist and Audience*, 2013
video stills
Bonner Kunstverein
Courtesy of the artist and PSM, Berlin

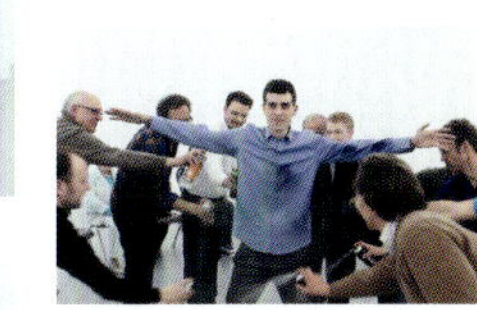

***P. 146** Male Behavior as a Result of Societal Power Relations between Artist and Audience*, 2013
video stills
Bonner Kunstverein
Courtesy of the artist and PSM, Berlin

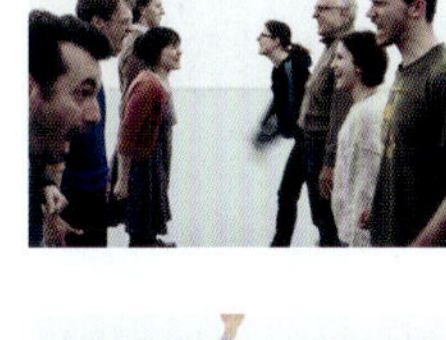
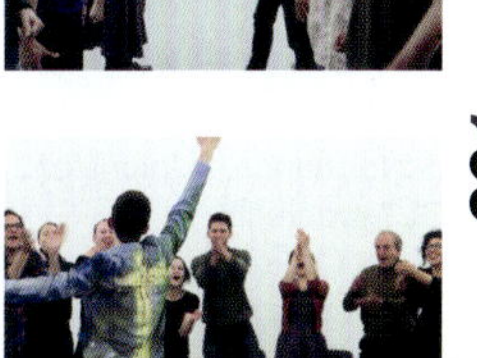
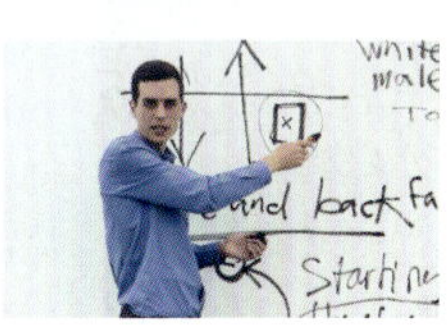
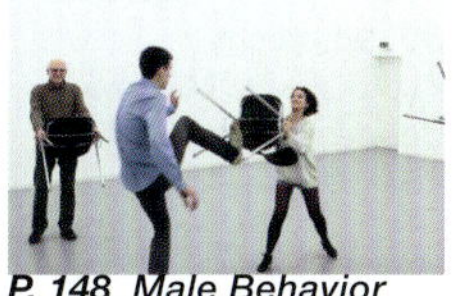

***P. 148** Male Behavior as a Result of Societal Power Relations between Artist and Audience*, 2013
video stills
Bonner Kunstverein
Courtesy of the artist and PSM, Berlin

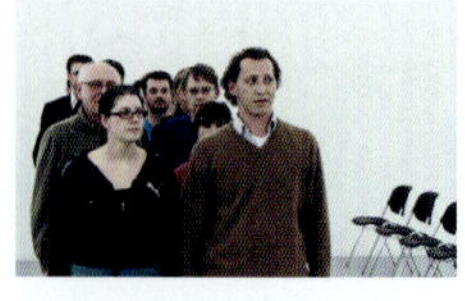

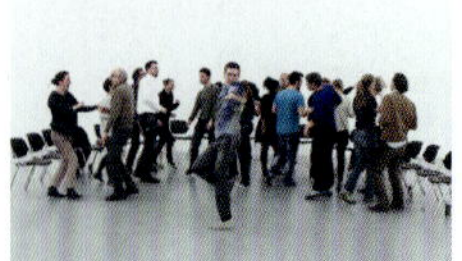

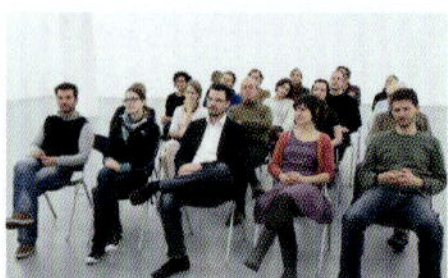

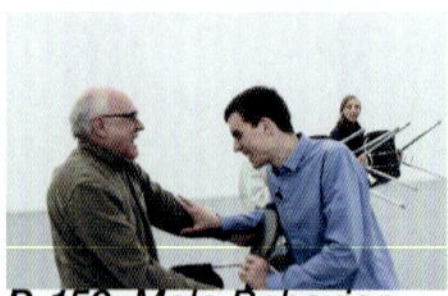

P. 150 Male Behavior as a Result of Societal Power Relations between Artist and Audience, 2013
video stills
Bonner Kunstverein
Courtesy of the artist and PSM, Berlin

INFLUENCE

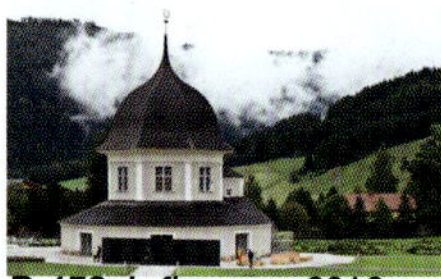

P. 152 Influence, 2012
performance, Regionale12, St. Lambrecht
Photo: Nikola Milatovic
Courtesy of the artist and PSM, Berlin

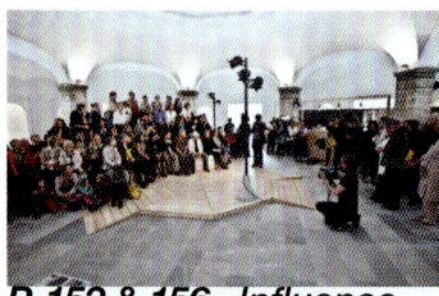

P. 152 & 156 Influence, 2012
performance, Regionale12, St. Lambrecht
Photo: Nikola Milatovic
Courtesy of the artist and PSM, Berlin

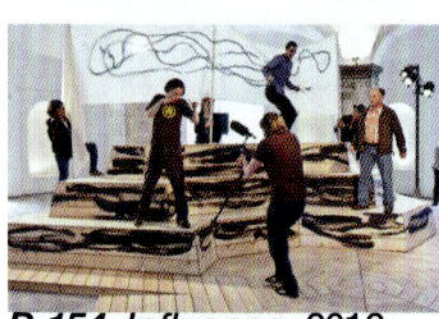

P. 154 Influence, 2012
performance, Regionale12, St. Lambrecht
Photo: Nikola Milatovic
Courtesy of the artist and PSM, Berlin

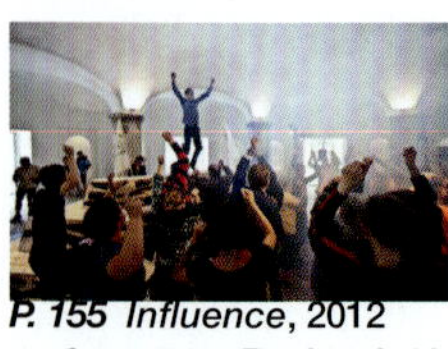

P. 155 Influence, 2012
performance, Regionale12, St. Lambrecht
Photo: Nikola Milatovic
Courtesy of the artist and PSM, Berlin

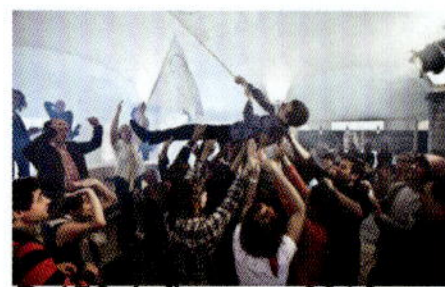

P. 156 Influence, 2012
performance, Regionale12, St. Lambrecht
Photo: Nikola Milatovic
Courtesy of the artist and PSM, Berlin

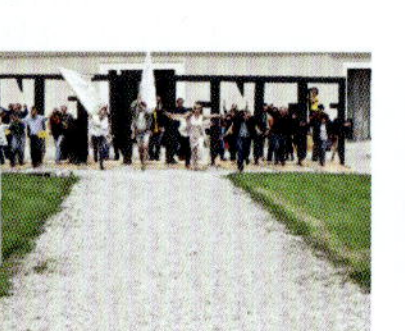

P. 158 Influence, 2012
performance, Regionale12, St. Lambrecht
Photo: Nikola Milatovic
Courtesy of the artist and PSM, Berlin

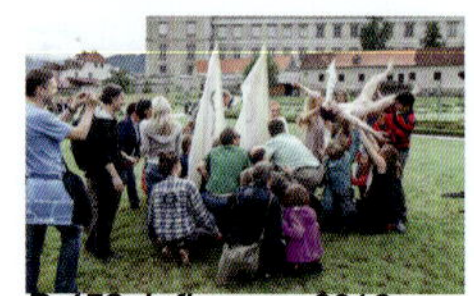

P. 158 Influence, 2012
performance, Regionale12, St. Lambrecht
Photo: Nikola Milatovic
Courtesy of the artist and PSM, Berlin

ELIXIR

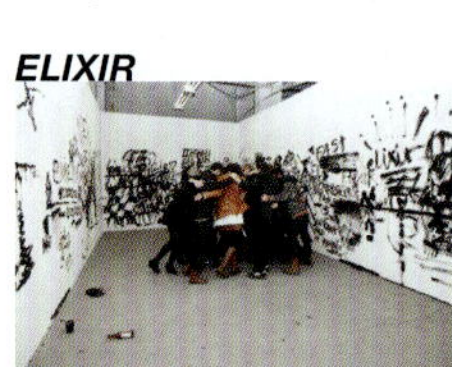

P. 160 & 166 ELIXIR, 2011
performance, PSM, Berlin
Photo: Dirk Dunkelberg
Courtesy of the artist and PSM, Berlin

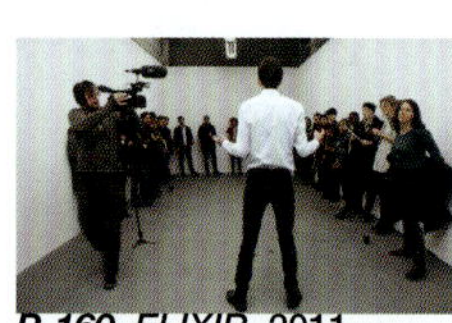

P. 160 ELIXIR, 2011
performance, PSM, Berlin
Photo: Dirk Dunkelberg
Courtesy of the artist and PSM, Berlin

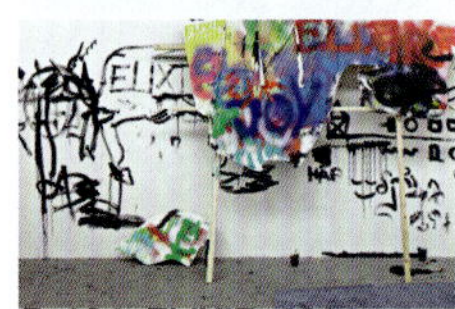

P. 164 ELIXIR, 2011
installation view (detail), PSM, Berlin
Photo: Hans-Georg Gaul
Courtesy of the artist and PSM, Berlin

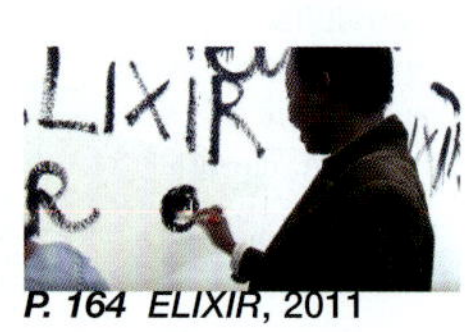

P. 164 ELIXIR, 2011
video still
Courtesy of the artist and PSM, Berlin

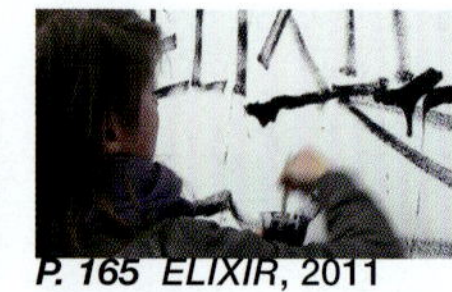

P. 165 ELIXIR, 2011
video still
Courtesy of the artist and PSM, Berlin

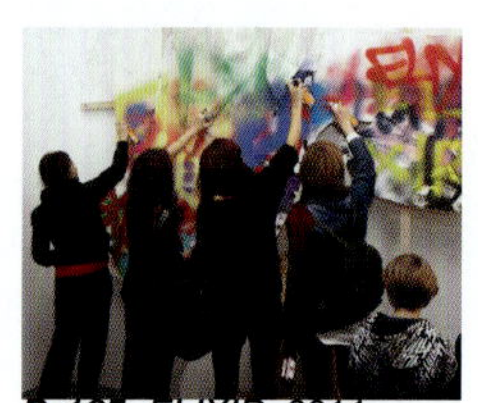

P. 165 ELIXIR, 2011
video still
Courtesy of the artist and PSM, Berlin

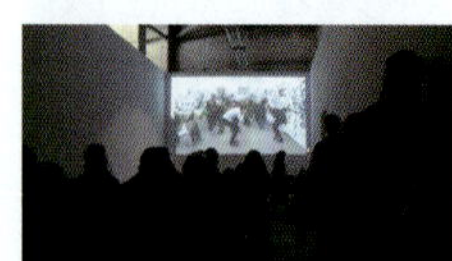

P. 168 ELIXIR, 2011
video still
Courtesy of the artist and PSM, Berlin

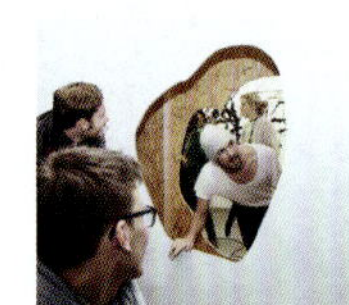

P. 168 ELIXIR, 2011
performance, PSM, Berlin
Photo: Dirk Dunkelberg
Courtesy of the artist and PSM, Berlin

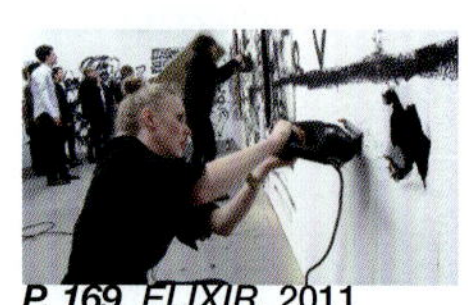

P. 169 ELIXIR, 2011
performance, PSM, Berlin
Photo: Dirk Dunkelberg
Courtesy of the artist and PSM, Berlin

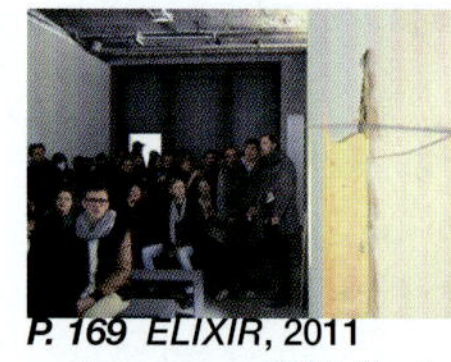

P. 169 ELIXIR, 2011
performance, PSM, Berlin
Photo: Dirk Dunkelberg
Courtesy of the artist and PSM, Berlin

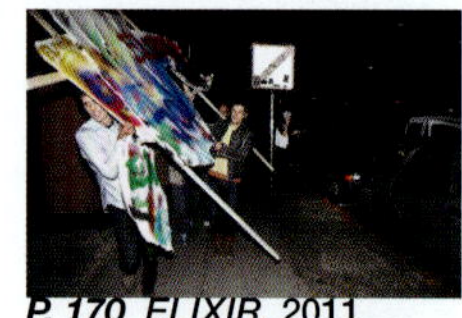

P. 170 ELIXIR, 2011
performance, PSM, Berlin
Photo: Dirk Dunkelberg
Courtesy of the artist and PSM, Berlin

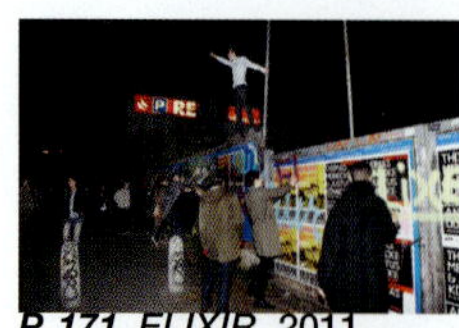

P. 171 ELIXIR, 2011
performance, PSM, Berlin
Photo: Dirk Dunkelberg
Courtesy of the artist and PSM, Berlin

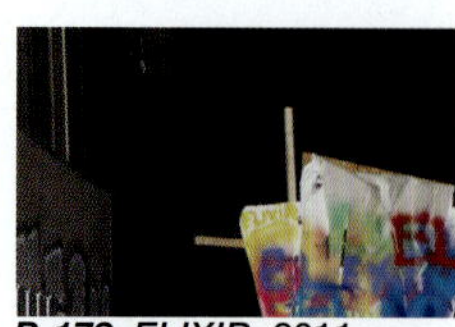

P. 172 ELIXIR, 2011
performance, PSM, Berlin
Photo: Dirk Dunkelberg
Courtesy of the artist and PSM, Berlin

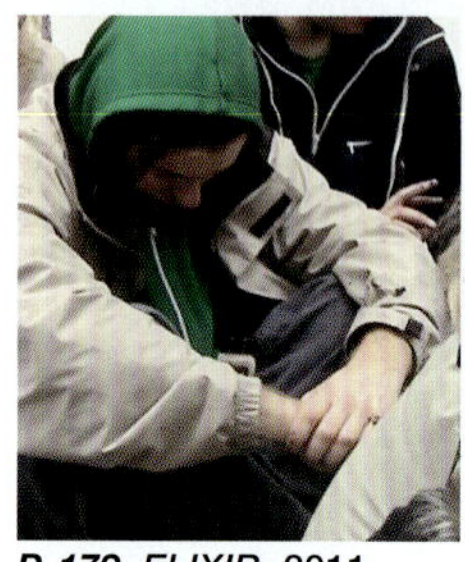

P. 172 ELIXIR, 2011
video still
Courtesy of the artist and PSM, Berlin

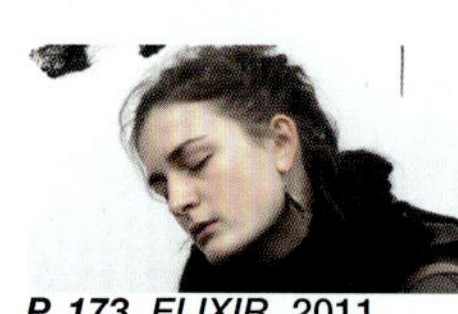

P. 173 ELIXIR, 2011
video still
Courtesy of the artist and PSM, Berlin

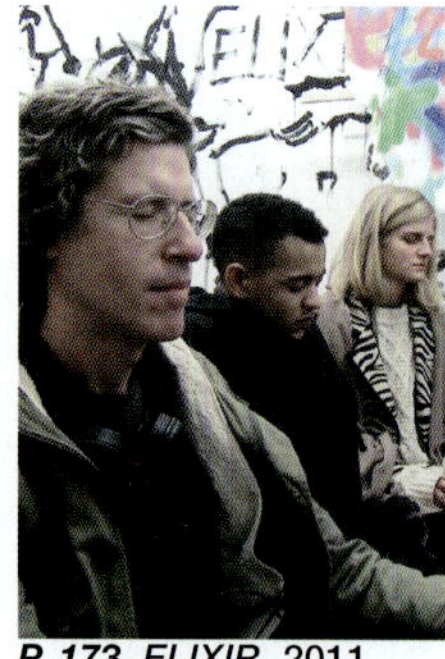

P. 173 ELIXIR, 2011
video still
Courtesy of the artist and PSM, Berlin

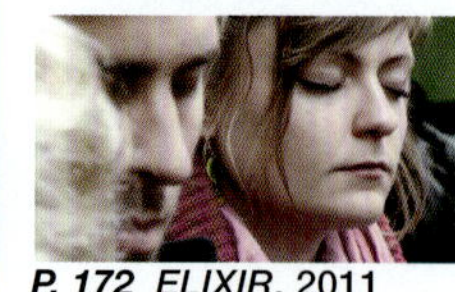

P. 172 ELIXIR, 2011
video still
Courtesy of the artist and PSM, Berlin

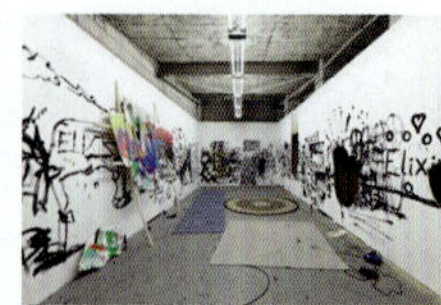

P. 174 ELIXIR, 2011
installation view (detail), PSM, Berlin
Photo: Hans-Georg Gaul
Courtesy of the artist and PSM, Berlin

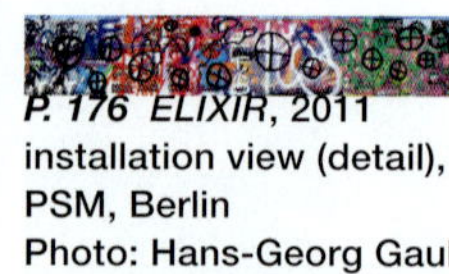

P. 176 ELIXIR, 2011
installation view (detail), PSM, Berlin
Photo: Hans-Georg Gaul
Courtesy of the artist and PSM, Berlin

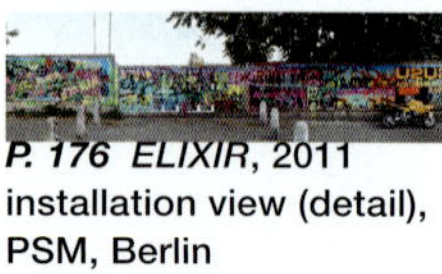

P. 176 ELIXIR, 2011
installation view (detail), PSM, Berlin
Photo: Hans-Georg Gaul
Courtesy of the artist and PSM, Berlin

P. 176 ELIXIR, 2011
installation view (detail), PSM, Berlin
Photo: Hans-Georg Gaul
Courtesy of the artist and PSM, Berlin

EXISTING THINGS

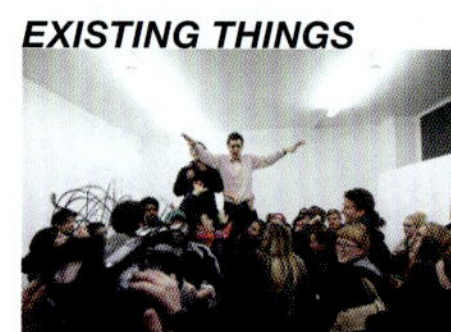

P. 178 Existing Things, 2010
performance, COCO, Vienna
Photo: esel.at
Courtesy of the artist and PSM, Berlin

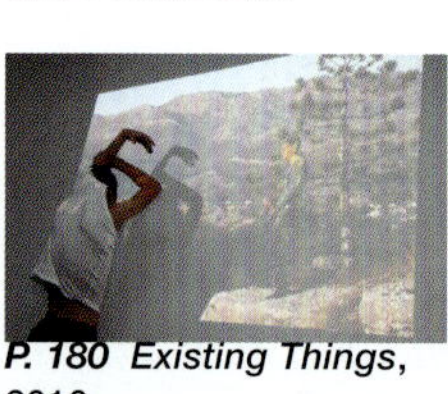

P. 180 Existing Things, 2010
performance, COCO, Vienna
Photo: esel.at
Courtesy of the artist and PSM, Berlin

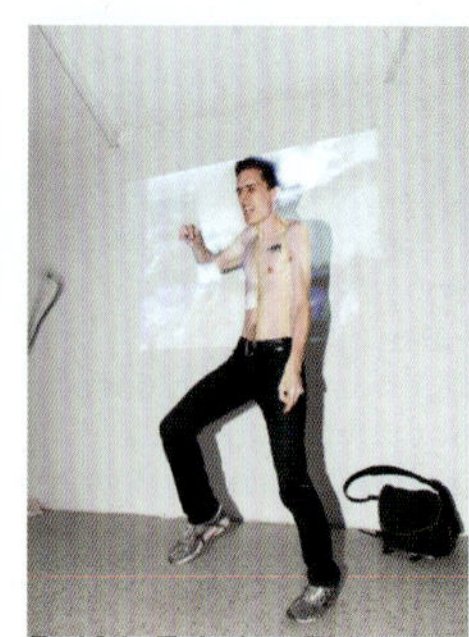

P. 181 Existing Things, 2010
performance, COCO, Vienna
Photo: esel.at
Courtesy of the artist and PSM, Berlin

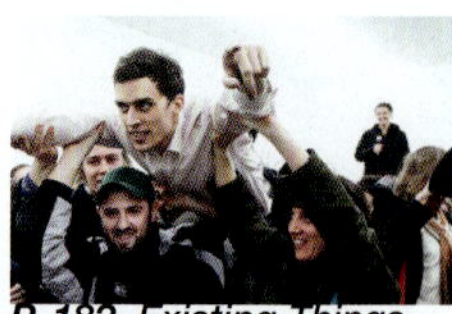

P. 182 Existing Things, 2010
performance, COCO, Vienna
Photo: esel.at
Courtesy of the artist and PSM, Berlin

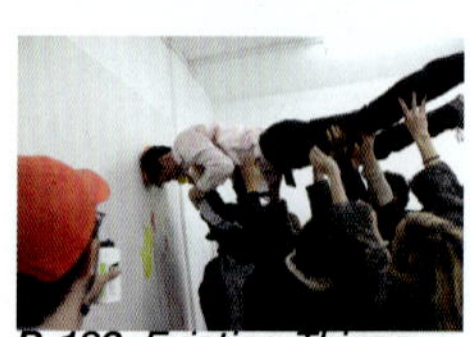

P. 182 Existing Things, 2010
performance, COCO, Vienna
Photo: esel.at
Courtesy of the artist and PSM, Berlin

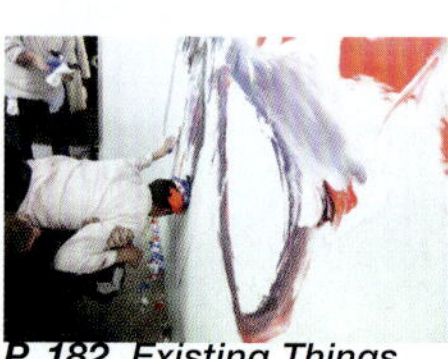

P. 182 Existing Things, 2010
performance, COCO, Vienna
Photo: esel.at
Courtesy of the artist and PSM, Berlin

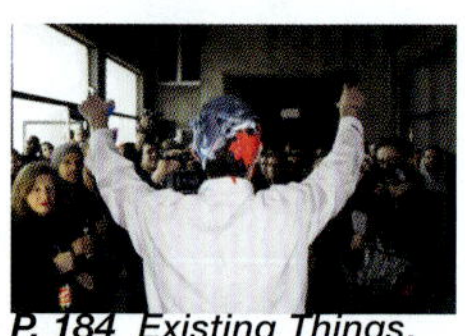

P. 184 Existing Things, 2010
performance, COCO, Vienna
Photo: esel.at
Courtesy of the artist and PSM, Berlin

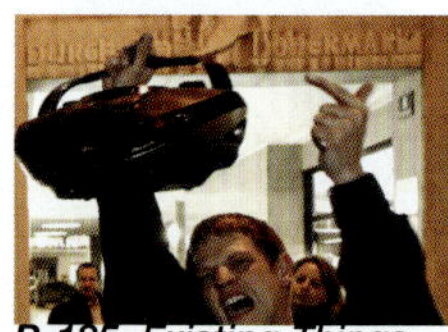

P. 185 Existing Things, 2010
performance, COCO, Vienna
Photo: esel.at
Courtesy of the artist and PSM, Berlin

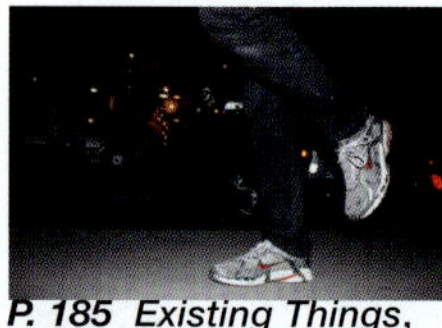

P. 185 Existing Things, 2010
performance, COCO, Vienna
Photo: esel.at
Courtesy of the artist and PSM, Berlin

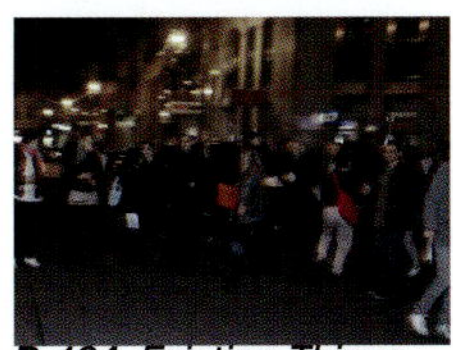

P. 184 *Existing Things*, 2010
performance, COCO, Vienna
Photo: esel.at
Courtesy of the artist and PSM, Berlin

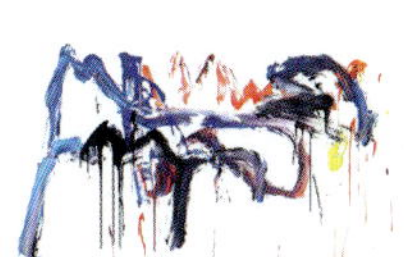

P. 186 *Existing Things*, 2010
acrylic on canvas, 200 x 280 cm
Collection of Juan and Patricia Vergez, Buenos Aires

THERE AND BACK

P. 188 *There and Back*, 2010
performance, Skånes Konstförening, Malmö
Photo: Lea Nielsen
Courtesy of the artist and PSM, Berlin

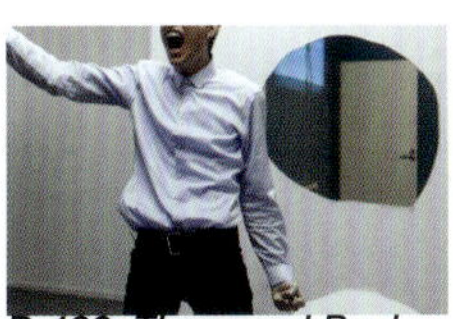

P. 190 *There and Back*, 2010
performance, Skånes Konstförening, Malmö
Photo: Lea Nielsen
Courtesy of the artist and PSM, Berlin

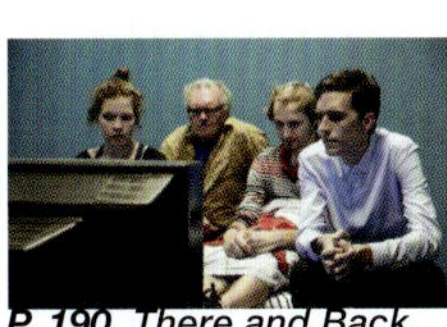

P. 190 *There and Back*, 2010
performance, Skånes Konstförening, Malmö
Photo: Lea Nielsen
Courtesy of the artist and PSM, Berlin

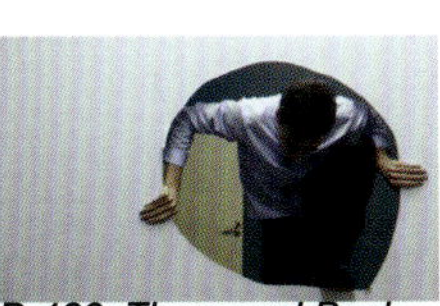

P. 190 *There and Back*, 2010
performance, Skånes Konstförening, Malmö
Photo: Lea Nielsen
Courtesy of the artist and PSM, Berlin

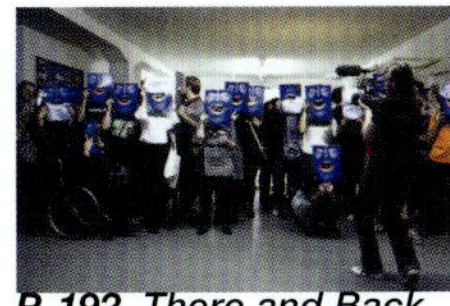

P. 192 *There and Back*, 2010
performance, Skånes Konstförening, Malmö
Photo: Lea Nielsen
Courtesy of the artist and PSM, Berlin

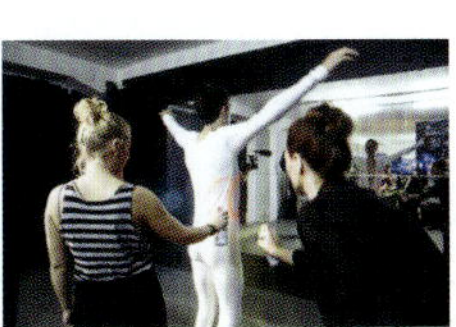

P. 190 *There and Back*, 2010
performance, Skånes Konstförening, Malmö
Photo: Lea Nielsen
Courtesy of the artist and PSM, Berlin

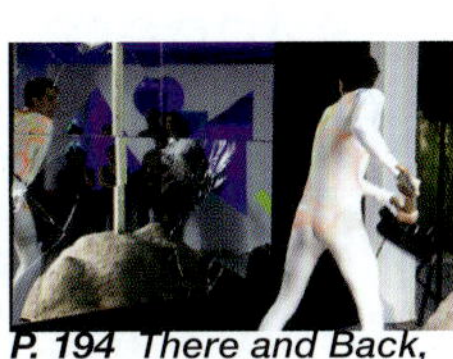

P. 194 *There and Back*, 2010
performance, Skånes Konstförening, Malmö
Photo: Lea Nielsen
Courtesy of the artist and PSM, Berlin

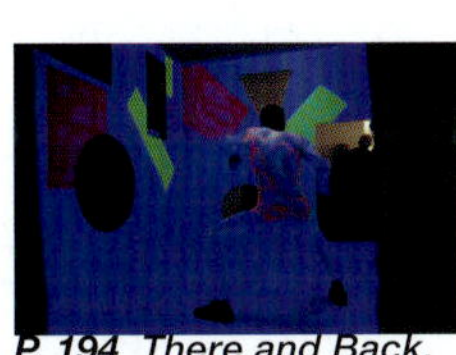

P. 194 *There and Back*, 2010
performance, Skånes Konstförening, Malmö
Photo: Lea Nielsen
Courtesy of the artist and PSM, Berlin

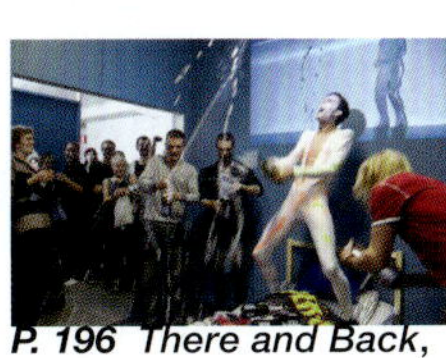

P. 196 *There and Back*, 2010
performance, Skånes Konstförening, Malmö
Photo: Lea Nielsen
Courtesy of the artist and PSM, Berlin

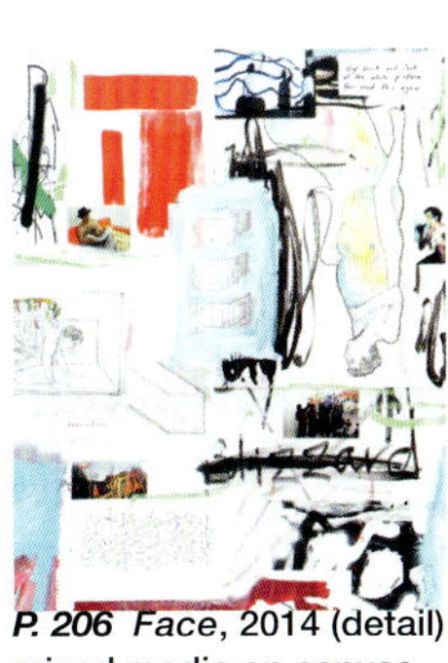

P. 206 *Face*, 2014 (detail)
mixed media on canvas, 150 x 200 cm
Private collection London

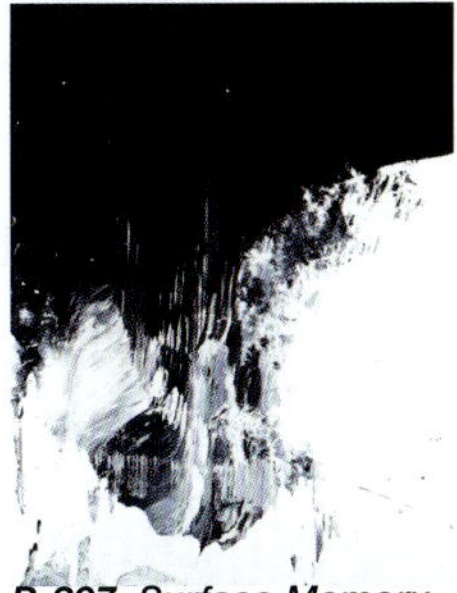

P. 207 *Surface Memory*, 2010 (detail)
oil on canvas, 110 x 90 cm
Courtesy of the artist and PSM, Berlin

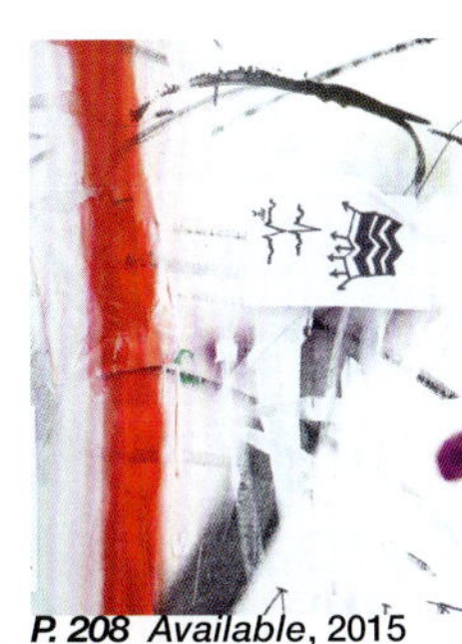

P. 208 *Available*, 2015
installation view (detail), Kunstverein Braunschweig
Photo: Stefan Stark
Courtesy of the artist and PSM, Berlin

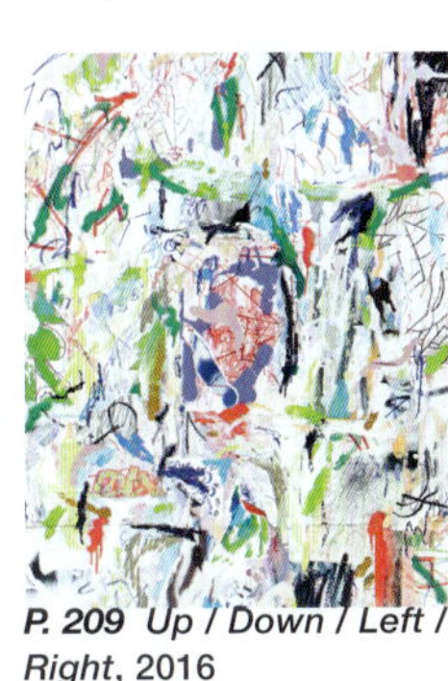

P. 209 *Up / Down / Left / Right*, 2016
mixed media on canvas, 160 x 120 cm
Courtesy of the artist and PSM, Berlin

COVER NO. 1

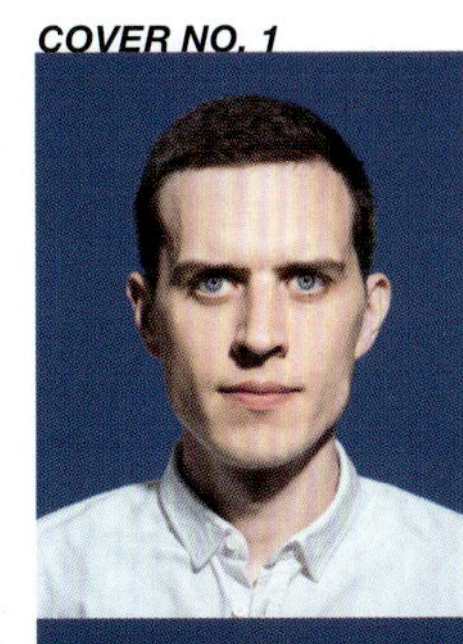

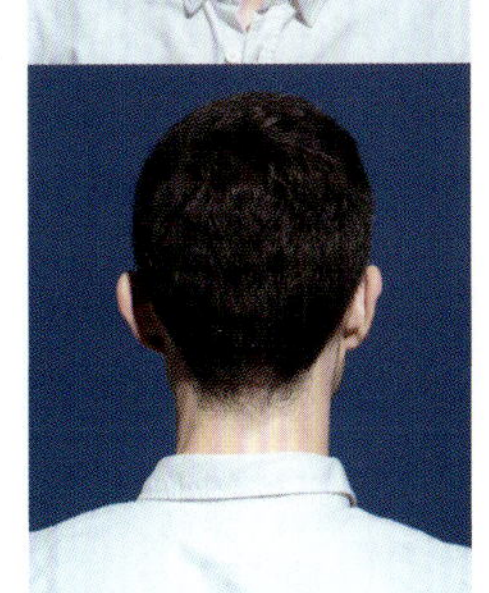

Christian Falsnaes, artist.
Photo: Jonas Lindstroem
Assistant: Kyra Wilhelmseder

COVER NO. 2

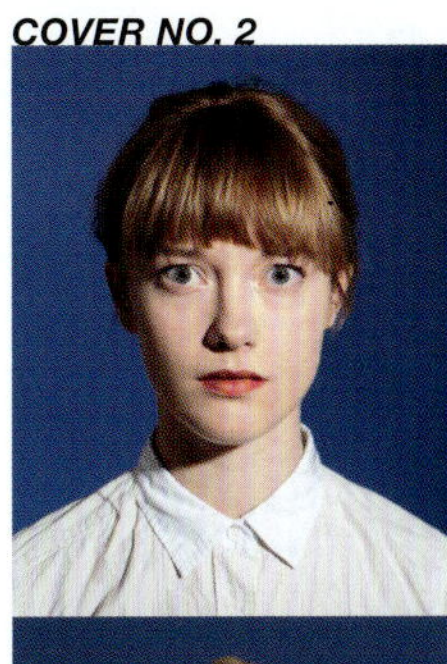

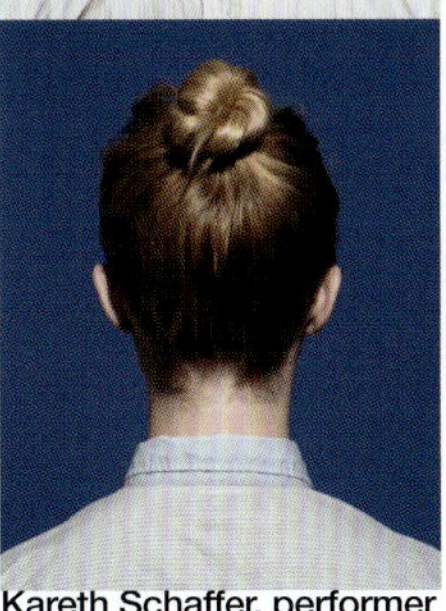

Kareth Schaffer, performer and choreographer.
Has performed works for Christian Falsnaes since 2013.
Photo: Jonas Lindstroem
Assistant: Kyra Wilhelmseder

COVER NO. 3

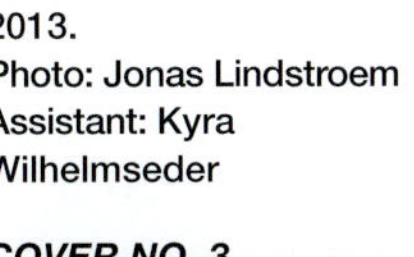

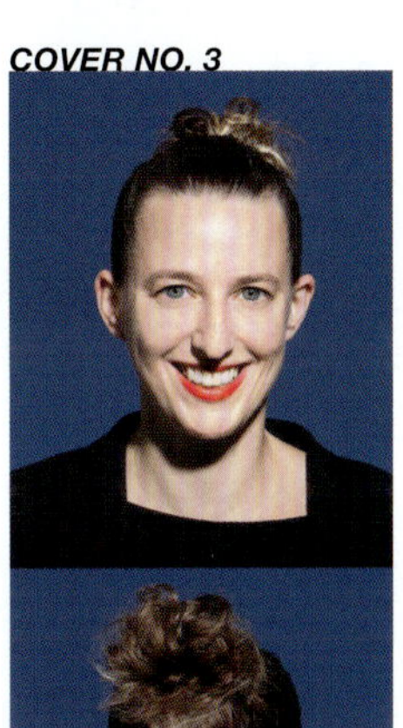

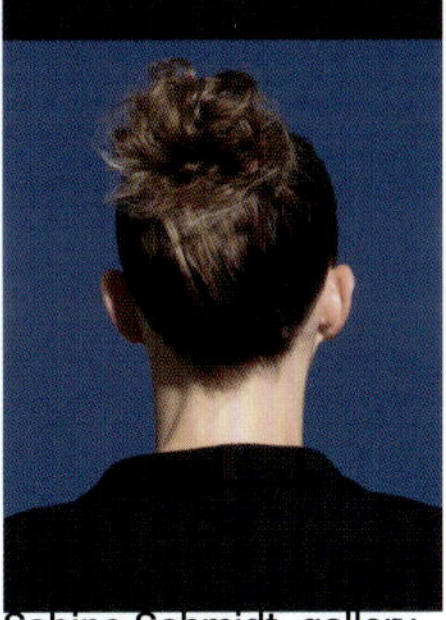

Sabine Schmidt, gallery owner.
Has co-produced and starred in works by Christian Falsnaes since 2011.
Photo: Jonas Lindstroem
Assistant: Kyra Wilhelmseder

COVER NO. 4

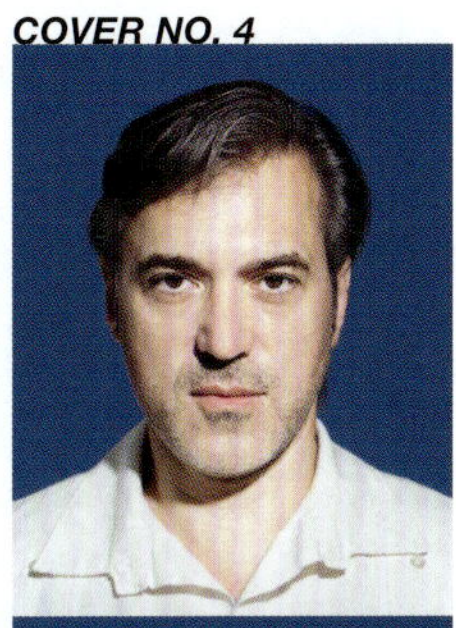

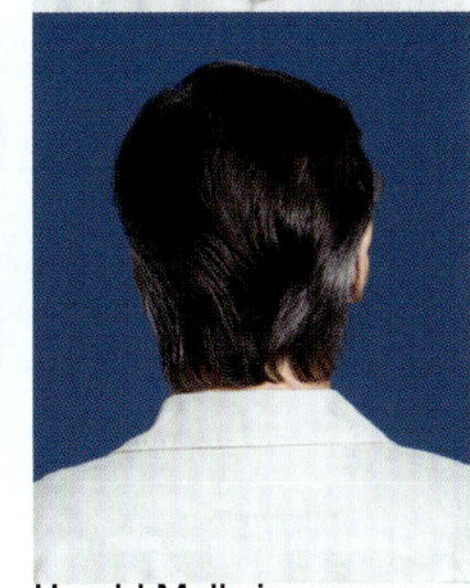

Harald Mellwig, cameraman.
Has been the director of photography for Christian Falsnaes since 2013.
Photo: Jonas Lindstroem
Assistant: Kyra Wilhelmseder

AUTHORS' BIOGRAPHIES

Carson Chan is an architecture writer and curator, pursuing a PhD in Architecture at Princeton University.

Anna-Catharina Gebbers is a writer, lecturer, and curator at Nationalgalerie im Hamburger Bahnhof – Museum für Gegenwart.

Jule Hillgärtner is Director of Kunstverein Braunschweig. She studied theater, film, and media sciences in Frankfurt am Main and completed her doctoral thesis on photography and video in embedded journalism in 2009.

Noemi Smolik studied in Cologne and New York. She is an art critic and curator with publications in *Artforum, Frieze, Frieze d/e*, and the *Franfurter Allgemeine Zeitung*. She teaches at the University of Cologne, and lives in Bonn and Prague.

Thomas Thiel is Director of the Bielefelder Kunstverein. He studied Cultural Sciences and Aesthetics in Hildesheim and Marseille.

ACKNOWLEDGMENTS

Christian would like to the thank the following people:
Søren Berner, Anne Bennike, Ellen Blumenstein, Aaron Bogart, Klaus Bürger-Ruxtorff, Carson Chan, Jessica David, Raphael Ducos, Peter Eiff, Anna-Catharina Gebbers, Sophie Goltz, Fanny Gonella, Uta Grosenick and the DISTANZ team, Markus Gugatschka, Sven Hausherr, Jule Hillgärtner, Luis Incera, Christian Kobald, Christina and Christian Kohorst, Harald Mellwig, Felicia Oschmann, Stella Plapp, Robert Ramsauer, Christiane Rekade, Dorothee Richter, Efrain Salas, Kareth Schaffer, Max Schaffer, Britta Schmidt, Sabine Schmidt, Calilo Sielecki, Noemi Smolik, Raimar Stange, Nik Suchentrunk, Thomas Thiel, Annabelle Tenèze, TRES, Nina Trippel and the CeeCee Creative team, Nazim Ünal Yilmaz, Christina Végh, Eileen Vergez, Juan and Patricia Vergez, Rita Vitorelli, Vilma and Richard Willmot, and Lea von Wintzingerode.

This publication was supported by:
Danish Arts Foundation
Kunstverein Braunschweig

DANISH ARTS FOUNDATION

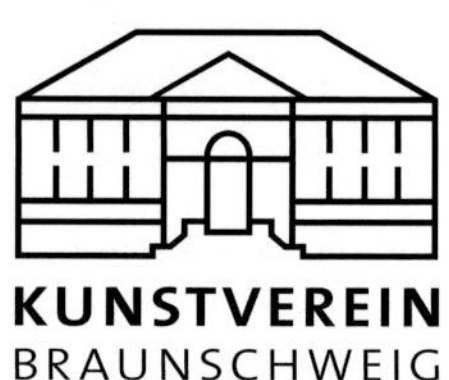

IMPRINT

Editors
Aaron Bogart and
Christian Falsnaes

Texts
Carson Chan, Anna-Catharina Gebbers, Jule Hillgärtner, Noemi Smolik, Thomas Thiel

Concept & Design
Cee Cee Creative
Creative Direction: Sven Hausherr; Art Direction & Design: Jessica David; Coordination: Nina Trippel

Paper
Multicard 250g (Cover),
LuxoArt Gloss 100g

Fonts
Noe Display, Helvetica Neue LT, Times

Production Management
DISTANZ Verlag, Sonja Bahr

Production
optimal media GmbH, Röbel/Müritz

Photo Credits
All images courtesy Christian Falsnaes and PSM, Berlin, unless otherwise noted in the Index

Distribution
Gestalten, Berlin
www.gestalten.com
sales@gestalten.com

ISBN 978-3-95476-151-7
Printed in Germany

Published by
DISTANZ Verlag
www.distanz.de

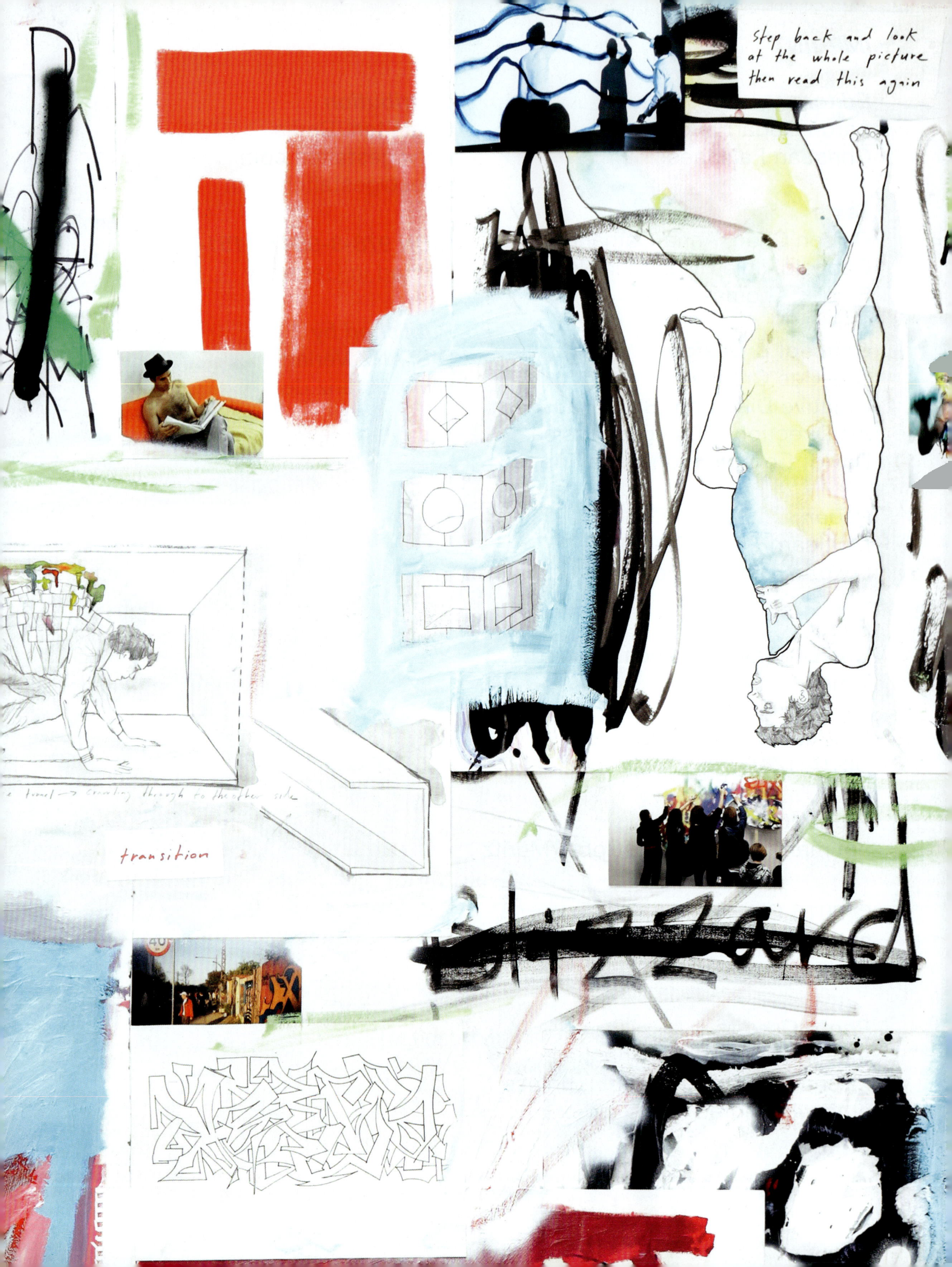
step back and look at the whole picture then read this again
transition